THE SOCIAL OUTCAST

The Sydney Symposium of Social Psychology series

This book is volume 7 in the Sydney Symposium of Social Psychology series. The aim of the *Sydney Symposia of Social Psychology* is to provide new, integrative insights into key areas of contemporary research. Held every year at the University of New South Wales, Sydney, each symposium deals with an important integrative theme in social psychology, and the invited participants are leading researchers in the field from around the world. Each contribution is extensively discussed during the symposium and is subsequently thoroughly revised into book chapters that are published in the volumes in this series. For further details see website at www.sydneysymposium.unsw.edu.au

Previous Sydney Symposium of Social Psychology volumes:

SSSP 1. FEELING AND THINKING: THE ROLE OF AFFECT IN SOCIAL COGNITION ISBN 0-521-64223-X (Edited by J. P. Forgas). Contributors: Robert Zajonc (Stanford), Jim Blascovich & Wendy Mendes (UC Santa Barbara), Craig Smith & Leslie Kirby (Vanderbilt), Eric Eich & Dawn Macauley (British Columbia), Len Berkowitz et al. (Wisconsin), Leonard Martin (Georgia), Daniel Gilbert (Harvard), Herbert Bless (Mannheim), Klaus Fiedler (Heidelberg), Joseph Forgas (UNSW), Carolin Showers (Wisconsin), Tony Greenwald, Marzu Banaji et al. (U.Washington/Yale), Mark Leary (Wake Forest), Paula Niedenthal & Jamin Halberstadt (Indiana).

Comments on 'Feeling and Thinking':

"At last a project that brings together the central findings and theories concerning the interface of social cognition and affect. This important new volume is sure to become the sourcebook . . . must reading for anyone interested in the vital role of affect in social life." **E. Tory Higgins, Columbia University**

"I can't imagine a more interesting collection of affect researchers under one roof! Joseph Forgas has brought together the best minds in psychology, young and old, to reflect on the interface between emotion and thought . . . this volume will make you wish you had traveled to Sydney to attend the original symposium. Excellent investigators showcase their best work." **Peter Salovey, Yale University**

SSSP 2. THE SOCIAL MIND: COGNITIVE AND MOTIVATIONAL ASPECTS OF INTERPERSONAL BEHAVIOR ISBN 0-521-77092-0 (Edited by J. P. Forgas, K. D. Williams, & Ladd Wheeler). Contributors: William & Claire McGuire (Yale), Susan Andersen (NYU), Roy Baumeister (Case Western), Joel Cooper (Princeton), Bill Crano (Claremont), Garth Fletcher (Canterbury), Joseph Forgas (UNSW), Pascal Huguet (Clermont), Mike Hogg (Queensland), Martin Kaplan (N. Illinois), Norb Kerr (Michigan State), John Nezlek (William & Mary), Fred Rhodewalt (Utah), Astrid Schuetz (Chemnitz), Constantine Sedikides (Southampton), Jeffrey Simpson (Texas A&M), Richard Sorrentino (Western Ontario), Dianne Tice (Case Western), Kip Williams & Ladd Wheeler (UNSW).

Comments on 'The Social Mind':

"At last . . . a compelling answer to the question of what is 'social' about social cognition. The editors have assembled a stellar cast of researchers . . . and the result is eye-opening and mind-expanding . . . the contributors to this project make a convincing case that, for human beings, mental life IS social life." **Marilynn B. Brewer, Ohio State University**

"The Sydney Symposium has once again collected some of social psychology's best researchers, and allowed them to . . . explore how the world within the mind represents, creates, interacts with, and is influenced by the world without. The bridge between social relations and social cognition has never been sturdier, and scientists on both sides of the divide won't want to miss this. . . ." **Daniel Gilbert, Harvard University**

SSSP 3. SOCIAL INFLUENCE: DIRECT AND INDIRECT PROCESSES* ISBN 1-84169-038-4. (Edited by J. P. Forgas & K. D. Williams). Contributors: Robert Cialdini (Arizona State), Eric Knowles, Shanon Butler & Jay Linn (Arkansas), Bibb Latane (Florida Atlantic), Martin Bourgeois (Wyoming), Mark Schaller (British Columbia), Ap Dijksterhuis (Nijmegen), James Tedeschi (SUNY-Albany), Richard Petty (Ohio State), Joseph Forgas (UNSW), Herbert Bless (Mannheim), Fritz Strack (Wurzburg), Eva Walther (Heidelberg), Sik Hung Ng (Hong Kong), Thomas Mussweiler (Wurzburg), Kipling Williams (Macquarie), Lara Dolnik (UNSW), Charles Stangor & Gretchen Sechrist (Maryland), John Jost (Stanford), Deborah Terry & Michael Hogg (Queensland), Stephen Harkins (Northeastern), Barbara David & John Turner (Australian National University), Robin Martin (Queensland), Miles Hewstone (Cardiff), Russell Spears & Tom Postmes (Amsterdam), Martin Lea (Manchester), Susan Watt (Amsterdam).

Comments on 'Social Influence':

"What a great new book. . . . In this cutting edge volume, . . . social cognition meets social influence, and the result is a big step forward for social psychology." **David Myers, Hope College**

"This Sydney Symposium volume, the third in a series, showcases the best research done by a collection of stellar scholars in social influence . . . from subliminal and cognitive effects to interpersonal and socio-cultural effects. [This book] will be of great interest to anyone concerned with social influence phenomena—students, researchers, practitioners and laypersons alike." **Elizabeth Loftus, University of Washington**

SSSP 4. THE SOCIAL SELF: COGNITIVE, INTERPERSONAL, AND INTERGROUP PERSPECTIVES* ISBN 1-84169-062-7 (Edited by J. P. Forgas & K. D. Williams). Contributors: Eliot R. Smith (Purdue), Thomas Gilovich (Cornell), Monica Biernat (Kansas), Joseph P. Forgas & Stephanie J. Moylan (UNSW), Edward R. Hirt & Sean M. McCrea (Indiana-Bloomington), Frederick Rhodewalt & Michael Tragakis (Utah), Mark Leary (Wake Forest), Roy F. Baumeister, Jean M. Twenge, & Natalie Ciarocco (Case Western), Dianne M. Tice, J. M. Twenge, & Brandon J. Schmeichel (Case Western), Bertram F. Malle (Oregon), William Ickes (Texas-Arlington), Marianne LaFrance (Yale), Yoshihisa Kashima, Emiko Kashima, & Anna Clark (Melbourne/Swinburne/Melbourne), Marilynn B. Brewer & Cynthia L. Pickett (Ohio State/Illinois), Sabine Otten (Jena), Christian S. Crandall (Kansas), Diane M. Mackie & Eliot R. Smith (UC Santa Barbara/Purdue), Joel Cooper & Michael Hogg (Princeton/Queensland), Stephen C. Wright, Art Aron, & Linda R. Tropp (UC Santa Cruz/SUNY-Stony Brook/Boston), Constantine Sedikides (Southampton).

Comments on The Social Self

"Those of us who are fascinated with how the self is constructed, maintained, and its impact on our everyday lives will find this volume enlightening and 'must' reading." **E. Tory Higgins, Columbia University**

"This collection showcases a fine array of recent social psychological research on the self. The focus here is explicitly social – examining self as a feature of the person's mind that is the hub of social relationships, a natural psychological link to specific others, to groups, and to social life. The volume reveals that the current study of the social self is vigorous and wide-ranging." **Daniel M. Wegner, Harvard University**

SSSP 5. SOCIAL JUDGMENTS: IMPLICIT AND EXPLICIT PROCESSES**. ISBN 0-521-82248-3. (Edited by J. P. Forgas, K. D. Williams, & W. von Hippel). Contributors: Herbert Bless (Mannheim), Marilynn Brewer (Ohio), David Buss (Texas), Tanya Chartrand (Ohio), Klaus Fiedler (Heidelberg), Joseph Forgas (UNSW), David Funder (UCRiverside), Adam Galinsky (Northwestern), Martie Haselton (UCLA), Denis Hilton (Toulouse), Lucy Johnston (Canterbury), Arie Kruglanski (Maryland), Matthew Lieberman (UCLA), John McClure (Wellington), Mario Mikulincer (Bar-Ilan), Norbert Schwarz (Michigan), Philip shaver (UCDavis), Diederik Stapel (Groningen), Jerry Suls (Iowa), William von Hippel (UNSW), Michaela Waenke (Basel), Ladd Wheeler (Macquarie), Kipling Williams (Macquarie), Michael Zarate (El Paso).

Comments on Social Judgments

"The editors should be congratulated for assembling in one volume an extraordinary range of perspectives from an outstanding set of authors. This is 'must' reading for all students and researchers interested in how people work together to make sense of the world in which they live" **E. Tory Higgins, Columbia University**

"The distinguished scholars assembled by the Sydney group have provided a vital collection of papers.. The bankable findings, the methodological innovations, and the unresolved controversies presented in these chapters will reward any scholar with an interest in social judgment" **Thomas Gilovich, Cornell University**

SSSP 6. SOCIAL MOTIVATION: CONSCIOUS AND UNCONSCIOUS PROCESSES** (in press). (Edited by Joseph P. Forgas & K. D. Williams). Contributors: Henk Aarts (Utrecht) & Ran Hassin (Hebrew Univ.), Trish Devine (Wisconsin), Joseph Forgas (UNSW), Jens Forster (Bremen) & Nira Liberman (Tel Aviv), Judy Harackiewicz (Wisconsin), Leanne Hing (Guelph) & Mark Zanna (Waterloo), Michael Kernis (Georgia), Paul Lewicki (Tulsa), Steve Neuberg (Arizona), Doug Kenrick & Mark Schaller (British Columbia), Tom Pyszczynski (Colorado State), Fred Rhodewalt (Utah), Jonathan Schooler (Pittsburgh), Steve Spencer (Waterloo), Fritz Strack & Roland Deutsch (Würzburg), Howard Weiss (Purdue) & Neal Ashkanasy (Queensland), Kip Williams, & Wayne Warburton (Macquarie), Wendy Wood & Jeffrey Quinn (Texas A&M), Rex Wright (Alabama) & Guido Gendolla (Nurnberg).

Comments on Social Motivation

"The exceptional contributors to this volume address questions ranging from the nature and characteristics of conscious and unconscious social motivation to the effects of implicit and explicit motivational processes on prejudice, aversive racism, self-regulation, work, and reactions to exclusion. Students and scholars in the social, behavioral, and neurosciences will find these contributions compelling reading." **John T. Cacioppo, University of Chicago**

"This wonderful book brings together chapters by leading researchers on two major forms of motivation -- conscious and unconscious. This book is a must-read for anyone interested in motivation." **Ed Diener, University of Illinois**

"This remarkable volume provides an integrative review of recent work on conscious and unconscious motivation. The excellent contributions...present truly original theories and empirical discoveries. I congratulate the authors for their valuable contribution to the reemergence of human motivation as a core field of inquiry in psychology." **Yaacov Trope, New York University**

*Published by Psychology Press; ** Published by Cambridge University Press

THE SOCIAL OUTCAST
Ostracism, Social Exclusion, Rejection, and Bullying

Edited by

Kipling D. Williams
Purdue University

Joseph P. Forgas
University of New South Wales

William von Hippel
University of New South Wales

Psychology Press
New York • Hove

Published in 2005 by
Psychology Press
Taylor & Francis Group
270 Madison Avenue
New York, NY 10016

Published in Great Britain by
Psychology Press
Taylor & Francis Group
27 Church Road
Hove, East Sussex BN3 2FA

© 2005 by Taylor & Francis Group, LLC
Psychology Press is an imprint of Taylor & Francis Group

Printed in the United States of America on acid-free paper
10 9 8 7 6 5 4 3 2 1

International Standard Book Number-10: 1-84169-424-X (Hardcover)
International Standard Book Number-13: 978-1-84169-424-5 (Hardcover)
Library of Congress Card Number 2005001560

Library of Congress Cataloging-in-Publication Data

The social outcast : ostracism, social exclusion, rejection, and bullying / edited by Kipling D.
    Williams, Joseph P. Forgas, and William von Hippel.
        p. cm. -- (Sydney Symposium of Social Psychology series)
    ISBN 1-84169-424-X (hardcover : alk. paper)
    1. Marginality, Social. 2. Social isolation. 3. Bullying. 4. Social psychology. I. Williams, Kipling
D. II. Forgas, Joseph P. III. Hippel, William von. IV. Series.

HM1136.S635 2005
302.3--dc22   2005001560

Taylor & Francis Group
is the Academic Division of T&F Informa plc.

Visit the Taylor & Francis Web site at
http://www.taylorandfrancis.com

and the Psychology Press Web site at
http://www.psypress.com

DEDICATION

To my parents, Dick, Evie, and Jack – K.W.
To Letitia – J.F.
To Courtney – WvH

Contents

II. DEEP ROOTS OF EXCLUSION: NEUROPSYCHOLOGICAL SUBSTRATES OF ISOLATION AND EXCLUSION

III. INDIVIDUAL AND POPULATION DIFFERENCES AND THE IMPACT OF SOCIAL EXCLUSION AND BULLYING

IV. INFLUENCES OF REJECTION ON EMOTION, PERCEPTION, AND COGNITION

V. EFFECTS OF SOCIAL EXCLUSION ON PRO- AND ANTI-SOCIAL BEHAVIOR

About the Editors

Kipling D. Williams received his BS at the University of Washington (Seattle). He then received his MA and PhD in social psychology at Ohio State University. There he began his collaboration with Bibb Latané and Stephen Harkins, working on the causes and consequences of social loafing. Before coming to Purdue University, Professor Williams held long-term positions at Drake University, University of Toledo, University of New South Wales, and Macquarie University. He is a Fellow of the American Psychological Society, the American Psychological Association, and the Society for Personality and Social Psychology. His current research focuses on ostracism, and he also has research interests in the area of psychology and law. Recent books include *Ostracism: The Power of Silence*, and *Psychology and Law: An Empirical Perspective* (co-edited with Neil Brewer).

Joseph P. Forgas is Scientia Professor of Psychology at the University of New South Wales, Sydney, Australia. He received his DPhil and subsequently a DSc from the University of Oxford. He has spent various periods of time working at the Universities of Giessen, Heidelberg, Stanford, Mannheim, and Oxford. His enduring interest is in studying the role of cognitive and affective processes in interpersonal behavior. His current projects investigate how mood states can influence everyday social judgments and interaction strategies. He has published some 16 books and more than 140 articles and chapters in this area. He has been elected Fellow of the Academy of Social Science in Australia, the American Psychological Society, the Hungarian Academy of Sciences and the Society for Personality and Social Psychology. He is recipient of the Distinguished Scientific Contribution Award (Australian Psychological Society), the Alexander von Humboldt Research Prize (Germany) and a Special Investigator Award from the Australian Research Council.

William von Hippel received his BA from Yale University, and his PhD from the University of Michigan. He taught at Ohio State University for over a decade prior to coming to the University of New South Wales in 2001. He has published some forty papers and served as Associate Editor of *Psychological Science and Personality and Social Psychology Bulletin*. His main research areas include stereotyping and prejudice, social cognitive aging, and evolutionary psychology.

Contributors

Roy F. Baumeister, Florida State University, USA

Marilynn B. Brewer, Ohio State University, USA

John T. Cacioppo, University of Chicago, USA

Kathleen R. Catanese, Florida State University, USA

Tanya L. Chartrand, Duke University, USA

C. Nathan DeWall, Florida State University, USA

Geraldine Downey, Columbia University, USA

Naomi I. Eisenberger, University of California, Los Angeles, USA

Susan T. Fiske, Princeton University, USA

Julie Fitness, Macquarie University, Australia

Joseph P. Forgas, University of New South Wales, Australia

Lowell Gaertner, University of Tennessee, USA

Marcello Gallucci, Free University, Amsterdam, The Netherlands

Wendi L. Gardner, Northwestern University, USA

Elishiva F. Gross, University of California, Los Angeles, USA

Louise C. Hawkley, University of Chicago, USA

Michael A. Hogg, University of Queensland, USA

Jonathan Iuzzini, University of Tennessee, USA

Jaana Juvonen, University of California, Los Angeles, USA

Norbert L. Kerr, Michigan State University, USA

Rachell Kingsbury, University of Queensland, Australia

Megan Knowles, Northwestern University, USA

Jessica L. Lakin, Drew University, USA

Mark R. Leary, Wake Forest University, USA

Matthew D. Lieberman, University of California, Los Angeles, USA

Geoff MacDonald, University of Queensland, Australia

Jaap W. Ouwerkerk, University of Amsterdam, The Netherlands

Cynthia L. Pickett, University of California–Davis, USA

Rainer Romero-Canyas, Columbia University, USA

Yonata S. Rubin, Baruch College—City University New York, USA

Stephanie Shaw, University of Queensland, Australia

Kristin L. Sommer, Baruch College—City University New York, USA

Dianne M. Tice, Florida State University, USA

Jean M. Twenge, San Diego State University, USA

Paul A.M. Van Lange, Free University, Amsterdam, The Netherlands

William von Hippel, University of New South Wales, Australia

Kipling D. Williams, Purdue University, USA / Macquarie University, Australia

Mariko Yamamoto, University of Tsukuba, Japan

Lisa Zadro, University of Sydney, Australia

Preface

*O*utcast. Exile. Banish. Pariah. Send to Coventry. Ignore. Snub. Recluse. The list of synonyms is seemingly endless, perhaps because the phenomenon is so important, so ingrained in society, so devastating to those who are targeted for such behavior, so powerful for those who use it.

In this book, we focus on four terms: ostracism, social exclusion, rejection, and bullying. One could argue that we have too many words, some might say we have too few. These terms envelop the burgeoning research area that directs attention to a fundamental social phenomenon that, until recently, has not enjoyed empirical investigation.

What does it feel like to be rejected by others, by family members, close friends, peers, and even others who are virtual strangers? Social psychology has long known that exclusion and rejection are such powerful fears that people will do all sorts of things to avoid them: they will conform to unanimous (but incorrect) others, they will refrain from helping someone in need, they will buy useless merchandise for which they had no desire, they will obey authorities to the point of harming others. But, what happens after the rejection, the exclusion, the ostracism, or the bullying? What does the person feel, think, and do then? This is what this volume is about.

Arguably, human beings are among the most socially dependent creatures. Our evolutionary success owes much to our ability to cooperate and collaborate with each other. It seems reasonable to argue that the need to interact with others, and the ability to form and maintain complex and rewarding social relationships are among the most fundamental human needs. Modern industrial mass societies with their fragmented social networks and often-superficial relationships present a particularly challenging social environment for many people. To be excluded, rejected, or ostracized is thus among the most devastating experiences a person can endure.

The contributors to this volume represent the top researchers in the field who are examining the psychology of the social outcast. Whereas they all share in common the appreciation for empirical research to help uncover answers to their questions, they come at their questions from a variety of perspectives and use a variety of research tools. Surveys, interviews, random assignment to experimental treatments within laboratories, role play, physiological and cognitive neuroscience measures combine to form a comprehensive and persuasive monograph that points to what we know, and what we need to know in the future about the social outcast.

No single volume could contain everything there is to know about a topic, but we believe we have assembled a uniquely important group of researchers here. Some are known for their research in this particular area, while others are better known more for their work in other domains that touch on the psychology of exclusion. We think this brings two advantages to this volume: core researchers who have developed over-arching theories to explain and understand the phenomena of ostracism, social exclusion, rejection, and bullying, and researchers whose expertise in developmental psychology, groups, relationships, personality, and physiological psychology offer complementary approaches that allows them to explore the relevance of being outcast to their particular domains of interest.

The chapters are arranged into five sections that deal with (1) theoretical foundations, (2) the neuropsychological substrates of isolation and exclusion, (3) individual and population differences and the impact of social exclusion and bullying, (4) the influence of rejection on emotion, perception, and cognition, and (5) effects of social exclusion on pro- and anti-social behavior. The introductory chapter presents a historical overview of research on the psychology of the social outcast, and outlines the goals we had and the chapters that are included to achieve these goals. We were especially fortunate to have Marilynn Brewer write a compelling and provocative summary integration chapter that examines themes and gives researchers a new charge for future investigations.

The chapters in Part I discuss the theoretical foundations of ostracism (Williams & Zadro), rejection (Leary), and exclusion (Baumeister & DeWall). These chapters present overarching theoretical perspectives on why and how being outcast has powerful effects on individuals. These chapters contain some points of commonality (being outcast threatens a need to belong) and points of contention (whether loss of control is a necessary aspect of being outcast).

In Part II, MacDonald, Kingsbury, and Shaw draw important similarities between the pain of exclusion and physical pain. The pain of isolation is further discussed by Cacioppo and Hawkley, who examine its chronic form: loneliness. Finally, Eisenberger and Lieberman consider the neuropsychological substrates of exclusion, how the brain reacts when excluded, and concomitant cognitive and affective responses by the individual. This research, too, demonstrates a strong link between the neuropsychology of social pain of rejection and that of physical pain.

In Part III, our contributors examine different reactions to being socially outcast. Not everyone reacts in the same way to being excluded, rejected, and bullied. A variety of factors play a role, such as rejection sensitivity levels in the individual (Romero-Canyas & Downey), developmental differences (Juvonen & Gross), self-esteem levels (Sommer & Rubin), and culture (Fiske & Yamamoto).

In Part IV, our contributors explore the ways that being socially outcast affects our emotions, perceptions, and cognitions. Our world changes once we are outcast; we feel differently, we see things differently, and we think differently. Twenge focuses on our emotions, Pickett and Gardner (and Gardner, Knowles, & Pickett) examine our perceptions and sense of self, Hogg considers its affect on our social self (or social identity), and Fitness discusses its effects on our emotions and cognitions especially within close relationships.

In Part V, our volume shifts toward one of the most important consequences of being socially outcast—how it makes us behave in our social world. As Steinbeck wrote in Cannery Row in 1945, "... there are two possible reactions to social ostracism — either a man emerges determined to be better, purer, and kindlier or he goes bad, challenges the world and does even worse things." Empirical research by social psychologists, although fifty years late, has arrived at the same conclusion. Whereas some research suggests pro-social reactions after being socially outcast (Lakin & Chartrand, Ouwerkerk, van Lange, Gallucci, & Kerr; see also Williams & Zadro in Chapter 2), others show an anti-social, even violent reaction to apparently the same cause (as discussed in this volume by Tice, and Gaertner & Iuzzini).

Finally, Brewer concludes the volume with a thoughtful integration and call for further research.

THE SYDNEY SYMPOSIUM OF SOCIAL PSYCHOLOGY SERIES

This book is the seventh in the Sydney Symposium of Social Psychology series, held every year in beautiful Coogee Bay, in Sydney, Australia. The University of New South Wales, Macquarie University, and the Australian Research Council sponsor the series, and we are very grateful for their support. We want to emphasize that this is not simply an edited book in the usual sense. Perhaps a few words are in order about the origins of this volume, and the Sydney Symposium of Social Psychology series in general. The objective of the Sydney Symposia is to provide new, integrative understanding in important areas of social psychology by inviting leading researchers in a particular field to a three-day residential Symposium in Sydney. Draft papers by all contributors were prepared months in advance and were made available to all participants before the March meeting in Sydney.

The critical part of the preparation of this book has been the intensive 3-day face-to-face meeting between all invited contributors (and several audience members). Sydney Symposia are characterized by open, free-ranging, intensive, and critical discussion between all participants, with the objective of exploring points of integration and contrast between the proposed papers. A further revision of each chapter was prepared soon after the symposium, incorporating many of the shared points that emerged in our discussions. Thanks to these collaborative procedures, the book does not simply consist of a set of chapters prepared in isolation (as apropos as that might be in for this particular volume). Rather, this Sydney Symposium volume represents a collaborative effort by a leading group of international researchers intent on producing a comprehensive and up-to-date review of research on the social outcast. We hope that the chapters will succeed in conveying some of the sense of fun and excitement we all shared during the symposium. For more information on the Sydney Symposium series and details of our past and future projects please see our Web site (www.sydneysymposium. unsw.edu.au). Six previous volumes of the Sydney Symposium series have been published. All Sydney Symposium books feature original contributions from leading international researchers on key issues in social psychology. Detailed information about our earlier volumes can be found on the series page in this book and on our Web site.

Given its comprehensive coverage, the present book should be useful both as a basic reference book and as an informative textbook to be used in advanced courses dealing with the social aspects of the individual, within relationships and groups. The main target audience for this book comprises researchers, students, and professionals in all areas of the social and behavioral sciences, such as social, cognitive, clinical, counseling, personality, organizational, and applied psychology, as well as sociology, communication studies, and cognitive science. The book is written in a readable yet scholarly style, and students at both the undergraduate and graduate levels should find it an engaging overview of the field and thus useful as a textbook or ancillary text in courses dealing with groups, close relationships, and social psychology. The book should also be of particular interest to people working in applied areas where acts of exclusion are not only common, but have profound consequences, as in industries, schools, institutions, clubs, and other organizations, and in areas of health psychology and counseling.

We want to express our thanks to people and organizations who helped to make the Sydney Symposium of Social Psychology series, and the seventh volume in particular, a reality. Producing a complex multi-authored book such as this is a lengthy and sometimes challenging task. We have been very fortunate to work with such an excellent and cooperative group of contributors. Our first thanks must go to them. Because of their help and professionalism, we were able to finish this project on schedule. Past friendships have not frayed, and no one has been ostracized. We hope that working together on this book has been as positive an experience for them as it has been for us.

The idea of organizing the Sydney Symposia owes much to discussions with and encouragement by Kevin McConkey and subsequent support by Chris Fell, Mark Wainwright, Peter Lovibond, and numerous others at the University of New South Wales. At Macquarie University, we appreciated the financial and social support of Judy Ungerer, Anne Burns, and John Loxton. And finally we would like to thank the Australian Research Council for their support. Our colleagues at Macquarie University and Purdue University, Nickie Newton and Kim Parish —have helped with advice, support, and sheer hard work to share the burden of preparing and organizing the symposium and the ensuing book. We also thank Paul Dukes at Psychology Press and Lynn Goeller at EvS Communications. Most of all, we are grateful for the love and support of our families, who have put up with us during the many months of work that went into producing this book.

Kipling Williams, Joseph Forgas, and William von Hippel, April 2005

1

The Social Outcast

An Overview

KIPLING D. WILLIAMS
JOSEPH P. FORGAS
WILLIAM VON HIPPEL
LISA ZADRO

INTRODUCTION

We are essentially social creatures. Throughout most of our evolutionary history, we lived, loved, and labored within the confines of small, intimate *groups* where we knew, and were known by, each member. Within these groups, we were sheltered from the elements, protected from predators, and

This work was supported by an Australian Research Council Grant to Kipling D. Williams and a Special Investigator award from the Australian Research Council, the Research Prize by the Alexander von Humboldt Foundation to Joseph P. Forgas. Address correspondence to: Kipling D. Williams, Department of Psychological Science, Purdue University, West Lafayette, IN, 47907-2004, USA. E-mail: kip@psych.purdue.edu

ultimately given the opportunity to propagate and prosper. To be rejected and excluded from the group, and thus from all the benefits of membership, would have been a death sentence—left alone without food, shelter, and vulnerable to outside attack, the life of a social outcast would have been brutal and brief. Hence our survival would have depended on our ability to detect imminent rejection and thereby act—cognitively, emotionally, and behaviorally—to regain our membership in the group.

As technology advanced and our civilization evolved, the dynamics of our day-to-day existence changed, and our social ties to those around us gradually became more complex and impersonal. Yet, despite this shift from face-to-face communities to sprawling metropolises, the potential for rejection and exclusion continues to permeate our society. Every aspect of our day-to-day lives contains the potential for some form of ostracism—for instance, in the workplace, our colleagues may deliberately or inadvertently fail to answer our e-mails, or may exclude us from after-hours social gatherings; in the home, our loved ones may punish us for some misdemeanor by leaving the room when we enter and refusing to meet our gaze over the dinner table; even in public transport, we may sit in such close proximity to a fellow passenger that we are forced to spend the entire journey uncomfortably wedged against one another, yet we will sit in silence and act as though we are traveling alone. Thus, it seems that regardless of whether it is socially sanctioned or personally directed, exclusion and rejection have remained a fundamental part of our social existence, as too has our very primitive and automatic adaptive sensitivity to even the slightest hint of social exclusion.

Understanding how people relate to each other, why they choose to exclude and ignore others, and what determines their response to rejection and exclusion has never been of greater importance than today. Recent research has linked being excluded to aversive psychological effects (e.g., depression, alienation, suicide), as well as to aversive behavioral outcomes (e.g., mass killings such as the shootings at Columbine High School; see Leary, Kowalski, Smith, & Phillips, 2003). Yet despite the far reaching implications of social exclusion on both the social outcast and on society as a whole, it was only in the last decade that social psychology began to regard social exclusion as an area worthy of investigation rather than merely an outcome to be avoided.

This book represents the culmination of a little more than a decade's worth of research, bringing together researchers across allied fields to understand more about the antecedents and consequences of social exclusion and rejection, and about the processes involved when they occurred. The subtitle of this book reflects the fact that as yet, four conceptually related topics exist that tap into the experience of being a social outcast: ostracism, social exclusion, rejection, and bullying. Not only are we not certain about the extent to which these phenomena overlap (see Leary, this volume, for an integrative attempt), but precise definitions for each are lacking. Generally speaking, ostracism refers to being ignored and excluded (Williams, 1997; 2001). Social exclusion refers to not being included within a given social network (but not necessarily ignored). Rejection is usually an explicit verbal or physical action that declares that the individual is not wanted as a member within a relationship or group. Bullying usually involves others' aversive focus on an individual, and often is accompanied by physical, verbal and nonverbal abuse of an individual.

THE BACKGROUND

Throughout the centuries, poets, writers, philosophers, and social commentators have often debated the nature of rejection and social exclusion, particularly when manifested through tactics such as the "silent treatment." Silence, when communication is expected, is inextricably tied to the act of ostracism. But it is clear from literature and science that silence, by itself, can mean many things. To some, silence is a noble act (e.g., "speech is silvern, silence is golden," [Swiss Inscription]; "nothing is more useful than silence," [Menander]; "well-timed silence has more eloquence than speech" [Martin Farquhar Tupper]), whereas others view silence as petty or malicious (e.g., "silence is the virtue of fools"[Sir Francis Bacon]; "in the end, we will remember not the words of our enemies, but the silence of our friends, " [Martin Luther King Jr.]). Silence has been conceived as an act of kindness toward others (e.g., "if you have nothing nice to say, say nothing at all," [Anonymous]; "a good word is an easy obligation; but to not speak ill requires only our silence which costs nothing," [John Tillston]), or as a deliberate and effective act of cruelty (e.g., "silence is the most perfect expression of scorn," [George Bernard Shaw]; "the cruelest lies are often told in silence," [Robert Louis Stevenson]). Thus, silence is ambiguous, and perhaps contributes to the difficulty people have coping with ostracism. On the one hand, targets of silence can pretend it is not happening, and can bask in the ambiguity by denying that they are being excluded. On the other hand, if individuals are "cast out" through silence, they may lack vital information they could use to correct their behavior, or to cope with their exclusion.

Of course, not all acts of rejection and social exclusion involve silence. Some forms of rejection involve hurtful words and explicit derogation; and at other times involve physical abuse. When being socially outcast is more explicit (and hence, less ambiguous) as is often the case in rejection and bullying, targets can at least *know* for certain that they are indeed being outcast. Whereas this prevents the ability to deny the experience, they may be better able to cope with it. They also know that they are not invisible and unworthy of attention, but instead, are important enough to be the objects of inattention and abuse.

Whether presented as an act of good or evil, virtue or sin, social exclusion is a complex phenomenon that, in its many guises, has transcended time, and has a place in our day-to-day lives from our first breath to our last gasp. Our experiences with social exclusion begin early in life. For most of us, we have some experience with being teased, bullied, silenced, excluded, and rejected by our peers from infancy (e.g., Barner-Barry, 1986; Sheldon, 1996) to adolescence (Cairns, Cairns, Neckerman, & Ferguson, 1989). As we grow older, the prevalence of ostracism is such that all individuals will be both a victim (i.e., a target) and a perpetrator (i.e., a source) of some form of social exclusion and rejection within almost all of their relationships, whether with loved ones, colleagues, or strangers. In our day-to-day lives, apparently innocuous episodes of ostracism in which we ignore and are ignored by strangers on the street or fellow passengers on elevators, buses, and trains are interwoven with more emotionally grueling episodes in which we choose to ignore or are ignored by those we love. In fact, 67% of a representative U.S. sample admitted using the silent treatment (deliberately not speaking to a person in their presence) on a loved one, and 75% indicated that they had been a target of the silent treatment by a loved one (Faulkner, Williams, Sherman, & Williams, 1997).

Even if our experience with ostracism in our personal life is minimal, we are bound to encounter other forms of ostracism in societal institutions, such as schools (e.g., time-outs, expulsion), the workplace (e.g., in the ostracism of "whistleblowers" by co-workers; Faulkner, 1998), the legal system (e.g., placing those guilty of a crime in prison; Lynn & Armstrong, 1996), and the church, where almost all religions punish non-compliance to ecclesiastical law with some form of excommunication (Zippelius, 1986).

The prevalence of ostracism throughout all aspects of our day-to-day life has led to a body of research that explores ostracism from various perspectives. Anthropologists, sociologists, biologists, physiologists, ethnologists, zoologists, and legal experts among others (see Gruter & Masters, 1986), have all examined the phenomenon across different cultures and species. Yet, it is surprising that there has been little *psychological* investigation into the nature, causes, or consequences of ostracism. Indeed, until the last decade, there were only a handful of studies that explicitly examined the consequences of being ignored, excluded or rejected, and most of these were stand-alone studies that were generally atheoretical, and varied in their conceptual and operational definitions of ostracism.

Many of the early studies typically focused on *physical isolation* to understand the psychological effects of exclusion. For instance, in what is probably the most radical of the studies examining the potential consequences of social exclusion, Schachter (1959) isolated five volunteers in a windowless room for as long as they could possibly endure being separated from others and found considerable individual differences in the amount of time participants tolerated the isolation.

Subsequent studies tended to study *psychological* rather than physical isolation. The underlying notion in these studies was that individuals could feel isolated even when in the presence of other people. These studies achieved psychological isolation through rejection, exclusion, or being ignored by others. In general, researchers tended to manipulate these forms of ostracism using a group social interaction, consisting of one participant (the target of social exclusion) and two or more confederates (the sources of exclusion).

These studies of psychological isolation varied in the way in which social exclusion was conceptualized. Some of these studies focused on examining the effects of being explicitly *rejected* from participation in a group activity (e.g., Dittes, 1959), whereas others conceptualized psychological isolation as being *ignored* (Geller, Goodstein, Silver, & Sternberg, 1974). Other researchers combined forms of social exclusion with other types of interpersonal rejection (e.g., argument or abuse). For instance, Mettee, Taylor, and Fisher (1971) examined "being shunned" in terms of physical avoidance and verbal abuse. Regardless of the nature of the paradigm used to induce ostracism, these studies have typically found that being rejected, excluded, and ignored had detrimental effects on the thoughts, feelings, and behaviors of targets (see also, the more general feeling of being lonely, as discussed by Cacioppo and Hawkley, this volume).

In addition to examining the psychological effects of ostracism on targets several of the early studies also investigated targets' thoughts and feeling toward their ostracizers. In some studies, participants who had been rejected rated the sources as less likeable (Pepitone & Wilpizeski, 1960), or less favorably (Geller et al., 1974) than those who were not ignored. Social exclusion was also found to affect the desire of targets to affiliate with their ostracizers. However, the findings on this point are somewhat contradictory. In some studies, targets preferred to avoid, or not work with, the ostracizers in the future (e.g., Mettee et al., 1971; Pepitone & Wilpizeski, 1960) whereas in other studies, targets expressed a desire to be with, or work with, those who had ostracized them (Snoek, 1962). These contradictory reactions are reflected in the various chapters in this book (see for instance, Williams & Zadro; Baumeister & DeWall; Twenge; Sommer, & Rubin, and Gaertner & Iuzzini; this volume).

Overall, these studies provide invaluable information about the nature of social exclusion. However, because many of these early studies were preliminary in nature, they present several limitations. The primary limitation is that the majority of these studies did not adequately acknowledge the complexity of ostracism. Hence, many of the early studies employed forms of social exclusion that may be phenomenologically different, yet treated them as equivalent (e.g., physically moving away versus ignoring the target) and thus did not ascertain whether different types of exclusion have different effects on the target. Second, these studies typically focused on the effects of social exclusion on targets, and thereby failed to explore the potential effects (beneficial or detrimental) of being a source of exclusion. Without an understanding as to why people use forms of ostracism, social exclusion, rejection, and bullying, there is little chance that we will be able to determine strategies that can be used to help individuals cope with these aversive experiences or for individuals who habitually use these aversive techniques to consider the benefits of using alternative constructive techniques. Finally, the early studies centered on examining the self-reported psychological effects of being excluded and ignored. Although this is an important first step, further research was clearly necessary to examine the effects of social exclusion on emotional, cognitive, and physiological processes in order to ascertain the range of potential consequences of social exclusion. These goals are now being realized in the work represented in this book. Physiological and social cognitive neuroscience paradigms are prevalent in the work of Eisenberger and Lieberman and MacDonald, Kingsbury, and Shaw. Emotional impact forms the substantial focus of Baumeister and DeWall, Twenge, Sommer and Rubin, and of Fitness.

Despite the limitations, the early studies provided a solid foundation for future social exclusion research. Yet amazingly, research in this area ground to a halt as social psychologists failed to acknowledge the importance of this complex phenomenon. It is only during the last decade that social exclusion research has experienced a renaissance of sorts, resulting in a surge of new theories on the nature of social exclusion, new models on which to base experimental research, and new paradigms that provide ingenious ways to explore the effects of being a target and/or source of social exclusion. Unlike the single-study approach of early research, current exclusion researchers often used a multi-method approach to conduct systematic programs of research into the nature, causes, and consequences of social exclusion. Moreover, these studies have aimed to broaden our understanding of the consequences of this phenomenon by examining not only the self-reported effects of exclusion, but also the behavioral, cognitive, and physiological effects of being excluded, rejected, and ignored.

This brings us to the organization of this book. Although the field of social exclusion is still in its infancy, the main objective of this book is to explore our current understanding of the powerful consequences of social exclusion, at the neurophysiological, emotional, cognitive, and behavioral levels. Part I will put forward grand integrative models and theories that try to encapsulate the experience of rejection and exclusion. As sweeping as these conceptualizations are, we also recognize that some individuals are more susceptible to acts of exclusion than are others, hence Part II will explore and explain these individual differences. Part III will examine how, once excluded, individuals perceive and respond to their social environments differently, leading them to interpret and attend to particular information that may help them cope, or often, that may perpetuate their state of exclusion. Part IV will discuss the nature and antecedents of adaptive and maladaptive reactions to social exclusion. Finally, Part V will report several research programs aimed at extricating the links between social exclusion and pro-social or anti-social behavior.

PART I: THEORETICAL FOUNDATIONS

In Chapter 2, Kip Williams and Lisa Zadro put forth a revised model of ostracism (originally developed by Williams, 1997), and summarize a program of research in their labs that seeks to describe the temporally changing reactions to ostracism. They begin by asserting that a considerable number of studies have now been conducted that appear to demonstrate that ostracism—being ignored and excluded—is immediately experienced as painful. They also argue that factors that ought to moderate this painful experience are inconsequential. For example, individuals report lower moods, threatened needs, and register physiological responses regardless of whether the ostracism is done by ingroup members or outgroup members, a computer or humans, or even by despised others. Additionally, individual differences such as social phobia, narcissism, self-esteem, and collectivism do not moderate the painful immediate experience. Williams and Zadro argue that reactions to ostracism follow three stages. In Stage 1, they propose an adaptive early indiscriminate detection system that warns individuals of the potential survival threat of being ignored and excluded. In Stage 2, individuals respond and cope with ostracism according to individual differences and moderating situational factors. For individuals who continue to be ostracized over the course of their life, the authors propose Stage 3, in which individuals are overly sensitized to detecting ostracism and whose resources to cope with it are depleted.

In Chapter 3, Mark Leary notes that several researchers have studied many different phenomena that involve, in one way or another, real, implied, or imagined interpersonal rejection, including exclusion, ostracism, stigmatization, bullying, childhood peer rejection, unrequited love, and jealousy. In his chapter, Leary offers an overarching conceptualization of interpersonal rejection that both identifies the common features of all rejecting events and that accounts for differences among different kinds of rejections. In addition, data are presented to demonstrate the utility of this conceptualization for understanding emotional responses to rejecting events. According to the proposed conceptualization, all rejection episodes involve the perception that one or more individuals do not value their relationships with the rejected person as much as the person desires. Two lines of research are described that examined the role of low perceived relational evaluation in the experience of rejection. One line suggests that low relational evaluation is the source of hurt feelings in response to rejecting events, but that other emotions that often accompany rejection (e.g., sadness, anger) spring from other factors. The other line of research shows that the strength of people's reactions to perceived rejection is directly related to the degree to which they feel that the perpetrator does not value their relationship.

In Chapter 4, Roy Baumeister and C. Nathan DeWall describe their (and their colleagues') original intent to study the effects of thwarting the need to belong, in which they predicted that rejection would cause strong emotional reactions that would, in turn, produce behavioral changes. They found plenty of behavioral changes but they were not mediated by emotion. Hence they had to reconsider what inner processes are changed in the wake of rejection. In this chapter, Baumeister and DeWall provide evidence that rejection impairs cognition and self-regulation. That is, intelligent thought is impaired among rejected people, though the impairments are specific to the more complex and volitional forms of thought (i.e., automatic processes seem unaffected). Furthermore, rejected subjects show impaired self-regulation, which could explain the rise in both selfish, impulsive actions and in self-defeating behavior.

PART II: DEEP ROOTS OF EXCLUSION: NEUROPSYCHOLOGICAL SUBSTRATES OF ISOLATION AND EXCLUSION

The detection of imminent or actual rejection is vital to survival in social beings such as humans, and early detection of exclusion allows us to take steps to be re-included in the group. Hence, it is not surprising that researchers have examined deeper processes involved in the detection of exclusion and rejection in their examination of the potency of this phenomenon, including physiological and dispositional bases.

In Chapter 5, Geoff MacDonald, Rachell Kingsbury, and Stephanie Shaw present evidence to connect detection of social pain with the detection of physical pain. According to social pain theory (MacDonald & Leary, 2005), the experience of social exclusion triggers painful feelings, and thus activates the physiological system that functions to protect individuals from physical threats. The authors present three studies supporting this view. In the first, they show that chronic pain patients report higher sensitivity to rejection than do controls, and that the relation between sensitivity to rejection and outcomes such as anxiety is partially mediated by reports of physical pain. In the second, they present evidence that individuals higher in rejection sensitivity are more vigilant for physical threat. In the third, they demonstrate that rejection sensitive individuals respond to social exclusion with decreased sensitivity to physical pain, a common response to physical injury. They conclude by discussing the implications of social pain theory for anti-social behavior such as relationship aggression.

In Chapter 6, John Cacioppo and Louise Hawkley present a model of the effects of loneliness on health and well being that emphasizes the mediational role of social perception and cognition. Specifically, lonely, compared to nonlonely, individuals are more likely to construe their world (including the behavior of others) as punitive or potentially punitive. Consequently, lonely individuals are more likely to be socially anxious, hold more negative expectations for their treatment by others, and adopt a prevention focus rather than a promotion focus in their social interactions. Relatedly, lonely, relative to nonlonely, individuals are more likely to appraise stressors as threats rather than challenges, and to cope with stressors in a passive, isolative fashion rather than an active fashion that includes actively seeking the help and support of others. Together, these differences in social cognition predictably result in an increased likelihood of lonely individuals acting in self-protective and, paradoxically, self-defeating ways.

In Chapter 7, Naomi Eisenberger and Matthew Lieberman begin by asserting that being socially excluded has damaging psychological, behavioral, and physiological effects. Being excluded, rejected, or separated from others is such a wounding experience that it is often described colloquially as "hurting" or "being painful." However, the neural systems underlying the pain associated with social separation ("social pain") have not yet been investigated. Because social distance from others is just as dangerous as hunger, thirst, or physical injury for mammalian species, Panksepp (1998) suggested a possible overlap between the systems that regulate social pain and the systems that regulate physical pain. In other words, the importance of regulating social distance led to the evolution of a social pain system that piggybacked onto the physical pain system, with the goal of minimizing social distance. Thus, the anticipation, experience, and recovery from physical and social pain may rely on the same neural machinery. Though provocative, there has been little empirical support for this overlap. Here the authors review several neuroimaging studies that provide evidence showing that the same neural circuitry plays a role in both physical and social pain. They also posit several novel hypotheses regarding how the same social factors that influence social pain would likely influence physical pain as well.

PART III: INDIVIDUAL AND POPULATION DIFFERENCES AND THE IMPACT OF SOCIAL EXCLUSION AND BULLYING

Although it appears that almost everybody reacts negatively to being cast out of their social network, research has also examined the extent to which some people are more likely to experience such social exclusion more negatively than others.

In Chapter 8, Geraldine Downey and Rainer Romero assert that it is not surprising that rejection by significant individuals and social groups triggers a variety of maladaptive reactions, including depression, suicidal behavior, and violence. Yet, they contend that although everyone experiences rejection at various points in their lives, such extreme responses are relatively uncommon. Why do some people respond to rejection in ways that compromise their well-being and relationships, whereas others do not? To help explain variability in people's responses to rejection, Downey and Romero propose a specific cognitive-affective processing disposition, rejection sensitivity (RS). They review the literature, and then describe their efforts to understand more fully why people who anxiously expect rejection behave in ways that lead to the realization of their worst fears. First, they describe research testing their guiding assumption that RS is a defensively-motivated system that gets elicited by rejection-relevant stimuli. Second, they describe the effects of being in this defensive state on the perception of rejection. Third, they describe laboratory research supporting the prediction that being in this defensive state triggers strenuous efforts to prevent rejection that involve over-accommodation, self-silencing, and excessive solicitousness. In the final section of the chapter, they discusses how the knowledge gained from this research program can potentially guide the development of interventions aimed at reducing the personal and interpersonal difficulties in which RS is implicated, including depression and interpersonal violence and hostility.

In Chapter 9, Jaana Juvonen and Elisheva Gross turn our attention to the very real and alarming phenomenon of bullying, specifically how it has been examined within the developmental psychology literature. The study of social outcasts has a long tradition in developmental psychology. This topic has received a great deal of attention in light of the robust empirical evidence showing that rejected and bullied youth are at high risk for adjustment problems. Juvonen and Gross provide insights from developmental research on the complex array of intrapersonal and interpersonal difficulties that both lead to and result from peer rejection. After a brief comparison of the last decade of relevant research published in developmental and social psychology's leading journals, they analyze the social function of rejection for the group. They then examine the personal consequences of rejection by focusing on the role that individual differences and social-contextual factors (e.g., witnessed incidents of bullying) play in moderating the association between rejection and social pain. They end the chapter by proposing a general conceptual model of the intrapersonal and group-level processes by which peer rejection places youth at risk for long-term maladaptive outcomes.

In Chapter 10, Kristin Sommer and Yonata Rubin begin by observing that rejection may cause people to question their overall desirability to others. Social expectancies, in turn, predict the cognitive and behavioral strategies that people employ to cope with rejection. Specifically, when people believe that others will like and accept them, they respond to rejection by reinforcing and strengthening their relationships. However, if they believe that others will not like and accept them, they respond by withdrawing from and devaluing their relationships. In support of this, Sommer and Rubin cite evidence showing that responses to rejection often depend on trait self-esteem, which reflects the extent to which people feel generally accepted by others. The authors also present recent experimental data showing that negative social expectancies following interpersonal rejection cause people to behave in ways that jeopardize their future attachments. Finally, they discuss how the emotional detachment and interpersonally-destructive behaviors of rejected people may reflect efforts to protect the self from additional harm.

In Chapter 11, Susan Fiske and Mariko Yamamoto examine reactions to rejection across cultures, but they begin by asserting that regardless of culture, a few core social motives are used to explain why people respond to others as they do. Chief among these is the motive for belonging. People live happier, healthier, longer lives if they are accepted by at least a small group of other people. From this follows two relatively cognitive motives, the need for a socially shared understanding, to coordinate with others, and the need for controlling, to influence one's outcomes that are contingent on others. Two more affectively focused motives are enhancing self, maintaining the feeling that one is worthy or at least improvable, and trusting, the comparable feeling about ingroup others. The BUCET (belonging, understanding, controlling, enhancing, trust) framework of motives organizes a range of research in social psychology. Fiske and Yamamoto present their explorations into the interplay of various core social motives in people's responses to rejection. They find that whereas American and Japanese college students both found rejection to be unpleasant, the Japanese responded with more emphasis on restoring harmony, whereas the Americans responded with more efforts at self-enhancing and understanding. They interpret their results in light of greater Japanese focus on the belonging self and trust in a long-term, focused ingroup. In comparison, Americans focus more on the individual self that maintains many positive but flexible social ties. If broad-brush cultural differences between American and Japanese responses depend on a more inflated or more modest sense of self in social belonging, these differences appear to be mirrored in American data on people with low and high self-esteem, such that low self-esteem participants who have been rejected respond in more socially desirable directions, whereas high self-esteem participants respond more negatively. The authors expand on these preliminary findings by examining people's meta-expectations and conscious motives concerning relationships and rejection as a function of culture and self-views.

PART IV: INFLUENCES OF REJECTION ON EMOTION, PERCEPTION, AND COGNITION

Not only does being a social outcast affect behavior, it also affects emotion, perception, and cognition. The chapters in this section are devoted to exploring these types of reactions.

In Chapter 12, Jean Twenge asks, does social rejection lead to a negative emotional state? She acknowledges that this should have been the easiest question to answer in our field of research, but it has turned out to be one of the most difficult. She describes two research groups (Williams and Leary) that have consistently found that rejection and/or ostracism causes negative emotions, whereas in her (and Baumeister's) labs, they have consistently found a null effect for emotion after rejection and exclusion. This, she suggests, could be because of differences in method and theory. Ostracism, for example, is a different experience than rejection, involving being ignored rather than explicit rejection. Participants in her experiments always meet their rejectors in person, but those in the Leary experiments typically do not. In her other technique, participants hear that they will be alone later in life, an ostensibly unchangeable condition that may create defensiveness. All labs have found that mood does not mediate effects of rejection on behavior. She presents experiments exploring the role of emotion after social rejection. She finds that excluded participants avoid emotion, regulate their mood, and although mood is sometimes affected, it does not mediate subsequent behaviors. Last, she presents new data in which she explores the effect of rejection severity on mood and aggression.

In Chapter 13, Cynthia Pickett and Wendi Gardner ask what are the processes and mechanisms that contribute to individuals' ability to recover from and avoid rejection? Pickett and Gardner provide a potential answer to this question by describing a model for the regulation of belonging needs. In this model, they propose that deficits in belonging will activate a mechanism (the social monitoring system) designed to attune individuals to social information and social cues in their environment. By noticing opportunities for social interaction and the contingencies of acceptance and rejection, individuals should be more successful at navigating their social world. They begin by describing the components of the model and the model's relation to other known processes involved in detecting and responding to social exclusion. They then summarize the evidence collected to date in their lab that bears upon various aspects of the model and discuss avenues for future research.

In Chapter 14, Wendi Gardner, Megan Knowles, and Cynthia Pickett assert that belonging needs are not always easily fulfilled through direct and positive social interaction. Actual physical distance from loved ones, psychological feelings of isolation, or even daily time demands may all set obstacles on the straightest path to social connection. In this chapter, they explore the more circuitous routes we may take in these circumstances by describing several indirectly social strategies used as fallbacks when direct social opportunities are temporarily thwarted. Some, such as using tangible social symbols, may be relatively common. Others, such as attachment to fictional social surrogates, may be better characterized as the belonging tactics of last resort. Importantly, all may hold important places within the broad portfolio of coping strategies that serve the regulation of belonging needs.

In Chapter 15, Michael Hogg discusses the paradox that, on the one hand, groups accentuate commonalities among members and are about fairness, equality, and inclusion; but, on the other hand, they are intolerant of diversity, contain sharp divisions that identify some members as marginal and of less worth than others, and engage in social exclusion. This paradox is also the background to Orwell's novel *Animal Farm* which is an attack on what he saw as the hypocrisy of Soviet communism, which he believed was actually a reincarnation of Tsarist Russia (inequality, privilege, and exclusion) merely under the guise of socialism (equality, tolerance, and inclusion). Hogg adopts a broad social identity perspective to discuss various aspects of social exclusion in groups. In addition to placing group prototypicality center stage, he develops ideas on uncertainty reduction motivation in groups to address the dynamics of marginal membership. There is a particular focus on deviates and deviant subgroups, and on extremist/pariah groups. One key idea in this chapter is that deviance processes are influenced by which group motivations are contextually prevalent—in particular, enhancement versus epistemic motivations. Hogg also discusses the role of leadership in marginalization processes—deviants and deviant groups are often highly functional for effective leadership, and therefore leaders engage in strategic marginalization processes. He reports current studies from his lab on deviance, leadership, and extremist groups, and make suggestions about positive aspects of deviance. Deviance can be re-characterized as diversity, and diversity has a number of distinct advantages for group functioning.

In Chapter 16, Julie Fitness asserts that families are fundamental to human existence and constitute the primary social group to which humans belong from birth. Further, she says that social psychologists know remarkably little about the causes and consequences of rejection in families. Following a discussion of laypeople's implicit theories about the "rules" of appropriate family conduct, Fitness presents the findings of two, exploratory studies of hypothetically unforgivable rule violations within parent–child, child–parent and sibling relationships—the kinds of violations considered by laypeople to be so serious as to warrant rejection or expulsion from the family. She discusses a variety of structural and dynamic features of families that may contribute to the rejection of children and siblings, including perceived viability, gender, birth order, degree of genetic relatedness, and scapegoating. Finally, Fitness presents the results of a recent study on family favorites and "black sheep" and proposes an agenda for future research.

PART V: EFFECTS OF SOCIAL EXCLUSION ON PRO- AND ANTI-SOCIAL BEHAVIOR

One particular question has become a central focus of many researchers interested in the behavior of social outcasts: do they behave pro-socially or anti-socially? The following chapters shed new light on this important theoretical and social question.

In Chapter 17, Jessica Lakin and Tanya Chartrand note that behavioral mimicry research suggests that mimicking others creates liking and rapport, which means that it may be one way for excluded people to affiliate with others. To explore this idea, Lakin and Chartrand excluded participants in a simulated ball-tossing game and then completed an ostensibly unrelated task with a confederate. In Experiment 1, they demonstrated that people who were excluded during the ballgame mimicked the behaviors of the confederate more than people who were included. In Experiment 2, they extended this finding by showing that participants excluded by an ingroup mimicked an ingroup member more in the subsequent interaction than participants who interacted with an outgroup member or those who were excluded by an outgroup. This effect was mediated by belongingness threat. They suggest that people may be able to address belongingness needs that have been threatened by exclusion by mimicking the behaviors of others, even though mimicry happens without intention, awareness, or conscious control.

In Chapter 18, Kathleen Catanese and Dianne Tice present research demonstrating that social exclusion and rejection can lead to aggressive and anti-social behavior. Excluded people issued a more negative job evaluation against someone who insulted them, and blasted a target with higher levels of aversive noise, both when the target had insulted them, and when the target was a neutral person and no interaction had occurred. However, excluded people were not more aggressive toward someone who issued praise. Not all bad news produced aggression. In their Misfortune Control group in one study, participants were told they would be prone to accidents and would suffer many injuries later in life. This forecast did not produce any perceptible rise in aggression. Apparently social exclusion is not just another kind of personal misfortune. Being alone is in some respects worse than having your bones broken. Aggressive responses were specific to social exclusion (as opposed to other misfortunes) and were not mediated by emotion.

Additional studies varied the exclusion status of the target of the aggression. Excluded participants were given an opportunity to aggress against another person who was described as also excluded by the same group that excluded the participant, excluded by another group, accepted by the group that excluded the participant, or control (not associated with the excluding group in any way). Aggressiveness varied with the exclusion status of the target.

In Chapter 19, Lowell Gaertner and Jonathan Iuzzini examine the possibility that social rejection and perceived entitativity (i.e., groupness) synergistically affect mass violence such that perpetrators are likely to harm multiple persons when rejection emanates from an entity-like group. Gaertner and Iuzzini present a laboratory experiment and a questionnaire study to provide evidence of this synergistic effect. The experiment manipulated whether a 3-person aggregate appeared to be an entity-like group crossed with whether a member of the aggregate rejected the participant. A noise-blast task revealed the predicted interaction: Participants issued the loudest noise against the aggregate when a member of the aggregate rejected the participant and the aggregate appeared to be an entity-like group. A questionnaire study conducted in a high school replicated the Rejection × Entitativity effect by demonstrating that the tendency for rejection to spawn fantasies about harming a social group increased with the perceived entitativity of the group. The authors discuss potential mediators and moderators of the synergistic effect.

And, in Chapter 20, Jaap Ouwerkerk, Paul van Lange, Marcello Gallucci, and Norbert Kerr argue that a threat of ostracism (as well as actual ostracism episodes) may have an important function—suppressing uncooperative behavior that is harmful to a group and its members. For this purpose, they review two of their research programs that demonstrate positive effects of (the threat of) ostracism on cooperative behavior in social dilemmas. More specifically, they show that a threat of ostracism attenuates the so-called "bad apple effect" in a public good dilemma. That is, it reverses the tendency to follow the behavior of a single non-cooperative group member rather than that of a single cooperative group member. Furthermore, a threat of ostracism strengthens our tolerance for multiple bad apples. They conclude with discussing the possible crucial role of ostracism in the evolution of cooperation.

INTEGRATION AND SYNTHESIS

Clearly, while research on the social outcast is burgeoning, conflicting results, differences in conceptualizations, and different foci for examinations of this phenomenon abound. Thus, even at this relatively early stage, it is important to attempt to synthesize that which can be synthesized, to find underlying themes, and overarching questions that should guide future research. Marilynn Brewer superbly handles this task of integration in the final chapter.

Her discussion draws on the conceptual framework of optimal distinctiveness theory of inclusion and belonging. The concept of optimal distinctiveness provides a motivational theory for understanding why social isolation has such powerful psychological effects and how members of groups might use exclusion of others as a mechanism for meeting their own needs for inclusion. A second conceptual framework for discussion is the distinction between interpersonal rejection/ostracism and group exclusion/ostracism. Social deprivation in the form of isolation or ostracism from a relationship partner and deprivation in the form of isolation or exclusion from a large social group may implicate different needs, motives, subjective experience, and reparation strategies. Brewer suggests that the different research paradigms for studying ostracism and its consequences can be examined in terms of this fundamental distinction between two types of social deprivation.

SUMMARY

Social exclusion, in its many forms and facets, permeates all of our relationships and almost every aspect of our lives. The chapters in this book highlight that social exclusion is a complex phenomenon—in many ways, still a mystery. However, the research evident in this book clearly details the deleterious emotional, cognitive, and physiological effects of even short episodes of exclusion and rejection, and hence goes a long way in changing the common perception that "silence is golden." With a phenomenon so ubiquitous, research into its nature and its social, physical, and economic cost is vital. For otherwise, our innate fear of being excluded and rejected, coupled with the rise of an increasingly automated and impersonal society, will ensure that social exclusion will continue to exert a significant personal, social, and economic toll—the extent of which has still to be fully explored.

REFERENCES

Barner-Barry, C. (1986). Rob: Children's tacit use of peer ostracism to control aggressive behavior. *Ethnology and Sociobiology, 7,* 281–293.

Cairns, R. B., Cairns, B. D., Neckerman, H. J., & Ferguson, L. L. (1989). Growth and aggression: I. Childhood to early adolescence. *Developmental Psychology, 25,* 320–330.

Dittes, J. E. (1959). Attractiveness of group as function of self esteem and acceptance by group. *Journal of Abnormal and Social Psychology, 59,* 77–82.

Faulkner, S. L. (1998). *After the whistle is blown: The aversive impact of ostracism.* Unpublished doctoral dissertation, University of Toledo.

Faulkner, S., Williams, K., Sherman, B., & Williams, E. (1997, May). *The "silent treatment:" Its incidence and impact.* Presented at the 69th Annual Midwestern Psychological Association, Chicago, IL.

Geller, D. M., Goodstein, L., Silver, M., & Sternberg, W. C. (1974). On being ignored: The effects of violation of implicit rules of social interaction. *Sociometry, 37,* 541–556.

Gruter, M., & Masters, R. D. (1986). Ostracism as a social and biological phenomenon: An introduction. *Ethology and Sociobiology, 7,* 149–158.

Leary, M. R., Kowalski, R. M., Smith, L., & Phillips, S. (2003). Teasing, rejection, and violence: Case studies of the school shootings. *Aggressive Behavior, 29,* 202–214.

Lynn, P., & Armstrong, G. (1996). *From Pentonville to Pentridge: A history of prisons in Victoria.* Victoria, Australia: State Library of Victoria.

Mettee, D. R., Taylor, S. E., & Fisher, S. (1971). The effect of being shunned upon the desire to affiliate. *Psychonomic Science, 23,* 429–431.

Panksepp, J. (1998). *Affective neuroscience.* New York: Oxford Univeristy Press.

Pepitone, A., & Wilpizeski, C. (1960). Some consequences of experimental rejection. *Journal of Abnormal and Social Psychology, 60,* 359–364.

Schachter, S. (1959). *The psychology of affiliation.* Stanford, CA: Stanford University Press.

Sheldon, A. (1996). You can be the baby brother but you aren't born yet: Preschool girls' negotiation for power and access in pretend play. *Research on Language and Social Interaction, 29,* 57–80.

Snoek, J. D. (1962). Some effects of rejection upon attraction to a group. *Journal of Abnormal and Social Psychology, 64,* 175–182.

Williams, K. D. (1997). Social ostracism. In R. M. Kowalski (Ed.), *Aversive interpersonal behaviors* (pp. 133–170). New York: Plenum.

Williams, K. D. (2001). *Ostracism: The power of silence.* New York: Guilford Press.

Zippelius, R. (1986). Exlusion and shunning as legal and social sanctions. *Ethology and Sociobiology, 7,* 159–166.

PART I

THEORETICAL
FOUNDATIONS

2

Ostracism
The Indiscriminate Early Detection System

KIPLING D. WILLIAMS
LISA ZADRO

INTRODUCTION

Animals who are ostracized inevitably face an early death. They are ostracized by their pack for being mentally or physically ill, or for any other behavioral displays that might threaten the survival of the group (Gruter & Masters, 1986). Once ostracized, they lack the resources to capture and secure their own food, no longer enjoy the protection of their group, and are prevented from forming bonds that provide social sustenance (Lancaster, 1986). They lag behind, become decimated, and eventually die through malnutrition or from attack. Detecting ostracism—being ignored and excluded—must be an invaluably adaptive response if it can guide the animal to alter its behaviors so that it will be re-embraced by its collective.

Address correspondence to: Kipling D. Williams, Department of Psychological Sciences, Purdue University, West Lafayette, IN 47907, USA. E-mail: kip@psych.purdue.edu

Although some humans ostracized by all groups have survived as hermits (Buchholz, 1995; Halpern, 1993), the infrequency of such occurrences suggests that for humans also, ostracism threatens survival. And if not a threat to the individual, it is certainly a threat to the continuance of their genetic line. Thus, it would be adaptive for humans to possess an early detection system in response to any signs that they are being ignored and excluded. When ostracism is detected, it is likely to be painful in order to motivate and activate a set of responses that will remove the pain. It would be maladaptive if humans showed wide variability in their detection of ostracism. To not perceive being ignored and excluded would be similar to not perceiving the pain of fire. Enduring it without responding would only ensure its devastating effects. Once it has been detected, then it is likely that individual differences and variations within and across cultures will determine what sort of responses are used to cope with the pain.

This analysis forms the basis for the studies reviewed in this chapter. We will first present a model of ostracism that integrates a variety of social motivational theories in psychology as they pertain to reactions to ostracism. We suggest that ostracism is unique in threatening four fundamental social motivations. Threats to these social motives are, for each motive, painful physically, emotionally, and socially. Individuals are then likely to remove the pain by actions or thoughts that will reduce the pain. Behavioral and/or cognitive responses are likely to re-establish optimal levels of one or more of these social motives. Highly adaptive responses should reduce the likelihood of continued ostracism. Responses that provide only an immediate salve to ostracism may relieve the pain temporarily, but may perpetuate further ostracism. Continued exposure to ostracism will eventually deplete the resources necessary to respond successfully, and may lead to an existence of loneliness (see Cacioppo, this volume) and despair.

A MODEL OF OSTRACISM

We are guided by a model of ostracism proposed first in 1997 (Williams, 1997), and revised subsequently in 2001 (Williams & Zadro, 2001; Williams, 2001). Our model attempts to provide an overarching framework within which to appreciate and conceptualize the complex varieties of ostracism, provide testable hypotheses, and direct research. This model continues to evolve, and at the end of this chapter we will offer suggestions for further revisions. Most of the model focuses on the perspective of the person or persons being ostracized—the targets. We will describe the model, as depicted in Figure 2.1, in a sequence that reflects first the core of the theory, then the periphery (Maddi, 1980). The core is presumed to be the effects that all individuals feel when being ostracized. The periphery distinguishes between types of ostracism and types of people that may moderate its affects.

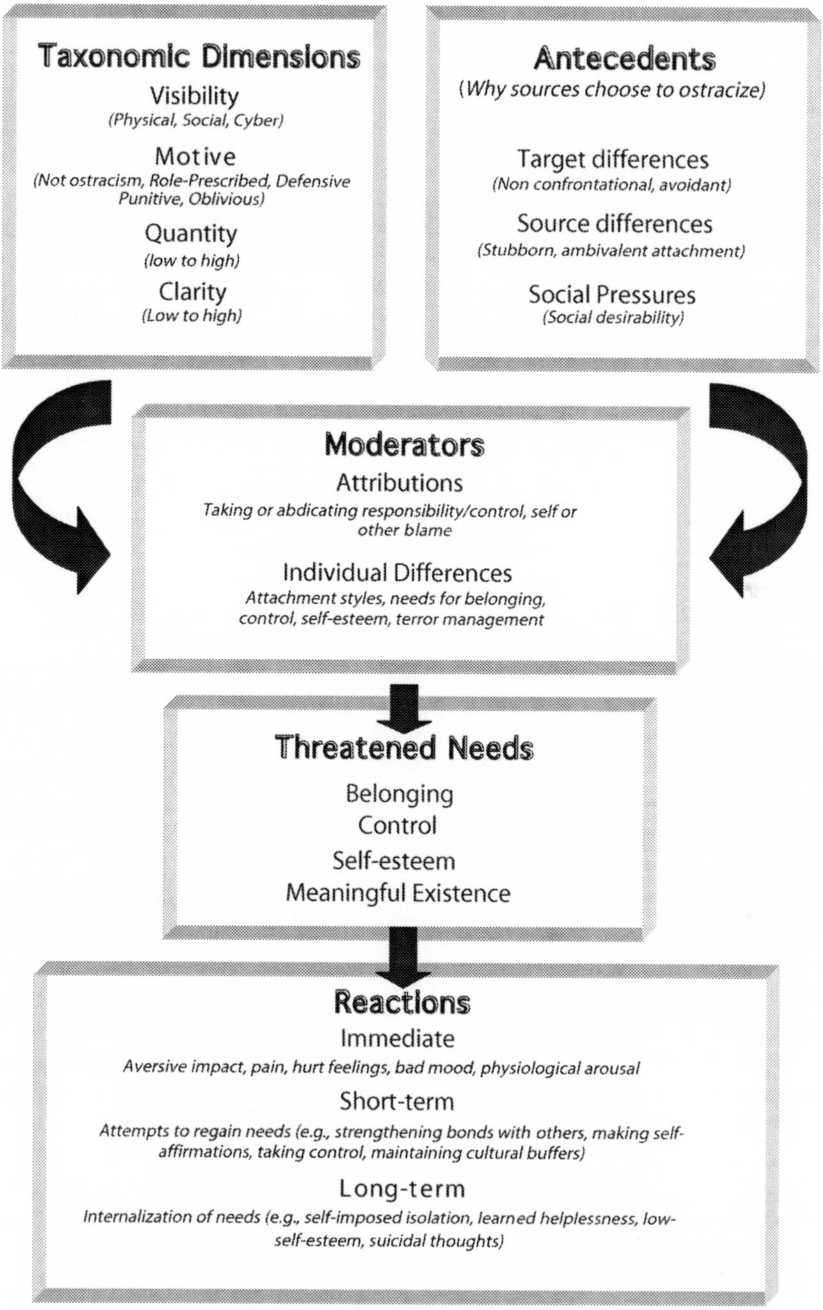

Taxonomic Dimensions

Visibility
(Physical, Social, Cyber)

Motive
(Not ostracism, Role-Prescribed, Defensive
Punitive, Oblivious)

Quantity
(low to high)

Clarity
(Low to high)

Antecedents
(Why sources choose to ostracize)

Target differences
(Non confrontational, avoidant)

Source differences
(Stubborn, ambivalent attachment)

Social Pressures
(Social desirability)

Moderators

Attributions
Taking or abdicating responsibility/control, self or
other blame

Individual Differences
Attachment styles, needs for belonging,
control, self-esteem, terror management

Threatened Needs

Belonging
Control
Self-esteem
Meaningful Existence

Reactions

Immediate
Aversive impact, pain, hurt feelings, bad mood, physiological arousal

Short-term
Attempts to regain needs (e.g., strengthening bonds with others, making self-
affirmations, taking control, maintaining cultural buffers)

Long-term
Internalization of needs (e.g., self-imposed isolation, learned helplessness, low-
self-esteem, suicidal thoughts)

FIGURE 2.1 Williams's (1997/2001) Model of Ostracism

Core—Threats and Reactions

As shown in the bottom two boxes in Figure 2.1, we postulate that there are four needs or social motives that are threatened when individuals are ostracized. In reaction to these threats, targets of ostracism pass through three stages of responding and coping. None of these needs or social motives are new inventions of the model; all enjoy considerable empirical support for their existence and importance in sustaining and motivating human behavior. The novel aspect of the model is that usually the literatures and interest in these four needs are separate and mutually exclusive. In some cases, there are attempts to engulf or subsume one or more needs into another, but from our observation, these proclamations are more provocative than testable. Our position is that all four needs are unique and important, but probably hold fuzzy boundaries.

Most researchers and theorists in the area of ostracism, social exclusion, and rejection acknowledge that these related aversive interpersonal behaviors threaten a fundamental need to belong (in this volume, see chapters by Baumeister, Gardner, Leary, Pickett, Tice, Sommer, and Twenge). The need to belong (Baumeister & Leary, 1995) has been shown to be of such importance that without it, people suffer mental and physical illness, and are rendered incapacitated. Baumeister and Leary hypothesized that people need to feel a sense of belonging no more than a few important others, but we believe that a threat to belonging, even to strangers, evokes a strong immediate warning.

One might argue that any sort of aversive interaction threatens belonging, but we find (Zadro, Williams, & Richardson, 2005) that ostracism threatens belonging more clearly and more strongly than other unpleasant social responses. Consider a comparison between being given the silent treatment (a form of ostracism) and being the target of a heated argument. Both are clearly aversive, but, within the argument, there is an interaction—one is still connected to the other(s). The connection is strained, but it exists. The same cannot be said for being the target of the silent treatment. There is an implicit, and perhaps explicit divorce between the source(s) and the target. There is no back-and-forth, no playing field on which to relate to the others. For all intents and purposes, it is as though the target no longer exists. There is no belonging.

Another need that enjoys some attention by other researchers is the threat to self-esteem, especially social self-esteem—how we perceive others to perceive our goodness and worth (see Leary's sociometer theory; e.g., Leary, Tambor, Terdal, & Downs, 1995). In one sense, from Leary's perspective, self-esteem is nothing more than a gauge for belonging and acceptance, thus self-esteem is a proxy for belonging. While we agree with this idea to a degree, we also think there is more to the threat of ostracism to self-esteem than simply as a means for estimating inclusionary status. Once again, let's compare argument to the silent treatment. In an argument, it is usually relatively clear what the target has done or said about which there is disapproval. This offense in question is usually the subject matter of the argument: the husband came home late without calling; the co-worker did not contribute sufficiently to the group task. Thus, although damaging to one's self-esteem, there is a sense of containment that makes coping with the problem relatively manageable. Even if one feels badly about a misdeed, other positive self-concepts can be brought forth to affirm the self (Steele, 1988). Ostracism, however, often (but not always) occurs without much in the way of an explanation. The target is usually left to surmise (a) that they are being ostracized, and (b) the reason for it. Without being given the specific reason, targets must generate plausible reasons for the occurrence of ostracism. This list might be comprised of one or two obvious infractions, or might extend to three, four, or more possibilities. Actively generating a list of wrong-doings that would warrant ostracism surely threatens self-esteem to a greater degree than does focused displeasure with a specific offense. In this sense, we think that self-esteem is threatened more by ostracism than by other forms of rejection.

A third need or social motive that has received considerable attention in social and clinical psychology is the need perceive *control* over one's (social) environment (Seligman, 1975, 1998.) Compared to belonging and self-esteem, however, relatively few social exclusion researchers have acknowledged the threat to control that comes with being ostracized (but see Twenge, this volume). To illustrate how control is affected by ostracism, let us again compare being the target of an argument with being a target of the silent treatment. In an argument, the target can influence intensity and course. One can choose calming or inflammatory words, which can either douse the flames with water or gasoline. Likewise, the content can be redirected by bringing up different topics, different perspectives, and different points. Thus, in an argument, the target still has control over the course of the interaction. Such is not the case when being subjected to the silent treatment; nothing one does or says evokes a reaction from the source. Reminiscent of the Uncle Remus fable, the target might just as well communicate with a lump of tar. There is no control when one is being ostracized.

Finally, we think that ostracism has the unique capacity to threaten one's sense of meaningful existence, and even serves as a mortality salience cue. Relying on the extensive research and theory by the terror management perspective (Greenberg, Pyszczynski, & Solomon, 1986), a prime motive for humans is to buffer the terror they feel in contemplating their mortality and insignificance. Even fleeting and unconscious exposures to various cues that remind people of their mortality have been shown to activate responses that shore up their worldviews, from which they derive worth and meaning. Why should ostracism be considered a mortality salience cue? In many tribes around the world, social ostracism is the most extreme form of punishment (Gruter & Masters, 1986; Case & Williams, 2004). The translation for this punishment often refers to death...as in "social death." William James (1897) referred to the terror of being ignored and excluded as being "cut dead." Indeed, we think that being ostracized is a glimpse into what life would be like if the target was nonexistent. To complete the comparison to argument, ostracism provides a very palpable metaphor for death, while argument does not.

Reactions to Threats to the Four Fundamental Needs. Research and theory on the sequence of reactions to threats to any of these four needs tends to follow the same path. The immediate reaction is one of pain and hurt. Then, individuals attempt to reduce the pain by fortifying the level of the need. Thus, if belonging is threatened, there is an attempt to increase a sense of belonging, which can be done cognitively (by reminding oneself about close ties one has with others, or by selective attending to social information) or behaviorally (by conforming to groups, working harder in groups, or even mimicking others—see Lakin & Chartrand, this volume). Similar reactions occur for temporary loss of self-esteem, control, and meaningful existence. If, however, the individual is continually exposed to threats to these needs, then the individual's capacity to cope becomes depleted, and acceptance and resignation take over. Probably the best evidence for this part of the sequence has been shown in the work on loss of control. Early responses are guided by reactance (Wortman & Brehm, 1975) as a means to regain control, but once the energy and means to react are depleted, then learned helplessness sets in (Seligman, 1975, 1998). We propose that targets of continuous ostracism face a similar fate. After coping responses are depleted, an overall despair envelops them; they feel alienated, depressed, helpless, and worthless.

Periphery—Taxonomy of Dimensions

As shown in the upper right box in Figure 2.1, there are several dimensions that capture the variety of types of ostracism. These include the modality, perceived motive, quantity, and clarity.

Modality. Individuals or groups can be *physically* ostracized by being exiled or otherwise removed from the physical presence of others. This includes the typical method employed in corporal punishment of children at home and in the schools—time out, assuming time out means the child is removed from the others and relocated in a private room. Physical ostracism also occurs in the case of banishment, exile, and solitary confinement. Social ostracism occurs when targets are ignored and excluded yet they remain in the presence of the others. At its extreme use, it is as though the target is invisible. Social ostracism is used commonly within relational disputes, otherwise known as the silent treatment. It also occurs informally in the classroom, playground, workplace, military institutions, and church. Cyber ostracism is the term we use to refer to instances of ostracism in which interaction is routinely expected outside face-to-face encounters. As the name suggests, this includes e-mails, chat rooms, text messaging, and interactive computer games, but it can also refer to phone calls and mail.

Motives. We have labeled five motives that can be applied to instances of ostracism, and these ascribed motives can match or mismatch the intended motives of the source(s) of ostracism. These motives have been grouped into two broad categories, intentional and unintentional (Sommer, Williams, Ciarocco, & Baumeister, 2001), but even this designation is a bit misleading. Those motives typically viewed as unintentional include the momentary and fleeting feeling or thought that one is being ignored, but upon closer examination, it becomes immediately clear that it was *not ostracism*. Thus, when someone you address does not answer back, but then you notice they are listening to music on their headset, it is clear that the act was not ostracism. *Role prescribed* ostracism refers to behaviors that appear to be ignoring and excluding, but that are permitted and typical within or across cultures. Standing in an elevator and not being acknowledged by the others, refilling water glasses in a restaurant and not being acknowledged by those being served, and remaining unacknowledged on a bus or train are examples of role-prescribed ostracism. These two designations were originally included because it was thought that they would be easily dismissed and coped with, or would not require any coping, and thus would not have painful affects. To steal the thunder a bit, we will present data that suggests that this assumption may have been incorrect. The so-called intentional acts of ostracism refer to being ostracized as a form of punishment. One perceives *defensive* ostracism as pre-emptive punishment or as self-protective. If your best friend chooses along with all the other co-workers to ostracize you after you have blown the whistle on the organization, one might attribute the motive to self-protection: If they continued talking with you, they, too, might be ostracized (Faulkner, 1998). *Punitive* ostracism is a straightforward attribution that ostracism is being employed to punish. A collection of individuals might perceive that the larger group is punitively ostracizing them because they wear different clothing, or enjoy different activities than the majority. The final motive is difficult to pigeonhole into being unintentional or intentional, as it seems to occupy a fuzzy space between the two. *Oblivious* ostracism refers to non role-prescribed instances in which an individual feels that they are of such low worth or importance to others that they are simply not noticed. They feel they do not matter and do not count. In this sense, they feel truly invisible and cannot even enjoy the thought that they matter enough to be punished.

Quantity. People can be barely ostracized, with subtle changes in language (leaving out personal pronouns of "I" and "you"), ostracized within a given domain (are acknowledged and spoken to about all matters *except* those related to a specific topic), or ostracized fully and completely, to the point they feel that they do not exist from the perspective of the source(s).

Causal Clarity. The reason for the ostracism can be explicit, as in a formal declaration of excommunication. Such as the case of the issuance of Meidung in the Amish community, in which the member is officially ostracized until their offending behavior is corrected. Or, more commonly in informal settings, ostracism can occur without explanation, rendering it frustratingly ambiguous. First, one must ascertain whether they are indeed being ostracized (rather than being, let's say, paranoid), and then one must try to figure out the reason.

These dimensions were explicated because of the belief that, depending upon how and why the ostracism occurred, it would differentially affect the target. Although in the future there may be evidence that such differentiation may be meaningful, our research suggests otherwise: The research we will summarize suggests that at least for immediate reactions, ostracism is painful regardless of mode, motive, quantity, or causal clarity.

Moderators

In the model (depicted in the box at the second level in Figure 2.1), we anticipated that ostracism would have differential impact on individuals depending upon various situational and dispositional factors. The situational factors all distill down to whether self-protective attributions can be made to deflect the hurt associated with ostracism. Thus, for example, being ostracized by an outgroup ought to be easier to handle (and dismiss) than being ostracized by an ingroup. Individual differences that are conceptually related to the four needs were also assumed to be likely moderators of responses to ostracism. For example, if individuals were particularly low in need for belonging or high in self-esteem, then ostracism should have less impact on them compared to those who are high in need for belonging or low in self-esteem. Again, as we shall see, our research to date does not offer much support for this proposition, at least as it applies to immediate responses to ostracism.

Antecedents

Why are people ostracized rather than confronted, ridiculed, or even physically attacked? The box in the upper right hand corner of Figure 2.1 describes potential antecedents for the use of ostracism. Employing ostracism rather than more confrontational methods has certain advantages; as already discussed, it may be more powerful in that it can simultaneously and perhaps more strongly threaten four fundamental needs. It is also relatively ambiguous compared to the other tactics and therefore its use can more easily be denied. In the workplace, for instance, ostracism is a very common response to whistleblowers (Miceli & Near, 1992), probably because it is difficult to prove as constituting illegal retaliation or abuse. Ostracism is stealth-like; it is something that can occur without the knowledge of onlookers. One could easily maintain the silent treatment of a spouse during a dinner party without others knowing it, but could not actively maintain verbal or physical abuse in front of others. So one antecedent of ostracism is that it is probably the best strategy to use in order to maintain a positive impression to others. Two other general categories of antecedents are source variables and target variables. People possessing certain traits may be more likely to ostracize than confront. In a preliminary study, Zadro (2004) found that two individual differences— low need for affiliation and insecure attachment—were significant predictors of the propensity to be a source of ostracism. We suspect that other traits may also play a role as antecedents of ostracism, for instance, stubbornness and avoidance, and these traits are still under investigation. Some targets are more likely to be ostracized than others. For instance, some may be perpetually ostracized due to negative personal qualities—there are undoubtedly some people who are so socially repugnant (e.g., the morally dubious or disturbingly lecherous) that they provoke ostracism in all they meet. Some people may react so negatively to confrontation that sources are left with ostracism as the last, but best, resort. Others may simply possess personality traits that increase their susceptibility to ostracism. Zadro (2004) found that those who possess a preoccupied attachment style (i.e., "I want to be completely emotionally intimate with others, but I often find others are as reluctant to get as close as I would like") was a significant predictor of the likelihood of being a target of ostracism. There are others, however, who may be ignored for positive qualities. For instance, in interviews with long-term targets and sources of ostracism, several sources stated that they often ignored targets who were better debaters than themselves in order to gain the upper hand in the conflict (Zadro, Williams, & Richardson, 2003). Moreover, some targets may be perpetually ostracized because they react so strongly to ostracism that others quickly note its power over them.

REACTIONS TO OSTRACISM ARE QUICK AND POWERFUL

There are now a substantial number of experiments that indicate the quick and powerful effects of relatively minor episodes of ostracism. In these studies, a variety of methods are used to manipulate ostracism (including role play, chat rooms, text messaging), but they share in common the fact that participants are randomly assigned to be ostracized or included. We will confine our review to the two most popular methods of inducing ostracism.

Ball-Toss Paradigm. In our early studies, ostracism was manipulated within the context of a face-to-face triadic ball tossing game. There are studies that employ this method in a face-to-face setting in which a seemingly unplanned game of ball toss ensues during the waiting period. In this method, there is one participant and two confederates, and the game appears unrelated to the experiment (indeed, unknown to the experimenter). Participants are either included, thrown the ball about one-third of the time, or ostracized, thrown the ball a few times at the beginning, then never again, for about 5 minutes. In addition, the confederates avoid all eye contact with ostracized participants, while maintaining appropriate eye contact with included participants. Williams and Sommer (1997) used the ball-toss paradigm (in same-sex triads) and observed nonverbal reactions during it. Following the ball tossing, participants (and confederates) worked either coactively or collectively generating as many uses for an object that they could in a given amount of time. While all included participants enjoyed the game and maintained their enthusiasm throughout, ostracized participants ended up slumping down and looking dejected by the time the 5-minute period had elapsed. During the 5 minutes, males tended to manipulate objects, look in their wallets, and engage in other presumably face-saving behaviors before resigning to their slumping positions. Females were more likely to maintain eye contact and smile, before they too slumped. During the group work task, females who were included loafed when working collectively compared to when they worked coactively, but if they had been ostracized, they socially compensated, working harder collectively than coactively. Regardless of whether they had been included or ostracized, males loafed. For females, the unusual behavior of social compensation (compared to the very typical response of social loafing, see Karau & Williams, 1993, for a review) was interpreted as evidence of an attempt to improve their inclusionary status—being good team players.

Using a similar paradigm, Williams and Lawson Williams (2003) found that following ostracism by two people who appeared to be friends with each other (as opposed to appearing to be strangers), male participants (in Study 1) exerted more social control over a newcomer, and female participants (in Study 2) reported a stronger desire for control. Both measures of control were low for included participants. At an attributional level, these results appear perplexing; one would think it would be easier to discount ostracism by two people who are friends with each other than by two people who are strangers to each other. But, from a control standpoint, the results are clearly supportive: An individual who finds him or herself in a triad with two people who are friends with each other is already stripped of a certain amount of control. When control is diminished further through ostracism, there is an increased motivation to fortify the lost control.

These two studies showed that a short period of ostracism produced behavioral consequences, and both supported the core predictions of the need-threat model: Ostracism increased attempts to fortify threatened needs (of belonging and control).

These demonstrations led to a new paradigm that served two purposes: The ball-toss paradigm was selected initially because it was a relatively clean and context-free method in which ignoring and exclusion could be manipulated. Casual observation of participants during the brief game indicated that it was powerful and aversive. We wondered if we minimized the drama by adding physical and psychological distance to the game, whether exclusion and ignoring would be enough to have negative consequences. Also, the face-to-face ball-toss paradigm was costly, requiring trained confederates. Thus, a new paradigm, Cyberball, was developed that would provide a stronger test of mere ignoring and exclusion by adding more distance, and that required no confederates.

Cyberball.   An Internet game of ball toss was developed by Williams, Cheung, and Choi (2000) in which participants logged on to a Web site that purportedly was interested in the effects of mental visualization on subsequent performance.

Led to believe they were logged on simultaneously with others and were formed into triads, participants were told that in order to stimulate their mental visualization skills they would first partake in a virtual game of toss. They were told that what mattered in the game was not who caught or threw or whether there were overthrows or drops, but that they engaged their mental visualization skills for the brief time of the game. They were to imagine the others players, where they were playing, the weather they were playing in, and anything else that would bring the experience to life. In fact, participants were randomly assigned to be included or ostracized, and the other participants were computer-generated. Minimal animations were employed showing icons for the others and the participant, and showing the ball (or, in the first study, the flying disk). Pre-measures and post-measures were taken, all from the Web site. Over 1,400 participants from over 67 countries participated. In Study 1, self-esteem was measured prior to being assigned to one of four levels of ostracism quantity: over-inclusion (being included more than one-third of the time in the triad), inclusion, partial ostracism, and complete ostracism. Post-measures of mood and self-reported need levels were taken, and the overall results indicated that the more that people were ostracized, the more negative the experience was for them. Self-esteem, while predicting overall distress (lower self-esteem individuals reported more negative experiences overall), did not interact with the ostracism manipulations. In Study 2, following either inclusion or ostracism by two others purported to be ingroup members (they reported using the same computer platform, PC or Mac), outgroup members (the others used a different platform), or mixed-group members (one PC and one Mac user), participants were ostensibly assigned to a new group of five other individuals (of unknown group membership), and they were asked to make perceptual judgments. Participants were always the last to make the judgments, and they could see the judgments of the other five prior to making their own answer. On 3 of the 6 trials, the others (who were really computer-generated) made unanimous correct judgments, but on the other 3 trials, they made unanimous incorrect judgments. Ostracized participants were more likely to conform to the incorrect decisions, especially if they had been ostracized by ingroup or mixed-group members. This result was interpreted as supporting the hypothesis that ostracized individuals would engage in behaviors aimed at increasing their inclusionary status: Conformity to a new group would increase the likelihood that others in the group would accept and like the individual. Interestingly, on measures immediately following the Cyberball game, regardless of who they had played with, ostracized participants reported more negative moods and lower needs. This suggests that factors that ought to moderate the affective reaction to ostracism did not matter, but that subsequent coping responses were sensitive to such factors (i.e., group membership).

Since the initial studies by Williams et al. (2000), Cyberball has not been conducted as a true Internet experiment, but has instead been conducted within laboratories with experimental participants (but the cover story and visual appearance suggest Intranet or Internet experiments to the participants).

The results of subsequent experiments using Cyberball indicate that even with more psychological and physical distance between group members, ostracism has quick and powerful negative effects. In many of these experiments, the power of ostracism overwhelmed factors that are believed to moderate the aversive effects of ostracism. For instance, Zadro, Williams, and Richardson (2005) showed that mood and self-reported needs decline for ostracized participants (compared to included participants) even when the participants are told (truthfully) that they are playing against the computer rather than other people, or when they are told that the game is scripted (i.e., the reason for ostracism is causally explicit).

In another study assessing potential moderators of ostracism, Abraham (2003) asked some participants to think of (implicitly or explicitly) close interpersonal bonds prior to ostracism or inclusion, and once again found strong negative impact on mood and need levels for those participants who were ostracized. Additionally, ostracized participants reported higher incidences of exclusionary themes in their interpretations of a TAT card. However, consistent with the other research, the buffering manipulations had no effect on these measures.

Recently, Eisenberger, Liebermann, and Williams (2003) found that ostracized participants playing Cyberball within an fMRI chamber also reported lower mood and need levels, even when they were told that their chamber had not yet been linked to the computers of other two players (thus, there was no way for the other two players to include them). Additionally, they found that when participants were ostracized, they showed significant increases in activity in their anterior cingulate cortexes, where people also show significant activity when enduring physical pain (for more elaboration on this research, see Eisenberger & Lieberman, this volume).

The search for moderators goes on. Can one imagine an instance in which people would not mind ostracism, or perhaps even prefer ostracism? We tested this by having people be ostracized by a hated outgroup, the Ku Klux Klan (KKK). Gonsalkorale and Williams (2004) convinced participants that in a study examining diverse groups in Australia, they were grouped according to social/political beliefs with ingroup members (Labor supporters paired with Labor supporters; Liberal supporters paired with Liberal supporters), rival, but respected outgroup members (Liberal with Labor and vice versa), or hated outgroup members (KKK of Australia). Regardless of group membership, even for a despised and disgusting outgroup, mood and self-reported need levels dropped with Cyberball ostracism.

In all of these Cyberball studies, the effects sizes of the ostracism manipulation on need satisfaction and mood questions are over 1.00 (often above 1.50) indicating strong effects, and subsequent meta-analyses (Case & Williams, 2003) indicate it takes only three people per condition to reach standard levels of significance. This negative reaction to ostracism appears to supercede any factors that would logically be hypothesized to moderate the impact of ostracism. In these and other studies using related paradigms (e.g., chat rooms, text messaging), personality factors have not interacted with reactions to ostracism. These include collectivism/individualism

(Smith & Williams, 2004), self-esteem (Williams et al., 2000), narcissism (Warburton, 2002), and extroversion (Nadasi, 1995). Situational factors that ought to diminish ostracism's impact are also rendered unimportant. Immediate negative reactions occur regardless of who is doing the ostracism (Gonsalkorale & Williams, 2004; Smith & Williams, 2004; Williams, et al., 2000; Williams, Govan, Croker, Cruickshank, Tynan, & Lam, 2002), when it is not known that the other two are interacting with each other (Smith & Williams, 2004) when the participant is being ostracized, and whether the ostracism is the result of being an under or over performer relative to the other group members (Kosasih, 2002). The results suggest that even a brief and seemingly innocuous exposure to ostracism is sufficient to be painful and activate warning signals. We take this as evidence for an adaptive response to ostracism: Ostracism signals a threat to survival to such a degree that it takes very little to engage individuals' ostracism detection system.

WHEN MIGHT SITUATIONAL OR INDIVIDUAL DIFFERENCE FACTORS MATTER?

Although immediate reactions to ostracism appear to be strong, negative, and invariant, we believe that subsequent coping responses (Stage 2) will be sensitive to situational and individual difference factors. There is some evidence supporting this hypothesis. First, as reported earlier (Williams & Sommer, 1997), participants' contributions to a group effort following ostracism—presumably a means to improve inclusionary status—were different for males and females. Females socially compensated while males did not. Second, Williams et al. (2000) found a trend toward more conformity—another means to improve inclusionary status—when individuals were ostracized by outgroup members. Warburton, Williams, and Cairns (in press) found that ostracized participants who were stripped of further control over the onset of exposure to aversive noise blasts were five times more aggressive than ostracized participants who were given control over the onset of the noise blasts. Zadro, Boland, and Richardson (2005) found that immediately following Cyberball, normals and socially anxious individuals responded similarly and negatively to ostracism. When their moods and self-reported needs were assessed 45 minutes later, normals bounced back to inclusion levels, whereas social phobics were still reported lower (but slightly improved) levels on these measures.

Further support for the presence of coping mechanisms comes from qualitative research that examines real-world instances of ostracism. In a series of interviews with targets of long-term ostracism, Zadro, Williams, and Richardson (2004) found that targets use several behavioral strategies (singly or in tandem) to cope with ostracism, specifically: seeking clarity, forgiveness-seeking, discussion, ingratiation, abuse, defensive ostracism, mediation, acceptance, and resignation. However, the success of each strategy tends to differ according to the ostracism situation, and ultimately, the willingness of the source to be coaxed into speech.

The results of all these studies suggest that in the time between immediate responses and coping responses, dispositional and situational factors can moderate the ostracism experience. Presumably, with time, ostracized individuals can call upon attributional information that can help deflect the negative experience of ostracism. Individuals who are especially sensitive to rejection (e.g., social phobics) are less able to use their cognitive and affective resources to cope than those who are not socially anxious. Becoming aggressive rather than displaying behaviors that increase acceptance and liking may also depend upon individual differences or situational factors (see also Baumeister; Gaertner; and Twenge, this volume). Thus, we think that immediate responses to ostracism are universally painful, but that coping with ostracism will depend on dispositional and situational factors. These coping responses may be oriented toward (a) cognitively diminishing the importance of the ostracism episode (as yet, this effect has not been tested), (b) increasing levels of belonging and self-esteem, in which we predict the responses will be relatively pro-social (see also Gardner, Knowles, & Pickett; Pickett & Gardner; and Ouwerkerk, van Lange, Gallucci, & Kerr, this volume), or (c) they may be oriented to increase control or recognition (aka meaningful existence), in which case anti-social responses may be as or more likely (see Warburton & Williams, 2004, for a thorough discussion of responses to competing need threats; for anti-social responses, see also Baumeister & DeWall; Catanese & Tice; Gaertner & Iuzzini; and Twenge, this volume).

At present, we feel that the crucial mechanism that will determine whether ostracism (or social exclusion or rejection) will lead to aggression or pro-social responses is the degree to which control has been thwarted. If the social outcast feels that he or she no longer has control over future social integration, they will resort to aggression. Thus, in the "life-alone" paradigm that Twenge, Tice, and Baumeister (see their chapters, this volume) use, participants are given a prognosis by a psychologist that they will lead a life alone, despite any attempt to the contrary. All control has been stripped away by this manipulation, if participants believe the feedback. Likewise, in the Leary paradigm (also used by Twenge, Baumeister, and Tice) in which participants first meet other naïve participants in a get-acquainted ice-breaker, participants are undoubtedly so perplexed about the feedback that none of the others wanted to work with them, that they might entertain the idea that their ability to perceive and control their own social behavior is substantially impaired. In other words, their "sociometer is broken." This, too, presents a lack of control that might be sufficiently frustrating to trigger an explosive reaction.

But what happens when coping mechanisms go awry? Our ability to detect forms of exclusion may be conceived of as an Ostracism Sensitivity Threshold (OST; see Zadro, 2004). The OST represents an innate, adaptive mechanism by which people recognize when they are being excluded or ignored. As previously stated, the ability to detect ostracism is essential for survival. Early detection of imminent rejection may allow us to act to maintain our group membership. However, those who have been repeatedly exposed to ostracism throughout their lives—what we refer to as Stage 3—show a lowered OST (Zadro, Williams, & Richardson, 2003).

That is, they become hypersensitive to all forms of potential ostracism, often seeing the potential for rejection in situations that are actually benign. Repeated or excessive exposure to ostracism will often lead targets to experience the aversive effects of ostracism in an accelerate cascade, thereby leading to an internalization of the four primary needs even after short periods of ostracism. Thus, a dysfunctional OST leads targets to experience ongoing psychological, somatic, and interpersonal distress that may reverberate throughout all segments of their life.

REFERENCES

Abraham, M. (2003). *Can a boost to belonging buffer the immediate painful effects of ostracism?: More evidence for no moderation.* Unpublished honors thesis, Macquarie University, Sydney, Australia.

Baumeister, R. F., & Leary, M. R. (1995). The need to belong: Desire for interpersonal attachments as a fundamental human motivation. *Psychological Bulletin, 117,* 497–529.

Buchholz, E. S. (1995). *The call of solitude: Alonetime in a world of attachment.* Boston: Beacon Press.

Case, T. I., & Williams, K. D. (2004). Ostracism: A metaphor for death. In J. Greenberg, S. L. Koole, & T. Pyszczynski (Eds.), *Handbook of experimental existential psychology* (pp. 336–351). New York: Guilford Press.

Eisenberger, N. I., Lieberman, M. D., Williams, K., D. (2003). Does Rejection Hurt? An fMRI Study of Social Exclusion. *Science, 302,* 290–292.

Faulkner, S. J. (1998). *After the whistle is blown: The aversive impact of ostracism.* Unpublished doctoral dissertation, University of Toledo.

Gonsalkorale, K., & Williams, K. D. (2004, April). *The KKK won't let me play: Ostracism by a despised outgroup hurts.* Presented at the 76th meeting of the Midwestern Psychological Association, Chicago.

Greenberg, J., Pyszczynski, T., & Solomon, S. (1986). The causes and consequences of the need for self-esteem: A terror management theory. In R. F. Baumeister (Ed.), *Public self and private self* (pp. 189–212). New York: Springer-Verlag.

Gruter, M., & Masters, R. D. (1986). Ostracism as a social and biological phenomenon: An introduction. *Ethnology and Sociobiology, 7,* 149–158.

Halpern, S. (1993). *Migrations to solitude: The quest for privacy in a crowded world.* New York: Vintage.

James, W. (1897). *Principles of psychology, Vol. 1.* New York: Dover Publications.

Karau, S. J., & Williams, K. D. (1993). Social loafing: A meta-analytic review and theoretical integration. *Journal of Personality and Social Psychology, 65,* 681–706.

Kosasih, M. (2002). *The effects of being ostracized for being a small versus tall poppy.* Honors thesis, Macquarie University, Sydney, Australia.

Lancaster, J. B. (1986). Primate social behavior and ostracism. *Ethnology and Sociobiology, 7,* 215–225.

Leary, M. R., Tambor, E. S., Terdal, S. K., & Downs, D. L. (1995). Self-esteem as an interpersonal monitor: The sociometer hypothesis. *Journal of Personality and Social Psychology, 2,* 518–530.

Maddi, S. R. (1980). *Personality theories: A comparative analysis.* Homewood, IL: The Dorsey Press.

Miceli, M. P., & Near, J. P. (1992). *Blowing the whistle: The organizational and legal implications for companies and employees.* New York: Lexington Books.

Nadasi, C. (1995). *The effects of social ostracism on verbal and non-verbal behavior in introverts and extraverts.* Honors thesis, University of Toledo, Toledo, OH.

Seligman, M. E. P. (1975). *Helplessness: On depression, development, and death.* San Francisco: Freeman & Co.

Seligman, M.E.P. (1998). *Learned optimism* (2nd ed.). New York: Pocket Books Simon and Schuster.

Smith, A., & Williams, K. D. (2004). R U There? Ostracism by cell phone text messages. *Group*

Dynamics: Theory, Research, and Practice, 8, 291–301.

Sommer, K. L., Williams, K. D., Ciarocco, N. J., & Baumeister, R. F. (2001). When silence speaks louder than words: Explorations into the intrapsychic and interpersonal consequences of social ostracism. *Basic and Applied Social Psychology, 23,* 225–243.

Steele, C. M. (1988). The psychology of self-affirmation: Sustaining the integrity of the self. In L. Berkowitz (Ed.), *Advances in experimental social psychology.* New York: Academic Press.

Warburton, W. A. (2002). *Aggressive responding to ostracism: The moderating roles of control motivation and narcissistic vulnerability, and the mediating role of negative affect.* Honors thesis. Macquarie University, Sydney, Australia.

Warburton, W. A., & Williams, K. D. (2004). Ostracism: When competing motivations collide. In J. P. Forgas, K. D. Williams, & S. M. Laham (Eds.), *Social motivation: Conscious and unconscious processes* (pp. 294–313). New York: Cambridge University Press.

Warburton, W. A., Williams, K. D., & Cairns, D. (in press). When ostracism leads to aggression: The moderating effects of control deprivation. *Journal of Experimental Social Psychology.*

Williams, K. D. (1997). Social ostracism. In R. M. Kowalski (Ed.), *Aversive interpersonal behaviors* (pp. 133–170). New York: Plenum.

Williams, K. D. (2001). *Ostracism: The power of silence.* New York: Guilford Press.

Williams, K. D., Cheung, C., & Choi, W. (2000). Cyberostracism: Effects of being ignored over the Internet. *Journal of Personality and Social Psychology, 79,* 748–762.

Williams, K. D., Govan, C., L., Croker, V., Tynan, D., Cruickshank, M., Lam, A. (2002). Investigations into differences between social and cyberostracism. *Group Dynamics: Theory, Research, & Practice, 6,* 65–77.

Williams, K. D., & Lawson Williams, H (2003). *Ostracism by friendship groups causes a desire to regain control.* Unpublished manuscript, Macquarie University, Sydney, Australia.

Williams, K. D., & Sommer, K. L. (1997). Social ostracism by one's coworkers: Does rejection lead to loafing or compensation? *Personality and Social Psychology Bulletin, 23,* 693–706.

Williams, K. D, & Zadro, L. (2001). Ostracism: On being ignored, excluded, and rejected. In M. R. Leary (Ed.), *Interpersonal rejection* (pp. 21–53). NY: Oxford University Press.

Wortman, C. B., & Brehm, J. W. (1975) Responses to uncontrollable outcomes: An integration of reactance theory and the learned helplessness model. In L. Berkowitz (Ed.), *Advances in experimental social psychology* (Vol. 8, pp. 277–336). San Diego CA: Academic Press.

Zadro, L. (2004). *Ostracism: Empirical studies inspired by real-world experiences of silence and exclusion.* Unpublished doctoral dissertation. University of New South Wales, Sydney, Australia.

Zadro, L., Boland, C., & Richardson, R. (2005, January). *How long does it last? The persistence of the effects of ostracism on the socially anxious.* Presented at the 2005 Annual Meeting of the Society of Personality and Social Psychology, New Orleans.

Zadro, L., Williams, K. D., & Richardson, R. (2004). How low can you go? Ostracism by a computer lowers belonging, control, self-esteem, and meaningful existence. *Journal of Experimental Social Psychology, 40,* 560–567.

Zadro, L., Williams, K. D., & Richardson, R. (2005). Riding the "O" train: Comparing the effects of ostracism and verbal dispute on targets and sources. *Group Processes and Interpersonal Relations, 8,* 125–143.

Zadro, L., Williams, K. D., & Richardson, R. (2003, April). *Ostracism in the real-world: Interviews with long-term targets and sources of ostracism.* Paper presented at the Society for Australasian Social Psychology, Sydney, Australia.

3

Varieties of Interpersonal Rejection

MARK R. LEARY

The Concept of Rejection
Dimensions of Rejection Episodes
Rejection-Related Constructs
Conclusions

*I*n a critique of scientists' use of conceptual definitions, the philosopher Bryan Magee (1985) wrote

> the amount of worthwhile knowledge that comes out of any field of inquiry (except of course language studies) tends to be in inverse proportion to the amount of discussion about the meaning of words that goes on in it. Such discussion, far from being necessary to clear thinking and precise knowledge, obscures both and is bound to lead to needless arguments about words instead of about matters of substance. (p. 49)

Social and behavioral scientists have been prone to the definitional debates that Magee cautions against, mostly out of the well-intentioned belief that scholars cannot have meaningful discussions without agreeing upon precise definitions of the constructs that they study. The problem, of course, is that matters of definition are not subject to objective verification or external corroboration, leaving open the possibility that researchers may hold different but equally defensible definitions of the same construct. Thus, behavioral scientists generally find it fruitless to debate

Address correspondence to: Mark R. Leary, Department of Psychology, Wake Forest University, Winston-Salem, NC 27109. Phone: 336-758-5750; Fax: 336-758-4733; email: leary@wfu.edu

conceptual definitions of the hypothetical constructs that they study—as if they could ever agree on what consciousness or love or intelligence or leadership *really* is. If consensus regarding definitions emerges, we are fortunate, but too much debate about terms can, as Magee noted, distract us from actually studying the phenomena to which the terms refer.

With Magee's (1985) admonition in mind, I must confess a certain degree of ambivalence about focusing this chapter on the constructs that psychologists use in the study of interpersonal rejection. Even so, I see three pressing reasons to do so. The first is that researchers who study rejection-related phenomena have gravitated toward different terms—such as rejection, ostracism, abandonment, and exclusion—often leaving it unclear whether various terms refer to the same general phenomenon or to different things. As a result, we have no conceptual basis for judging whether theoretical ideas or empirical findings involving any particular construct are relevant to any of the others. A careful conceptual examination of the constructs may help to clarify this.

Second, researchers' conceptual definitions of a construct inform how they operationalize that construct in a particular study. Yet, without clear conceptualizations of various rejection-related phenomena, researchers have operationally manipulated and measured rejection in a variety of ways that do not, on the surface, appear to refer to the same psychological construct. A close examination of these constructs may clarify how various rejection-related experiences should be measured, manipulated, and studied, as well as whether the results obtained using a particular paradigm are relevant to those obtained with another.

Third, closely examining the rejection-related constructs in the literature may identify distinctions among rejection-related phenomena that are obscured if we simply assume that all of these terms refer to the same phenomenon. As we will see, examining various rejection-related constructs brings to light new distinctions that may guide future theorizing and research.

Thus, my goal in this chapter is to examine the concept of interpersonal rejection, parsing it into fundamental components that may help us to describe more clearly the ways in which people are rejected. I will deal both with concepts that relate directly to rejection—such as exclusion, ostracism, and rejection—as well as with those that involve rejection indirectly—such as bullying, stigmatization, and betrayal.

THE CONCEPT OF REJECTION

As I have written and spoken about rejection during the past 10 years, I have often found myself painted into semantic corners by the everyday terms that we use to refer to these phenomena. Aside from wrestling with the plethora of terms (which we will address later), three problems frequently arise.

The first is that most terms that refer to interpersonal rejection—including the three most commonly used (rejection, exclusion, and ostracism)—connote something of a dichotomy between the states of acceptance and rejection. That is, writers have tended to talk about acceptance and rejection in rather absolute terms because the English language does not permit easy discussions of degrees of acceptance and rejection. In everyday life, of course, shades of acceptance and rejection are quite real. One may be partly accepted by one person but fully accepted by another, suffer different degrees of exclusion by different groups (one of which denies admission whereas another allows admission as a second-class citizen), and one's love for another person may be more or less reciprocated. Yet, our language does not allow us to easily capture gradations of acceptance and rejection. Using adverbial or numerical qualifiers to refer to degrees of acceptance and rejection is both awkward and vague. It is not clear precisely what it would mean to say that someone was "partly rejected," "halfway excluded," or "mostly ostracized," or that an unrequited lover's love was, in fact, actually only three-fourths unrequited. The words do not easily lend themselves to describing the degrees of acceptance and rejection that exist in everyday social life, suggesting that researchers may need another way to talk about rejection.

A second problem is that terms such as "acceptance" and "rejection" are commonly used to refer both to subjective evaluations of, feelings about, and commitment to other people as well as to overtly accepting and rejecting behaviors. For example, we may not accept someone in our minds, finding them objectionable, unacceptable, and not worthy of our concern or respect, yet not reveal these feelings in our behavior. Clearly, we do not fully accept such an individual, but it seems awkward to say that we have rejected them. Likewise, we may exclude someone we like and accept from a particular social context, but this seems to be a very different sort of rejection than if we hated them instead. Using the same terms for subjective and behavioral rejection creates confusion.

Third, research on the cognitive, emotional, and interpersonal consequences of being rejected shows that people's perceptions of acceptance and rejection do not always map onto how accepted or rejected they objectively are (Leary, Haupt, Strausser, & Chokel, 1998). This is not necessarily a conceptual problem; we have many instances in psychology in which people's perceptions do not mirror reality. Even so, this discrepancy raises the question of whether rejection should be defined in terms of how a person is treated or how a person feels. In part, this confusion arises because writers use the same terms to refer to objective rejection as well as to people's subjective feelings of being rejected. When we say that people are "rejected" (or "ostracized" or "excluded"), are we referring to how others have treated them or to how they feel they have been treated? And, if people feel and act as if they are rejected even though others like and accept them, should be consider them to be "rejected" or not?

These considerations suggest that we would benefit from a fine-grained analysis of what interpersonal rejection actually entails, the psychological processes that underlie it, and the different varieties of rejection. With due respect to Magee (1985), the conceptual confusion is so rampant that some "discussion about the meaning of words" that relate to rejection is needed.

Inclusionary Status

My first effort to reconceptualize rejection involved an index of what I called "inclusionary-status," which is based on the effort to which other people go to include versus exclude an individual (Leary, 1990). This inclusionary-status continuum ranges from "maximal inclusion," in which people actively seek the individual's company, to "maximal exclusion," in which people deliberately reject, ostracize, or abandon the individual. In between are instances in which people accept or reject the individual but do not go too far out of their way to do so. For example, this index characterizes rejection as "passive" when we simply ignore other people (but do not physically avoid or reject them), "active" when we avoid them (but tolerate their presence when necessary), or "maximal" when we overtly eject the individual from a social encounter (such as throwing an individual out of the house or expelling him from an organization). Similarly, acceptance may be "passive" (allowing the person to be present), "active" (welcoming the individual), or "maximal" (exerting effort to seek out the individual's company).

This index of inclusionary-status may be useful when studying the effort people exert to accept or reject others, but I have not found it helpful in understanding people's reactions to rejection. The problem is that the psychological impact of an acceptance or rejection episode is only weakly related to how passively or actively people accept or reject us. A person who is passively rejected by a romantic partner may feel far more rejected than one who is maximally rejected by an acquaintance.

Relational Evaluation

More recently, I have suggested that what we colloquially call acceptance and rejection may be understood in terms of *relational evaluation*. Relational evaluation refers to the degree to which a person regards his or her relationship with another individual as valuable, important, or close (Leary, 2001). People value their relationships with others to varying degrees. Some relationships are exceptionally valuable and important, others are moderately valuable, and others have little or no value (and, in fact, may have a negative value if they bring nothing but pain). What we typically call "acceptance" and "rejection" may be seen as regions along this continuum of relational evaluation. Acceptance involves a state of relatively high relational evaluation in which a person regards his or her relationship with another individual to be valuable, important, or close. In contrast, rejection is a state of relatively low relational evaluation in which a person does not regard his or her relationship with another individual as valuable, important, or close.

Defining acceptance and rejection in terms of relational evaluation provides a relatively clear, explicit way to conceptualize the degree to which people psychologically accept and reject one another and provides a unifying construct that underlies all rejection-related phenomena. All phenomena that involve interpersonal rejection—such as ostracism, unrequited love, childhood peer rejection, betrayal, stigmatization, and so on—involve instances in which one person does not regard his or her relationship with another individual as valuable, important, or close. Although these phenomena differ in important ways, which I discuss later, each involves low relational evaluation.

Perceived Relational Evaluation

Most of the literature on interpersonal rejection focuses not on rejection per se but rather on the effects of rejection on people's emotions, self-evaluations, social judgments, and behaviors. Elsewhere, I have suggested that the subjective experiences of acceptance and rejection are tied directly to a person's perception of the degree to which another individual regards his or her relationship with the person to be valuable, important, or close—that is, to perceived relational evaluation (Leary, 2001). People feel accepted when *perceived relational evaluation*—their inferred relational value in another person's eyes—falls above some minimum criterion but feel rejected when perceived relational evaluation falls below that criterion. Conceptualized in this manner, others' actions toward an individual will make him or her feel rejected to the extent that they connote a lower level of relational evaluation than the individual desires. Such actions sometimes involve explicit rejections (as with romantic break-ups, ostracism, and banishment), but even relatively unimportant actions, such as an unreturned phone call or a missed birthday, can lead people to feel rejected if those events connote lower-than-desired relational value.

Conceptualizing rejection in terms of perceived relational evaluation makes it clear that some cases of mere exclusion do not constitute rejection. If people are excluded at random or because space does not permit more people to be included, they should not feel rejected because there is no implication of low relational evaluation (Leary, Tambor, Terdal, & Downs, 1995). Such exclusions may lead people to feel frustrated or envious if group membership provides some benefit but should not make them feel rejected. In contrast, being excluded in precisely the same way would induce a strong sense of rejection if the person interpreted the exclusion as evidence of having low relational value. Hence, we must be careful not to equate social exclusion per se with either actual or perceived rejection because some exclusions do not implicate the person's relational value. Likewise, cases of social inclusion do not involve acceptance unless they occur because of high relational value. The teenager who begrudgingly includes a younger sibling in his plans because of parental pressure does not actually "accept" him or her in this context, and the sibling is unlikely to feel accepted despite being included. Here, then, is an important conceptual distinction among rejection-related terms: social exclusion does not necessarily involve rejection, and the terms should not be used interchangeably.

To take this point one step further, people may feel rejected and display the emotional, cognitive, and behavioral effects of rejection even though they have not been excluded in any sense and, in fact, recognize that the other person accepts and, perhaps even likes or loves them! This is not necessarily a matter of people misperceiving rejection where there is none. Rather, this discrepancy suggests that whether people are ostracized or excluded in an objective, behavioral sense is not as important as whether they perceive that their relational value in another's eyes is lower than they desire. In many cases, people who are clearly valued and accepted may experience a sense of rejection because they perceive that others do not adequately value their relationship. For example, a woman may know that her husband loves her and is committed to their marriage yet feel rejected because she perceives that he does not value his relationship with her as much as she would like.

Williams (1997, 2001) suggested that ostracism threatens basic human needs for belongingness, self-esteem, control, and meaningful existence, and that the emotional and behavioral effects of ostracism are responses to these threatened needs. The relational evaluation perspective qualifies this idea slightly, suggesting that threats to relational value (and, thus, belongingness) are the central feature of ostracism and all other forms of rejection. Rejection may also threaten people's sense of control and meaningfulness, and thwart other desires (such as for attention, status, or physical security), but these effects are not specific to rejection. These secondary effects can be quite powerful and certainly deserve attention, but they should be distinguished from the fundamental threat that all rejection episodes bring to relational value and belongingness. To say it differently, it will help as we proceed to distinguish the central feature of all rejection episodes—low perceived relational evaluation—from secondary effects that are not specific to rejection.

DIMENSIONS OF REJECTION EPISODES

The concept of relational evaluation provides a first step toward a common language for talking about rejection-related experiences. As noted, all instances in which people feel rejected involve perceived low relational value. However, rejection episodes differ in a number of ways that have implications for how people respond and that allow us to distinguish among various constructs that are used to refer to rejection. In this section, I examine four basic dimensions of rejection episodes: the rejected person's prior belongingness status (Was the person initially accepted prior to the rejection?); the valence of the rejector's evaluation of the person (Was the person rejected for possessing positive versus negative attributes?); disassociation (Did the rejection involve psychological or physical withdrawal by other people?); and the comparative nature of the judgment (Was the person rejected outright or simply preferred less than other individuals?). As we will see, these four dimensions highlight important distinctions among varieties of rejection episodes and raise questions about whether various research paradigms for studying rejection are interchangeable.

Prior Belongingness Status

The first dimension involves the individual's belongingness status prior to the rejection episode—that is, whether the person was accepted (and, presumably, relationally valued) prior to the rejecting event. More concretely, we may ask whether the individual was rejected from a group or relationship to which he or she already belonged or was merely not accepted into the group or relationship in the first place. Experimental paradigms have used both approaches to induce rejection without considering the possibility that being rejected from an existing group or relationship is quite different than not being accepted. (As with most of the criticisms of previous research that I raise in this chapter, I am personally guilty of this particular offense.) In the case of a rejection that follows a period of acceptance, the individual experiences a net loss of belongingness, whereas in the case of nonacceptance nothing is lost, but there is no increase in belongingness or relational value.

Both kinds of episodes can have powerful effects, but the loss of a previously existing membership or relationship is arguably worse than nonacceptance. Being fired from a job is usually worse than not being hired, romantic rejection in an established relationship is usually worse than unrequited love, and being expelled from a group is more traumatic than not having been admitted to it. Aside from the fact that losses are typically more negative experiences than equal-sized gains are positive experiences (e.g., losing $100 is worse than failing to win $100), losses of belongingness appear to be particularly aversive. People seem acutely attuned to decrements in their relational value, display a strong inclination to protect their relationships and memberships, and react strongly when existing relationships are threatened (Baumeister & Leary, 1995). Even when one's relational value is positive (and the person is still somewhat accepted), a decline in perceived relational value compared to some previous time—relational *devaluation*—is typically hurtful and traumatic. It may be small consolation to learn that, although one's romantic partner still loves you, his or her love for you is less than it once was.

Aronson and Linder (1965) made a similar point in their description of gain–loss theory, which deals with people's reactions to patterns of being liked and disliked over time. The theory suggests that changes in evaluations over time have a greater effect on people's reactions than evaluations that are constantly positive or negative. Thus, according to the theory, we like others more when they evaluate us increasingly positively over time than when they constantly rate us positively, and we dislike people more when they evaluate us more negatively over time than when they are consistently negative. Despite the intuitive plausibility of this idea, experimental support for it has been mixed (Aronson & Linder, 1965; Hewitt, 1972; McAllister & Bregman, 1983; Mettee, 1971).

To explore the effects of increasing versus decreasing patterns of relational evaluation on perceived rejection and emotion, Buckley, Winkel, and Leary (2003, Experiment 2) had participants talk about themselves into a microphone for 5 minutes while receiving bogus feedback on a computer screen from another individual who was ostensibly listening from an adjacent room. The feedback, which arrived at 1-minute intervals as the participant was talking about him- or herself, indicated the degree to which the listener wished to get to know the participant on a 7-point scale (1 = I do not wish to get to know the speaker at all; 7 = I wish very much to further get to know the speaker) and, thus, was a rather direct manipulation of relational evaluation. Participants received one of four patterns of feedback that reflected either constant acceptance (ratings of 5s and 6s), increasing rejection (an initial rating of 6 followed by ratings that decreased to 2 over time), constant rejection (ratings of 2s and 3s), or increasing acceptance (an initial rating of 2 that increased over time to 6).

As expected, participants' responses varied as a function of the pattern of feedback they received. Interestingly, increasing rejection was perceived as somewhat more rejecting than constant rejection despite the fact that increasingly rejected participants actually received fewer rejecting evaluations overall. Furthermore, participants who were increasingly rejected felt more sad, hurt, and angry than those who were constantly rejected. These findings are consistent both with the suggestion that relational devaluation is more troubling than low relational evaluation per se (Leary, 2001) and with gain–loss theory's suggestion that losses in esteem have a greater impact than continuously low esteem (Aronson & Linder, 1965). They are not, however, consistent with Hewitt's (1972) prediction, based on reinforcement theory, that constant rejection should have a greater impact because constantly rejected participants receive a larger number of punishing ratings. Although few differences were obtained between constantly and increasingly accepted participants in the Buckley et al. (2003) study, constantly accepted participants had higher state self-esteem than increasingly accepted participants. Immediate and sustained acceptance may suggest that one is more relationally valued than an initially negative evaluation that improves over time (Leary & Baumeister, 2000).

Given the importance of prior belongingness status to the experience of rejection, we should distinguish clearly between rejections that occur after an initial period of acceptance and rejections that do not (which might be more accurately called *nonacceptance*). So, for example, romantic rejections and betrayals that cause people to feel rejected by someone who once cared for them fall into the first category, where as unrequited love and bullying generally fall into the second. Likewise, being fired from a job or expelled from a group results in a loss of prior belonging, whereas failing to be hired for the job or admitted to the group does not.

Evaluative Valence

In most cases, people are rejected because they have low relational value stemming from the fact that others perceive them to possess attributes that make them an undesired relational partner or group member. For example, people are commonly rejected because they are socially unpleasant or difficult to interact with, lack important abilities, possess stigmatizing characteristics, or are physically unattractive (Baumeister & Leary, 1995).

However, researchers have generally overlooked the fact that people may also be rejected because they possess exceptionally desirable characteristics. People who are very competent, talented, attractive, or wealthy, for example, may be ignored or ostracized either because they pose a threat to other, more average individuals or because people assume that highly desirable individuals do not wish to associate with the mediocre masses. For example, people in close relationships may distance themselves from partners whose accomplishments exceed theirs (O'Mahen, Beach, & Tesser, 2000), and people tend to pair with friends, dating partners, and spouses who match them in intelligence and appearance (Murstein, 1986), often ignoring highly desirable partners in favor of less desirable ones. Furthermore, people who appear to be "perfect" may be liked less than those who display human foibles (Aronson, Willerman, & Floyd, 1966), and those who stand out by virtue of their accomplishments are sometimes targeted to be cut down (Feather, 1989).

The distinction between being rejected for possessing desirable versus undesirable characteristics became obvious to me while watching the final episode of the first season of the television show, *Survivor*. (Although I had not previously watched the show, I tuned into the 2-hour finale because a colleague suggested that I would find the social psychological dynamics interesting, and she was correct.) On the show, 16 contestants were divided into two tribes and left to fend for themselves on a tropical island while competing against one another in various tests of endurance and skill. After each competition, the losing tribe was forced to select one member to expel from the group, with each rejection occurring during a tribal council in which a vote was taken and the loser ceremoniously banished from the tribe. The last person remaining after several weeks of competition won a sizable amount of money and other prizes.

Watching the season recapped in a single show, I was intrigued by how the criteria for voting people off the island changed as the game progressed. Early in the show, the tribal members selected for expulsion were typically weak or unskilled (and, thus, compromised the tribe's ability to win the competitions) or were interpersonally unpleasant (being bossy, whiny, petty, untrustworthy, or otherwise insufferable). However, as the show progressed, contestants began to focus on eliminating the strongest and most skilled of the remaining players—those members of their tribe who constituted the greatest threat to their own success in the game. In watching rejection after rejection unfold over the course of the show, it struck me that the experience of being voted off the island for being an undesirable group member must have been quite different than being voted off because one was a potent player who was perceived as a threat by other contestants. In all cases, the tangible consequences of being rejected were the same: The person suffered the public indignity of being excluded from the tribe (and the show), his or her torch was snuffed out to signal the end of his or her participation, and the grand prize was forfeited. Yet, contestants who were voted out because they posed a potential threat to other competitors must have felt differently about being excluded than those who were voted off because they were weak, ineffectual, or disliked.

Intrigued by this possibility, Carrington Rice and I designed an experiment to compare the reactions of people who were rejected for possessing positive versus negative qualities (Leary, Rice, & Schreindorfer, 2004; Experiment 2). In this study, participants completed a questionnaire about themselves and a bogus measure of intellectual ability that were ostensibly shown to two individuals who were to decide which participants to admit to a laboratory group. Participants then received feedback informing them that the other individuals had either accepted or rejected them for the group, and that the decision was based on the fact that the participant was either superior or inferior to the other candidates. (A cover story was created to justify why superior members were sometimes rejected.) In addition, one-third of participants received no justification as to why they were accepted or rejected.

Not surprisingly, participants responded most positively when they were accepted for being the best candidate and most negatively when rejected for being the worst candidate. Of greater interest, however, was how they reacted when rejected for being good versus bad. Participants who were rejected for being the best candidate experienced greater positive affect and thought they had made a better impression on the other individuals than participants who were rejected for being the worst or who received no information regarding why they were rejected. Furthermore, participants felt angrier, sadder, more hurt, and less happy when informed that they were the worst candidate than when informed of being the best candidate. In both instances, participants were socially excluded, yet they reacted quite differently depending on the degree to which the rejectors appeared to evaluate them positively.

In one particular condition, social inclusion was experienced as more negative than being rejected. Among participants who thought that the other two individuals judged them among the worst of the potential members, those who were accepted (for being the worst) reacted more negatively than those who were rejected. Being included for possessing negative attributes was apparently perceived as more rejecting than being excluded for having positive attributes. People may not always be happy about being excluded for being "too good," but they will not feel or act rejected in the same way as when they are also evaluated negatively.

Behavioral Disassociation

As noted, people feel rejected when they perceive that their relational value to one or more other individuals is low. In many cases, people convey low relational evaluation by ignoring, avoiding, excluding, or otherwise disassociating from the person, whereas in other cases, low relational evaluation is not accompanied by behavioral disassociation. I may feel rejected when I know that a person who interacts regularly with me regards me as worthless, or I may feel rejected when a person who I know likes me excludes me from her plans. In both cases, my feelings of rejection stem from my perception that my relational value is not as high as I would like, yet they differ in the degree to which the precipitating event involves actual disassociation.

Research on rejection has failed to distinguish rejections that involve disassociation from those that do not. In many experimental studies of rejection, participants in the "rejection" condition are not, in fact, ignored, avoided, or excluded. For example, Bourgeois and Leary (2001) led participants to feel rejected by telling them that they were selected last for a 5-person laboratory team. In this instance, the "rejected" participants were, in fact, included as team members, although they understandably concluded that they had relatively low relational value compared to team members who were selected before them. Similarly, Snapp and Leary (2001) had participants talk about themselves over an intercom to a confederate who alternated between listening to them and to another participant. Participants who believed that they held the confederate's attention only about 20% of the time felt rejected and hurt despite the fact that the confederate had paid a certain amount of attention to them.

In other studies, participants in the "rejection" condition have actually been excluded from groups or interactions. Paradigms in which participants are voted out of a group (or are not admitted into the group to begin with) fall in this category (Leary et al., 1995; Nezlek, Kowalski, Leary, Blevins, & Holgate, 1997; Twenge, Baumeister, Tice, & Stucke, 2001), as do studies in which participants are completely ignored during group tasks, conversations, or interactive games (e.g., Williams, Cheung, & Choi, 2000).

Although researchers have not explicitly examined the effects of rejections that do versus do not involve behavioral disassociation or exclusion, it seems likely that disassociation introduces an added, very powerful element into rejection episodes. If nothing else, people are likely to feel more rejected when they think that their relational value to another person is low *and* that the person disassociates from them than when disassociation is not present. (In fact, disassociation may be interpreted as evidence that one has low relational value even in the absence of other corroborating evidence.) In addition, Williams (1997; Williams & Zadro, this volume) proposed that some of the negative consequences of ostracism arise from its effects on people's needs for control and meaningful existence, both of which are more greatly undermined when people are not only relationally devalued but also excluded or avoided.

Comparative Versus Noncomparative Judgment

Sometimes, rejection occurs when people "lose" their bid for acceptance to one or more other individuals. Unsuccessful job applicants face this type of rejection, as do jilted lovers whose partners leave them for another person, aspiring athletes who are not chosen for a team, politicians who lose elections, and contestants on television shows in which players choose which individuals to accept versus reject (e.g., *The Dating Game, Survivor, Joe Millionaire, The Weakest Link*). In each case, the rejection involves a comparative judgment in which one person is rejected in lieu of one or more others. In other instances, rejection occurs without reference or comparison to other people. The lone job applicant who is not hired for the position, a person whose romantic partner ends their relationship with no prospect of an alternative, an athlete who is dismissed from the team, and a child who is ostracized by a parent each experiences this sort of absolute, noncomparative rejection.

Experimental studies of rejection have used both comparative and noncomparative paradigms. In comparative rejection designs, participants have been led to believe that other individuals chose to exclude them from among a set of possible group members (Leary et al., 1995; Nezlek et al., 1997; Twenge et al., 2001), assigned them a lower number of "membership points" than assigned to other group members (Leary, Cottrell, & Phillips, 2001), opted to play an interactive game with another person (Williams et al., 2000), or preferred to interact with another participant rather than them (Snapp & Leary, 2001). In such studies, rejected participants know that the decision to reject them was based on a comparison with other individuals. In noncomparative rejection designs, in contrast, participants receive information indicating that another person simply decided not to interact with them, had no interest in getting to know them further, or chose to work alone on a task rather than with them (Buckley et al., 2003).

No research has explicitly compared the effects of comparative versus noncomparative rejections, but we may speculate that rejections that are noncomparative are probably more hurtful. The person who receives a comparative rejection may maintain the belief, whether accurate or illusory, that the rejector's choice reflected a preference among valued options. Thus, although the person's relational value was lower than another individual's, it was not necessarily low in absolute terms. However, the recipient of a noncomparative rejection can harbor no such beliefs; such a rejection indicates that the rejected individual's relational value is so low that the rejector opted to go it alone rather than interact with him or her.

REJECTION-RELATED CONSTRUCTS

Having described four fundamental dimensions of rejection episodes—prior belongingness, evaluative valence, disassociation, and comparative judgment—we are now in the position to discuss how various rejection-related constructs map onto these dimensions and, thus, are similar to and different from one another. As we will see, although all rejection-related constructs involve low relational evaluation, they differ in important ways and should not be considered synonymous.

Varieties of Rejection

Let us first consider terms that refer directly to types of rejection. To begin, the term exclusion should be used to describe instances of interpersonal disassociation without respect to the cause of the disassociation or the excluded individual's relational value. Exclusion is a purely behavioral descriptor that does not necessarily connote low relational evaluation and, thus, may or may not constitute rejection. I may be excluded from a group to which I belong (which obviously connotes low relational evaluation and qualifies as rejection) as well as from an overcrowded subway car that can not accommodate me (which does not). Note that the term, exclusion, applies both when people are removed from groups and relationships to which they previously belonged as well as from incipient groups and relationships (i.e., prior belongingness status may be either included or excluded). In many everyday cases of exclusion, people believe they are excluded for having low relational value, but, given that this is not always the case, we should not treat exclusion and rejection as synonymous.

Abandonment is a special case of exclusion. Abandonment connotes absolute disassociation by an individual who is legally or ethically obligated to maintain an ongoing relationship with another person. Thus, abandonment necessarily involves the existence of a prior relationship. Typically, the term is used in cases of parents abandoning their children or people abandoning their spouses or other romantic partners. Abandonment does not necessarily imply low relational evaluation (e.g., a fugitive may abandon his beloved family in order to evade the police), but the abandoned individual will often perceive that his or her relational value is lower than desired and, thus, feel rejected.

Rejection is the broadest, most generic term for instances in which people perceive that their relational value is lower than they desire. Rejection may occur with either prior belonging or nonbelonging, may be accompanied by either positive or negative evaluations of the rejected person, may or may not involve actual disassociation, and may result from either comparative or noncomparative judgments. Specific forms of rejection that have been studied—such as peer rejection, romantic rejection, and unrequited love—may be viewed as instances of rejection experienced in particular types of relationships. These constructs may differ (for example, romantic rejection assumes prior belongingness, whereas unrequited love does not), but they all involve low perceived relational evaluation and, thus, rejection.

Ostracism is a particular type of rejection in which the rejector necessarily disassociates from the rejected person. Williams (2001, p. ix) defined ostracism as "any act or acts of ignoring and excluding of an individual or groups," which comes close to the definition offered here. Like all rejection, ostracism involves low relational value (people do not ostracize those whose relationships they value) combined with actions that dramatically increase one's psychological and/or physical distance from the rejected person. Ostracism connotes extreme disassociation in which the rejector does not accord the rejected individual even minimal social acknowledgment or civility, such as by completely ignoring, avoiding, or excluding the individual (Williams & Zadro, 2001; this volume). Defined in this manner, ostracism is a type of rejection, but not all episodes of rejection constitute ostracism.

Constructs with Real or Perceived Rejection as a Secondary Feature

Other terms do not refer to rejection per se but nonetheless involve interpersonal rejection as a secondary feature, and it is instructive to consider how these constructs relate to the four dimensions of rejection.

Stigmatization has been defined in a variety of ways. For example, stigma has been defined in terms of possessing characteristics that discredit the individual or spoil his or her identity (Goffman, 1963), convey a devalued social identity (Crocker, Major, & Steele, 1998), or cause other people to conclude that a person is not a legitimate participant in an interaction (Elliott, Ziegler, Altman, & Scott, 1982). In my view, stigmatization occurs "when a shared characteristic of a category of people becomes consensually regarded as a basis for disassociating from (that is, avoiding, excluding, or otherwise minimizing interaction with) individuals who are perceived to be members of this category" (Leary & Schreindorfer, 1997, p. 15). Put differently, people are stigmatized when other people agree, often implicitly, that relationships with members of a particular category ought not to be valued.

Traditionally, *bullying* and *malicious teasing* have been studied primarily as categories of aggressive behavior (Kowalski, Howerton, & McKenzie, 2001; Olweus, 1996), but it is clear that much of the psychological impact of being bullied or teased comes from the fact that these actions connote interpersonal rejection (Juvonen & Gross, this volume). The targets of bullying and teasing invariably conclude that the perpetrator does not value his or her relationship with them (and would not torment them if their relational value was higher). Along with the fear and humiliation that accompany bullying and teasing, perceived rejection is usually present as well.

Although *betrayal* is usually conceptualized in terms of disloyalty and the violation of trust, Fitness (2001) proposed that betrayal occurs when one person in a relationship "acts in a way that favors his or her own interests at the expense of

Table 3.1 Rejection-Related Constructs

Construct	Prior Belonging	Evaluative Valence	Disassociation	Comparison
Exclusion	Sometimes	Any	Yes	Sometimes
Abandonment	Yes	Any	Yes	No
Rejection	Sometimes	Very positive or very negative	Sometimes	Sometimes
Unrequited love	No	Less positive than desired	Sometimes	Sometimes
Ostracism	Sometimes	Negative	Yes	No
Stigmatization	No	Negative	Yes	No
Bullying/ malicious teasing	No	Negative	No	No
Betrayal	Yes	Any	No	No
Loneliness	Sometimes	Any	Yes	Sometimes

the other party's interests" (p. 74). When this occurs, "betrayal sends an ominous signal about how little the betrayer cares about, or values his or her relationship with the betrayed person" (p. 74). Viewed in this way, betrayal nearly always involves low perceived relational evaluation and, thus, a sense of rejection.

Loneliness is typically defined as the subjective experience that one's social relationships are deficient (Peplau & Perlman, 1982). More precisely, loneliness arises when people who value their relationships with us are not available for social interaction and support. In some cases, people have no one, anywhere, who adequately values their relationship, whereas in other cases, those who value their relationship are not currently available for interaction or support. People may certainly feel lonely without being rejected, yet rejection often induces loneliness, and loneliness, whatever its source, inherently involves the status of people's relationships with those who they believe relationally value them.

Table 3.1 shows how each of these constructs relate to the four dimensions of rejection described earlier. Clearly, each of these terms refer to a somewhat different phenomenon and should not be used interchangeably.

CONCLUSIONS

Only the reader can now judge whether I should have heeded Magee's (1985) warning about the risks of discussing the meaning of theoretical terms. Indeed, if Magee is correct that "the amount of worthwhile knowledge that comes out of any field of inquiry . . . tends to be in inverse proportion to the amount of discussion about the meaning of words that goes on in it," I have not only obscured clear thinking about these constructs, but the reader now possesses less worthwhile knowledge regarding rejection than before reading this chapter.

I hope that this is not the case and that, in fact, I have achieved three goals. First, by showing how various rejection-related phenomena relate both to the underlying construct of relational evaluation and to one another, I hope that researchers who study rejection may begin to refer to these constructs in clear and consistent ways. In doing so, we may be able to see more clearly when and why effects obtained with one construct may generalize to another.

Second, by identifying four fundamental components of rejection episodes, researchers can begin to explore the effects of these various dimensions on the affective, self-evaluative, cognitive, and behavioral consequences of rejection. Different features of rejection episodes may impact different psychological outcomes. Incidentally, I do not mean to imply that these are the only dimensions on which rejection episodes differ, and future research will undoubtedly identify more. But, it is a first step toward a componential analysis of the features of rejection episodes that underlie their psychological and social effects.

Third, I hope that these distinctions will inform methodological decisions regarding how rejection should be manipulated and measured. As we have seen, various research paradigms create experiences of rejection that differ in terms of prior belongingness status, evaluative valence, disassociation, and judgmental comparison. Clearly, not all paradigms induce the same experience, and we should not assume that all methods of inducing rejection are socially and psychologically equivalent. By considering the basic dimensions on which these paradigms differ, researchers can make more careful and informed decisions regarding how best to study interpersonal rejection in all of its forms.

REFERENCES

Aronson, E., & Linder, D. (1965). Gain and loss of esteem as determinants of interpersonal attraction. *Journal of Experimental Social Psychology, 1*, 156–171.

Aronson, E., Willerman, B., & Floyd, J. (1966). The effect of a pratfall on increasing interpersonal attractiveness. *Psychonomic Science, 4*, 227–228.

Baumeister, R. F., & Leary, M. R. (1995). The need to belong: Desire for interpersonal attachments as a fundamental human motivation. *Psychological Bulletin, 117*, 497–529.

Bourgeois, K. S., & Leary, M. R. (2001). Coping with rejection: Derogating those who choose us last. *Motivation and Emotion, 25*, 101–111.

Buckley, K. E., Winkel, R. E., & Leary, M. R. (2003). Reactions to acceptance and rejection: Effects of level and sequence of relational evaluation. *Journal of Experimental Social Psychology, 40*, 14-28.

Crocker, J., Major, B., & Steele, C. (1998). Social stigma. In D. T. Gilbert, S. T. Fiske, & G. Lindzey (Eds.), *The handbook of social psychology* (Vol. 2, 4th ed., pp. 504–553). New York: Oxford University Press.

Elliott, G. C., Ziegler, H. L., Altman, B. M., & Scott, D. R. (1982). Understanding stigma: Dimensions of deviance and coping. *Deviant Behavior, 3*, 275–300.

Feather, N. T. (1989). Attitudes towards the high achiever: The fall of the tall poppy. *Australian Journal of Psychology, 41*, 239–267.

Fitness, J. (2001). Betrayal, rejection, revenge, and forgiveness: An interpersonal script approach. In M. R. Leary (Ed.), *Interpersonal rejection* (pp. 73–103). New York: Oxford University Press.

Goffman, E. (1963). *Stigma: Notes on the management of spoiled identity.* Englewood Cliffs, NJ: Prentice-Hall.

Hewitt, J. (1972). Liking and the proportion of

favorable evaluations. *Journal of Personality and Social Psychology, 22,* 231–235.

Kowalski, R. M., Howerton, E., & McKenzie, M. (2001). Permitted disrespect: Teasing in interpersonal interactions. In R. M. Kowalski (Ed.), *Behaving badly: Aversive behaviors in interpersonal relationships* (pp. 177–202). Washington, DC: American Psychological Association.

Leary, M. R. (1990). Responses to social exclusion: Social anxiety, jealousy, loneliness, depression, and low self-esteem. *Journal of Social and Clinical Psychology, 9,* 221–229.

Leary, M. R. (2001). Toward a conceptualization of interpersonal rejection. In M. R. Leary (Ed.), *Interpersonal rejection* (pp. 3–20). New York: Oxford University Press.

Leary, M. R., & Baumeister, R. F. (2000). The nature and function of self-esteem: Sociometer theory. In M.P. Zanna (Ed.), *Advances in experimental social psychology* (Vol. 32, pp. 1–62). San Diego: Academic Press.

Leary, M. R., Cottrell, C. A., & Phillips, M. (2001). Deconfounding the effects of dominance and social acceptance on self-esteem. *Journal of Personality and Social Psychology, 81,* 898–909.

Leary, M. R., Haupt, A. L., Strausser, K. S., & Chokel, J. T. (1998). Calibrating the sociometer: The relationship between interpersonal appraisals and state self-esteem. *Journal of Personality and Social Psychology, 74,* 1290–1299.

Leary, M. R., Rice, S. C., & Schreindorfer, L. S. (2004). *When rejection isn't hurtful: Distinguishing disassociation from low relational evaluation.* Manuscript under review.

Leary, M. R., & Schreindorfer, L. S. (1998). The stigmatization of HIV and AIDS: Rubbing salt in the wound. In V. J. Derlega & A. P. Barbee (Eds.), *HIV and social interaction* (pp. 12-29). Thousand Oaks, CA: Sage.

Leary, M. R., Tambor, E. S., Terdal, S. K., & Downs, D. L. (1995). Self-esteem as an interpersonal monitor: The sociometer hypothesis. *Journal of Personality and Social Psychology, 68,* 518–530.

Magee, B. (1985). *Philosophy and the real world: An introduction to Karl Popper.* La Salle, IL: Open Court Publishing.

McAllister, H. A., & Bregman, N. J. (1983). In search of gain-loss effects: The role of control groups. *Representative Research in Social Psychology, 13,* 23–30.

Mettee, D. R. (1971). Changes in liking as a function of the magnitude and affect of sequential evaluations. *Journal of Experimental Social Psychology, 7,* 157–172.

Murstein, B. L. (1986). *Paths to marriage.* Newbury Park, CA: Sage.

Nezlek, J. B., Kowalski, R. M., Leary, M. R., Blevins, T., & Holgate, S. (1997). Personality moderators of reactions to interpersonal rejection: Depression and trait self-esteem. *Personality and Social Psychology Bulletin, 23,* 1235–1244.

Olweus, D, (1996). Bullying at school: Knowledge base and an effective intervention program. In C. Ferris & T. Grisso (Eds.), *Understanding aggressive behavior in children* (pp. 265–276). New York: New York Academy of Sciences.

O'Mahen, H. A., Beach, S., & Tesser, A. (2000). Relationship ecology and negative communication in romantic relationships: A self-evaluation maintenance perspective. *Personality and Social Psychology Bulletin, 26,* 1343–1352.

Peplau, L. A., & Perlman, D. (Eds.) (1982). *Loneliness: A sourcebook of current theory, research, and therapy.* New York: John Wiley and Sons.

Snapp, C. M., & Leary, M. R. (2001). Hurt feelings among new acquaintances: Moderating effects of interpersonal familiarity. *Journal of Personal and Social Relationships, 18,* 315–326.

Twenge, J. M., Baumeister, R. F., Tice, D. M., & Stucke, T. S. (2001). If you can't join them, beat them: Effects of social exclusion on aggressive behavior. *Journal of Personality and Social Psychology, 81,* 1058–1069.

Williams, K. D. (1997). Social ostracism: The causes and consequences of "the silent treatment." In R. Kowalski (Ed.), *Aversive interpersonal behaviors* (pp. 133-170). New York: Plenum.

Williams, K. D. (2001). *Ostracism: The power of silence.* New York: Guilford Press.

Williams, K. D., Cheung, C., & Choi, W. (2000). Cyberostracism: Effects of being ignored over the internet. *Journal of Personality and Social Psychology, 79,* 748–762.

Williams, K. D., & Zadro, L. (2001). Ostracism: On being ignored, excluded and rejected. In M. R. Leary (Ed.), *Interpersonal rejection* (pp. 21–53). New York: Oxford University Press.

4

The Inner Dimension of Social Exclusion

Intelligent Thought and Self-Regulation Among Rejected Persons

ROY F. BAUMEISTER
C. NATHAN DEWALL

Cognitive information processing and self-regulation provide people with the basic tools for becoming useful and productive members of society. Millions of years of evolution have endowed humans with large and powerful brains, full of mechanisms specifically selected for adaptive purposes and problems. These a priori knowledge structures allow humans to categorize the infinite number of decisions they are faced with every day and to organize that information on the basis of its functionally specialized importance, the specific category into which it most suitably fits, and the appropriate response to be expected from such incoming information. In addition, people possess an ability to modify their behavior in order to conform to socially defined standards. This ability, better known as self-

Address correspondence to: Roy F. Baumeister, Department of Psychology, Florida State University, Tallahassee, FL 32306-1270, USA

regulation, enables people to sacrifice their selfish inclinations for the sake of securing and maintaining acceptance in their group.

The need to belong is one of the most basic and powerful motives in the human psyche. What happens when that need is thwarted? This chapter focuses on two intertwined sets of inner processes, namely cognitive information processing and self-regulation; both may be drastically changed in the immediate aftermath of a rejection or exclusion experience.

The need to belong is probably such a pervasive and influential motive because human beings evolved to rely on group interaction as their main biological strategy. With no fangs, no claws, no fur, other physical vulnerabilities, and a very extended childhood, human beings are not well suited to living alone in the forest. All over the world, people live together in small groups, sometimes (but not necessarily) connected to large groups. Given the importance of maintaining membership in social groups, it is hardly surprising that people react strongly to rejection or exclusion. Some years ago, one of the present authors set out to study the behavioral and inner reactions to social exclusion. The simple theory was that rejection would evoke strong emotional distress, which would have a variety of effects on behavior. This program of work had some successes and some failures. The successes were in the behavioral domain: Excluded or rejected people were shown to become much more aggressive (Twenge et al., 2001; also Catanese & Tice, this volume; Twenge, this volume), more self-defeating or self-destructive (Twenge, Catanese, & Baumeister, 2003, less cooperative and helpful (Twenge et al., 2003), and less prone to effortful and meaningful thought in a broad time context (Twenge, Catanese, & Baumeister, 2003). Moreover, these effects were often quite large in comparison with the typical results of laboratory studies, typically running to more than a standard deviation. The failures, on the other hand, pertained to the inner processes. We generally found little or no evidence of emotional distress among the rejected, excluded participants, nor did emotion or mood show any sign of mediating the behavioral effects. We were therefore left with the question: What is going on inside rejected people to produce the huge changes in behavior? If emotion is not driving the shift in behavior, what is?

Apart from emotion, other major inner processes include cognitive information processing and self-regulation. The most distinctively human form of information processing is intelligent thought, including reasoning. Self-regulation is another trait that seems much more powerful and much more centrally important in human beings than in other species. As this chapter will review, recent studies have led us to conclude that thwarting the need to belong leads to significant impairments in both self-regulation and intelligent performance.

The idea that social exclusion can impair both intelligent thought and self-regulation is itself somewhat surprising and possibly controversial. By one line of reasoning intelligence enables people to solve problems in their physical environment and therefore make life safer and more comfortable for themselves. A person who is living alone should have the greatest need for such solutions, insofar as the loner cannot rely on others for help, for solutions to problems, and the like. Hence it would seem adaptive for intelligent thought to increase in the wake of social rejection, rather than decreasing.

Likewise, self-regulation is crucial for enabling the self to alter itself so as to conform to ideals, expectations, values, norms, and other standards. Social rejection is often based on the fact that other people object to one's behavior, and in order to gain acceptance (either into a new group or back into the same group from which one was recently rejected), altering oneself would seemingly be a very sensible and adaptive thing to do. Hence one might also predict that social exclusion or rejection would stimulate greater efforts at self-regulation.

Simply put, it would be unsurprising and adaptive if socially rejected people responded to their exclusion by increasing their intelligent thinking and their effectiveness at self-regulation. As this chapter will show, however, that is not at all what we have found.

The chapter is organized into five main sections. First, social rejection is discussed in terms of its relationship with fundamental motives of social acceptance (Baumeister & Leary, 1995). Next, a brief overview of our approach to the study of social rejection is provided, including the methods employed to manipulate social rejection. Third, we review research findings on the impact of social exclusion on information processing and intelligent thought. Fourth, we review findings regarding the impact of social exclusion on self-regulation. We conclude with an integrative theoretical discussion and directions for further research.

SOCIAL REJECTION AND THE NEED TO BELONG

Human social life makes considerable and complex demands on the psyche. Every day people are faced with numerous decisions, most of which include taking into account the thoughts and feelings of other people. However, like any organism, human beings are naturally inclined to seek their own pleasure and to avoid pain. In a complex society, people may still have these basic, selfish inclinations to seek pleasure and to avoid pain, but there are two complications. First, they may need to negotiate through complex social realities and relationships in order to do so. Second, in order to avoid conflict with other people, they sometimes need to restrain their own selfish inclinations. The socialization of prosocial behavior entails learning to respect the rights and feelings of others even when that means restraining one's own impulses. Although this self-restraint does involve some sacrifice, it may also be compensated by the rewards that come with belonging to the social group. There is thus a potential tradeoff: Selfishness and antisocial behavior go with unpleasant social isolation, whereas unselfish and prosocial behavior can bring social acceptance and its rewards. Nearly all human beings find that some degree of self-restraint is a reasonable price to pay for having a social network of supportive relationships. To a substantial extent, the development of the self is geared toward learning to manage the self so as to secure some degree of social acceptance and belongingness.

Thus, we think, the self develops its executive functions for the sake of pursuing the goal of social acceptance. Complex, intelligent thought and reasoning, restraint of selfish impulses, restraint of aggression, and self-sacrificing prosocial behavior all reflect the ability of the self to renounce immediate gratification and self-interest for the sake of others, which is to be rewarded by belongingness. Satisfying the need to belong is one of the most basic and pervasive human motivations (Baumeister & Leary, 1995), so it frequently takes precedence over other goals.

From this perspective, social exclusion represents a powerfully disruptive phenomenon because it undermines the implicit "bargain" on which the entire intrapsychic system is based. The self-restraint and sacrifices that are made for the sake of belongingness are decidedly not worth while if the anticipated reward of belongingness is not forthcoming. And because the self is fundamentally oriented toward seeking belongingness, the impact of social exclusion is disorienting: A major overarching goal is gone, and along with it the basis for many other behaviors is swept away. Even a seemingly limited social rejection or exclusion may produce this effect to some degree, because the exclusion brings up the possibility that other rejections will follow (see Romero-Canyas & Downey, this volume; Sommer & Rubin, this volume). Indeed, social rejection may set into motion a vicious cycle in which the need to belong, having been thwarted once, may appear more vulnerable to future attack than if the individual had not been rejected.

As a result, the self's executive function may temporarily cease its normal functions in the immediate aftermath of social rejection. From this perspective, self-regulation will be impaired, leading to impulsive and selfish behaviors. Active responses may be reduced, with the person becoming more passive. Complex thought, including controlled processes, may also be significantly impaired, whereas automatic responses and habits may continue as usual (and may even prevail more than they normally would).

One important implication of this theory is that exclusion will not simply produce sweeping deficits in all manner of performances, such as would happen if exclusion merely had a broad effect on motivation or cognition generally. Instead, the deficits may relate more closely to responses that depend on the self's executive function such as logical, systematic thought and self-regulation processes.

MANIPULATIONS OF REJECTION AND EXCLUSION

Within our program of research, two different methods have been employed to manipulate social exclusion and rejection. In one, participants complete a personality inventory and later are provided with bogus feedback about its results. To bolster credibility, each participant is accurately given his or her score on introversion/extraversion. Then the experimenter delineates another crucial prediction, ostensibly based on the participant's responses to the personality inventory. In the Future

Belonging condition, the participant is told, "You're the type who has rewarding relationships throughout life. You're likely to have a long and stable marriage and have friendships that will last into your later years. The odds are that you'll always have friends and people who care about you."

In contrast, people in the Future Alone condition are told that "You're the type who will end up alone later in life. You may have friends and relationships now, but by your mid-twenties most of these will have drifted away. You may even marry or have several marriages, but these are likely to be short-lived and not continue into your thirties. Relationships don't last, and when you're past the age where people are constantly forming new relationships, the odds are you'll end up being alone more and more." This condition is, of course, of central interest because it makes people anticipate a future in which their need to belong will be thwarted.

A Misfortune Control condition is included, in which people are told that "You're likely to be accident prone later in life—you might break an arm or a leg a few times, or maybe be injured in car accidents. Even if you haven't been accident prone before, these things will show up later in life, and the odds are you will have a lot of accidents." This last group was added so that there would be a group whose future was forecast to be unpleasant but not in a way that involved belongingness versus exclusion. In this way, we can distinguish any cognitive, affective, or behavioral reactions to the rejection manipulation that are specific to social rejection from reactions that apply broadly to any sort of bad news.

Last, some of our studies have also used a control group in which participants receive no feedback about their ostensible futures. This is in a sense the purest control group, but, of course, if it were to differ from the others, the findings would reflect the impact of receiving any sort or any valence of feedback.

The second type of manipulation we have used relies on current, immediate exclusion rather than bogus feedback about a lack of relationships in the distant future. We developed this on our own, but similar manipulations had been used by Nezlek, Kowalski, Leary, Blevins, and Holgate (1997). In this manipulation, participants arrive in a group, conduct a get-acquainted discussion, and are then asked to list which other members they would most like to work with in a dyadic task. Each participant is then informed that he or she would have to work alone, based on one of two explanations (assigned at random). Half were told that everyone else in the group had chosen to work with them. The others were told that no one had chosen them. The latter is the focus of interest because it constitutes a direct and palpable rejection by several other people.

There is room for debate about how powerful these manipulations should be in comparison with rejection experiences from everyday life. The news that one will end up alone in life may seem like a sweeping, powerful, and potentially devastating blow, but then again it is only a few words from a research assistant ostensibly based on one's paper-and-pencil responses to a questionnaire. Some data suggest that participants are often skeptical of psychological tests and of messages about the future in particular. Many participants may occasionally fill out magazine questionnaires or read their horoscopes, thereby obtaining some predictions about their future but not necessarily believing them very deeply. The other manipulation is at least a genuine rejection, but still it is hardly a profound indictment of one's personality: Several strangers whom one has just met for 10 minutes decided to work with each other rather than with you. To the extent that the important message in rejection is relational devaluation (Leary, this volume), it is much less painful to be rejected by strangers than by people with whom one has an important relationship.

It is indisputable that these manipulations do have some psychological impact on research participants. As we shall see, the typical effect sizes on behavior have been exceptionally large by the standards of laboratory studies of social behavior. Then again, these manipulations must seem fairly trivial when compared to substantive rejections from everyday life. Hearing that several strangers chose to work with each other rather than with you can hardly be expected to have the same impact as being dumped by a romantic partner after a long, intimate relationship (or, for that matter, even after a short intimate relationship!). Likewise, hearing that responses to a paper-and-pencil predict a lonesome future can hardly compare with learning that one's application to medical or law school or for employment in a desired firm has been turned down. At very least, our laboratory manipulations have no actual, lasting consequences, and, in this respect, they should have somewhat less impact than do most actual rejections.

Some features of these rejections are worth noting because they may diverge from what other laboratories do, and these differences could possibly lead to somewhat different results. First, the rejection comes as a surprise: The subject does not know that an acceptance or rejection is about to happen until it comes. This may produce more disorientation and confusion than, say, a rejection that comes on a day that has been anticipated for weeks, such as during fraternity or sorority rush. Second, it is a single event, rather than an unfolding sequence of acts. Procedures that study ostracism, in contrast, involve a series of events in which the person may strive to gain acceptance or recognition and repeatedly fail to get it, thereby allowing reactions to build over time (see Williams & Zadro, this volume; Lakin & Chartrand, this volume; Gardner, Pickett, & Knowles, this volume). Third, our manipulations are presented with some degree of finality, and the subject is not offered any prospect of being reintegrated into the group or of gaining some prospect of future acceptance, and giving rejected people a palpable option to re-connect might drastically alter the structure of the situation and the subject's responses (see especially Twenge, this volume; Ouwerkerk, Kerr, Van Lange, & Gallucci, this volume).

In summary, two ways of manipulating social exclusion have been developed. The first consists of giving false feedback to say that based on questionnaire results, we can confidently estimate that the participant is likely to end up alone much of the time in later life. The second involves telling the participant that no group members rated the participant as someone they wanted to work with on a dyadic task.

SOCIAL REJECTION AND ITS INFLUENCE ON COGNITION

Initially, we had thought that emotional distress would mediate the consequences following social exclusion. This is not a particularly novel hypothesis, especially insofar as anxiety has consistently been shown to play an integral role in responding to social rejection (Baumeister & Tice, 1991, for a review; Leary, 1990) and ostracism (Williams, Cheung, & Choi, 2000). Being rejected or excluded may trigger emotional distress, which may in turn produce short-term cognitive impairment. Despite the apparent connection between social rejection and emotional distress, however, research from our laboratory has consistently failed to find much in the way of emotional distress following our manipulations of social rejection (see also Catanese & Tice, this volume; Lakin & Chartrand, this volume; Twenge, this volume). Rejected participants have not reported much emotional distress, and even when we have occasionally found a significant difference in self-reported emotion between accepted and rejected participants, the emotion has failed to mediate the behavioral consequences. Hence, we began to consider the possibility that inner processes other than emotional distress mediated the behavioral consequences of social rejection. Decrements in cognitive functioning and self-regulation seemed plausible candidates.

We had three plausible theories that might explain how social exclusion might affect cognitive processing. First, social exclusion could cause arousal, with a corresponding narrowing of attention and potentiation of dominant responses. Second, exclusion could cause people to ruminate about the experience of being rejected, thereby distracting them from processing new information. Third, excluded people might devote their cognitive resources to suppressing their emotional distress, and this would preoccupy the executive function. Self-regulation would therefore be impaired, along with other controlled processes, whereas automatic processes would remain relatively unaffected. We conducted a series of studies (Baumeister, Twenge, & Nuss, 2002) in part to distinguish among these theories. The first task, however, was simply to confirm that social exclusion would have any sort of negative effect on intellectual functioning.

In a preliminary study, participants completed a portion of the General Mental Abilities Test, which includes measures of verbal reasoning, mathematical ability, and spatial ability (Janda, 1996; Janda, Fulk, Janda, & Wallace, 1995). Before completing the intelligence test, participants completed a personality inventory and received bogus feedback about its results. Participants first received accurate feedback regarding their scores on extraversion and then received bogus feedback regarding their future belongingness. Following a procedure developed by Twenge et al. (2001), participants were randomly assigned to one of three social feedback conditions: Future Alone, Future Belonging, and Misfortune Control (see previous section for details). This served as the social exclusion manipulation.

Participants then completed a 1-item mood measure and were asked to complete as many items as they could on the intelligence test. When 6 minutes had elapsed, the experimenter collected the test and scored the responses in terms of the number of correct and incorrect responses and the number of attempts made.

Results from this study indicated that anticipated social exclusion produced a dramatic drop in intelligent performance. Participants who were told they were going to end up alone later in life performed significantly worse than participants who believed their future would be filled with many meaningful relationships or those who anticipated a future that would be plagued with several accidents. Social exclusion impaired performance in both speed and accuracy. That is, Future Alone participants attempted fewer questions than Future Belonging or Misfortune Control participants. In terms of accuracy, Future Belonging participants performed the most accurately, whereas Future Alone and Misfortune Control participants did not differ in their accuracy. Thus, social exclusion produced significant decrements in the ability to process information in an efficient and intelligent manner.

As usual, we also tested for mediation by emotion. There was no sign that any of the observed decrements in general intelligence were due to emotional distress.

Encoding and Memory

Next, Baumeister et al. (2002) investigated the effects of social exclusion on learning and memory. If exclusion results in cognitive impairment dependent on the self's executive function, then excluded individuals should remain unhindered in their encoding of information. Such cognitive activity requires little effort and should therefore remain relatively facile to individuals depleted of their regulatory resources through exclusion. Activities requiring recall of information, however, necessitate substantially more cognitive effort than encoding of information and should present excluded individuals with greater difficulty than individuals who anticipate belongingness or misfortune in their future.

The design of this study closely resembled that of the first study. Participants completed a personality test and were given bogus feedback regarding their future belongingness (and a brief mood measure). Participants then completed a portion of the Reading Comprehension section of the Graduate Record Examination (GRE). Participants were given two reading passages, one that was long and complex and another that was short and comparatively easy. The GRE protocol for testing was also followed, with participants being presented with both easy and difficult problems. Participants were given 3 minutes to read the passages but were given an unlimited amount of time for the memory recall task. (Experts on testing disagree as to whether timed or untimed tests provide the best measure, and so we sought to use both in different studies.) The recall task consisted of 12 multiple choice questions—7 about the difficult passage and 5 about the easier passage.

In addition to manipulating social exclusion, this study varied whether participants received the exclusion feedback before encoding the information (recall affected) or afterward (encoding affected). In the former case, they were debriefed before taking the test. Put another way, some participants first received the exclusion manipulation, then read the passage, then were debriefed as to the bogus nature of the exclusion feedback, and then took the memory test. Others first read the passage, then received the exclusion feedback, and then took the memory task (and then were debriefed). The exclusion manipulation was thus in force only during the encoding or during the recall phase of the study.

If social exclusion impairs cognitive processing dependent on the self's executive function, Future Alone participants in the recall affected condition should perform worse than either Future Belonging or Misfortune Control participants. Such decrements in performance should be observed for only the difficult questions, as easier questions rely less on cognitive control and self-regulated thinking. Encoding information requires significantly less effort than memory recall and, as a result, excluded participants in the encoding affected condition should not differ significantly in performance compared to the other two social feedback groups. Future Belonging and Misfortune Control participants should perform equally well regardless of whether they receive their personality feedback before or after encoding the passages.

As predicted, excluded participants in the recall affected condition performed significantly worse than participants in all other conditions. Further analysis revealed that the observed differences were largely due to excluded participants performing poorly on questions that required executive functioning (i.e., difficult questions). Performance on the easy questions did not differ significantly between social feedback groups. For the difficult questions, the interaction between sequence and feedback was significant, with Future Alone participants in the recall affected condition performing worse than all other participants. The size of effect between Future Alone and Misfortune Control participants on the difficult questions was large ($d = 1.01$). This provides additional support that the observed cognitive impairments were due to a future diagnostic forecast of exclusion and not merely a response to hearing bad news about one's future.

The observed decrements in performance among excluded participants were also dependent on the order in which they received the social exclusion feedback. Future Alone participants in the encoding affected condition performed as well as Future Belonging and Misfortune Control participants on both the easy and difficult questions. The change in sequence did not affect Future Belonging and Misfortune Control participants, who performed equally well in both the encoding affected and recall affected conditions. Thus, these results further corroborated the hypothesis that social exclusion produces cognitive impairments unique to the self's executive function, such as memory retrieval, but they leave less taxing processes, such as encoding information, relatively unhindered.

Simple comparisons and mediational analyses again provided no support for the mood mediation hypothesis. Future Alone participants did not differ from Future Belonging or Misfortune Control participants in their reported mood, and mood ratings were not related to cognitive performance.

Social exclusion impairs memory retrieval processes on tasks that require cognitive control and self-regulated thinking. Does exclusion also produce similar deficiencies in complicated tasks that involve active thinking? A final study tested whether exclusion inhibits performance on tasks that require processing information in a serial fashion (e.g., logical reasoning), leaving tasks that involve more automatic, parallel processing unimpaired (e.g., rote memory).

This study was needed because the results of the second study could be interpreted in two ways. One obvious interpretation was that exclusion affects recall but not encoding. (As stated above, people who merely read the passage after receiving the exclusion feedback, and then were debriefed before the memory test, performed quite well on the memory test.) Alternatively, those results could indicate that exclusion affects executive function tasks such as answering difficult questions based on recalled information, while it leaves simple and automatic tasks such as encoding relatively unaffected. Hence we designed the third study to compare performance on automatic versus controlled processes in intellectual performance.

This study used the same personality exclusion feedback paradigm that was employed in the previous two studies. Participants were randomly assigned between two tasks. One group completed either a logical reasoning task, while the rest memorized a list of 15 nonsense syllable words. After receiving the social exclusion feedback and reporting their mood, participants in the logical reasoning condition received 12 problems from the GRE Analytical section (5 questions on one logic problem, 3 reasoning questions, and 4 questions on an additional logic problem) and were given 12 minutes to complete them. Participants assigned to the nonsense syllable condition were given 60 seconds to memorize 15 three-letter nonsense syllables ranging in difficulty of pronunciation (e.g., FUM, TYJ, JEF, PIH), completed a filler task of math problems for 90 seconds, received the social exclusion feedback, completed the mood measure, and were then given 90 seconds to recall as many nonsense syllables as possible.

The results of this study indicated that social exclusion impairs cognitive processes that require active volition by the self, such as logical reasoning, but leaves more automatic and overlearned responses (such as rote memory) unaffected. Future Alone participants performed significantly worse than Future Belonging and Misfortune Control participants on the logical reasoning task. Future Alone participants attempted the fewest problems and answered the most problems incorrectly. In contrast, no significant variation was observed between the three social feedback groups for the rote memory task. Future Alone participants were able to store and remember information as well as Future Belonging or Misfortune Control participants.

Although this study employed a more comprehensive and detailed measure of mood than in previous studies (Positive and Negative Affect Scale; PANAS; Watson, Clark, & Tellegan, 1988), mood was not related to performance on either the logical reasoning or rote memory task.

In sum, three studies demonstrated that social exclusion produces significant impairments in intelligent thought. Participants who believed they were likely to spend their future alone had impaired performance on a general intelligence test, were less able to retrieve information from memory on a difficult reading comprehension passage, and they performed worst on a logical reasoning task, as compared to participants who received a future diagnostic forecast of belongingness or one of physical misfortune. These cognitive impairments were limited to processes that required cognitive control and self-regulated thinking. Excluded participants were not impaired in their ability to perform tasks that involved less active thinking, such as encoding and retrieval of simple information. Mood was not found to mediate any of the observed effects and the three social feedback groups did not reliably differ with regard to their reported mood.

SOCIAL EXCLUSION INHIBITS EFFECTIVE SELF-REGULATION

The studies covered in the preceding section found cognitive impairments among rejected participants. These followed a pattern suggesting that only processes depending on executive control were impaired by social exclusion. Hence we turned our attention to the possibility that social exclusion has a major impact on executive control. Because self-regulation is a prominent, centrally important form of executive control (e.g., Baumeister, 1998), we conducted a series of studies designed to see whether self-regulation would deteriorate among people who received messages of social rejection or exclusion (Baumeister, DeWall, Ciarocco, & Twenge, in press).

Self-regulation, defined as the ability to alter or modify one's thoughts, feelings, or behaviors, enables people to override their naturally selfish inclinations in order to remain in line with the standards set by their social group. Eating healthfully, abstaining from emotional outbursts, and other self-regulation processes require people to take into account the interests of the group before satisfying their selfish interests. Effective self-regulation therefore increases the possibility of acceptance by one's group. Failure to self-regulate effectively, in contrast, should decrease the likelihood of acceptance and instead should lead to possible rejection and exclusion from the group.

What happens to self-regulation processes when an individual is abruptly rejected or excluded by a group? Because people have an innate need to belong, it would seem adaptive and reasonable that excluded or rejected individuals would be naturally motivated to self-regulate all the more effectively in an effort to regain a semblance of acceptance and belongingness from others. After all, to the extent that acceptance or rejection is controllable by the individual, then rejection indicates that one has not behaved in socially desirable ways—changing the self would be optimal. Changing the self , and especially changing oneself toward more socially desirable lines of action, is the essence of self-regulation.

Hence one might expect self-regulation to improve among excluded or rejected people. However, by the time we ran these studies, we had seen enough other results to doubt that responses to social exclusion are generally adaptive or optimal (or socially desirable). Moreover, the studies showing decrements in cognitive functioning among excluded individuals all pointed toward poorer self-regulation. Hence our main prediction was that self-regulation would deteriorate in the wake of social exclusion or rejection.

Taking Care of One's Health

Two initial studies tested whether people who experienced social exclusion or rejection would effectively regulate their intake of healthy and unhealthy foods and drinks. We manipulated acceptance versus exclusion and then measured consumption in an ostensibly separate, unrelated context.

The first study used the personality feedback exclusion paradigm, with participants assigned either to the Future Alone, Future Belonging, or Misfortune Control conditions. The method used to measure self-regulatory failure was the number of ounces each participant was willing to drink of a bad-tasting yet healthy beverage, consisting of vinegar, water, and artificial unsweetened fruit flavoring (Muraven, 1998). Self-regulation was required to overcome the bad taste of the healthy drink. Persistence at a task that brings immediate costs to the self for the sake of a beneficial future outcome represents the cornerstone of self-regulation and can be seen in numerous other self-regulatory behaviors, such as forcing oneself to eat bland tasting but healthy foods, studying for an exam instead of procrastinating, and saving money from a paycheck each month instead of spending it all.

Participants were also offered a modest monetary reward of 5 cents for every ounce of the bad tasting but healthy beverage the participant drank. This helped not only to motivate participants to drink more but also framed the act of imbibing the bad tasting beverage as desirable but not entirely pleasant (thus necessitating an extrinsic reward).

Results from this study indicated that participants who received a future diagnostic forecast of social exclusion persisted less on the self-regulation task than participants in the other two conditions. Future Alone participants drank substantially less of the bad tasting but healthy beverage than participants who anticipated belongingness or general misfortune. As usual, the effects were not mediated by mood.

A second study sought to test whether social exclusion produces an inability to regulate the consumption of unhealthy, fattening foods. Participants entered the laboratory in small groups and completed a brief relationship closeness induction task (questions were taken from Sedikides, Campbell, Reeder, & Elliot, 1999). Each participant was then led to a separate room, completed a brief demographic questionnaire, and stated how long it had been since he or she had last eaten. Participants were then told that the next part of the study involved forming small groups of people that like and respect each other and that they could pick the two people with whom they would most like to work. For participants assigned to the rejected condition, the experimenter returned to tell them that no one had listed them as a person with whom they would like to work and that they would have to go ahead and complete the next task alone. Participants assigned to the accepted condition, on the other hand, were told that everyone had expressed interest in them as a desirable partner but because there could not be a group so large that they would have to complete the next task alone.

The next part of the study was framed as a taste-testing task. All participants were given a small bowl of 35 bite-size chocolate chip cookies and were instructed to taste-test the cookies by eating as many as they needed to provide an accurate judgment the smell, taste, and texture. In order to avert attention away from the number of cookies eaten, participants were given a brief questionnaire on which they rated the taste of the cookies and the likelihood that they would purchase a box of them. Participants were given 10 minutes to complete the taste-testing task and questionnaire. Self-regulatory failure was measured by the number of cookies eaten during the study. This measure was based on the general societal perception that eating cookies is bad for you and should be restrained; moreover, previous data with a similar sample confirmed that most students in our subject population viewed eating cookies as an unhealthy and undesirable behavior that ought to be regulated (Tice, Bratslavsky, & Baumeister, 2001). Hence we assumed that as self-regulation deteriorates, people will eat more cookies.

Consistent with the view that social rejection impairs self-regulation, we found that participants who had been rejected by the group seemed less able to override their inclination to eat good-tasting yet fattening foods. Rejected participants consumed an average of nearly nine cookies, which was about twice as many cookies as accepted participants consumed.

Actually, rejection apparently made the cookies taste better too. Rejected participants gave the cookies more favorable ratings on taste. However, the improvement in taste did not mediate the increased eating, and many rejected participants who ate the most cookies rated them as relatively unappealing. In the accepted condition, taste ratings correlated positively with the number eaten, which suggests that accepted participants ate more cookies the more they enjoyed the taste of them. In contrast, taste ratings and amount eaten were uncorrelated among the rejected participants. Thus, they ate a relatively high number of cookies regardless of their quality of taste.

Mood was measured in both studies using a 1-item mood measure. In the first study, Future Belonging participants reported a significantly better mood than Future Alone participants. Misfortune Control participants also reported a (marginally) better mood than socially excluded (Future Alone) ones. The second study showed that accepted participants reported a significantly better mood than rejected participants, who reported a neutral mood. The mood effects were small, unlike the behavioral (self-regulation) effects, which were large. Results from mediational analyses, however, revealed that mood did not mediate the observed decrements in self-regulation in either study.

The next study in this series tested whether socially excluded participants would persist less than other people at a frustrating and discouraging task. Persistence in the face of failure has long been regarded as a virtue in our society. It is relevant to self-regulation because it often requires overriding the desire to quit working on the frustrating task so as to do something more satisfying.

The task in this study consisted of puzzles that required the person to trace a geometric figure without double-tracing any lines and without lifting one's pen from the paper. Thus it requires spatial reasoning. The puzzles were rigged so as to be unsolvable. The measure was how long the participant continued to try to solve the puzzles, as opposed to quitting.

This study used the same personality feedback exclusion paradigm used in previous studies. Participants entered the laboratory, completed a personality test, and were given false feedback about the implications of their personality for their future belongingness. A no-feedback control group was added in addition to the Future Alone, Future Belonging, and Misfortune Control groups. Participants then reported their mood on the Brief Mood Introspection Scale (BMIS; Mayer & Gaschke, 1988) and completed the State Self-Esteem Scale (SSES; Heatherton & Polivy, 1991).

The main dependent measure was duration of work on an unsolvable puzzle. Using a procedure developed by Baumeister, Bratslavsky, Muraven, and Tice (1998), participants were instructed to trace a pair of geometric figures without retracing any lines or picking up his or her pencil from the paper. The experimenter showed each participant how to complete the task with an example figure, and the participant completed a practice trial while the experimenter was present. Both of these figures were solvable. When the experimenter was convinced that the participant understood the task, the participant was given a pair of geometric figures to trace. Unlike the practice figures, these were unsolvable. Participants were told that they could take as much time as they needed to complete the puzzles and that they could a ring a bell to signal to the experimenter when they had completed the task.

Participants who anticipated a future devoid of meaningful relationships gave up significantly faster than participants in all other conditions. Future Alone participants gave up on the unsolvable puzzles before both Future Belonging and Misfortune Control participants and also participants who did not receive any feedback about their future belongingness. When comparing Future Alone participants with participants in the two other conditions, the size of effect for task persistence was over a full standard deviation ($d = 1.31$).

No main effects for mood or state self-esteem were found. Mediational analyses failed to demonstrate any relationship between self-regulation failure and mood or state self-esteem.

Thus, again, social exclusion impaired self-regulation. Hearing that one's future would likely lack close relationships made people give up more readily on unsolvable puzzles.

In our next study, we turned to dichotic listening as a measure of self-regulation. Attention control is an important self-regulation process that provides people with benefits in several domains. Being a good listener or student, for example, often involves diverting attention away from personal thoughts for the sake of understanding another person, article, or other source of information. Increased attention also provides people with signals of possible environmental variables that pose a threat to effective self-regulation. Recovering addicts, for example, often become greatly attuned to environmental cues that "trigger" or activate impulses to partake in unwanted, self-destructive behaviors (Pomerleau, Fertig, Baker, & Cooney, 1983; Laberg, Hugdahl, Stormark, Nordby, & Aas, 1992). Thus, the ability to regulate one's attention can be important for securing individual social approval and acceptance. This ability may suffer a dramatic decrease in effectiveness following social exclusion, if self-regulation is broadly impaired among people who experience rejection.

This study used the same personality exclusion manipulation paradigm employed in previous studies. Participants entered the laboratory, completed a personality test, and were given bogus feedback about their future belongingness, aloneness, or accident proneness. After reporting their mood, participants were instructed to sit at a desk at the opposite end of the room in order to complete a brief listening game. The experimenter explained to each participant that he or she would be presented with a brief audio recording on which there would be a different voice in each ear. In the right ear, there would be a speech regarding a policy issue. The left ear would contain a female voice speaking a series of words. Participants were instructed to pay close attention to the female voice in the left ear and try their best to ignore the policy speech in their right ear. In addition, participants were given a recording sheet and were asked to write down each word spoken in the left ear that contained the letters "m" or "p" anywhere in the word.

Participants who believed they would spend their future alone were less able to regulate their attention than participants in the two other conditions. Future Alone participants identified significantly fewer correct words than Future Belonging and Misfortune Control participants. Comparing the performance of Future Alone and Misfortune Control participants yielded a large size of effect ($d = 1.17$). This provides further support that the observed self-regulation failure was due to a future diagnostic prediction of social exclusion as opposed to merely hearing bad news about one's future.

Participants did not differ significantly in their mood and mediational analyses again failed to demonstrate a significant relationship between self-regulation failure and emotional distress. Social exclusion feedback, on the other hand, remained significantly related to task performance even after controlling for mood.

In sum, this series of studies found a broad pattern of impaired self-regulation among people who experienced social exclusion (Baumeister, DeWall, Ciarocco, & Twenge, in press). Rejected or excluded people ate more unhealthy foods, drank less of a bad-tasting but healthy beverage, quit sooner on a frustrating task, and were less effective at screening out distractions so as to focus their attention on a target message.

DECREMENTS IN COGNITION AND SELF-REGULATION FOLLOWING SOCIAL EXCLUSION AND REJECTION: WHY?

The studies reviewed in this chapter demonstrate that social exclusion and rejection produce inner disruption sufficient enough to produce reduced intelligent thought and self-regulation failure. Participants who believed they were likely to spend their future alone performed poorly on a general intelligence measure, had impaired memory for difficult reading passages, and were unable to successfully process information in a logical manner. Socially excluded and rejected participants also failed to effectively regulate their intake of healthy and unhealthy foods and beverages, quit prematurely on a frustrating and discouraging exercise, and failed to regulate their attention on a dichotic listening task. These effects were in most cases substantial, exceeding Cohen's (1977) criteria for large effect sizes. These deficiencies in intelligent thought and self-regulation were also unique to participants who experienced exclusion or rejection. Participants who were told that they could expect a future where they would likely break many bones and be injured in accidents did not suffer the same inner disruption as excluded and rejected participants. Specifically, their performance on cognitive and self-regulation tasks was statistically indistinguishable from participants who believed their future would be filled with meaningful and lasting relationships. Participants who received no feedback on a personality test performed as effectively at a self-regulation task as participants who anticipated future belongingness or becoming accident prone.

Social exclusion and rejection did not produce much in terms of emotional distress in any of our studies. Excluded participants occasionally reported a less positive mood than accepted or control participants, but these differences did not mediate the observed decrements in self-regulation and intelligent performance. Participants who anticipated a future marred by frequent accidents (in the Misfortune Control conditions) reported moods similar to those of socially excluded participants. Their intelligent performance and self-regulation ability, however, closely resembled that of participants in the Future Belonging condition. Thus, our studies demonstrate that people who experience a slightly negative mood (as did the Misfortune Control participants) maintain their ability to perform intelligently and to self-regulate effectively. A direct threat to belongingness, in contrast, renders individuals less capable of intelligent thought and effective self-regulation.

We noted earlier that the decrements in intelligent thought and self-regulation are maladaptive responses to rejection. The likelihood of social acceptance increases with intelligent, regulated, socially desirable behavior, and if rejected people would want to gain such acceptance, they should increase those behaviors. But our findings repeatedly indicated that they do not. Indeed, our findings suggest that many people may experience a downward spiral in which rejection may lead to socially disvalued behavior which may, in turn, elicit further rejection. Poor self-regulation leads to social exclusion, and if exclusion also causes poorer self-regulation, it is hard to see how individuals can escape from the downward spiral so as to gain or re-gain acceptance.

HOW AND WHY DOES REJECTION IMPAIR SELF-REGULATION?

The deficits in intelligent thought and self-regulation may help explain some of the behavioral consequences of self-regulation—but they call for explanation in turn. We found some evidence that the decrements in self-regulation and executive function may contribute to the decreases in intelligent thought (Baumeister, Twenge, & Nuss, 2002), but what inner processes contribute to self-regulation failure? Our current work has begun to explore these factors.

Self-awareness is one mechanism that helps self-regulation succeed (Carver & Scheier, 1981, 1982). It is difficult, if not impossible, to exert effortful control over responses of which one is unaware. Our earlier work found some evidence that social exclusion leads to a motivated avoidance of self-focused attention. That is, Twenge, Catanese, and Baumeister (2003) found that rejected people preferred to sit in chairs facing away from mirrors, as opposed to facing toward mirrors. Could avoidance of self-focused attention contribute to self-regulatory failures?

To test this, we used a standard manipulation of self-awareness, namely the presence of a mirror. Unlike our previous study, in which participants were offered the choice of seats facing either toward or away from a mirror, we randomly assigned people to sit facing a mirror or not. The procedure closely followed that of the dichotic listening study described earlier (Baumeister, DeWall, Ciarocco, & Twenge, in press) in which participants received bogus feedback about their ostensible futures and then performed the dichotic listening task. The mirror manipulation was introduced after the bogus feedback manipulation, and participants performed the dichotic listening task while either facing the mirror or not. We found that the presence of the mirror eliminated the self-regulation problems. That is, even people who were told that they would likely end up alone in life were able to screen out the distracting voice and count stimulus words successfully if they were facing a mirror while they performed the task.

Another approach focuses on the motivation to self-regulate. Our theoretical analysis proposed that self-regulation is essentially a mechanism that enables individuals to make sacrifices so as to perform socially desirable behavior to gain social acceptance. Hence when social acceptance is denied, people may lose the motivation to make such sacrifices. We are currently conducting a study in which we attempt to provide an alternate source of motivation that might substitute or compensate for the loss of anticipated belongingness. That is, we expose participants to the manipulation of future aloneness versus belongingness, and then some of them perform the dichotic listening task with a cash incentive to do well. Preliminary findings indicate that people who are led to anticipate being alone in life can perform effectively on the dichotic listening task if they are given a monetary incentive to do so.

Further research is needed, but these findings have begun to suggest some processes by which social exclusion can damage self-regulation. Rejected people seem to lose the will to regulate their behavior. They also lose or avoid self-awareness, without which self-regulation is difficult to achieve.

CONCLUSION

Our program of research has begun to uncover some of the inner processes that are set in motion by social exclusion or rejection. Our initial theories and assumptions have been proven wrong in many cases, but we think that we are finally moving toward a more accurate understanding.

It is easy to propose how people ideally or optimally would respond to social exclusion. They ought to redouble their efforts to secure acceptance. Toward that end, they should reduce their aggressive and antisocial tendencies and increase prosocial behavior. They should improve at self-regulation so as to perform more socially desirable actions. And even if improved social acceptance is not a promising option, they ought at least to become more thoughtful and intelligent and should avoid self-defeating behaviors, so as to fare better on their own if necessary. Yet, our laboratory studies have found the opposite of all of these to be closer to the truth.

The finality of our rejection manipulations may have contributed to the gloomy outcomes. Other work has suggested that when rejected people are given a good opportunity to re-connect with those who excluded them or possibly with others, people behave in a more prosocial, adaptive manner (see Twenge, this volume; Ouwerkerk et al., this volume, Williams & Zadro, this volume). Conversely, when the prospects for gaining acceptance are especially dim, such as when one has been rejected by a well-defined category of people that one has no chance of joining, aggressive and antisocial responses are especially intense (Gaertner & Iuzzini, this volume).

Initially we thought that emotional distress would be the central feature of the impact of social rejection, and all behavioral consequences would flow from this distress. This too has been disconfirmed. Across many studies we have found large behavioral effects but small and inconsistent emotional effects, and even when we did find significant differences in emotion these have failed to mediate the behaviors. Indeed, the sweeping failure of our emotion mediation theories has led us to question the role of emotion in causing behavior generally (but that is another story). The erratic nature of emotional responses and their general irrelevance to the behavioral consequences of rejection have been confirmed in other laboratories (see Lakin & Chartrand, this volume). If anything, the immediate impact of an unexpected rejection experience seems to be one of emotional numbness, which may be linked to the body's naturally analgesic response to physical pain, and which could possibly help explain some of the socially insensitive behavior exhibited by rejected individuals (MacDonald, Kingsbury, & Shaw, this volume; see also Eisenberger & Lieberman, this volume).

Self-regulation and cognition, instead of emotion, have emerged from our most recent data as the most important inner processes to change in response to social exclusion. Rejected or excluded people exhibit poorer self-regulation in many spheres. They also show impairments in intelligent thought, though these are limited to forms of thought that are linked to self-regulation (i.e., thinking processes that depend on effortful control by the self's executive functioning).

Further research is needed. Now that we know self-regulation and cognition are damaged by social exclusion, it is necessary to establish that these decrements do indeed help mediate the behavioral responses. For example, does aggression increase among rejected individuals because, and to the extent that, they fail to self-regulate their aggressive impulses?

Nonetheless, the findings from this work have helped shed light on both the inner and outer responses to exclusion. They help illuminate why many troubled individuals may engage in maladaptive or seemingly self-destructive behaviors (see Romero-Canyas & Downey, this volume). They may also have relevance to the responses of groups to perceived exclusion from society as a whole. Although there are some exceptions, such as the intellectually vigorous culture maintained by Jews during the centuries of discrimination and ghettoization, many groups who felt excluded or rejected by society have shown patterns similar to those we find in our laboratory studies: high aggression, self-defeating behaviors, reduced prosocial contributions to society as a whole, poor performance in intellectual spheres, and impaired self-regulation. Our findings suggest that if modern societies can become more inclusive and tolerant, so that all groups feel they are welcome to belong, many broad social patterns of pathological and unhealthy behavior could be reduced.

Most creatures get what they need to live from their physical surroundings. Humans, in contrast, get what they need from each other and from their culture (see Baumeister, 2005, for extended treatment). The human psyche is therefore designed with elaborate mechanisms that help it obtain and maintain belongingness. These mechanisms include motivations (e.g., the need to belong), cognitions (e.g., theory of mind and social cognition), and self-regulation. Social exclusion is therefore not a misfortune like any other. Rather, it seems to violate the very purpose for which the human psyche is designed. That perspective seems vital to understanding the large and widely assorted changes in behavior, cognition, and self-regulation that we have found even in response to seemingly relatively minor laboratory manipulations that thwart the need to belong.

REFERENCES

Baron, R. M., & Kenny, D. A. (1986). The moderator-mediator variable distinction in social psychological research: Conceptual, strategic, and statistical considerations. *Journal of Personality and Social Psychology, 51,* 1173–1182.

Baumeister, R. F. (1998). The self. In D. T. Gilbert, S. T. Fiske, & G. Lindzey (Eds.), *Handbook of social psychology* (4th ed.; pp. 680–740). New York: McGraw-Hill.

Baumeister, R. F. (2005). *The cultural animal: Human nature, meaning, and social life.* New York: Oxford University Press.

Baumeister, R. F., Bratslavsky, E., Muraven, M., & Tice, D. M. (1998). Ego depletion: Is the active self a limited resource? *Journal of Personality and Social Psychology, 74,* 1152–1265.

Baumeister, R. F., DeWall, C. N., Ciarocco, N. J., & Twenge, J. M. (in press). Social exlusion impairs self-regulation. *Journal of Personality and Social Psychology.*

Baumeister, R. F., & Leary, M. R. (1995). The need to belong: Desire for interpersonal attachments as a fundamental human motivation. *Psychological Bulletin, 117,* 497–529.

Baumeister, R. F., & Tice, D. M. (1990). Anxiety and social exclusion. *Journal of Social and Clinical Psychology, 9,* 165–195.

Baumeister, R. F., Twenge, J. M., & Nuss, C. K. (2002). Effects of social exclusion on cognitive processes: Anticipated aloneness reduces intelligent thought. *Journal of Personality and Social Psychology, 83,* 817–827.

Carver, C. S., & Scheier, M. F. (1981). *Attention and self-regulation: A control theory approach to human behavior.* New York: Springer-Verlag.

Carver, C. S., & Scheier, M. F. (1982). Control theory: A useful conceptual framework for personality-social, clinical and health psychology. *Psychological Bulletin, 92,* 111–135.

Cohen, J. (1977). *Statistical power analysis for the behavioral sciences.* New York: Academic Press.

Heatherton, T. F., & Polivy, J. (1991). Development and validation of a scale for measuring state self-esteem. *Journal of Personality and Social Psychology, 60,* 895–910.

Janda, L. H. (1996). *The psychologist's book of self-tests.* New York: Berkley.

Janda, L. H. , Fulk, J., Janda, M., & Wallace, J. (1995). *The development of a test of General Mental Abilities.* Unpublished manuscript, Old Dominion University.

Laberg, J. C., Hugdahl, K., Stormark, K. M., Nordby, H., & Aas, H. (1992). Effects of visual alcohol cues on alcoholics' autonomic arousal. *Psychology of Addictive Behaviors, 6,* 181–187.

Leary, M. R., & Kowalski, R. (1995). *Social anxiety.* New York: Guilford Press.

Mayer, J. D., & Gaschke, Y. N. (1988). The experience and meta-experience of mood. *Journal of Personality and Social Psychology, 55,* 102–111.

Muraven, M. (1998). *Mechanisms of self-control failure: Motivation and limited resources.* Doctoral dissertation, Case Western Reserve University, Cleveland, OH.

Muraven, M., Tice, D. M., & Baumeister, R. F. (1998). Self-control as limited resource: Regulatory depletion patterns. *Journal of Personality and Social Psychology, 74,* 774–789.

Nezlek, J. B., Kowalski, R. M., Leary, M. R., Blevins, T., & Holgate, S. (1997). Personality moderators of reactions to interpersonal rejection: Depression and trait self-esteem. *Personality and Social Psychology Bulletin, 23,* 1235–1244.

Pomerleau, O. F., Fertig, J., Baker, L., & Cooney, N. (1983). Reactivity to alcohol cues in alcoholics and non-alcoholics: Implications for a stimulus control analysis of drinking. *Addictive Behaviors, 8,* 1–10.

Sedikides, C., Campbell, W. K., Reeder, G. D., & Elliot, A. J. (1999). The relationship closeness induction task. *Representative Research in Social Psychology, 23,* 1–4.

Tice, D. M., Bratslavsky, E., & Baumeister, R. F. (2001). Emotional distress regulation takes precedence over impulse control: If you feel bad, do it! *Journal of Personality and Social Psychology, 80,* 53–67.

Twenge, J. M., Baumeister, R. F., Tice, D. M., & Stucke, T. S. (2001). If you can't join them, beat them: Effects of social exclusion on aggressive behavior. *Journal of Personality and Social Psychology, 81,* 1058–1069.

Twenge, J. M., Catanese, K. R., & Baumeister, R. F. (2003). Social exclusion and the deconstructed state: Time perception, meaninglessness, lethargy, lack of emotion, and self-awareness. *Journal of Personality and Social Psychology, 85,* 409–423.

Twenge, J. M., Ciarocco, N. J., Cuervo, D., & Baumeister, R. F. (2003). *Social exclusion reduces prosocial behavior.* Unpublished manuscript.

Watson, D., Clark, L. A., & Tellegen, A. (1988). Development and validation of brief measures of positive and negative affect: The PANAS scales. *Journal of Personality and Social Psychology, 54,* 1063–1070.

Williams, K. D., Cheung, C. K. T., & Choi, W. (2000). CyberOstracism: Effects of being ignored over the Internet. *Journal of Personality and Social Psychology, 79,* 748–762.

PART *II*

DEEP ROOTS
OF EXCLUSION:
NEUROPSYCHOLOGICAL
SUBSTRATES OF ISOLATION
AND EXCLUSION

5

Adding Insult to Injury
Social Pain Theory and
Response to Social Exclusion

GEOFF MACDONALD
RACHELL KINGSBURY
STEPHANIE SHAW

Study 1: Hurt Feelings and Reaction to Depictions of Injury
Study 2: Pain Sensitivity Following Rejection
Study 3: Persistent Pain and Hurt Feelings
Summary and Conclusions

I know it was wrong, but I got hecka suspicious about her and Charles so I went into her e-mail one day and I saw a letter that she sent to Charles...And after I saw that, it was over. I was so fucking mad and so fucking hurt, mostly mad. I wanted to throw EVERYTHING and just punch everything I saw...That night that I found out, I couldn't even sleep. I thought I was just gonna die in bed that night, it was just hella hurting. I was just lying there, and the heartache was hurting so bad, it's unexplainable. It starts from the heart, and it spreads throughout your body so the whole body hurts. The heart, the mind, everything about me was dying. (uclamangoboy, 2003)

The jilted lover is a role most adults have played at one time or another, and so the reactions described above may have a certain familiarity for many readers. From a researcher's point of view, however, such a statement highlights two striking qualities of reactions to rejection. The first is the extremity of the reaction. If romantic break-up is a common experience, then it seems unduly

---

Address correspondence to: Geoff MacDonald, School of Psychology, University of Queensland, St. Lucia, Qld., 4072, geoff@psy.uq.edu.au.

harsh to feel something akin to death in response to relationship dissolution. The second is the apparent nonfunctionality of the reactions. If a rejected individual's primary goal is to increase inclusionary status, it seems difficult to understand what wanton aggressiveness, sleeplessness, and full-body pain do to subserve that goal. Although the reasons for the extremity and nonfunctionality of such rejection experiences are not well understood, in this chapter we strive to demonstrate that the motivations behind such reactions are not, in fact, unexplainable. Specifically, we will present evidence, including three studies, that the experience of social exclusion can activate the physiological system that functions to protect individuals from physical threats, thus leading to a cascade of physical defense responses.

In modern life, it is relatively easy to view our social needs as separate from our physical needs. But in the environment that forged human nature, as well as that of our pre-human ancestors, social needs and physical needs were intimately related. Inclusion in social groups meant access to nutrition, security, and mates while exclusion undermined survival not just of an individual but also of its genetic lineage (Baumeister & Leary, 1995). As a result, social animals required mechanisms that could warn of threats to inclusion and guide appropriate action. Social pain theory (MacDonald & Leary, 2005) posits that aspects of the physical pain system provided the foundation for some of the physiological mechanisms that regulate social behavior. Specifically, the experience of pain can be separated into two components—pain sensation and pain affect (Melzack & Casey, 1968; Price, 2000). Pain sensation mechanisms function to detect physical injury through specialized receptors, with tissue damage signaled via the nociceptive system. Pain affect mechanisms function to promote the sense of unpleasantness that often accompanies pain sensation, as well as triggering emotions relating to the possible future consequences of the injury (Price, 2000). It is pain affect mechanisms that connote a sense of aversiveness, draw attention to injury, and provide motivation to end exposure to the noxious stimulus (Melzack & Casey, 1968; Price, 1999). Social pain theory proposes that perceptions of exclusion or relational devaluation lead to the experience of pain affect, but not pain sensation (see also Eisenberger & Lieberman, this volume; Eisenberger, Lieberman, & Williams, 2003).

In particular, social pain has been defined as, "a specific emotional reaction to the perception that one is being excluded from desired relationships, or being devalued by desired relationship partners or groups" (MacDonald & Leary, 2005, p. 202). Exclusion refers to being denied a relationship with an individual or group for any reason, such as rejection, death of a loved one, or forced separation. Relational devaluation refers to feeling less valued as a relational partner (e.g., friend, romantic partner, group member) than one desires (Leary & Springer, 2000). Devaluation is considered to be experienced as aversive because it is a cue related to ultimate exclusion. Leary and Springer (2000) suggest that hurt feelings is the specific emotion felt in response to relational devaluation. However, other affective states such as embarrassment, shame, guilt, or jealousy can also be indicators that one may be disappointing important others, and thus may also accompany hurt feelings.

MacDonald and Leary (2005) argue that painful feelings came to be associated with cues predictive of exclusion experiences because evolutionary pressures made the regulation of inclusionary status critical to survival. Specifically, social pain theory suggests that the pain system provided two important preadaptations to aid in response to exclusion threats—pain promotes quick reaction in response to threat and provides a source of punishment to teach organisms to avoid threatening stimuli. Although these two functions are related, this chapter will focus more exclusively on the former. We will discuss evidence suggesting that shared physiological mechanisms underlie behavioral responses to socially and physically threatening stimuli, and that these mechanisms promote rapid responses to general threats as opposed to tailored responses to specific threats. That is, we will argue that both social and physical pain lead to reactions that prepare an organism for quick reaction to non-specific danger. Such a response facilitates timely reaction to threat, but may, at times, lead to inappropriate and self-defeating reactions to social exclusion.

If response to social exclusion is regulated by the same system that manages response to physical threat, understanding the physical threat response system should provide insight into reactions to exclusion. According to Gray and McNaughton (2000), behavior in response to threat is regulated according to the state of two key variables. The first variable, defensive distance, refers to the degree of perceived threat in a given situation (Blanchard & Blanchard, 1990). Defensive distance should be perceived as relatively high when a stimulus is viewed as having little capacity to inflict harm or when a potentially harmful stimulus is not nearby. Defensive distance should be perceived as relatively low when a stimulus that has the potential to inflict harm is in close proximity. For example, encountering an individual with a gun should promote perceptions of low defensive distance, whereas recognizing the gun as only a toy should promote perceptions of high defensive distance. The second variable, defensive direction, refers to whether or not motivation exists to approach a potentially dangerous stimulus (Gray & McNaughton, 2000). For example, an individual may perceive walking alone at night as being threatening, but may need to do so in order to get home (i.e., approach a threatening situation to reach a desired goal). According to Gray and McNaughton's (2000) model, the emotional response to approaching a potentially threatening stimulus is *anxiety*, which encourages cautious approach behavior (e.g., carefully attending to other pedestrians). Anxiety and cautious approach behavior should be increased as defensive distance (e.g., distance from a stranger) is reduced. When a dangerous stimulus is detected at high levels of defensive distance, and motivation to approach the stimulus exists, the defense system promotes *fearful avoidance* of the stimulus (e.g., avoiding eye contact with strangers walking on the other side of the road). However, threatening stimuli perceived at low defensive distance (e.g., the individual is accosted), leads to a panic response, with accompanying fight, flight, or freezing behavior geared towards finding the quickest possible route to safety. This response has been shown to be reliably elicited by such factors as immediate predators, high levels of carbon dioxide, and physical pain (Gray & McNaughton,

2000). Physical pain often signals highly proximal threat, as it typically associated with ongoing tissue damage. In this way, pain is an important activator of the fight/flight/freezing response (Berkowitz, 1993; Berkowitz, Cochran, & Embree, 1981; Merskey, 2000). Importantly, such fight/flight/freezing behavior is highly reactive and relatively undirected—coordination and planning are bypassed in order to provide a rapid response to danger. To facilitate quick reaction, panic induces a set of physiological changes such as increased heart rate, increased blood clotting factor, and analgesia (Gray & McNaughton, 2000).

Just as the physical world contains rewards and threats that must be negotiated, so too does the social world. While the need to belong (Baumeister & Leary, 1995) and sexual desire provide social approach motivation, the dangers of rejection and exclusion provide social avoidance motivation. Accordingly, the concepts of defensive distance and defensive direction may be useful in understanding social behavior. Defensive distance in a social context may be thought of as a function of one's perceptions of the likelihood of exclusion from a relationship, and the value that inclusion in that relationship holds. That is, impending exclusion from important relationships should promote perceptions of low defensive distance from threat in social situations. In attachment theory terms, defensive distance may be comparable to the dimension of anxious attachment, or the degree to which one fears ultimate exclusion from close others (e.g., Feeney, Noller, & Hanrahan, 1994). Defensive direction may be thought of as the degree to which one is motivated to become emotionally close with others. Again, in terms of attachment, defensive distance may be comparable to the dimension of discomfort with closeness, or the extent to which closeness from others is considered desirable. Consistent with these speculations, hurt feelings appear to promote anxious, fearful, and panic responses consistent with those seen in response to physical threat. For example, Vangelisti and Crumley (1998) factor analyzed responses to hurtful communication into three categories. The first, "acquiescent," consisted of behaviors such as apologizing that appear to facilitate safety from hurt via cautious approach. The second, labeled "invulnerable," consisted of behaviors such as ignoring the source of hurt that serve to help one avoid or withdraw from a hurtful exchange. Finally, the response labeled "active verbal" consisted of behaviors such as verbally attacking the source of hurt that seem to reflect aggressive responses. These classes of responses seem to match well with the anxiety, fear, and panic components of the physical defense system, respectively.

There is a large body of evidence supporting the notion that avoidance responses to social and physical threat are managed by the same physiological system (for a review see MacDonald & Leary, 2005). One line of evidence especially relevant to the current discussion comes from research involving the midbrain periaqueductal gray (PAG). In general, the PAG is considered an important site for the management of autonomic and motor responses to threats (Fanselow, 1991; Gray & McNaughton, 2000; Lonstein & Stern, 1998). Gray and McNaughton (2000) argue that the PAG serves as the coordinator of the panic response, integrating a variety of physiological changes into a relatively coherent response pattern.

Indeed, direct stimulation of the lateral PAG in non-human animals has been shown to instigate panic behaviors such as undirected escape, defensive aggression, and freezing (Bandler & Shipley, 1994; Fanselow, 1991). Natural elicitors of PAG activation appear to include both physical pain and social separation cues. The PAG receives input from the nociceptive system (Craig & Dostrovsky, 1999) and has been shown to play a role in response to physical pain (Fields, 2000). The PAG also receives input from the anterior cingulate cortex (An, Bandler, Öngür, & Price, 1998), which has been shown to be involved in processing the affective component of physical pain (Rainville, 2002), and to be active in response to social exclusion in humans (Eisenberger et al., 2003). The PAG has also been shown to be related to bonding (Lonstein, Simmons, & Stern, 1998; Stack, Balakrishnan, Numan, & Numan, 2002) and infant proximity-seeking behavior (Panksepp, 1998). In fact, Panksepp (1998), based on the physical proximity of PAG areas that can be stimulated to produce separation distress vocalizations and physical pain responses in non-human animals, concluded that, "This affirms that separation distress is related to perceptions of (physical) pain..." (p. 267).

As discussed, one reason pain may have been adopted as a signal of threat to social inclusion status is that pain triggers quick reaction to threat. It is fairly evident why quick reaction to physical threat is an adaptive trait. Such reactivity allows for fight, flight, or freezing behavior to occur in the small window of time an organism may have to save itself. Threats to inclusionary status also frequently require similar quick reactions. For example, inappropriate comments that are halted on the first sign of disapproval from others are likely to do less damage to inclusionary status than inappropriate comments that continue despite warning signs of disapproval. In some cases, stopping one word or one action too late can mean the difference between inclusion and exclusion. We suggest that the same base fight/flight/freezing motivation involved in response to physical threat may underlie response to social threat because it promotes adaptive reactions in these circumstances. For example, "social freezing" motivation could promote behaviors such as ceasing inappropriate remarks and increasing vigilance to the social situation. "Social flight" motivation may promote withdrawal from hurtful exchanges, and the pursuit of interaction with safer relational partners. Finally, "social fight" motivation may promote assertiveness when one's inclusionary status is challenged.

However, because the threat response system is designed to prepare an organism for generalized threat, rather than specific classes of social or physical threats, threat to social inclusion status should lead to physiological changes consistent with preparation for a physical threat. Research on the effects of social exclusion supports this suggestion. The experience of exclusion has been shown to lead to increases in plasma cortisol (a marker of stress) and blood pressure (Stroud, Tanofsky-Kraff, Wilfley, & Salovey, 2000), to interfere with higher order cognitive processing while not affecting more base mental tasks (Baumeister & DeWall, this volume; Baumeister, Twenge, & Nuss, 2002), to hinder self-regulation (Baumeister & DeWall, this volume), to automatically prime anger (Williams, Case,

& Govan, 2003), and to promote aggression (Buckley, Winkel, & Leary, 2003; Catanese & Tice, this volume; Twenge, this volume; Twenge, Baumeister, Tice, & Stucke, 2001). Although this constellation of responses to exclusion appears to have little connection to effective social behavior, the set of responses makes more sense when considered as part of the activation of a general threat response system. Specifically, these physiological changes appear designed to prepare an organism for quick reactions to any type of threat that may manifest itself. This analysis suggests that when high degrees of rejection are perceived (i.e., defensive distance is low), a social threat may be treated equivalently to a physical threat. That is, excluded individuals' threat response systems may become so highly active that they react to a source of relational devaluation as if the excluder is a proximate physical threat. This notion may help explain why relationship conflicts often devolve into violence or chronic withdrawal.

More fundamentally, the above analysis suggests that because responses to social and physical threat are processed by similar mechanisms, perceived threats to inclusion should lead to increased sensitivity to and physiological preparation for physical threats. Three recent studies, described below, support this hypothesis. In the first study, we investigated whether concern over social rejection would promote sensitivity to physical threat. In the second study, we investigated whether social exclusion would lead to analgesia, or decreased sensitivity to physical pain. In the third study, we looked for evidence that feelings of pain are a mechanism by which hurt feelings promote cautious and defensive behavior.

STUDY 1: HURT FEELINGS AND REACTION TO DEPICTIONS OF INJURY

If concerns about social exclusion prepare an individual to respond to generalized threat, then greater concern over rejection should be related to higher sensitivity to physical threat. That is, if the threat response system is activated by perceived rejection from others, then rejection concerns should also cause physical safety threats to become more salient and to be taken more seriously. Some existing research supports this notion. Romero-Canyas and Downey (this volume) report a study in which the fear-potentiated startle reaction is amplified in highly rejection sensitive individuals when viewing depictions of rejection. In Study 1, we further tested the notion that social pain sensitivity is related to physical defensiveness by investigating the responses of individuals varying in their proneness to hurt feelings to video clips of physically painful events.

Eighty undergraduate students (60 females and 20 males) were recruited for a study on reactions to video images. The study began with participants completing an initial questionnaire booklet, including a measure of hurt feelings proneness (Leary & Springer, 2000). The last page of the questionnaire package asked participants to describe a recent incident wherein they felt rejected or isolated by an individual close to them. Specifically, they were asked to write about what occurred and what were their feelings relating to this experience. This item was included so as to prime rejection concerns within the participants, and thus activate the threat response system. Participants then viewed eight video clips featuring images of individuals or groups of individuals experiencing varying degrees of pain. Two of the clips involved negligible pain to individuals, for example, an ice hockey player scoring a goal. The remaining six clips involved pain ranging from low to moderately high levels, for example an American football player being shown in an obvious amount of pain, following a strong hit. The incidents featured within the clips were spontaneous rather than staged events, and were chosen so as to be relatively novel to the participants within this study. Following the presentation of each individual clip, participants completed our two dependent measures. The first consisted of 4 items measuring how aversive participants found the clips, for example, "How much discomfort did you feel when watching this incident?" The second was a single item asking participants, "How funny did you find this incident?" We reasoned that if participants were more sensitive to physical threat, they should perceive less defensive distance from the painful images and thus report the clips to be more aversive and less humorous. In short, participants more sensitive to threat should take the painful clips more seriously. Thus, we hypothesized that those more prone to hurt feelings would report the painful images to be more aversive and less humorous than those less prone to hurt feelings.

The data were analyzed by regressing hurt feelings on to the aversiveness and humor ratings for the pain clips after the variance accounted for by the ratings of the non-pain clips had been partialed out. This method was chosen so that participants acted as their own controls. As predicted, after controlling for ratings of the non-pain clips, individuals higher in proneness to hurt feelings reported the painful images to be both more aversive and less humorous. We interpret these results as suggesting that individuals highly prone to hurt feelings are more sensitive to physical threat than those less prone to hurt feelings. That is, hurt prone individuals appeared to have especially strong avoidance reactions to depictions of physically threatening stimuli, suggesting a reduced perception of defensive distance from physical threat. Thus, the data suggest that individuals more sensitive to rejection are also more sensitive to the presence of physically threatening stimuli.

STUDY 2: PAIN SENSITIVITY FOLLOWING REJECTION

As discussed earlier, one physiological change stimulated by the threat response system is analgesia, or decreased pain sensitivity. Analgesia aids in fight, flight, and freezing behavior by allowing an organism to ignore physical injury until its safety is secured. There is also evidence that social threat can lead to analgesia, as decreases in pain sensitivity have been shown to occur in non-human animals as a result of social isolation. Such reduced pain sensitivity in response to isolation has been demonstrated in rat pups (Kehoe & Blass, 1986), adult rats (Schwandt, 1993), mice (Konecka & Sroczynska, 1990), cows (Rushen, Boissy, Terlouw, &

de Passillé, 1999), and chicks (Sufka & Hughes, 1990). Study 2 was designed to test whether social exclusion could lead to analgesia in humans as well.

Ninety-six people (66 females and 30 males) were recruited for a study on reactions to physical discomfort. Participants began by completing the hurt feelings proneness scale (Leary & Springer, 2000), then were seated at a computer and given instructions that they would play an online ball tossing game with three other participants. In fact, this game was an exclusion manipulation (Williams, Cheung, & Choi, 2000). In the inclusion condition, participants received a ball toss on 10 of the 40 total throws, but in the exclusion condition participants received the ball only twice in 40 throws. Following the exclusion manipulation, participants were asked to place their non-dominant arm in a container filled with water cooled to 1°C for as long as they were able, up to 3 minutes. For our key dependent measure, participants were asked to indicate the point at which they first felt pain, referred to hereafter as their pain threshold. We predicted that highly hurt prone individuals randomly assigned to experience social exclusion would demonstrate higher pain thresholds, or decreased sensitivity to physical pain. That is, we predicted that social exclusion would prime the threat system especially strongly in those who perceive low defensive distance from rejection, and thus prepare them more strongly for fight/flight/freezing responses. Consistent with our hypothesis, participants high in hurt feelings proneness evidenced a higher pain threshold (i.e., less pain sensitivity) in the exclusion than the inclusion condition.

The results of Study 2 are strongly supportive of the notion that social exclusion triggers a general threat response system that prepares an individual for physical and social threats alike. Highly hurt prone individuals who were randomly assigned to experience exclusion evidenced a significant increase in pain threshold during the cold pressor task relative to those assigned to the inclusion condition. Thus, similar to many non-human animals, highly hurt prone people appeared to demonstrate analgesia in response to social threat. Interestingly, this effect was not significant for individuals less prone to hurt feelings. This suggests that individuals low in hurt feelings proneness experienced less threat, or higher defensive distance, when excluded. That is, exclusion appears to be more threatening for individuals with higher levels of hurt proneness, and thus triggers the threat response system more strongly.

STUDY 3: PERSISTENT PAIN AND HURT FEELINGS

If pain serves as a warning signal of both physical injury and social exclusion, then individuals experiencing higher levels of physical pain should also report higher levels of social pain. Further, not only should both types of pain be related to higher levels of caution and defensiveness, but feelings of pain should be one mechanism by which sensitivity to rejection leads to such caution and defensiveness. In Study 3, we tested these ideas by surveying both persistent (i.e., chronic) pain patients and community members in order to test the degree to which reports of physical pain were related to hurt feelings proneness. In addition, we used mediational analyses to test whether reports of physical pain were a mechanism by which hurt feelings led to increased caution and defensiveness.

Sixty-four participants (34 females, 29 males, 1 gender not listed) were recruited from a multidisciplinary pain center located at the Royal Brisbane and Women's Hospital (Australia). Potential participants from the pain center were recruited either prior to a regular group information session, or through a mailing to patients who had received treatment during the preceding 6-month period. A community sample of 92 respondents (48 females and 44 males) was recruited from a shopping center resulting in a total of 156 participants. Participants completed measures of hurt feelings, current pain, anger, depression, anxiety, and stress. These final three measures were highly correlated, and so were combined into an index of general defensiveness.

Initial analyses indicated significant differences in age and education between the pain center and community samples, thus analyses were conducted controlling for these variables. Via regression analysis, reports of physical pain were found to relate significantly to hurt feelings proneness. This suggests that feelings of pain are, in fact, related to the tendency to feel emotionally hurt. Further, both physical pain and hurt feelings related significantly to anger and general defensiveness. These data provide support for the notion that both physical pain and social pain are functionally related as defenses against harm. Finally, mediational analyses revealed that reports of physical pain were a significant partial mediator of the relation between hurt feelings and anger, as well as the relation between hurt feelings and general defensiveness. This suggests that feelings of pain are one mechanism by which hurt feelings lead to increases in anger and defensivenss. That is, this supports the suggestion that it is a sense of pain that promotes caution in response to perceived rejection.

SUMMARY AND CONCLUSIONS

The three studies reported here are supportive of social pain theory. Specifically, the results provide evidence that responses to social and physical threat share common mechanisms, with social threat resulting in increased sensitivity to and physiological preparation for physical threat. In Study 1, participants more prone to hurt feelings were particularly averse to depictions of physical pain and found these depictions relatively humorless, suggesting a decrease in perceived defensive distance from physically threatening stimuli. In Study 2, highly hurt prone individuals displayed decreased pain sensitivity following social exclusion, suggesting strongly that social threat led to the priming of more generalized threat-response mechanisms. These data suggest that we can add increased sensitivity to physical threat and analgesia to the previously reported increases in cortisol, blood pressure, anger, aggressiveness, reliance on less complex cognitive processing, and diminished self-regulation capacity as physical threat defenses shown to be spurred by social exclusion (Buckley et al., 2003; Baumeister & DeWall, this volume; Baumeister et al., 2002; Stroud et al., 1998; Twenge, this volume; Twenge et al., 2001; Warburton, Williams, & Cairns, in press). Further, Study 3 demonstrated a link between reports of physical pain and hurt feelings, and showed that pain appears to be one mechanism by which perceived rejection promotes increased caution and defensiveness. Together, these findings support the notion that social exclusion leads to physiological preparation for quick action in response to non-specific danger.

The pain sensitivity results in particular may have important consequences for behavior in response to social exclusion. Social pain theory suggests that the affective component of pain serves as a signal to help regulate social behavior. Behavior that threatens inclusiveness should lead to painful feelings, thus encouraging the individual to alter that behavior. However, if rejection sensitive individuals experience analgesia in response to exclusion, then the warning signal that pain provides may not be as prominent during exclusion episodes. Thus, highly rejection sensitive individuals may not experience the same restraints on anti-social behavior following exclusion as less rejection sensitive individuals. For example, higher levels of rejection sensitivity have been related to higher rates of abuse in romantic relationships (Dutton, 2002; Holtzworth-Munroe, Bates, Smutzler, & Sandin, 1997). If rejection sensitive individuals are less sensitive to social pain as a result of perceived exclusion, this may contribute to abusive tendencies by making the abusive behavior feel less inclusion-threatening to the attacker. More generally, the degree of analgesia experienced in response to exclusion threat may play an important role in guiding an individual toward either pro- or anti-social behavior. Of course, in pursuing this hypothesis it will be important to investigate whether exclusion-related analgesia functions via the dulling of pain affect, pain sensation, or both.

The finding that exclusion by unknown others during a meaningless game can lead to decreased pain sensitivity for hurt prone individuals argues strongly that exclusion is treated as a very serious threat. Consistent with this notion are the findings by Williams and colleagues (Williams & Zadro, this volume) showing that even ostracism by a computer or by disliked outgroup members can lead to distress. Social pain theory is potentially useful in explaining why rejection appears to lead to social pain even under such minimal conditions. LeDoux (1994) has argued that detection of threat occurs in multiple stages. In the early stages, partially processed information is sent to the defensive system such that basic stimulus features are analyzed for threat potential. This "quick and dirty" analysis allows for the priming of defense mechanisms so preparation for threat response can begin. If subsequent, more complex, processing disconfirms the presence of a threat, defense responses can be down-regulated. This mechanism is especially useful when threatening stimuli are embedded in a complex environment, as response can begin before the existence of a threat is fully confirmed. It seems reasonable to assume that social threat information may be processed in a similar manner. This seems especially likely given that cues to social exclusion are often located within highly complex social environments, such that long delays between exclusion cues and reactions would be likely unless the defense system was triggered by partially processed information. Such "quick and dirty" social information processing may be focused mainly on detecting the presence of any cues to exclusion, however minimal, with later information processing refining the evaluation of defensive distance from exclusion from important relationships. That is, exclusion even from unimportant sources may initially lead to social pain, with the degree of pain changing over time as more social information is processed. This reasoning suggests that initial reactions to rejection may have different properties than reactions following the passage of time.

In this sense, an argument could be made that the social pain system is miscalibrated, signaling an undue amount of threat and potentiating counterproductive behavior such as aggression against close others. However, it is important to consider that social pain may play its most important role during infancy. During this period, the child is almost totally reliant on its caregivers, and thus separation from important others truly is extremely threatening. Response to separation from caregivers initially involves strong protest, including the expression of anger, which functions to alert the caregiver to the child's separation distress (Bowlby, 1973). The strong reaction of children separated from caregivers certainly does not seem miscalibrated as the degree of threat and the lack of effective alternative responses necessitates the protest response. However, it is possible that as an individual grows older, this strong perception of threat from social exclusion remains despite the individual's increasing self-reliance. Thus, social pain may function optimally during the crucial period of childhood, but become somewhat less functional as an individual matures.

A potentially fruitful strategy for future research would involve the examination of whether other consequences of physical pain also result from social exclusion. For example, research has shown that physical pain taxes attentional resources. Specifically, in order to draw attention to threat, pain, "interrupts, distracts, and is difficult to disengage from" (Eccleston & Crombez, 1999, p. 356). Thus, it seems reasonable to suggest that social exclusion may cause attention to be heavily focused on the exclusion episode. For example, Pickett and Gardner (this volume) have shown that both a chronic need to belong and transient rejection experiences appear to increase vigilance for social information. Such a focus of attention on exclusion may have important consequences. Research has shown that increased focus on rejection concerns as a result of experimentally manipulated self-focus, trait self-focus, or alcohol intoxication leads romantic partners to experience feelings of decreased relationship security (MacDonald, Leary, & Boksman, 2003; MacDonald, Zanna, & Holmes, 2000). Such "rejection-myopia" appears to threaten security by removing attentional focus from information that would mitigate rejection fears such as a partner's past reassurances of affection. Further, increased focus on rejection concerns has also been tied to an increased risk of partner violence for those low in felt security (MacDonald, Holmes, Zanna, Leary, & Agrawal, 2003). Thus, if perceptions of social exclusion in themselves promote extreme focus on an individual's insecurities, then such attentional vigilance may be an important mediator of reactions to exclusion. If true, this analysis suggests that one means for reducing the destructive aspect of response to exclusion may be distraction from the exclusion episode, or intentional focus on security-enhancing information.

In general, we believe that social pain theory can help in understanding reactions to social exclusion by highlighting the notion that such exclusion is processed at a very basic level as a strong survival threat. As a result, the excluded individual becomes physiologically prepared to respond to not just social threat, but to physical threat as well. Although this process is likely often functional, we also believe that there is significant room for error as social and physical threats often require very different response patterns. At the extreme, we believe that social threats may be treated as physical threats, resulting in fight (e.g., partner abuse), flight (e.g., demand/withdraw conflict patterns), and freezing (e.g., shyness) responses to perceived social exclusion. Overall, we believe social pain theory reaffirms the notion that our social and physical needs are deeply interwoven, and helps to explain why, "a sense of separation is a condition that makes being a mammal so painful" (MacLean, 1993, p. 74).

REFERENCES

An, X., Bandler, R., Öngür, D., & Price, J. L. (1998). Prefrontal cortical projections to longitudinal columns in the midbrain periaqueductal gray in macaque monkeys. *The Journal of Comparative Neurology, 401,* 455–479.

Bandler, R., & Shipley, M. T. (1994). Columnar organization in the midbrain periaqueductal gray: Modules for emotional expression? *Trends in Neurosciences, 17,* 379–389.

Baumeister, R. F., & Leary, M. R. (1995). The need to belong: Desire for interpersonal attachments as a fundamental human motivation. *Psychological Bulletin, 117,* 497–529.

Baumeister, R. F., Twenge, J. M., & Nuss, C. K. (2002). Effects of social exclusion on cognitive processes: Anticipated aloneness reduces intelligent thought. *Journal of Personality and Social Psychology, 83,* 817–827.

Berkowitz, L. (1993). Pain and aggression: Some findings and implications. *Motivation and Emotion, 17,* 277–293.

Berkowitz, L., Cochran, S. T., & Embree, M. C. (1981). Physical pain and the goal of aversively stimulated aggression. *Journal of Personality and Social Psychology, 40,* 687–700.

Blanchard, R. J. & Blanchard, D. C. (1990). An ethoexperimental analysis of defense, fear and anxiety. In N. McNaughton & G. Andrews (Eds.), *Anxiety* (pp. 124–133). Dunedin: Otago University Press.

Bowlby, J. (1973). Attachment and loss (Vol. 2). New York: Basic Books.

Buckley, K. E., Winkel, R. E., & Leary, M. R. (2003). Reactions to acceptance and rejection: Effects of level and sequence of relational evaluation. *Journal of Experimental Social Psychology,* 14–28.

Craig, A. D., & Dostrovsky, J. O. (1999). Medulla to thalamus. In P. Wall & R. Melzack (Eds.), *Textbook of pain* (pp. 183–214). New York: Churchill Livingstone.

Dutton, D. G. (2002). The neurobiology of abandonment homicide. *Aggression and Violent Behavior, 7,* 407–421.

Eccleston, C., & Crombez, G. (1999). Pain demands attention: A cognitive-affective model of the interruptive function of pain. *Psychological Bulletin, 125,* 356–366.

Eisenberger, N. I., Lieberman, M. D., & Williams, K. D. (2003). Does rejection hurt? An fMRI study of social exclusion. *Science, 302,* 290–292.

Fanselow, M. S. (1991). The midbrain periaqueductal gray as a coordinator of action in response to fear and anxiety. In A. Depaulis & R. Bandler (Eds.), *The midbrain periaqueductal gray matter* (pp. 151–173). New York: Plenum Press.

Feeney, J.A ., Noller, P., & Hanrahan, M. (1994). Assessing adult attachment. In M. B. Sperling & W. H. Berman (Eds.), *Attachment in adults: Clinical and developmental perspectives* (pp. 128–152). New York: Guilford Press.

Fields, H. L. (2000). Pain modulation: Expectation, opioid analgesia and virtual pain. In E. Mayer & C. Saper (Eds.), *Progress in Brain Research* (Vol. 122, pp. 245–254). New York: Elsevier.

Gray, J. A., & McNaughton, N. (2000). *The neuropsychology of anxiety.* New York: Oxford University Press.

Holtzworth-Munroe, A., Bates, L., Smutzler, N., & Sandin, E. (1997). A brief review of the research on husband violence: I. Maritally violent versus nonviolent men. *Aggression and Violent Behavior, 2,* 65–99.

Kehoe, P., & Blass, E. M. (1986a). Opioid-mediation of separation distress in 10-day-old rats: Reversal of stress with maternal stimuli. *Developmental Psychobiology, 19,* 385–398.

Konecka, A. M. & Sroczynska, I. (1990). Stressors and pain sensitivity in CFW mice: Role of opioid peptides. *Archives Internationales de Physiologie et de Biochimie, 98,* 245–252.

Leary, M. R., & MacDonald, G. (2003). Individual differences in trait self-esteem: A theoretical integration. In M. Leary & J. Tangney (Eds.), *Handbook of self and identity* (pp. 401–418). New York: Guildford Press.

Leary, M. R., & Springer, C. A. (2000). Hurt feelings: The neglected emotion. In R. Kowalski (Ed.), *Aversive behaviors and interpersonal transgression* (pp. 151–175). Washington, DC: American Psychological Association.

LeDoux, J. E. (1994). Emotion, memory, and the brain. *Scientific American, 270,* 50–59.

Lonstein, J. S., Simmons, D. A., & Stern, J. M. (1998). Functions of the caudal periaqueductal gray in lactating rats: Kyphosis, lordosis, maternal aggression, and fearfulness. *Behavioral Neuroscience, 112,* 1502–1518.

Lonstein, J. S., & Stern, J. M. (1998). Site and behavioral specificity of periaqueductal gray lesions on postpartum sexual, maternal, and aggressive behaviors in rats. *Brain Research, 804,* 21–35.

MacDonald, G., Holmes, J. G., Zanna, M. P., Leary, M. R., & Agrawal, A. (2003). *Relationship insecurity, alcohol, and aggression against romantic partners.* Manuscript under review.

MacDonald, G., & Leary, M. R. (2005). Why does social exclusion hurt? The relationship between social and physical pain. *Psychological Bulletin, 131,* 202–223.

MacDonald, G., Leary, M. R., & Boksman, K. (2003). *Self-myopia: Self-focused attention, self-esteem, and feelings of security in romantic relationships.* Manuscript under review.

MacDonald, G., Zanna, M. P., & Holmes, J. G. (2000). An experimental test of the role of alcohol in relationship conflict. *Journal of Experimental Social Psychology, 36,* 182–193.

MacLean, P. D. (1993). Cerebral evolution of emotion. In Lewis, M. & Haviland, J. M. (Eds.), *Handbook of emotions* (pp. 67–83). New York: Guilford Press.

Melzack, R., & Casey, K. L. (1968). Sensory, motivational, and central control determinants of pain: A new conceptual model. In D. Kenshalo (Ed.), *The skin senses.* Springfield, IL: Chas C. Thomas.

Merskey, H. (2000). History of psychoanalytic ideas concerning pain. In R. Gatchel & J. Weisberg (Eds.), *Personality characteristics of patients with pain* (pp. 25–35). Washington, DC: American Psychological Association.

Panksepp, J. (1998). *Affective neuroscience: The foundations of human and animal emotions.* London: Oxford University Press.

Price, D. D. (2000). Psychological and neural mechanisms of the affective dimension of pain. *Science, 288,* 1769–1772.

Price, D. D. (1999). *Psychological mechanisms of pain and analgesia.* Seattle: I.A.S.P. Press.

Rainville, P. (2002). Brain mechanisms of pain affect and pain modulation. *Current Opinion in Neurobiology, 12,* 195–204.

Rushen, J., Boissy, A., Terlouw, E. M., & de Passillé, A. M. (1999). Opioid peptides and behavioral and physiological responses of dairy cows to social isolation in unfamiliar surroundings. *Journal of Animal Science, 77,* 2918–2924.

Schwandt, L. M. (1993). Individual versus group housing affects nociception independently of housing status during development. *Bulletin of the Psychonomic Society, 31,* 525–528.

Stack, E. C., Balakrishnan, R., Numan, M. J., & Numan, M. (2002). A functional neuroanatomical investigation of the role of the medial preoptic area in neural circuits regulating maternal behavior. *Behavioural Brain Research, 131,* 17–36.

Stroud, L. R., Tanofsky-Kraff, M., Wilfley, D. E., & Salovey, P. (2000). The Yale Interpersonal Stressor (YIPS): Affective, physiological, and behavioral responses to a novel interpersonal rejection paradigm. *Annals of Behavioral Medicine, 22,* 204–213.

Sufka, K. J., & Hughes, R. A. (1990). Dose and temporal parameters of morphine-induced hyperalgesia in domestic fowl. *Physiology and Behavior, 47,* 385–387.

Twenge, J. M., & Baumeister, R. F. (2002). Self-control: A limited yet renewable resource. In Y. Kashima & M. Foddy (Eds.), *Self and identity: Personal, social, and symbolic* (pp. 57–70). Mahwah, NJ: Lawrence Erlbaum Associates.

Twenge, J. M., Baumeister, R. F., Tice, D. M., & Stucke, T. S. (2001). If you can't join them, beat them: Effects of social exclusion on aggressive behavior. *Journal of Personality and Social Psychology, 81,* 1058–1069.

uclamangoboy (2003). Breakup story of Vinh and Julia. Retrieved November 17, 2003, from http://www.livejournal.com/users/uclamangoboy/25030.html.

Vangelisti, A. L., & Crumley, L. P. (1998). Reactions to messages that hurt: The influence of relational contexts. Communication Monographs, 65, 173–196.

Warburton, W. A., Williams, K. D., & Cairns, D. R. (in press). When ostracism leads to aggression: The moderating effects of control deprivation. *Journal of Experimental Social Psychology.*

Williams, K. D., Case, T. I., & Govan, C. (2003). Impact of ostracism on social judgments and decisions: Explicit and implicit responses. In J. Forgas, K. Williams, & W. von Hippel (Eds.), *Responding to the social world: Implicit and explicit processes in social judgments and decisions* (pp. 325–342). New York: Psychology Press.

Williams, K. D., Cheung, C. K. T., & Choi, W. (2000). CyberOstracism: Effects of being ignored over the Internet. *Journal of Personality and Social Psychology, 79,* 748–762.

6

People Thinking About People

The Vicious Cycle of Being a Social Outcast in One's Own Mind

JOHN T. CACIOPPO
LOUISE C. HAWKLEY

Social Isolation Elevates Feelings of Loneliness
Personality, Affective Orientations, and Social Dispositions
Social Cognition
Conclusion

*T*he increasing number of people living alone is changing the face of post-industrial societies. The average household size over the past two decades in the United States declined by about 10% to 2.5 (Hobbs & Stoops, 2002). By 1990, more than one in five family households with children under 18 was headed by a single parent, and within a single decade, the proportion of single parent households rose from 21% to 29% of all households in the United States (Hobbs & Stoops, 2002). Family households were not the only residential unit to become more socially isolated. There are also now more than 27 million people living alone in the United States, 36% of whom are over the age of 65 (Hobbs & Stoops, 2002). According to the middle projections by the Census Bureau (1996), the number of people living alone by 2010 will reach almost 29,000,000—more

This research was supported by the John D. and Catherine T. MacArthur Foundation (Mind-Body Integration Network) and the National Institute of Aging Grant No. PO1 AG18911 (Social isolation, loneliness, health, and the aging process). Address correspondence to: John T. Cacioppo, Department of Psychology, University of Chicago, Chicago, IL 60637, USA. E-mail Cacioppo@uchicago.edu

than a 30% increase since 1980, with a disproportionate share of these being individuals over 65 years of age.

Despite these changes in the structure of society, little attention has been given to the effects of social isolation on people's perceived social isolation, social cognition, interpersonal relationships, and health. Our goal in this chapter is to begin to address this deficit. Specifically, we outline a model in which social isolation can promote loneliness, which in turn promotes passive coping and people construing their world, including the behavior of others, as threatening or punitive. We further propose that these differences in social cognition result in an increased likelihood of lonely individuals acting in self-protective and, paradoxically, self-defeating ways. These dispositions, in turn, activate social neurobehavioral mechanisms that may contribute to the association between loneliness and mortality.

SOCIAL ISOLATION ELEVATES FEELINGS OF LONELINESS

Loneliness is a complex set of feelings encompassing reactions from romantic events to social isolation. Ceteris paribus, as objective social isolation increases, intimate and social needs are less likely to be met adequately, and loneliness is the experience elicited or exacerbated by these life circumstances (Weiss, 1973). De Jong-Gierveld (1987), in a semi-structured interview of single, married, divorced, and widowed individuals 25 to 75 years of age, reported that living with a partner predicted the lowest levels of loneliness. Similarly, elderly individuals who lived alone were lonelier than were age-matched individuals living with others, despite reporting comparable social interaction frequency and personal network adequacy (Henderson, Scott, & Kay, 1986). Tornstam (1992), in a random sample in Sweden of 2,795 individuals 15 to 80 years of age, found that married individuals were, on average, less lonely than unmarried individuals. Among elderly independently living individuals (60 to 106 years), frequency of telephone contact with others predicted feelings of loneliness (Fees, Martin, & Poon, 1999). Conversely, lonely, compared to nonlonely, individuals have fewer friends and fewer close friends, see their friends as less similar to themselves, and are less likely to have a romantic partner (Bell, 1993).

Significant individual differences in loneliness abound within these relationship categories (e.g., single, married; Tornstam, 1992; Barbour, 1993; de Jong-Gierveld, 1987), as people also can live what feels to them to be an isolated existence even when around others (Cacioppo et al., 2000; Mullins & Elston, 1996; Van Baarsen, Snijders, Smit, & van Duijn, 2001). For this reason, loneliness is characterized as feelings of social isolation, absence of companionship, and rejection by peer groups (Adams, Openshaw, Bennion, Mills, & Noble, 1988; Austin, 1983), with feelings of an isolated life in a social world forming the dominant experience (e.g., Russell, Peplau, & Cutrona, 1980; Hays & DiMatteo, 1987).

Feelings of loneliness are aversive and, like many negative emotional states, motivate individuals to alleviate these feelings, for instance, by trying to form connections with others (Weiss, 1973). The motivational potency of the absence of personal ties and social acceptance is reminiscent of the potency of a presumably more basic need such as hunger (Harlow & Harlow, 1973). Solitary confinement is one of humankind's most severe punishments (Felthous, 1997). Ostracism, the exclusion by general consent from common privileges or social acceptance, is universal in its aversive and deleterious effects (Williams, 1997; see Williams & Zadro, this volume; Pickett & Gardner, this volume), and the neural processes underlying social rejection have common substrates to those involved in physical pain (Eisenberger, Lieberman, & Williams, 2003; see Eisenberger & Lieberman, this volume).

Negative motivational states such as hunger require only that an individual do something (e.g., eat food in the case of hunger) to reduce the aversive state. In the case of a motivation to form a social relationship or alliance, however, all of the individuals involved must be willing to join into the *desired* relationship, able to do so, and agree to do so in a coordinated fashion. In some circumstances, such as betrayal by or the loss of a loved one, the desired social connection by one individual is either denied or impossible. As a result, loneliness also tends to be characterized by low perceived personal control, despair, and depression (see review by Ernst & Cacioppo, 1998).

Because loneliness can result not only if an individual is socially isolated, but if other individuals involved are not willing or able to join into the desired relationship or alliance, qualitative aspects of social interactions are at least as predictive of loneliness as are quantitative aspects of social interactions. Using a daily diary methodology, Wheeler, Reis, and Nezlek (1983) found that an individual's rating of the meaninglessness of their interpersonal interactions was the most important predictor of loneliness. Amount of time, frequency of interactions, and other quantitative descriptors of the social interactions were not found to add to the prediction of loneliness. For older adults, the average closeness of the social network, and not its size, predicted loneliness (Green, Richardson, Lago, & Schatten-Jones, 2001). In a study of young adults in college, Cacioppo et al. (2000) found no differences between lonely and nonlonely young adults in the time spent alone, and an experience sampling study of a normal day in the life of these students revealed qualitative rather than quantitative differences in interpersonal relationships (Hawkley et al., 2003).

Although objective social isolation can create and exacerbate feelings of loneliness, this link is not the only factor operating. People can be a social outcast in their own minds even while living amongst others. Indeed, our experience sampling study of young adults revealed that average momentary feelings of loneliness were significantly higher for lonely than for nonlonely students regardless of social context (Hawkley et al., 2003). Significant individual differences in loneliness exist within each kind of relationship (e.g., marriage, families, coworkers, group members), and loneliness, as well as objective social isolation, has been found to be significant risk factors for broad based morbidity and mortality (e.g., Seeman, 2000). Given the evidence that feelings of loneliness are in part influenced by genetic constitution (McGuire & Clifford, 2000) or early childhood experiences (e.g., Asher & Wheeler, 1985; Juvonen & Gross, this volume), we next examine whether personality, affective styles, and social dispositions differ as a function of loneliness, and we address whether these characteristics are fixed or they vary with a person's feelings of loneliness or connectedness.

PERSONALITY, AFFECTIVE ORIENTATIONS, AND SOCIAL DISPOSITIONS

In a large study conducted by the National Opinion Research Center, individuals who reported having contact with five or more intimate friends in the prior six months were 60% more likely to report that their lives were "very happy" (Burt, 1986). In a similar study, Berscheid (1985) found that when asked "what is necessary for happiness?" the majority of respondents rate "relationships with family and friends" as most important. Perhaps it should not be surprising that Aristotle's observation of the importance of positive interpersonal relationships holds for the post-industrial world of the United States as well as the ancient Greeks. The classic work of Harlow and Harlow (1958; 1973) demonstrated that positive tactile contact is a stronger determinant of mother-infant attachment in monkeys than feeding, and that deprivation of such contact produces adult animals with behavioral problems different than those resulting from physical restraint or stressors (Seeman, 2000; see Gardner, Gabriel, & Diekman, 2000; Gardner, Knowles, & Pickett, this volume).

Physical attractiveness, height, body mass index, age, education, and intelligence can affect a person's interpersonal attractiveness (Berscheid & Reis, 1998), yet these features provide little if any protection against loneliness (Cacioppo & Hawkley, 2003; Cacioppo et al., 2000; see, also, Fitness, this volume). The absence of a relationship between an individual's physical attractiveness and their feelings of loneliness may be surprising to some. In advertisements and media portrayals, the achievement of physical beauty, wealth, status, and success is associated with living happily ever after. Yet celebrities ranging from Marilyn Monroe to Princess Diana have been haunted by intensely lonely lives, a condition that seemed incomprehensible given their immense popularity. These biographies make more sense when one recalls that qualitative aspects of social interactions are at least as strongly, if not more strongly, predictive of loneliness as are quantitative aspects of social interactions.

Although there are gripping states of loneliness that everyone experiences transiently in specific circumstances or interactions (e.g., see Lakin & Chartrand, this volume), some individuals live in the devastating clutches of loneliness. These individuals tend to be characterized by poor attachment in early childhood (Shaver & Hazan, 1987), poor social skills (Segrin & Flora, 2000), a strong distrust of others (Rotenberg, 1994), hostility, and negative affectivity and reactivity (e.g., Cacioppo et al., 2000; Russell et al., 1980; see review by Berscheid & Reis, 1998;

Marangoni & Ickes, 1989, Ernst & Cacioppo, 1999; Twenge, this volume). In an illustrative study of young adults, we found lonely, relative to nonlonely, individuals differed in their personality traits (e.g., lonely individuals are higher in shyness, lower in sociability, surgency, agreeableness, conscientiousness, emotional stability than nonlonely individuals) and affective moods and states (e.g., lonely individuals are higher in negative mood, anxiety, and anger, lower in optimism and positive mood; Cacioppo et al., in press).

Recent research on positive psychology suggests that individuals who score very low on dimensions such as loneliness, that is, individuals who harbor few feelings of social isolation or rejection, are not simply the antithesis of those who score high on a dimension but instead are characterized by a unique and adaptive profile. In light of this perspective, we selected three groups of young adults to study based on the prior measurement of over 2,600 students levels of loneliness as gauged by the UCLA-R loneliness scale administered approximately a month earlier (Russell et al., 1980): a group of young adults who had scored high in loneliness (top 20%), a group of individuals who had scored average in loneliness (middle 20%), and a group who had scored low in loneliness (bottom 20%). When we tested these individuals approximately a month later, the results revealed that the individuals who had scored low in loneliness differed from those who had scored average in loneliness and high in loneliness on four of the five dimensions of the Big 5 (more outgoing, agreeable, conscientious, and non-neurotic); the individuals who had been selected for study because they had scored low in loneliness were also found to score higher on optimism, positive mood, social skills, self-esteem, and social support, and lower in anger, anxiety, shyness, fear of negative evaluation, and negativity. Importantly, the individuals who had been selected for study because they had scored average in loneliness were indistinguishable on these scales from those who had been selected for study because they had scored high in loneliness. Manipulation checks on loneliness further confirmed that the differences remained as apparent for those who had scored average and low in loneliness as for those who had scored average and high in loneliness. Finally, analyses indicated that, although loneliness is an aversive experience, with but a few exceptions these results were attributable to loneliness, not negative affect.

One interpretation of these findings is that the individuals who rarely feel socially isolated or rejected are people who are charismatic. The notion that people who are publicly adored are not immune to living intensely lonely lives should give us pause before accepting this interpretation uncritically. An alternative view on these findings is that most individuals, when he or she feels intimate, companionship, and affiliative needs are fulfilled, express a constellation of states and dispositions that elevate the person above the average. If this interpretation is correct, then two predictions follow. First, loneliness, if manipulated, should produce changes in psychological states and dispositions similar to those observed between-subjects. Second, the average states and dispositions would be "average" because most individuals, although capable of achieving these more pleasant states and dispositions, do not remain so, perhaps because they may not know how to do so, they may have no control over critical aspects (e.g., the acceptance of significant others), or they may value or choose to pursue incompatible objectives or goals.

Despite the putative centrality of social connectedness/loneliness, little is known about what occurs when feelings of loneliness change. Russell et al. (1980) suggested that "(e)mpirical research (on loneliness) has been hampered by a variety of problems . . . A major hindrance is that loneliness, unlike aggression, competition, and crowding, cannot be readily manipulated by researchers" (p. 472). To address this obstacle, Russell et al. (1980) developed a measure of loneliness to investigate differences among those who contrasted in terms of the feelings and experiences of individuals who are lonely. This approach has dominated the field, but it does not adequately address the centrality or causal role of loneliness in terms of priming specific characteristics of an individual. We, therefore, designed a study to examine whether, and if the extent to which affective states and dispositions, and even traits such as shyness and sociability, would vary with experimental manipulations of loneliness.

If manipulations of high versus low feelings of loneliness elicited different sets of characteristics in the same person, then explanations of loneliness that tied it to invariant factors (e.g., simple genetic determinism as in gender and eye color) could be rejected. To manipulate loneliness within the same person, we used a procedure similar to that used by Kosslyn, Thompson, Costantini-Ferrando, Alpert, and Spiegel (2000). Kosslyn et al. (2000) recruited highly hypnotizable participants for a study of picture processing. Following hypnotic induction, participants were exposed to color and gray scale pictures and patterns under the hypnotic suggestion that the stimulus would be presented in color or gray scale. Results revealed that the participants reported seeing a color pattern when they had been told one was being presented whether the pattern actually presented was a color or a gray scale pattern. Similarly, the participants reported seeing a gray scale pattern when they had been told a gray scale pattern was being presented whether the pattern actually presented was a color or a gray scale pattern.

Results in which hypnotized individuals have reported what the hypnotist instructed them to feel have been criticized in the past as not producing changes in psychological content or experience, but only in producing compliance in terms of what the participants said they saw (i.e., role playing behavior). However, in the Kosslyn et al. (2000) study, the authors also performed positron emission tomography scanning by means of [15O]CO2 during the presentation of the pictures. Results of the PET data indicated that the classic color area in the fusiform or lingual region of the brain was activated when participants were asked to perceive color, whether the participant had actually been shown the color or the gray scale stimulus, and these brain regions showed decreased activation when the participants were told they would see gray scale, whether they were actually shown the color or gray scale stimuli. Thus, observed changes in subjective experience achieved during hypnosis were reflected by changes in brain function similar to those that occur in perception, supporting the claim that hypnosis can produce actual changes in psychological experience in highly hypnotizable participants.

To manipulate loneliness within-subjects, we recruited a sample of highly hypnotizable participants, used the same hypnotic induction procedure, and performed the hypnotic induction with the same experimenter/hypnotist as used by Kosslyn et al. (2000). We developed scripts that induced individuals to recall and re-experience a time when they felt lonely (e.g., a high sense of isolation, absence of intimacy or companionship, and feelings of not belonging), or nonlonely (e.g., a high sense of intimacy, companionship, friendships, and belonging; Cacioppo et al., in press).

When the participants were induced to feel lonely, compared to nonlonely, they also scored higher on measures of shyness, negative moods, anger, anxiety, and fear of negative evaluation; and lower on measures of social skills, optimism, positive mood, social support, and self-esteem. Individuals in our earlier cross-sectional study of lonely and nonlonely young adults did not differ on measures of avoidant or intrusive thinking about a major stressor (Cacioppo et al., in press), and neither did participants in the hypnosis study. This makes it less likely that participants in the hypnosis study were simply reporting what they thought the experimenter wanted to them to say, but rather—as in the Kosslyn et al. (2000) study, they reported what they experienced. Finally, in response to a manipulation check (the UCLA-R scale), participants scored much higher on the loneliness scale when hypnotized and induced to feel lonely than when they were hypnotized and induced to feel nonlonely.

The results not only suggest that states of loneliness might be manipulated experimentally but, more interestingly, that the states and dispositions that we had found to differentiate lonely and nonlonely individuals also varied with manipulated feelings of loneliness. Additional analyses confirmed that loneliness is an aversive experience, but again with few exceptions the results from the experimental manipulation of loneliness were attributable to feelings of loneliness, not the dysphoric experience that the participants felt when lonely. Together, the results of these studies support the view that, despite a possible genetic component, loneliness is not an invariant genetically determined trait. When feelings of loneliness change substantially—for instance, when individuals feel intimate, companionship, and social needs are being fully met, they also become characterized by a constellation of states and dispositions that are generally more positive and engaging. The experimental study suggests that loneliness has features of a central trait—central in the sense that it influences how individuals construe themselves and others in the omnipresent social world, as well as how others view and act toward these individuals.

More specifically, explicit social factors that can promote or intensify feelings of loneliness include relocation (or homelessness), discrimination and other forms of social rejection or ostracism, divorce or bereavement, and loss of employment (e.g., de Jong-Gierveld, 1987; Shaver, Furman, & Buhrmester, 1985), but powerful, ubiquitous, and less visible social forces appear also at work to hold people in their orbit of an isolated existence (Cacioppo et al., 2000). Lonely people, for instance, are recognizable by others and are viewed more negatively—in terms of their psychosocial functioning and in terms of their interpersonal attraction or acceptance—than are nonlonely people (Lau & Gruen, 1992; Rotenberg & Kmill, 1992). Once people in a lonely person's social environment form the impression that he or she is lonely, their behaviors toward that individual can reinforce his or her negative social expectancies (Rotenberg, Gruman, & Ariganello, 2002), promote hostile or antagonistic behavior, and sustain the lonely individual's isolated existence. In an illustrative study, Rotenberg et al. (2002) found that individuals rated opposite-gender partners who they expected to be lonely as less sociable, and these individuals behaved toward their partners in a less sociable manner, than they did toward partners they expected to be nonlonely. The opposite social forces appear to preserve the superior life of individuals very low in loneliness, in that they are perceived and treated more positively and are more likely to be given a benefit of the doubt in uncertain or ambiguous situations.

The implication of this analysis is that people may *become* lonely due to an unfortunate event but *remain* lonely because of the manner in which they and others think about each other—their social cognition—their social expectations and aspirations, the way in which they perceive others, and the manner in which they process, remember, appraise, and act on social information. Lonely individuals are cognizant that their social needs are not being met and perceive that they do not have a great deal of control over the extent to which they can fulfill these social needs (Solano, 1987). They tend to be more anxious, pessimistic, and fearful of negative evaluation than nonlonely individuals, and consequently, they are more likely to act and relate to others in anxious, self-protective fashion which, paradoxically, results in their also acting in self-defeating ways. To the extent that the health consequences of loneliness unfold over decades (cf. heart disease rather than suicide), the factors that have deleterious effects on physiological functioning may be tied more closely to social cognition than personality traits. The final implication is that the escape from loneliness may be through changes in social cognition rather than through plastic surgery, financial success, designer jeans, or powerful stations in life. We turn to these issues in the next section.

SOCIAL COGNITION

The world is seldom simple. The striking development of the frontal regions in the brain has enhanced dramatically the human capacity for reasoning, planning, and performing mental simulations, but human information processing capacities remain woefully insufficient in light of the torrents of information in which people live. When one also considers the amount and complexity of the information that comes from other individuals, groups, alliances, and cultures—and the potential for treachery from each—it is perhaps understandable why social cognition is rife with the operation of self-interest, self-enhancement, and self-protective processes.

Among the curiosities in the way in which people think are that people overestimate their strengths and underestimate their faults; they overestimate the importance of their input (Kruger & Gilovich, 1999), the pervasiveness of their beliefs (Ross, Greene, & House, 1977), and the likelihood of a desired event to occur (McGuire, 1981), all while underestimating the contributions of others (Ross & Sicoly, 1979) and the likelihood that risks in the world apply to them (Vaughan, 1993). Events that unfold unexpectedly are not reasoned as much as they are rationalized, and the act of remembering itself is far more of a biased reconstruction than an accurate recollection of events. Because there is more information than people can possibly process, people tend to search for and attend to evidence that confirms what they already believe to be true. This capacity means that neither an individual's capacity to argue for something, nor their level of confidence in its truth, makes it so. Subtle reminders of their mortality can push people to blame the victim and to risky behaviors as if to prove the world is just and that such threats do not apply to them. And, despite the fact people believe they know how much and for how long things they do will make them feel good or bad, their beliefs about the causes and consequences of their behavior are stunningly poor. People believe they know, for instance, that opposites attract, just as assuredly as they know birds of a feather flock together. Yet both of these cannot be simultaneously true—a point that many may miss without a moment of reflective thought.

For centuries human nature has been conceived as dual: A rational, admirable side versus an emotional, darker side. Aristotle, St. Thomas Aquinas, and Freud all espoused such a view. A more interactive, unified view is now emerging, however. The same irrational processes that at times act as our downfall are also the foundation of our finest qualities as humans (Cacioppo, 2002a). Hope entails irrationality. Positive illusions of one's spouse produce longer and happier marriages. Without a biased weighting of the odds, few would begin a new business, run for public office, or seek to change society for the better. Simply going by statistics alone, it is irrational for individuals to assume that they can paint a masterpiece, make a breakthrough in science, or marry for life. Each individual is the guardian of their own rational and irrational processes, even if most are deployed without their intention or realization.

People nevertheless have much more influence in the creation of their lives and social relationships than they often realize. If an individual believes a new acquaintance is fun and nice, the individual behaves in a fashion that draws out pleasant and enjoyable behaviors from the person. If parents think their child is intelligent, they do and say things that make a smarter child than would result if the parents thought the child was of more normal intelligence. When people think they will fail at an important task or social relationship, they may self-handicap. By subtly producing insurmountable obstacles to success, they can attribute their subsequent failure to these obstacles rather than to themselves. In each of these instances, the individuals are totally oblivious to the fact that *they* are the architects of their own social realities.

The inherent complexity and treachery of interpersonal relationships, together with the automatic deployment of self-interest, self-enhancement, and self-protective processes, mean that thoughtless acts, partial truths, minor betrayals, and incomplete recognition of the contributions of another are inevitable. Unkind social inferences and negative causal attributions, while potentially serving a self-protective function, tend to diminish happiness while also justifying more negative actions toward others; on the other hand, positive social expectations and positive illusions of a partner—for instance, exaggerations of the extent to which a partner is wonderful, trustworthy, and caring—contribute to longer and happier marriages (Murray & Holmes, 1999). When an individual's negative social expectations elicit behaviors from others that validate these expectations, the expectations are buttressed and increase the likelihood of the individual behaving in ways that pushes away the very people he or she most want to be close to better fulfill their social needs (cf. Murray, Bellavia, Rose, & Griffin, 2003; see, also Downey & Romero, this volume).

Although these processes operate generally, lonely individuals may be at special risk for acting in this fashion. Specifically, we review evidence for the following propositions:

1.   Lonely, compared to nonlonely, individuals are more likely to construe their world, including the behavior of others, as punitive or potentially punitive. Consequently, lonely individuals are more likely to be socially anxious, to hold more negative expectations for their treatment by others, and to adopt a prevention focus rather than a promotion focus in their social interactions.
2.   Lonely, relative to nonlonely, individuals are more likely to appraise stressors as threats rather than challenges, and to cope with stressors in a passive, isolative fashion rather than an active fashion that includes seeking the help and support of others. Together, these differences in social cognition predictably result in an increased likelihood of lonely individuals acting in self-protective and, paradoxically, self-defeating ways.

As we saw in the preceding section, there is ample evidence that ego-protective processes might be especially likely in individuals high rather than low in loneliness. Lonely individuals, for instance, are more likely to have low self-esteem, high anxiety, fears and expectancies of negative evaluation by others, and pessimistic outlooks. There is also clear evidence that, on average, lonely individuals form more negative social impressions of others than nonlonely individuals. Wittenberg and Reis (1986) reported that lonely individuals held more negative perceptions of their roommates than did nonlonely individuals. Cacioppo et al. (2000) replicated this finding and further found that the divide between lonely and nonlonely undergraduates' perceptions of others in their residence hall existed for roommates, was even larger for suitemates, was larger yet for floormates, and was larger yet again for hallmates. That is, individuals in the social environment with whom lonely students had relatively little exposure or few interactions were liked the least relative to their nonlonely counterparts in the residence halls.

Both social perception and social memory appear to contribute to these results. For instance, Duck, Pond, and Leatham (1994) asked participants to interact with a friend. The participants rated the quality of the relationship and the quality of the communication immediately after their interaction with the friend, and they repeated these ratings after watching a videotape of their interaction with the friend. In a session held at a later date, the participants were reminded of their previous interaction with their friend in the laboratory, and were asked to rate the quality of the interaction and the communication. Participants were next shown the videotape of their interaction and were again asked to rate the quality of the interaction and the communication.

The results indicated that lonely individuals are primed to interpret the behavior of others in a more negative light than nonlonely individuals. At all four measurement points, lonely individuals rated relationship quality more negatively than did nonlonely individuals, but lonely, compared to nonlonely, individuals rated the communication quality of the interaction more negatively during this second session and they were especially negative about the quality of their friendship after viewing the videotape during the second session (Duck et al., 1994). When lonely individuals rated the interaction soon after it occurred, their social perceptions were somewhat biased negatively, but the effects of their negative bias in social cognition was constrained by the apparent reasons for their friend's behavior. As time passes and memory for the underlying subtext fades, however, reality constraints are lessened, and lonely individuals remember the relationship and the communication more negatively than immediately following their interaction with the friend. As Duck et al. (1994) suggested, lonely individuals may filter social information through a negative lens, seeing others in a more negative light, especially as the memory for the actual lighting on the facts of the social exchange dims.

Social interactions, perhaps especially between strangers or acquaintances, are replete with opportunities for treachery, negative attributions, mistrust, and conflict, just as they are full or opportunities for positive attributions, understanding, hope, trust, and support. Just as a hungry person might delight in less palatable food than would a sated individual, a lonely person who seeks to fulfill unmet social needs might rationally be expected to seek and accept less from new acquaintances than nonlonely individuals whose social needs are satisfied. This is not what is found, however. Instead, self-protective processes operate to produce in lonely individual's pattern of social information processing and behavior that paradoxically pushes others away. Indeed, Rotenberg and Kmill (1992) found that lonely perceivers were less accepting of nonlonely targets than were nonlonely perceivers.

In another illustrative study, Rotenberg (1994) examined the manner in which lonely and nonlonely individuals interacted with a stranger in a prisoner's dilemma game. The rules of the game are such that both players make a small and equal amount of money when they cooperate with one another, one player makes a large amount of money at the expense of the other if the former competes when the other cooperates, and both players do poorly when both compete. In the Rotenberg (1994) study, players made known to their opponent before each trial whether they intended to play the trial cooperatively or competitively.

Recall that one of the foibles of social cognition is that people tend to search for and attend to evidence that confirms what they already believe to be true. Given lonely individuals are more socially anxious, hold more negative social expectations, and have stronger fears of negative evaluation, it follows that the tendency for lonely individuals to cooperate and trust others can be undermined much more easily than the trust and cooperation of their nonlonely counterparts. This is what Rotenberg (1994) found. At the outset and during the early trials, lonely and nonlonely individuals were equally likely to cooperate. As play continued and occasional betrayals occurred, however, the lonely individuals were more likely to become competitive and untrustworthy than nonlonely individuals. The heightened social anxiety and vulnerability felt by individuals who are lonely (Segrin & Kinney, 1995) apparently led to social perceptions and expectations of the relationship that produce relatively hostile, intolerant behaviors.

Similarly, Anderson and Martin (1995) found that lonely students were less responsive to their classmates during class discussions, and that lonely students provided less appropriate and effective feedback than nonlonely students. Consequently, lonely students are less popular with their peers (Nurmi et al., 1996) and have relatively impoverished social networks compared to nonlonely students (Damsteegt, 1992). Differences in social cognition and behavior result in lonely individuals being less likely than their nonlonely counterparts to succeed in their dire efforts to develop and maintain constructive, meaningful, or intimate relationships.

Lonely individuals appear to possess the requisite social skills to relate effectively to others, but they are not as likely to deploy these skills effectively or, if they do, they are not as likely to realize their efficacy, as are nonlonely individuals. In an illustrative study, Vitkus and Horowitz (1987) asked lonely and nonlonely individuals to adopt either the role of listening to another individual describe a personal problem or the role of describing a personal problem to another. Both lonely and nonlonely individuals displayed equivalent social skills regardless of role. Individuals in the listener role were more active listeners, generated more help, and conversed longer than those who were describing a personal problem. Lonely individuals, however, rated themselves as having poorer social skills than nonlonely individuals. More recently, Vandeputte et al. (1999) coded same-age and mixed-age dyadic conversations and found no relationship between loneliness and social skill. The social-skills deficit of lonely individuals, therefore, appear to have more to do with their willingness or ability to select appropriate social behaviors rather than their ability to adopt a given social role when explicitly instructed to do so.

Evidence was also provided by Anderson et al. (1994) that lonely individuals are more fragile and self-critical than nonlonely individuals. Participants performed experimental tasks after which they received success or failure feedback. The typical finding in the attribution literature is that people tend to attribute failures to something external to themselves (e.g., the situation or difficulty of the task) and success to something about themselves (e.g., their competence or effort)—causal reasoning that may not be entirely rational but generally fosters effective adaptation, persistence, and well being (Taylor et al., 2003). Anderson et al. (1994), in contrast, found that the higher an individual's loneliness, the more likely was the individual to attribute the failure to something about themselves and success to something about the situation. To the extent that lonely individuals perceive little control over external circumstances, the less likely they are to attempt to actively cope. It should be no surprise, therefore, that lonely individuals are also more likely to deploy self-protective processes even though doing so often proves to be self-defeating (cf. Twenge, Catanese, & Baumeister, 2002; Baumeister & DeWall, this volume).

Together, these data suggest that lonely individuals are more likely than nonlonely individuals to act and relate to others in an anxious, self-protective fashion with the paradoxical effect of pushing others away. Indeed, research has confirmed that lonely individuals are high in social avoidance and low in social approach (Nurmi et al., 1996). Crandall and Cohen (1994) found that lonely individuals were more likely to be socially rejected than nonlonely individuals. The main predictors of social rejection were identified by Damsteegt (1992) as a cynical worldview consisting of alienation, loneliness, and little faith in others. Finally, Nurmi and Salmelo-Aro (1997) found that lonely students were more likely to use a "pessimistic-avoidant" than approach-oriented social strategy, and that the use of the pessimistic-avoidant social strategy both predicted future loneliness and was predicted by concurrent loneliness. In sum, lonely, compared to nonlonely, individuals tend to construe their world, including the behavior of others, as punitive or potentially punitive, be cynical and socially anxious, hold more negative expectations for their treatment by others, and adopt avoidance than approach focus in their social interactions.

The negative, self-protective lens through which lonely individuals view their social world should promote insular, self-protective appraisals and coping strategies rather than active and interactive modes of appraisal and coping. To test this hypothesis, we assessed the coping mechanisms deployed in response to stressors by individuals who were high, average, or low in loneliness. Our study confirmed that lonely individuals were more likely to behaviorally disengage or to withdraw from the stressor, whereas nonlonely individuals were more likely to actively cope (e.g., problem solve), seek instrumental support from others, and seek emotional support from others (Cacioppo et al. 2002b). Similar results were reported by others who, using somewhat different measures of coping (Overholser, 1992), and were more likely to think about missed opportunities, finances, and death but less likely to think about opportunities for forming new and constructive social connections such as parenthood (Ben-Artzi et al., 1995).

Passively coping or withdrawing from stressful tasks, interactions, or circumstances is reasonable in certain instances (e.g., when one has no control or low efficacy to learn or cope), but when applied generally to everyday hassles and stressors it at best can retard learning and personal growth and, at worst, can lead to an accumulation of tasks and stressors that become increasingly taxing and oppressive. Individuals who are low in loneliness, on the other hand, not only are more likely to actively cope with everyday stressors, but they are more likely to seek the support and assistance of others to do so. Relatedly, Larose, Guay, and Boivin (2002) relied not only on self-reports of support-seeking, but also on a friend's evaluation of how often the participant sought emotional and social support. Results revealed that the participant's attachment style at Time 1 and the friend's report of emotional support seeking at Time 2 predicted lower loneliness at Time 2. It appears that using social ties is associated with strengthened connections, perhaps in part through increased accessibility and in part through the development of reciprocal obligations and trust. Thus, the growth of feelings of personal control, efficacy, and optimism may be fueled by these small daily triumphs, which further decreases the likely operation of self-protective processes in nonlonely, compared to lonely, individuals.

In sum, lonely, in contrast to nonlonely, individuals tend to view their social world as unfulfilling. They seek to address this deficit in a context fraught with treachery and betrayal. Their expectations, impression formation, and attributional reasoning, and actions toward others are less charitable than shown by nonlonely individuals, differences that are based at least in part in actual differences in the way in which they are viewed and treated. But lonely individuals are not simply passive victims in their social world; they are active participants in a fragile interpersonal dance that cultivates both self-protective and paradoxically self-defeating interactions with others. The continual social deficit felt by lonely individuals, and the caustic nature of their social cognition (e.g., threat appraisals and passive coping processes) and based on their self-absorbing rather than socially enhancing behavior, activate transduction pathways with deleterious effects on physiological functioning that unfold over time.

CONCLUSION

The notion that a human can be modeled as a discrete personal computer dominated psychology and the cognitive sciences in the latter half of the twentieth century. Our research, and that of others presented in this volume, calls this notion into question, as ironically have technological developments over the past decade. The notion of a computer disconnected from others is already passé, and it is becoming apparent that humans share much more in common with mobile computers that are linked through ubiquitous broadband wireless connections than tethered disconnected personal computers. However, important differences exist, as illustrated by the predictable effects of sociodemographic changes reviewed above, and the consequent effects on social cognition and behavior.

A second dominant metaphor from the latter half of the twentieth century—the notion of the selfish gene—should also be questioned as a model of human behavior. The genetic constitution of species characterized by large litter sizes or brief periods of dependency is reducible essentially to the reproductive success of individual members of the species. Simply stated, if an organism survives to reproduce, the genes of the organism are more likely to be included in the gene pool of the species. The genetic constitution of Homo sapiens, in contrast, derives not simply from an individual's reproductive success but more critically from the success of one's children to reproduce. The human infant is born individually to an extended period of abject dependency. If infants do not elicit nurturance and protection from caregivers, or if caregivers are not motivated to provide such care over an extended period of time, the infants perish along with the genetic legacy of the parents. Even as adults, humans are not particularly strong, fast, or stealthy relative to other species. It is only the ability to think, to seek meaning and purpose, and to work together that makes Homo sapiens such a formidable species. Hunter/gatherers who, in times of danger or famine, chose not to return to share their food with mother and child may have survived to hunt another day but the genetic constitution that enabled them to feel so little humanity also made it less likely their genes were propagated. In contrast, those who yearned to return despite personal hardship, and individuals who protected and nurtured those close to them, were more likely to have offspring who survived to propagate. Because genetic transmission is based not on one's ability to reproduce but on the success of one's children to reproduce, Homo sapiens evolved to be an inherently social, meaning-making species with qualities ascribable to a human spirit. In short, we posit that humans have evolved a brain and biology whose functioning benefits from the formation and maintenance of sociality, spirituality, and meaning making. The deprivation of any of these ingredients—such as a relocation that is distant from friends and family or the loss of purpose in life—produces a dysphoria and a motivation to reinstate connections reminiscent of our evolutionary heritage. Recent research has confirmed that loneliness/sociality has a sizeable heritable component (Boomsma, Willemsen, Hawkley, & Cacioppo, 2004; McGuire & Clifford, 2000).

From this perspective, it is clear why social isolation might promote loneliness. In the present chapter, we have outlined a model in which loneliness in turn promotes people construing their world, including the behavior of others, as threatening or punitive. Consistent with this model, lonely individuals are more likely to be socially anxious, hold more negative expectations for their treatment by others, and adopt a prevention focus rather than a promotion focus in their social interactions. Lonely, relative to nonlonely, individuals are also more likely to appraise stressors as threats rather than challenges, and to cope with stressors in a passive, isolative fashion rather than an active fashion that includes actively seeking the help and support of others. We further hypothesized that these differences in social cognition result in an increased likelihood of lonely individuals acting in self-protective and, paradoxically, self-defeating ways, which is in turn buttressed by the confirmation of their expectations and by the behavioral confirmation processes of others. Finally, the ways in which lonely individuals reason about people and cope with stress activate social neurobehavioral mechanisms that may contribute to the association between loneliness and mortality (Cacioppo, Hawkley, & Berntson, 2003).

REFERENCES

Adams, G. R., Openshaw, D. K., Bennion, L., Mills, T., & Noble, S. (1988). Loneliness in late adolescence. *Journal of Adolescent Research, 3*, 81–96.

Anderson, C. M., & Martin, M. M. (1995). The effects of communication motives, interaction involvement, and loneliness on satisfaction: A model of small groups. *Small Group Research, 26*, 118–137.

Anderson, C. A., Miller, R. S., Riger, A. L., Dill, J. C., et al. (1994). Behavioral and characterological attributional styles as predictors of depression and loneliness: Review, refinement, and test. *Journal of Personality & Social Psychology, 66*, 549–558.

Austin, B. A. (1983). Factorial structure of the UCLA Loneliness Scale. *Psychological Reports, 53*, 883–889.

Asher, S., & Wheeler, V. A. (1985). Children's loneliness: A comparison of rejected and neglected peer status. *Journal of Consulting & Clinical Psychology, 53*, 500–505.

Barbour, A. (1993). Research report: Dyadic loneliness in marriage. *Journal of Group Psychotherapy, Psychodrama & Sociometry, 46*, 70–72.

Bell, B. (1993). Emotional loneliness and the perceived similarity of one's ideas and interests. *Journal of Social Behavior & Personality, 8*, 273–280.

Ben-Artzi, E., Mikulincer, M., & Glaubman, H. (1995). The multifaceted nature of self-consciousness: Conceptualization, measurement, and consequences. *Imagination, Cognition & Personality, 15*, 17–43.

Berscheid, E. (1985). Interpersonal attraction. In G. Lindzey & E. Aronson (Eds.), *The Handbook of Social Psychology* (3rd ed., pp. 413-484). New York: Random House.

Berscheid, E., & Reis, H. T. (1998). Attraction and close relationships. In D. T. Gilbert, S. T. Fiske, et al. (Eds.), *The Handbook of Social Psychology: Vol. 2* (4th ed., pp. 193–281). New York: McGraw Hill.

Boomsma, D. I., Willemsen, G., Dolan, C. V., Hawkley, L. C., & Cacioppo, J. T. (under review). Genetics and enviornmental contributions to loneliness in adults: The Netherlands Twin Register Study.

Burt, R. S. (1986). Strangers, friends, and happiness. *GSS Technical Report No. 72*. Chicago: National Opinion Research Center, University of Chicago.

Cacioppo, J. T. & Hawkley, L. C. (2003). Social isolation and health, with an emphasis on underlying mechanisms. *Perspectives in Biology and Medicine, 46*, S39–S52.

Cacioppo, J. T., Hawkley, L. C., & Berntson, G. G. (2003). The anatomy of loneliness. *Current Directions in Psychological Science, 12*, 71–74.

Cacioppo, J. T., Ernst, J. M., Burleson, M. H., McClintock, M. K., Malarkey, W. B., Hawkley, L. C., Kowalewski, R. B., Paulsen, A., Hobson, J. A., Hugdahl, K., Speigel, D., & Berntson, G. G. (2000). Lonely traits and concomitant physiological processes: The MacArthur Social Neuroscience Studies. *International Journal of Psychophysiology, 35*, 143–154.

Cacioppo, J. T., Hawkley, L. C., Berntson, G. G., Ernst, J. M., Gibbs, A. C., Stickgold, R., & Hobson, J. A. (2002a). Do lonely days invade the night?: Potential social modulation of sleep efficiency. *Psychological Science, 13*, 385–388.

Cacioppo, J. T., Hawkley, L. C., Crawford, L. E., Ernst, J. M., Burleson, M. H., Kowalewski, R. B., Malarkey, W. B., Van Cauter, E., & Berntson, G. G. (2002b). Loneliness and health: Potential mechanisms. *Psychosomatic Medicine, 64*, 407–417.

Cacioppo, J. T., Hawkley, L. C., & Berntson, G. G. (2004). The anatomy of loneliness. In J. B. Ruscher & E. Y. Hammer (Eds.), *Current directions in social psychology: Readings from the American Psychological Society*. Washington, DC: Prentice Hall.

Cacioppo, J. T., Hawkley, L. C., Ernst, J. M., Burleson, M. H., Berntson, G. G., Nouriani,

B., & Spiegel, D. (in press). Lonliness within a nomological net: An evolutionary perspective. *Journal of Research in Personality.*

Crandall, C. S, & Cohen, C. (1994). The personality of the stigmatizer: Cultural world view, conventionalism, and self-esteem. *Journal of Research in Personality, 28,* 461–480.

Damsteegt, D. (1992). Loneliness, social provisions and attitude, *College Student Journal, 26*(1), 135–139.

de Jong-Gierveld, J. (1987). Developing and testing a model of loneliness. *Journal of Personality and Social Psychology, 53,* 119–128.

Duck, S., Pond, K., & Leatham, G. (1994). Loneliness and the evaluation of relational events. *Journal of Social & Personal Relationships, 11,* 253–276.

Eisenberger, N. I., Lieberman, M., & Williams, K. D. (2003). Does rejection hurt? An fMRI study of social exclusion. *Science, 302*(10 October), 290–292.

Ernst, J. M. & Cacioppo, J. T. (1999). Lonely hearts: Psychological perspective on loneliness. *Applied and Preventive Psychology, 8,* 1–22.

Fees, B. S., Martin, P., & Poon, L. W. (1999). A model of loneliness in older adults. *Journal of Gerontology: Psychological Sciences, 54B,* P231–P239.

Felthous, A. R. (1997). Does "isolation" cause jail suicides? *Journal of the American Academy of Psychiatry & the Law, 25,* 285–294.

Gardner, W. L., Gabriel, S., & Diekman, A. B. (2000). Interpersonal processes. In J. T. Cacioppo, L. G. Tassinary, & G. G. Berntson (Eds.), *Handbook of psychophysiology* (pp. 643–664). New York: Cambridge University Press.

Green, L. R., Richardson, D. S., Lago, T., & Schatten-Jones, E. C. (2001). Network correlates of social and emotional loneliness in young and older adults. *Personality and Social Psychology Bulletin, 27,* 281–288.

Harlow, H. F. (1973). *Learning to love.* Oxford, UK: Ballantine.

Harlow, H. F., & Harlow, M. K. (1973). Social deprivation in monkeys. In W. T. Greenough (Compiler), *The nature and nurture of behavior: Readings from the Scientific American* (pp. 108–116). San Francisco: Freeman.

Hawkley, L. C., Burleson, M. H., Berntson, G. G., & Cacioppo, J. T. (2003). Loneliness in everyday life: Cardiovascular activity, psychosocial context, and health behaviors. *Journal of Personality & Social Psychology, 85,* 105–120.

Hays, R. D., & DiMatteo, M. R. (1987). A short-form measure of loneliness. *Journal of Personality Assessment, 51,* 69–81.

Henderson, A. S., Scott, R., & Kay, D. W. (1986). The elderly who live alone: Their mental health and social relationships. *Australian & New Zealand Journal of Psychiatry, 20,* 202–209.

Hobbs, F. & Stoops, N. (2002). *Demographic Trends in the 20th Century.* U.S. Census Bureau, Census 2000 Special Reports, Series CENSR-4. Washington, DC: U.S. Government Printing Office.

Kosslyn, S. M., Thompson, W. L.; Costantini-Ferrando, M. F.; Alpert, N. M.; & Spiegel, D. (2000). Hypnotic visual illusion alters color processing in the brain. *American Journal of Psychiatry, 157,* 1279–1284.

Kruger, J., & Gilovich, T. (1999). "Naive cynicism" in everyday theories of responsibility assessment: On biased assumptions of bias. *Journal of Personality & Social Psychology, 76,* 743–753.

Larose, S., Guay, F., & Boivin, M. (2002). Attachment, social support, and loneliness in young adulthood: A test of two models. *Personality and Social Psychology Bulletin, 28,* 684–693.

Lau, S., & Gruen, G. E. (1992). The social stigma of loneliness: Effect of target person's and perceiver's sex. *Personality & Social Psychology Bulletin, 18,* 182-189.

McGuire, W. J. (1981). The probabilogical model of cognitive structure and attitude change. In R. E. Petty, T. M. Ostrom, and T. C. Brock (Eds.), *Cognitive responses in persuasion* (pp. 291–307). Hillsdale, NJ: Erlbaum.

McGuire, S., & Clifford, J. (2000). Genetic and environmental contributions to loneliness in children. *Psychological Science, 11,* 487–491.

Marangoni, C., & Ickes, W. (1989). Loneliness. A theoretical review with implications for measurement. *Journal of Social and Personal Relations, 6,* 93–128.

Mullins, L., & Elston, C. (1996). Social determinants of loneliness among older Americans. *Genetic, Social, and General Psychology Monographs, 122,* 455–469.

Murray, S. L., & Holmes, J. G. (1999). The (mental) ties that bind: Cognitive structures that predict relationship resilience. *Journal of Personality & Social Psychology, 77,* 1228–1244.

Murray, S. L., Bellavia, G. M., Rose, P., & Griffin, D.W. (2003). Once hurt, twice hurtful: How perceived regard regulates daily marital interactions. *Journal of Personality and Social Psychology, 84,* 126–147.

Nurmi, J-E., & Salmela-Aro, K. (1997). Social strategies and loneliness: A prospective study. *Personality & Individual Differences, 23,* 205–215.

Nurmi, J-E., Toivonen, S., Salmela-Aro, K., & Eronen, S. (1996). Optimistic, approach-oriented, and avoidance strategies in social situations: Three studies on loneliness and peer relationships. *European Journal of Personality, 10,* 201–219.

Overholser, J. C. (1992). Sense of humor when coping with life stress. *Personality and Individual Differences, 13,* 700–804.

Ross, L., Greene, D., & House, P. (1977). The false consensus effect: An egocentric bias in social perception and attributional processes. *Journal of Experimental Social Psychology, 13,* 279–301.

Ross, M., & Sicoly, F. (1979). Egocentric biases in availability and attribution. *Journal of Personality & Social Psychology, 37,* 322–336.

Rotenberg, K. J., & Kmill, J. (1992). Perception of lonely and non-lonely persons as a function of individual differences in loneliness. *Journal of Social & Personal Relationships, 9,* 325–330.

Rotenberg, K. J., Gruman, J. A., & Ariganello, M. (2002). Behavioral confirmation of the loneliness stereotype. *Basic & Applied Social Psychology, 24,* 81–89.

Russell, D., Peplau, L. A., & Cutrona, C. E. (1980). The revised UCLA loneliness scale: Concurrent and discriminant validity evidence. *Journal of Personality and Social Psychology, 39,* 472–480.

Seeman, T. E. (2000). Health promoting effects of friends and family on health outcomes in older adults. *American Journal of Health Promotion, 14,* 362–370.

Segrin, C., & Flora, J. (2000). Poor social skills are a vulnerability factor in the development of psychosocial problems. *Human Communication Research, 26,* 489–514.

Segrin, C., & Kinney, T. (1995). Social skills deficits among the socially anxious: Rejection from others and loneliness. *Motivation & Emotion, 19,* 1–24.

Shaver, P., & Hazan, C. (1987). Being lonely, falling in love: Perspectives from attachment theory. *Journal of Social Behavior & Personality, 2,* 105–124.

Shaver, P., Furman, W., & Buhrmester, D. (1985). Transition to college: Network changes, social skills, and loneliness. In S. Duck & D. Perlman (Eds.), *Understanding personal relationships: An interdisciplinary approach* (pp. 193–219). London: Sage.

Solano, C. H. (1987). Loneliness and perceptions of control: General traits versus specific attributions. *Journal of Social Behavior and Personality, 2*(2, Pt 2), 201–214.

Taylor, S. E., Lerner, J. S., Sherman, D. K., Sage, R. M., & McDowell, N. K. (2003). Portrait of the self-enhancer: Well-adjusted and well-liked or maladjusted and friendless? *Journal of Personality and Social Psychology, 84,* 165–176.

Tornstam, L. (1992). Loneliness in marriage. *Journal of Social & Personal Relationships, 9,* 197–217.

Twenge, J. M., Catanese, K. R., & Baumeister, R. F. (2002). Social exclusion causes self-defeating behavior. *Journal of Personality and Social Psychology, 83,* 606–615.

Van Baarsen, B., Snijders, T. A. B., Smit, J. H., & van Duijn, M. A. J. (2001). Lonely but not alone: Emotional isolation and social isolation as two distinct dimensions of loneliness in older people. *Educational and Psychological Measurement, 61,* 119–135.

Vandeputte, D. D., Kemper, S., Hummert, M. L., Kemtes, K. A., Shaner, J., & Segrin, C. (1999). Social skills of older people: Conversations in same- and mixed-age dyads. *Discourse Processes, 27,* 55–76.

Vaughan, E. (1993). Chronic exposure to an environmental hazard: Risk perceptions and self-protective behavior. *Health Psychology, 3,* 431–457.

Vitkus, J., & Horowitz, L. M. (1987). Poor social performance of lonely people: Lacking a skill or adopting a role? *Journal of Personality & Social Psychology, 52,* 1266–1273.

Weiss, R. S. (1973). Loneliness: The experience of emotional and social isolation. Cambridge: MIT Press.

Wheeler, L., Reis, H., & Nezlek, J. (1983). Loneliness, social interaction, and sex roles. *Journal of Personality and Social Psychology, 45,* 943–953.

Williams, K. D. (1997). Social ostracism. In R. M. Kowalski (Ed.), *Aversive interpersonal behaviors* (pp. 133–170). New York: Plenum.

Wittenberg, M. T., Reis, H. T. (1986). Loneliness, social skills, and social perception. *Personality and Social Psychology Bulletin, 12,* 121–130.

7

Why It Hurts to Be Left Out
The Neurocognitive Overlap Between
Physical and Social Pain

NAOMI I. EISENBERGER
MATTHEW D. LIEBERMAN

> *Without friends no one would choose to live, though he had all other goods.*
>
> Artistotle

Replace the word "friends," as quoted above, with the word "air," "water," or "food" and Aristotle's claim is indisputable. Without amending his statement, however, Aristotle's claim seems more hyperbolic than truthful. If granted all the 'real' necessities of life, such as air, water, and food, would we not be able to live or, at least, not want to live, without the companionship of others? Are social relationships something we actually need or are they better

Address correspondence to: Naomi Eisenberger, Department of Psychology, Franz Hall, University of California, Los Angeles, Los Angeles, California 90025, USA. E-mail: neisenbe@ucla.edu

described as desirable but not necessary? In this chapter we will suggest that social connection is a need as basic as air, water, or food and that like these more basic needs, the absence of social connections causes pain. Indeed, we propose that the pain of social separation or rejection may not be very different from some kinds of physical pain.

We are not alone in this claim. For centuries, writers, musicians, playwrights, and poets have noted that the loss of social bonds can unleash the most profound forms of human pain and suffering. The legal systems of many countries have also recognized this, as evidenced by their use of social isolation as one of the most extreme forms of punishment, at times issued interchangeably with the death penalty for the most severe crimes (Baumeister, 2000). Likewise, the pain of broken social bonds permeates the English language, illustrated by the use of physical pain words to describe episodes of socially painful experiences, such as when speaking of "broken hearts" or "hurt feelings" (MacDonald & Shaw, this volume). Could Aristotle have been right?

Until a half-century ago, most psychologists would have responded with a resounding "no." Psychologists believed that an infant's attachment to his or her caregiver was exclusively the result of the association of the caregiver's face or form with the alleviation of certain drive states such as hunger or thirst (Dollard & Miller, 1950). However, in a series of seminal studies, Harlow (1958) demonstrated that infant rhesus monkeys separated from their natural mothers preferred a cloth surrogate mother that provided them with contact comfort to a wire-mesh mother that provided them with food, indicating the existence of a need, over and above the need for food. This study, along with the others that have followed, emphasized the importance of a mammalian drive that is primarily social, unrelated to hunger or thermoregulation, aimed at maintaining social closeness or social contact. Though it is possible that this need for social closeness may have originally evolved to support a drive for food or warmth, Harlow's studies indicate that it is now clearly a separate, autonomous need.

We propose that along with the evolution of mammals, a species unique in their need for early nurturance and care, came a corresponding lifelong need for social connection (Baumeister & Leary, 1995; see also, Pickett & Gardner; Williams & Zadro; this volume). Indeed, this need has proved so essential to survival that social separation, like other unmet needs, is experienced as painful. We hypothesize that the pain mechanisms involved in preventing physical harm were co-opted during our evolution to prevent social separation. In this chapter, we suggest that social and physical pain share the same underlying system and that this overlap has several consequences for the way that these types of pain are detected, experienced, and overcome (see also MacDonald & Shaw, this volume). We will refer to this theory as *pain overlap theory* and will present evidence for four hypotheses derived from this proposed overlap.

PAIN OVERLAP THEORY

Pain overlap theory proposes that social pain, the pain that we experience when social relationships are damaged or lost, and physical pain, the pain that we experience upon physical injury, share parts of the same underlying processing system (Eisenberger & Lieberman, 2004). This system is responsible for detecting the presence or possibility of physical or social harm and recruiting attention once something has gone wrong in order to fix it. Evolutionarily, this overlap makes good sense. Based on mammalian infants' lengthy period of immaturity and their critical need for substantial maternal contact and care, it is possible that the social attachment system, the system that keeps us near close others, may have piggybacked onto the pre-existing pain system, borrowing the pain signal to signify and prevent the danger of social separation (Nelson & Panksepp, 1998; Panksepp, 1998).

This evolutionary hypothesis was first proposed to explain the similar effects of opiates on both physical and social pain. Panksepp (1998) noted that opiate-based drugs, known for their effectiveness in alleviating physical pain, were also effective in alleviating distress vocalizations emitted by the young of different mammalian species when separated from others. Panksepp suggested that the social attachment system may have co-opted the opiate substrates of the physical pain system to maintain proximity with others, eliciting distress upon separation and comfort upon reunion (Nelson & Panksepp, 1998).[1]

For most mammalian species, an initial connection between mother and child is essential for survival as mammalian infants are born relatively immature, without the capacity to feed or fend for themselves. The Latin root of the word *mammal* is *mamma* which means *breast* and bears a striking resemblance to the first word uttered by many infants across many countries, namely the colloquial word for *mother* (English: *mom, mommy*; Spanish: *mami, mama*; French: *maman*; German: *mami, mama*; Hindi: *ma*; Korean: *ama*; Hebrew: *ima*). Thus, the need to maintain closeness with the mother is so critical that the first word uttered by many human infants typically reflects this important underlying motivation, the need for the mother.

Because maintaining closeness with caregivers for food and protection is necessary for the survival of mammalian young, a system that monitors for distance from the caregiver and alerts the individual once a certain distance has been exceeded is critical. Indeed, the pain system may have been co-opted for just this purpose. Due to its aversiveness, pain grabs attention, interrupts ongoing behavior, and urges actions aimed at mitigating painful experience (Williams, 2002). To the extent that social distance is harmful to survival, experiencing pain upon social separation would be an adaptive way to prevent social distance.

The value of pain overlap theory, however, comes primarily from its corollary hypotheses. In this chapter, we will present four of these hypotheses along with the evidence relevant to each. Pain overlap theory provides an overarching structure and organization to these findings that on their own tend to be interesting but atheoretical. The first hypothesis is that physical and social pain should share a common phenomenological basis and should rely on some of the same neural structures. Second, if both types of pain rely on some of the same neural structures, they should also share some of the same underlying cognitive or computational mechanisms. Third, potentiating or regulating one type of pain should similarly influence the other type of pain. Fourth, traits related to a heightened sensitivity to one type of pain should also relate to a heightened sensitivity to the other type of pain. Before examining these hypotheses, we will first define the terms "physical pain" and "social pain."

Physical pain has previously been defined as "an unpleasant sensory and emotional experience associated with actual or potential tissue damage, or described in terms of such damage" (International Association for the Study of Pain, 1979). For social pain, however, there is no pre-existing definition of this term that captures our intended meaning. We conceptualize social pain as analogous to Bowlby's description of the separation distress that occurs when an infant feels distress due to separation from a caregiver (Bowlby, 1969). In a similar manner, we define social pain as *the distressing experience arising from actual or potential psychological distance from close others or from the social group.*

Psychological distance could include perceptions of rejection, exclusion, non-inclusion, or any socially-relevant cue that makes an individual feel unimportant to, distant from, or not valued by important relationship partners (see also Leary; Baumeister, & DeWall, this volume). Whereas infants may only be capable of detecting actual physical distance from a caregiver, emergent cognitive capacities soon enable young children with the ability to monitor not only objective distance from the caregiver, but also perceived psychological distance from the caregiver, an assessment that relies on a more complex understanding of socio-relational information. In short, social pain can be thought of as the distressing experience associated with *perceived social distance.*

Two factors make social pain a broader and more expansive social experience than Bowlby's conception of separation distress. First, unlike separation distress, social pain is posited to be an experience that persists throughout the life span. Typically, separation distress is thought to diminish as a child matures and becomes capable of taking care of himself (Bowlby, 1969). However, if the social attachment system borrowed the mechanisms underlying the physical pain system, perceived social distance should continue to cause social pain for as long as the physical pain system is in tact. Indeed this seems to be the case, as evidenced by the occurrence of grieving responses, social anxiety disorders, and depression from social isolation in individuals of all ages. Whether this continued sensitivity to social distance remains adaptive in adulthood or is merely a vestige of the merging of these two systems is not yet known.

Second, based on expanding cognitive capacities that allow certain species to represent, manipulate, imagine, and predict complex social information, many more cues may be capable of eliciting social pain in mature humans than are capable of eliciting separation distress in infants or other mammals. For example, human adults can experience social pain not only based on the perception of psychological distance from an individual but also based on the perception of psychological distance from a *social group*, a more complex mental representation. In addition, humans can experience social pain or anxiety at the mere *possibility* of social distance. The capacity to represent complex ideas such as the social group or the possibility of social distance may only be possible for those species with cognitive resources that allow symbolic and propositional representations (Deacon, 1992; Lieberman et al., 2002). For instance, human infants can only begin to show fear of *anticipated* situations once they have undergone a critical period of prefrontal cortex maturation, at the end of their first year (Bowlby, 1973; Schore, 2001). Species that show the most expansion of neocortical areas, such as primates, humans, and possibly cetaceans (whales and dolphins; Panksepp, 1998) may be the only mammals capable of showing distress at these more subtle cues of social distance. In the remainder of this chapter, we will present evidence for the four corollary hypotheses derived from pain overlap theory.

HYPOTHESIS #1: PHYSICAL AND SOCIAL PAIN SHARE A COMMON PHENOMENOLOGICAL AND NEURAL BASIS

The first hypothesis proposes that physical and social pain share a common phenomenological and neural basis. We have already mentioned one reason to believe that these two types of pain share a common phenomenological experience; they share a common vocabulary. In the English language, the same words are used to describe instances of both physical and social injury. Thus, we can have a *broken* bone or a *broken* heart; we can feel the pain of a stomach*ache* or of heart*ache*; and we can be *hurt* by a dog's *bite* or by another's *biting* remark. Indeed, the use of pain words to describe episodes of physical and social pain is a phenomenon common to many different languages (MacDonald & Shaw, this volume). However, linguistic evidence alone does not substantiate the claim that physical pain and social pain share the same underlying phenomenology. A "broken heart" could simply be a figure of speech and might not actually be experienced as physically painful. Showing that the same neural regions are involved in the experience of both physical and social pain provides more substantial evidence that these two types of pain share a common phenomenological experience.

In this section, we will review neuropsychological and neuroimaging research suggesting that the dorsal anterior cingulate cortex (dACC), a large structure on the medial wall of the frontal lobe, is one of the key neural structures involved in the affective distress associated with the physical-social pain overlap. Though there are undoubtedly several other neural structures involved in this overlap, such as the insula and periaqueductal gray, we will focus primarily on the role that the dACC plays in the affective component of physical and social pain.

Physical Pain and the dACC

For nearly a century, it has been known that the dACC plays a role in the experience of physical pain. Since the mid-1930s, neurosurgeons have used cingulotomy, a circumscribed lesioning of the dACC, for the treatment of intractable chronic pain disorders (Davis et al., 1994). Following cingulotomy for chronic pain, patients report still being able to feel the intensity of pain but that the pain itself no longer bothers them (Foltz & White, 1968).[2]

Pain researchers have subsequently subdivided painful experience into two components: the intensity and the unpleasantness of painful experience (Price, 2000; Rainville et al., 1997). Rating the *intensity* of pain can be likened to rating the loudness of the volume on a radio; whereas rating the *unpleasantness* of pain can be likened to rating the extent to which the volume on the radio is perceived as bothersome. While the dACC has been shown to be involved in the perceived unpleasantness of physical pain, other neural regions such as the somatosensory cortex and posterior insula have been shown to be involved in processing the sensory-discriminative aspects of pain (Peyron, Laurent, & Garcia-Larrea, 2000). Pain disorders involving damage to somatosensory areas leave patients unable to identify where the pain is coming from or how intense it is but still able to experience the distress associated with having the pain in the first place (Nagasako, Oaklander, & Dworkin, 2003).

The first neuroimaging study linking pain distress to dACC activity used hypnotic suggestion to alter the perceived unpleasantness of painful stimulation without changing the perceived intensity (Rainville et al., 1997). Using positron emission tomography (PET), it was observed that dACC activity corresponded to changes in the perceived unpleasantness of painful stimuli whereas the activity of primary somatosensory cortex, typically associated with the perceived intensity of painful stimulation, remained unaltered. Since then, several neuroimaging studies have linked the increasing unpleasantness of painful stimulation with dACC activation (Peyron et al., 2000). In a similar manner, pain-sensitive individuals, who report more pain unpleasantness to less intense pain, show significantly more dACC activity to painful stimulation than do less pain-sensitive individuals (Coghill, McHaffie, & Yen, 2003).

Social Pain and the dACC

Social Pain in Animals.   The cingulate gyrus has no distinctive counterpart in the reptilian brain, appearing for the first time, phylogenetically, in mammalian species (MacLean, 1985a, 1993).[3] Several behavioral characteristics accompany the evolution of mammals as well. These newly emerged characteristics, differentiating mammals from their reptilian ancestors, include audiovocal communication for maintaining maternal-offspring contact and the nursing of young along with maternal care.[4] As the cingulate appeared on the evolutionary scene at the same time as these characteristics, it may be a contributor to these uniquely mammalian behaviors.

One of these uniquely mammalian behaviors is the production of distress vocalizations, which are considered to be the most primitive and basic mammalian vocalization with the original purpose of maintaining mother-infant contact (MacLean, 1985a). Typically, infants emit distress vocalizations when separated from their caregivers and the sound of these vocalizations elicits distress in the mother, motivating her to retrieve her young. Consistent with the idea that distress vocalizations evolved in the context of parent–child relations, reptilian newborns, which receive no parenting as they are born almost completely mature, do not produce distress vocalizations (MacLean, 1985b).

To establish that the cingulate gyrus plays a causal role in the distress of social distance and the production of distress vocalizations, lesions to the cingulate gyrus should lead to: (a) fewer distress vocalizations when socially separated, and (b) fewer attempts at maintaining social closeness if social distance is no longer distressing. Consistent with this causal role, ablation of the dACC in squirrel monkeys leads to decreased distress vocalizations (Kirzinger & Jurgens, 1982; MacLean & Newman, 1988). Additionally, cingulate lesions in macaques lead to decreases in affiliative behavior, as indicated by a reduction in the amount of time spent in social interactions or in proximity with other macaques (Hadland et al., 2003). This drop-off in social affiliation may be the result of a reduced need for social closeness because social distance is no longer experienced as aversive.

Additionally, if the dACC is one of the primary neural regions involved in the production of distress vocalizations, localized stimulation of the dACC should elicit distress vocalizations while stimulation of other language areas should not. To this end, electrical stimulation of the dACC leads to the spontaneous production of distress vocalizations in rhesus monkeys (Robinson, 1967; Smith, 1945); whereas, stimulation of the area corresponding to Broca's area in monkeys and in apes, an area known to be involved in speech production, elicits movement of the vocal chords but no distress vocalizations (Leyton & Sherrington, 1917; Ploog, 1981).

The cingulate gyrus also plays a role in caregiver responses to infant distress vocalizations. Ablation of the cingulate gyrus in adult female rats results in deficits in maternal behavior, including the nursing and retrieval of pups (Stamm, 1955). Following cingulate ablation in females, rat mothers become less responsive to the distress vocalizations of their pups. In one study, the survival rate of rat pups with cingulate-lesioned mothers was only 12%, compared to a 95% survival rate in rat pups with sham-lesioned mothers (Stamm, 1955).

Social Pain in Humans.   Much less is known about the neural correlates of social pain in humans. However, if the dACC is involved in social pain in other mammals, it is reasonable to suggest that it is involved in human social pain as well. If this is true, lesioning the dACC in humans should have social consequences, making individuals less sensitive to social pain and potentially less interested in social affiliation as social closeness is no longer relieving. An early study noted that lesioning the dACC for chronic pain or anxiety disorders had social consequences. Following cingulotomy, patients became less socially inhibited, less shy, and less socially sensitive (Tow & Whitty, 1953). In other words, these patients became less socially concerned and more socially uninhibited.

Another frequent consequence of cingulotomy is akinetic mutism, in which patients temporarily do not initiate vocalization based on a lack of desire rather than a lack of ability (Laplane et al., 1977). While highly speculative, the disinclination to initiate vocalization may reflect a reduction in the concern for social connection. Destroying the portion of the cingulate associated with detecting social separation and vocalizing to reestablish connection, may result in the temporary absence of self-initiated vocalizations.

Perhaps the most direct evidence for the role of the dACC in human social pain comes from a neuroimaging study investigating the neural correlates of one type of social pain: social exclusion (Eisenberger, Lieberman, & Williams, 2003). In this study, participants were led to believe that they would be playing a virtual ball-tossing game with two other players over the Internet while in the fMRI scanner. In reality, there were no other players; rather, the computer images of the other players were preprogrammed to include the participant during one round of the ball-tossing game and to exclude the participant in another round of the game by not throwing the ball to the participant. Upon being excluded from the game, compared to when being included, participants showed increased activity in dACC, the region most often associated with the affective distress of physical pain. In addition, the amount of activity in this area correlated strongly ($r = .88$) with the amount of self-reported social distress participants felt during the exclusion episode. Thus, mirroring the animal research, the dACC seems to play a role in the distress associated with perceived social distance in humans as well.

HYPOTHESIS #2: PHYSICAL AND SOCIAL PAIN RELY ON THE SAME COMPUTATIONAL MECHANISMS

Because the dACC is involved in the experience of both physical and social pain, it is plausible that the underlying computational processes of the dACC are relevant in the processing of both types of pain. Understanding the computations underlying this shared neural circuitry is important for building a more complete model of the physical-social pain overlap.

Cohen and colleagues have shown that the dACC acts as a conflict or discrepancy monitor, detecting when an automatic habitual response is contextually inappropriate or conflicts with current goals (Botvinick et al., 2001). One simple example of conflict, often used to elicit dACC activation, is the Stroop task in which the automatic word-reading response conflicts with the goal of color naming (e.g., name the ink color of the word R-E-D printed in blue ink; MacDonald et al., 2000).

A number of other studies suggest that the dACC may be sensitive to goal conflicts and unexpected events more generally (Weissman et al., 2003), detecting discrepancies between automatic responses and current goals, between actual and expected events, and between new stimuli and pre-existing representations that do not map onto each other. When the dACC detects these discrepancies, the prefrontal cortex is notified of the problem so that it can exert executive control (Miller & Cohen, 2001) by overriding automatic processes.

Though much research supports this account of the dACC as a discrepancy detector, it is not clear how this function relates to physical or social pain processes. On the one hand, the dACC has been characterized as a discrepancy detector, producing activity to simple response conflicts such as those evidenced in the Stroop task (Botvinick et al., 2001). On the other hand, the dACC has been characterized as a distress center, producing activity to instances of both physical and social pain (Eisenberger et al., 2003; Rainville et al., 1997). How can these two characterizations of dACC function be reconciled?

If one conceptualizes the dACC as a neural alarm system (Eisenberger & Lieberman, 2004), the connection between discrepancy detection and the experience of physical and social pain quickly makes more sense. Most real world alarm systems (e.g., fire alarms) have two components. The first component is the sound of the alarm bell, the part of the alarm that signals that there is a problem, interrupts ongoing activity, and directs attention at solving the problem. This part of the alarm may be analogous to the experience of physical or social pain, which is also distressing, attention-getting, and disruptive. The second component of the alarm is the machinery that detects when something has gone wrong or has strayed from a desired set point (e.g., too much smoke in the room). In essence, this part of the alarm system detects discrepancies from some standard, initiates the sounding of the bell, and may be analogous to the discrepancy detection function of the dACC. Rather than discrepancy detection and distress being two competing accounts of dACC functioning, the analogy to an alarm system suggests that they may actually be two sides of the same coin: the two complementary processes of a neural alarm system. Based on this account, this multi-purpose alarm should be triggered once the underlying machinery has detected either physical damage, a discrepancy from the healthy state of the body, or social distance, a discrepancy from the desired state of social connection.

Though it seems reasonable that the dACC might act as a neural alarm system, detecting discrepancy and producing the subsequent feelings of distress, these two properties of dACC activity have yet to be linked. Typically, studies of the dACC as a discrepancy detector do not assess phenomenological distress and studies of the dACC's involvement in distress do not assess discrepancy detection. In order to examine whether these two properties of dACC function are two sides of the same coin, we examined two hypotheses: (1) whether individuals who tend to be distressed more often are more sensitive to discrepancy as evidenced by increased dACC activation during a discrepancy detection task, and (2) whether activating discrepancy detection processes heightens an individual's sensitivity to distress.

To test the first hypothesis, we examined whether individuals high in neuroticism, those who tend to experience distress more often, are more sensitive to discrepancy detection, as evidenced by more dACC activity to a simple discrepancy detection task (Eisenberger, Lieberman, & Satpute, in press). Because neuroticism is often defined as the tendency to experience negative affect (Costa & McCrae, 1980; Eysenck, 1967), neurotics should show a greater sensitivity to discrepancy, if discrepancy detection and distress go hand-in-hand.

In this study (Eisenberger et al., in press), participants were scanned while performing an "oddball" task, a simple discrepancy detection task in which a sequence of letters is presented, one at a time, on a computer screen. In this task, 80% of the letters are the letter "X", but participants are instructed to press a button only when they see a letter other than X. Because the base-rate expectation of seeing an X is 80%, seeing other letters violates this expectation and leads to activation of the dACC (Braver et al., 2001; Weissman et al., 2003).

It was found that heightened dACC reactivity to the oddball trials, relative to non-oddball trials, was significantly correlated with higher levels of self-reported neuroticism ($r = .76$). In other words, individuals higher in neuroticism showed more dACC reactivity to this simple discrepancy detection task, implying that heightened levels of distress and a more sensitive alarm system go hand-in-hand.

The second study investigated whether increasing the activity of the alarm system's discrepancy detector would simultaneously make distress-related cognitions more accessible, particularly in neurotics who may have a more sensitive alarm system to begin with. In this study (Eisenberger & Gable, 2004), participants were exposed to either a normal Stroop task involving discrepancy detection or a modified Stroop task containing no discrepancy (neutral task), in which individuals were simply asked to name the color of different shapes. Following the manipulation of discrepancy detection processes, participants completed a lexical decision task in which reaction times to different categories of words were assessed. Faster reaction times to a certain class of words were presumed to be indicative of cognitions that were more readily accessible. Participants were exposed to five categories of words including: (1) social rejection words ("abandonment," "rejection"); (2) negative trait words ("lazy," "dullness") to control for the negativity of the social rejection words without the social relationship component; (3) social comfort words ("love," "support"); (4) positive trait words ("charming," "clever") to control for the positivity of the social comfort words without the social relationship component; and (5) non-words ("tlinking," "worls").

In general, participants did not become more sensitive to social rejection words following discrepancy. However, individuals higher in neuroticism did. It was found that after controlling for reaction times to negative trait words, individuals higher in neuroticism were significantly faster to social rejection words following the discrepancy detection task compared to the neutral task. There were no between-group differences in reaction times to social comfort words after controlling for positive trait words, and there were no neuroticism by condition interactions. Thus, inducing minimal discrepancy detection processes made neurotics more sensitive to social rejection, suggesting that activating this system can make certain individuals more sensitive to distressing cues such as those indicating social pain. This study, along with the one described before it, provides evidence for the notion that discrepancy detection and distress are two complementary processes that underlie the functioning of the dACC.

HYPOTHESIS #3: INDUCING OR REGULATING ONE TYPE OF PAIN SIMILARLY INFLUENCES THE OTHER

In this section, we will provide evidence showing that enhancing one type of pain or its predictors should heighten an individual's sensitivity to the other type of pain (pain potentiation effects). Alternatively, reducing one type of pain or its predictors should diminish an individual's sensitivity to the other type of pain (pain regulation effects).

Pain Potentiation Effects

Whereas it seems quite intuitive that physical harm produces physical pain and that social harm produces social pain, the notion that experiencing or enhancing sensitivity to one type of pain might potentiate one's sensitivity to the other type of pain is far from obvious. However, there is at least some evidence supporting this hypothesis. Correlational accounts suggest that the experience of one kind of pain directly correlates with a heightened sensitivity to the other. For example, Bowlby noted that when children feel physical pain, they become much more sensitive to the whereabouts of their caregiver and experience distress more frequently and easily upon noting distance from the caregiver (Bowlby, 1969). Similarly, compared to healthy controls, adults with chronic pain are more likely to have an anxious attachment style, characterized by a heightened sense of concern with their partner's relationship commitment (Ciechanowski et al., 2003).

To date, no studies have experimentally manipulated physical pain to investigate the consequences for social pain or have manipulated social pain to investigate the consequences for physical pain. However, several studies have investigated the effects of failure on the experience of physical pain. If the perceived consequence of failing is that one would not be accepted or liked by others, failure could trigger feelings of social pain. This might occur for individuals who have been told that they have failed at something that they consider important for their social identity or for their acceptance or inclusion in a certain group.

In line with this, college-age participants who were informed that they performed far below average on a college entrance exam, reported heightened pain ratings to a cold-pressor task (van den Hout et al., 2000). For the college undergraduates who participated in this study, intelligence is likely to be a characteristic that is valued by themselves and their families. Failing on an academic test could signify that their family or other important social relationship members would disapprove or reject them, thus eliciting social pain and a corresponding sensitivity to physical pain. In a similar study, college-age participants who were given computerized feedback indicating that they had performed poorly on a reading comprehension task, also reported higher pain ratings to a cold-pressor task (Levine, Krass, & Padawer, 1993).

Pain Regulation Effects

Diminishing one type of pain or diminishing an individual's sensitivity to one type of pain has been shown to reduce an individual's sensitivity to the other type of pain as well. A great deal of correlational research has shown that individuals with more social support experience less cancer pain (Zaza & Baine, 2002), take less pain medication, are less likely to suffer from chest pain following coronary artery bypass surgery (King et al., 1993; Kulik & Mahler, 1989), report less labor pain, and are less likely to use epidural anasthesia during childbirth (Kennell et al., 1991). Thus the perception or presence of social support, presumably indicative of a lesser likelihood of social harm, is associated with reduced physical pain in several different health domains.

Experimental evidence has demonstrated similar effects. Animal research has shown that the presence of another animal lessens the distressing experience of painful stimulation (Epley, 1974). For example, electric shock punishment was less effective in training rats that were tested in groups than rats that were tested alone (Rasmussen, 1939), suggesting that the shocks were less aversive and thus a less effective training device when the rats were in a social group. In addition, a rat's immobility due to electric shocks was reduced by the presence of a companion rat (Davitz & Mason, 1955). Finally, baby goats displayed fewer emotional reactions to electric shock when their mother was present than when she was absent (Liddell, 1954).

Human research has shown similar effects as well (Epley, 1974). The presence of companions has been shown to reduce the amount of self-reported fear associated with electric shocks (Amoroso & Walters, 1969; Buck & Parke, 1972) and to increase participant's tolerance of intense electric shock, suggesting that painful stimulation is experienced as less painful when in the presence of a companion (Seidman et al., 1957). More recently it has been shown that participants in the presence of either a friend or a supportive stranger reported less pain to a cold-pressor task than when alone (Brown et al., 2003). In short, experimentally manipulating the presence of supportive others can reduce pain sensitivity.

More evidence for pain regulation effects comes from drug studies. Opiate-based drugs, known to reduce physical pain, have also been shown to reduce separation distress vocalizations, elicited by infant mammals when separated from their caregivers or the social group (Nelson & Panksepp, 1998; Panksepp, 1998). In fact, one of the surest ways to increase a rat's consumption of opiates (especially for female rats) is through social isolation (Alexander, Coambs, & Hadaway, 1978), as the increased consumption of opiates seems to regulate the animal's experience of isolation distress.

Antidepressant medications or selective serotonin reuptake inhibitors (SSRIs) also have similar effects on both physical and social pain. Antidepressants, typically prescribed for treating anxiety and depression, often related to or resulting from social pain, are effective in alleviating physical pain as well (Nemoto et al., 2003; Singh, Jain, & Kulkarni, 2001). In fact, antidepressants are now regularly prescribed to treat chronic pain conditions.

HYPOTHESIS #4: TRAIT DIFFERENCES RELATING TO ONE TYPE OF PAIN RELATE TO THE OTHER TYPE AS WELL.

The last hypothesis that will be considered in this chapter is that trait differences related to the sensitivity to one type of pain should also relate to the sensitivity to the other type of pain. Because neuroticism has been shown to link to both aspects of the alarm, a heightened sensitivity to discrepancy (Eisenberger et al., 2004) and heightened distress (Costa & McCrae, 1980; Eisenberger & Gable, 2004), neuroticism may well represent a trait amplification of this alarm system. As such, neuroticism should be associated with a greater sensitivity to and a more distressing experience of both physical and social pain.

Some observational evidence already exists that suggests this might be the case. Beck noted that the two of the most frequent types of anxious thoughts that neurotic individuals had, revolved around the possibility of physical harm (being attacked, being in a car accident) and the possibility of social harm (being rejected, ostracized; Beck, Laude, & Bohnert, 1974). In addition, Twenge (2000) has shown that increases in the levels of neuroticism and anxiety in the United States, over the past 40 years, directly correspond with increases in indicators of social distance (divorce rates) and increases in the prevalence of physical dangers (crime rates). In the following section, we will review evidence suggesting that neuroticism is associated with a heightened sensitivity to both physical and social pain.

Neuroticism and Physical Pain Sensitivity

Neuroticism is frequently associated with the tendency to be hypersensitive to physical symptoms, such as pain or discomfort, and to be distressed by these symptoms more often (Watson & Pennebaker, 1989). Epidemiological studies report that 50% of patients seeking treatment for medically unexplained physical symptoms, often visceral or somatic pain, are either anxious or depressed (Katon, Sullivan, & Walker, 2001). Neuroticism, along with similar constructs such as trait negative affect and trait anxiety, has also been shown to be associated with lower pain thresholds (Bisgaard et al., 2001; Pauli, Wiedemann, Nickola, 1999; Phillips & Gatchel, 2000; Shiomi, 1978; Wade & Price, 2000) and higher pain unpleasantness ratings (Wade et al., 1992). In addition, neuroticism predicts greater levels of postoperative pain following cholecystectomy (Bisgaard et al., 2001), is associated with higher pain severity ratings to chest pain symptoms (Costa et al., 1985), and is associated with higher levels of psychological distress due to pain in individuals with low back pain (BenDebba, Torgerson, & Long, 1997).

Neuroticism and Social Pain Sensitivity

Perhaps less intuitive than the neuroticism-physical pain link, is the hypothesis that neuroticism is associated with a heightened sensitivity to social pain as well. Though some have made the claim that the experience of anxiety is fundamentally a fear of social rejection or exclusion (Baumeister, 1991; Baumeister & Tice, 1990), most do not intrinsically equate neuroticism or trait anxiety with a specific sensitivity to social rejection. However, studies suggest that neuroticism is at least partly associated with a heightened sensitivity to the possibility or actuality of social pain.

Several studies have shown that neuroticism correlates well with measures assessing sensitivities to social pain, such as measures of rejection sensitivity or interpersonal sensitivity. Rejection sensitivity is defined as the tendency to expect rejection and is assessed by questions such as "How concerned or anxious would you be over whether or not this person would want to go out with you?" (Downey & Feldman, 1996; see also Romero-Canyas & Downey, this volume). Interpersonal sensitivity is defined as the tendency to react with excessive sensitivity to the interpersonal behavior of others or the perceived or actual negative evaluation by others and is assessed by statements such as "I worry about what others think of me" (Boyce & Parker, 1989). Recent studies have demonstrated that self-reported neuroticism is correlated positively with rejection sensitivity ($r = .36$; Downey & Feldman, 1996) and with interpersonal sensitivity ($r = .48$ to $r = .61$; Boyce & Parker, 1989; Gillespie, et al., 2001; Luty et al., 2002; Smith & Zautra, 2002). Self-reported neuroticism also correlates highly with self-reported generalized social anxiety ($r = .58$; Norton et al., 1997). Similarly, substance abusers who are high in neuroticism are more likely to relapse specifically from episodes of social rejection ($r = .47$; McCormick et al., 1998). Lastly, not only are neurotics more sensitive to the possibility of social rejection but they can also experience greater and longer-lasting episodes of grief following the actual loss of close others (Bailley, 2001; Ogrodniczuk et al., 2003).

CONCLUSION

There is something in staying close to men and women, and looking on them, and in the contact and odor of them, that pleases the soul well...

Walt Whitman, "I Sing the Body Electric," 1855

We began this chapter with a quote from Aristotle, who suggested that no individual would want to live without social connections. We now end this chapter with a quote by Walt Whitman, written nearly 2,000 years later, indicating a similar idea—that part of what makes life worth living is being close to others. Indeed, if asked to pinpoint the best and worst experiences of life, most of us would pick those experiences involving the making and breaking of social bonds. For most, no occasion could be happier than a marriage or the birth of a child, and none could be more painful than the loss of the ones we love. Increasingly, evidence is pointing to the importance of social connections not only for our happiness and well-being but for our survival as well. Through the studies reviewed here, we are beginning to appreciate that the need for social connection is so essential to survival, at least in mammalian species, that being left out or disconnected from the social group is processed by the brain in a manner similar to physical pain. Just as physical pain has evolved to alert us that something has gone wrong with our bodies, social pain is a similarly potent signal that alerts us when something has gone wrong with our social connections to others, an equally important threat to the survival of our species.

In this chapter we have reviewed pain overlap theory, which advances the notion that physical and social pain rely on parts of the same underlying system for their operation. We have also provided evidence for several hypotheses that can be derived from this theory. We have shown that the dACC acts as one of the neural substrates of the physical-social pain overlap and that it is involved in both the detection of physical and social danger and in the alarming experience that follows. We have shown that potentiating or regulating one of these forms of pain influences the other form of pain in a congruent manner. Lastly, we have provided some evidence to suggest that neuroticism is associated with a heightened sensitivity to indicators of both types of pain. These are not the only implications that can be derived from this theory. Other hypotheses that remain to be explored include whether physical and social pain have similar behavioral consequences, result in similar health outcomes, or share other common neural structures or neurotransmitters not reviewed here. Continuing to explore the underlying commonalities between physical and social pain may provide us with new ways of treating physical pain and new techniques for managing social pain. Perhaps most importantly, understanding this overlap may provide us with answers to two of our most fundamental questions: why it hurts to lose those we love and why being close to others "pleases the soul well."

NOTES

1. Although we will focus more specifically on the common neural structures underlying physical and social pain, we recognize that the shared opiate substrates are an important part of the physical-social pain overlap and will refer to them in a general manner throughout the chapter.

2. Although we can use the behavioral consequences of cingulotomy to inform our working knowledge of the phenomenology of ACC activation, it should be kept in mind that cingulotomies are only performed in the most extreme and severe cases of pain or anxiety. Thus, one should use caution when extrapolating from

cingulotomy patients to the general population as the functioning of this neural region may be different for healthy individuals.

3. In non-primates, the cingulate gyrus is the primary unit of analysis; whereas in primates and humans, anterior and posterior sectors of the gyrus are treated separately.

4. The evolution of play is also a uniquely mammalian behavior; however, a complete discussion of the evolution of play behavior will not be discussed here (for a full review and discussion of play, see MacLean, 1985a or Panksepp, 1998, Chapter 15).

REFERENCES

Alexander, B. K., Coambs R. B., & Hadaway P. F. (1978). The effect of housing and gender on morphine self-administration in rats. *Psychopharmacology, 58*, 175–179.

Amoroso, D. M., & Walter, R.H. (1969). Effects of anxiety and socially mediated anxiety reduction on paired-associated learning. *Journal of Personality and Social Psychology, 11*, 388–396.

Bailley, S. E. (2001). *Personality and grieving in a university student population.* Unpublished doctoral dissertation.

Baumeister, R. F. (1990). Anxiety and deconstruction: On escaping the self. In J. M. Olson & M. P.; Zanna (Eds.), *Self-inference processes: The Ontario symposium, vol. 6. Ontario symposium on personality and social psychology* (pp. 259–291). Hillsdale, NJ: Lawrence Erlbaum Associates.

Baumeister, R. F., & Tice, D. M. (1990). Anxiety and social exclusion. *Journal of Social and Clinical Psychology, 9*, 165–195.

Beck, A. T., Laude, R., & Bohnert, M. (1974). Ideational components of anxiety neurosis. *Archives of General Psychiatry, 31*, 319–325.

BenDebba, M., Torgerson, W. S., & Long, D. M. (1997). Personality traits, pain duration and severity, functional impairment, and psychological distress in patients with persistent low back pain. *Pain, 72*, 115–125.

Bisgaard, T., Klarskov, B., Rosenberg, J., & Kehlet, H. (2001). Characterisitics and prediction of early pain after laparoscopic cholecystectomy. *Pain, 90*, 261–269.

Botvinick, M. M., Braver, T. S., Barch, D. M., Carter, C. S., & Cohen, J. D. (2001). Conflict monitoring and cognitive control. *Psychological Review, 108*, 624–652.

Bowlby, J. (1969). *Attachment & Loss, Vol. I: Attachment.* New York: Basic Books.

Boyce, P., & Parker, G. (1989). Development of a scale to measure interpersonal sensitivity. *Australian and New Zealand Journal of Psychiatry, 23*, 341–351.

Braver, T. S., Barch, D. M., Gray, J. R., Molfese, D. L., & Snyder, A. (2001). Anterior cingulate cortex and response conflict: effects of frequency, inhibition and errors. *Cerebral Cortex 11*, 825–836.

Brown, J. L., Sheffield, D., Leary, M. R., & Robinson, M. E. (2003). Social support and experimental pain. *Psychosomatic Medicine, 65*, 276–283.

Buck, R. W., & Parke, R. D. (1972). Behavioral and physiological response to the presence of a friendly or neutral person in two types of stressful situations. *Journal of Personality and Social Psychology, 24*, 143–153.

Ciechanowski, P., Sullivan, M., Jensen, M., Romano, J., & Summers, H. (2003). The relationship of attachment style to depression, catastrophizing and health care utilization in patients with chronic pain. *Pain, 104*, 627–637.

Coghill, R. C., McHaffie, J. G., & Yen, Y. (2003). Neural correlates of interindividual differences in the subjective experience of pain. *Proceedings* of the *National Academy of Sciences, 100,* 8538–8542.

Costa, P. T., & McCrae, R. R. (1980). Influence of extraversion and neuroticism on subjective well-being: Happy and unhappy people. *Journal of Personality and Social Psychology, 38,* 668–678.

Costa, P. T., Zonderman, A. B., Engel, B. T., Baile, W. F., Brimlow, D. L., & Brinker, J. (1985). The relation of chest pain symptoms to angiographic findings of coronary artery stenosis and neuroticism. *Psychosomatic Medicine, 47,* 285–293.

Davis, K. D., Hutchison, W. D., Lozano, A. M., & Dostrovsky, J. O. (1994). Altered pain and temperature perception following cingulotomy and capsulotomy in a patient with schizoaffective disorder. *Pain, 59,* 189–199.

Davitz, J. R., & Mason, D. J. (1955). Socially facilitated reduction of a fear response in rats. *Journal of Comparative and Physiological Psychology, 48,* 149–151.

Deacon, T. W. (1997). *The symbolic species: The co-evolution of language and the brain.* New York: W.W. Norton.

Dollard, J., & Miller, N. E. (1950). *Personality and psychotherapy.* McGraw-Hill, New York.

Downey, G., & Feldman, S. I. (1996). Implications of rejection sensitivity for intimate relationships. *Journal of Personality and Social Psychology, 70,* 1327–1343.

Eisenberger, N. I., & Gable, S. L. (2004). *Individual differences in social distress cognitions following conflict.* Unpublished data.

Eisenberger, N. I., & Lieberman, M. D. (2004). Why rejection hurts: The neurocognitive overlap between physical and social pain. *Trends in Cognitive Sciences, 8,* 294–300.

Eisenberger, N. I., Lieberman, M. D., & Williams, K. D. (2003). Does rejection hurt: An fMRI study of social exclusion. *Science, 302,* 290–292.

Eisenberger, N. I., Lieberman, M. L., & Satpute, A. B. (2004). *Personality from a controlled processing perspective: An fMRI study of neuroticism, extraversion, and self-consciousness.* Under review.

Epley, S. W. (1974). Reduction of the behavioral effects of aversive stimulation by the presence of companions. *Psychological Bulletin, 81,* 271–283.

Eysenck, H. J. (1967). *The biological basis of personality.* Springfield, IL: Charles C. Thomas.

Foltz, E. L., & White, L. E., (1968). The role of rostral cingulotomy in "pain" relief. *International*

Journal of Neurology, 6, 353–373.

Gillespie, N. A., Johnstone, S. J., Boyce, P., Heath, A. C., & Martin, N. G. (2001). The genetic and environmental relationship between interpersonal sensitivity measure (IPSM) and the personality dimensions of Eysenck and Cloninger. *Personality and Individual Differences, 31,* 1039–1051.

Hadland, K. A., Rushworth, M. F. S., Gaffan, D., & Passingham, R. E. (2003). The effect of cingulate lesions on social behaviour and emotion. *Neuropsychologia, 41,* 919–931.

Harlow, H. F. (1958). The nature of love. *American Psychologist, 13,* 673–685.

International Association for the Study of Pain Task Force On Taxonomy (1994). *Classification of Chronic Pain: Description of Chronic Pain Syndromes and Definition of Pain Terms,* 2nd ed., H. Merskey & N. Bogduk. (eds.). Seattle, IASP Press.

Katon, W., Sullivan, M., & Walker, E. (2001). Medical symptoms without identified pathology: relationship to psychiatric disorders, childhood and adult trauma, and personality traits. *Annals of Internal Medicine, 134,* 917–925.

Kennell, J., Klaus, M., McGrath, S., Robertson, S., & Hinkley, C. (1991). Continuous emotional support during labor in U.S. hospital: A randomized control trial. *Journal of the American Medical Association, 265,* 2197–2201.

King, K. B., Reis, H. T., Porter, L. A., & Norsen, L. H. (1993). Social support and long-term recovery from coronary artery surgery: Effects on patients and spouses. *Health Psychology, 12,* 56–63.

Kirzinger, A., & Jurgens, U. (1982). Cortical lesion effects and vocalization in the squirrel monkey. *Brain Research, 233,* 299-315.

Kulik, J. A., & Mahler, H. I. (1989). Social support and recovery from surgery. *Health Psychology, 8,* 221–238.

Laplane, D., Talairach, J., Meininger, V., Bancaud, J., & Orgogozo, M. (1977). Clinical consequences of corticectomies involving the supplementary motor area in man. *Journal of the Neurological Sciences, 34,* 301–316.

Levine, F. M., Krass, S. M., & Padawer, W. J. (1993). Failure hurts: the effects of stress due to difficult tasks and failure feedback on pain report. *Pain, 54,* 335–340.

Leyton, A. S. F., & Sherrington, C. S. (1917). Observations of the excitable cortex of the chimpanzee, orangutan, and gorilla. *Quantitative Journal of Experimental Physiology, 11,* 135–222.

Liddell, H. S. (1954). Conditioning and emotions. *Scientific American, 190,* 48–57.

Lieberman, M. D., Gaunt, R., Gilbert, D. T., & Trope, Y. (2002). Reflection and reflexion: A social cognitive neuroscience approach to attributional inference. In M. Zanna (Ed.), *Advances in experimental social psychology,* 34 (pp. 199–249). New York: Academic Press.

Luty, S. E., Joyce, P. R., Mulder, R. T., Sullivan, P. F., & McKenzie, J. M. (2002). The interpersonal sensitivity measure in depression: associations with temperament and character. *Journal of Affective Disorders, 70,* 307–312.

MacDonald A. W., Cohen J. D., Stenger, V. A., & Carter C. S. (2000). Dissociating the role of the dorsolateral prefrontal and anterior cingulate cortex in cognitive control. *Science, 288,* 1835–1838.

MacLean, P. D. (1985a). Brain evolution relating to family, play, and the separation call. *Archives of General Psychiatry, 42,* 405–417.

MacLean, P. D. (1985b). Evolutionary psychiatry and the triune brain. *Psychological Medicine, 15,* 219–221.

MacLean, P. D. (1993). Perspectives on cingulate cortex in the limbic system. In B. A. Vogt & M. Gabriel (Eds.), *Neurobiology of cingulate cortex and limbic thalamus: A comprehensive handbook.* Birkhauser: Boston.

MacLean P. D., & Newman, J. D. (1988). Role of midline frontolimbic cortex in production of the isolation call of squirrel monkeys. *Brain Research, 45,* 111–123.

McCormick, R. A., Dowd, E. T., Quirk, S., & Zegarra, J. H. (1998). The relationship of NEO-PI performance to coping styles, patterns of use, and triggers for use among substance abusers. *Addictive Behaviors, 23,* 497–507.

Miller, E. K., & Cohen, J. D. (2001). An integrative theory of prefrontal cortex function. *Annual Review of Neuroscience, 24,* 167–202.

Nagasako, E. M., Oaklander, A. L. & Dworkin, R. H. (2003). Congenital insensitivity to pain: an update. *Pain, 101,* 213–219.

Nelson, E. E., & Panksepp, J. (1998). Brain substrates of infant-mother attachment: Contributions of opioids, oxytocin, and norepinephrine. *Neuroscience and Biobehavioral Reviews, 22,* 437–452.

Nemoto, H., Toda, H., Nakajima, T., Hosokawa, S., Okada, Y., Yamamoto, K., Horiuchi, R., Endo, K., Ida, I., Mikuni, M., & Goto F. (2003). Fluvoxamine modulates pain sensation and affective processing of pain in human brain. *Neuroreport, 14,* 791–797.

Norton, G. R., Cox, B. J., Hewitt, P. L., & McLeod, L. (1997). Personaltiy factors associated with generalized and non-generalized social anxiety. *Personality and Individual Differences, 22,* 655–660.

Ogrodniczuk, J. S., Piper, W. E., Joyce, A. S., McCallum, M., Rosie, J. S. (2003). NEO-five factor personality traits as predictors of response to two forms of group psychotherapy. *Internal Journal of Group Psychotherapy, 53,* 417–442.

Panksepp, J. (1998). *Affective neuroscience.* New York: Oxford University Press.

Pauli, P., Wiedemann, G., & Nickola, M. (1999). Pain sensitivity, cerebral laterality, and negative affect. *Pain, 80,* 359–364.

Peyron, R., Laurent, B., & Garcia-Larrea, L. (2000). Functional imaging of brain responses to pain. A review and meta-analysis. *Neurophysiological Clinics, 30,* 263–288.

Ploog, D. (1981). Neurobiology of primate audio-vocal behavior. Brain Research, 3, 35–61.

Price, D. D. (2000). Psychological and neural mechanisms of the affective dimension of pain. *Science, 288,* 1769–1772.

Rainville, P. (2002). Brain mechanisms of pain affect and pain modulation. *Current Opinions in Neurobiology, 12,* 195–204.

Rainville, P., Duncan, G. H., Price, D. D., Carrier, B., & Bushnell, M. D. (1997). Pain affect encoded in human anterior cingulate but not somatosensory cortex. *Science, 277,* 968–971.

Rasmussen, E. W. (1939). Social facilitation. *Acta Psychologica, 4,* 275–291.

Robinson, B. W. (1967). Vocalization evoked from forebrain in Macaca mulatta. *Physiology and Behavior, 2,* 241–255.

Schore, A. N. (2001). Effects of secure attachment relationship on right brain development, affect regulation, and infant mental health. *Infant Mental Health Journal, 22,* 7–66.

Seidman, D., Bensen, S. B., Miller, I., & Meeland, T. (1957). Influence of a partner on tolerance for a self-administered electric shock. *Journal of Abnormal and Social Psychology, 54,* 210–212.

Shiomi, K. (1978). Relations of pain threshold and pain tolerance in cold water with scores on

Maudsley Personality Inventory and Manifest Anxiety Scale. *Perceptual & Motor Skills, 47,* 1155–1158.

Singh, V. P., Jain, N. K., Kulkarni, S. K. (2001). On the anitnociceptive effect of fluoxetine, a selective serotonin reuptake inhibitor. *Brain Research, 915,* 218–226.

Smith, W. (1945). The functional significance of the rostral cingular cortex as revealed by its responses to electrical excitation. *Journal of Neurophysiology, 8,* 241–255.

Smith, B. W., & Zautra, A. J. (2002). The role of personality in exposure and reactivity to interpersonal stress in relation to arthritis disease activity and negative affect in women. *Health Psychology, 21,* 81–88.

Stamm, J. S. (1955). The function of the medial cerebral cortex in maternal behavior of rats. *Journal of Comparative Physiological Psychology, 47,* 21–27.

Tow, P. M., & Whitty, C. W. M. (1953). Personality changes after operations of the cingulate gyrus in man. *Journal of Neurology, Neurosurgery, and Psychiatry, 16,* 186–193.

Twenge, J. M. (2000). The age of anxiety? The birth cohort change in anxiety and neuroticism, 1952–1993. *Journal of Personality & Social Psychology, 79,* 1007–1021.

van den Hout, J. H. C., Vlaeyen, J. W. S., Peters, M.L., Engelhard, I. M., & van den Hout, M. A. (2000). Does failure hurt? The effects of failure feedback on pain report, pain tolerance and pain avoidance. *European Journal of Pain, 4,* 335–346.

Wade, J. B., Dougherty, L. M., Hart, R. P., Rafii, A., & Price, D. D. (1992). A canonical correlation analysis of the influence of neuroticism and extraversion on chronic pain, suffering, and pain behavior. *Pain, 51,* 67–73.

Wade, J. B., & Price, D. D. (2000). Nonpathological factors in chronic pain: Implications for assessment and treatment. In R. Gatchell & J. Weisberg (Eds.), *Personality characteristics of patients with pain* (pp. 89–107). Washington, DC: American Psychological Association.

Watson D., & Pennebaker J. W. (1989). Health complaints, stress, and distress: exploring the central role of negative affectivity. *Psychological Review, 96,* 234–254.

Weissman, D. H., Giesbrecht, B., Song, A. W., Mangun, G. R., & Woldorff, M. G. (2003). Conflict monitoring in the human anterior cingulate cortex during selective attention to global and local object features. *Neuroimage, 19,* 1361–1368.

Williams, A. C. (2002). Facial expression of pain: An evolutionary account. *Behavioral and Brain Sciences, 25,* 439–488.

Zaza, C., & Baine, N. (2002). Cancer pain and psychosocial factors: A critical review of the literature. *Journal of Pain and Symptom Management, 24,* 526–542.

PART III

INDIVIDUAL AND POPULATION DIFFERENCES AND THE IMPACT OF SOCIAL EXCLUSION AND BULLYING

8

Rejection Sensitivity as a Predictor of Affective and Behavioral Responses to Interpersonal Stress
A Defensive Motivational System

RAINER ROMERO-CANYAS
GERALDINE DOWNEY

THE LEGACY OF REJECTION

*A*s much of the research in this volume attests, the need to secure acceptance and avoid rejection from others, especially from significant and valued others is a powerful motivational drive (Baumeister & Leary, 1995; and see in this volume Fiske & Yamamoto; Sommer & Rubin; Williams & Zadro). While the need to secure acceptance and avoid rejection is universal, people differ

Address correspondence to: Geraldine Downey, 406 Schermerhorn Hall, 1190 Amsterdam Avenue. MC 5501, New York, NY 10027

considerably in how they process information about acceptance and rejection. People's history of acceptance and rejection can lead them to develop particular cognitive-affective networks that are activated in social situations where issues of acceptance and rejection are of particular salience. The activation of this network, in turn, gives rise to particular coping strategies and behaviors that individuals have learned can prevent rejection or gain acceptance. One such system is the cognitive affective processing dynamic known as sensitivity to rejection (Downey & Feldman, 1996).

In this chapter we present some of the work that we have conducted to explore the impact of rejection sensitivity on people's reactions to the real or imagined threat of rejection, as well as to actual experiences of rejection. We will show evidence in support of the idea that the rejection sensitivity (RS) processing dynamic can serve as a defense motivational system (DMS) that impacts and sometimes dictates what the individual thinks is the appropriate response to the possibility of rejection and to an actual rejection experience. Much of the work on social exclusion shows the existence of systems that allow individuals to monitor and process information about acceptance and belongingness (Pickett & Gardner, this volume; Williams & Zadro, this volume). These systems also impact the way that people respond to their social environment. We believe that rejection sensitivity is one of these systems, one that has developed from a history of repeated rejection. Rejection sensitivity generally leads to maladaptive responses to rejection, responses that ultimately bring about exclusion and rejection.

What Is RS?

Downey and Feldman conceptualized rejection sensitivity as a cognitive-affective processing dynamic or disposition to anxiously expect, readily perceive and react in an exaggerated manner to cues of rejection in the behavior of others (Downey & Feldman, 1996; Downey, Freitas, Michaelis, & Khouri, 1998). As a cognitive-affective, information-processing framework, RS affects individuals' perception of their social reality by means of expectations, perceptual biases, and encoding strategies activated in interpersonal contexts. Generally, individuals who are highly sensitive to rejection approach a social situation with anxious expectations of rejection that make them hypervigilant for signs of potential rejection. When environmental or interpersonal cues are interpreted as rejection, the high RS individual actually experiences feelings of rejection, which are likely to incite an affective or behavioral overreaction such as hostile behavior, depression, or socially inappropriate efforts to prevent, or in some way obviate the rejection (Downey & Feldman, 1996; Downey et al., 1998; Ayduk, Mendoza-Denton, Mischel, Downey, Peake, & Rodriguez, 2000). These efforts, in turn, often elicit rejection from the target of the behavior, and so the feared outcome becomes a reality for the rejection sensitive person. Because additional experiences of rejection serve to perpetuate the expectations of rejection, the RS dynamic is strengthened.

Much of the work that we have carried out over the past 10 years has investigated the functioning of the RS dynamic. Through a gamut of survey, experimental, and diary studies, we have sought to map the mechanisms that are activated in rejection sensitive individuals during social interactions. We have sought to identify the strategies that rejection sensitive people deploy in anticipation or in response to social encounters.

Consistent with our conceptualization of RS and reflecting our adoption of an expectancy-value framework (Bandura, 1986), we measure RS by looking at the expectations of rejection the individual experiences in particular situations, as well as the concern with the possibility of being rejected in the situation. Throughout our studies we have used the Rejection Sensitivity Questionnaire (the RSQ), the psychometric properties of which were documented by Downey & Feldman (1996). The RSQ for adults consists of 18 situations in which rejection by a significant other is possible. For each situation, respondents are first asked to indicate the degree of anxiety or concern about the outcome of the situation on a 6-point scale ranging from 1 (very unconcerned) to 6 (very concerned). Using a 6-point scale ranging from 1 (very unlikely) to 6 (very likely), respondents then indicate the likelihood that the other person in the situation would respond to the respondent's request in an accepting fashion. To compute the overall RS score the ratings of expectations of acceptance are reverse-coded to transform them into ratings of expectation of rejection. This score is then weighted by the rating of anxiety by multiplying the two ratings for each situation. A total, cross-situational score is obtained by averaging the product score of all, 18 situations in the measure. RSQ scores are normally distributed and reflect a relatively enduring and coherent information-processing disposition (Downey & Feldman, 1996).

When studying children, we employ the Children's Rejection Sensitivity Questionnaire (CRSQ), which is quite similar in structure to the adult RSQ (Downey, Lebolt, Rincon, & Freitas, 1998). Unlike the RSQ for adults, the CRSQ asks respondents to make a rating of how angry they would be in each of the 12 theoretical situations that constitute the measure. By multiplying the ratings of expected rejection times the anxiety score, the CRSQ yields a score of anxious expectations of rejection. Multiplying the rating of anger times the rating of expectations of rejection generates an angry expectations of rejection score.

We have used the RSQ and the CRSQ in a wide range of projects that explore the impact of RS on affective, interpersonal, and cognitive functioning. We begin a summary of this work with a theoretical account of the origins of RS and the empirical evidence in support of this theory.

THE ORIGINS OF RS

The origins of the rejection sensitivity dynamic lie in early experiences of rejection (Feldman & Downey, 1994) that teach the individual to anxiously expect rejection from significant others, and from people in general. Rejection from caretakers is one important source of these anxious expectations. Parental rejection is conveyed to children through abuse, cruelty, hostility, and physical and emotional neglect and abuse, all of which carry a message of rejection. These experiences are internalized into a legacy of rejection experiences that will impact the person's functioning in interpersonal relationships (Feldman & Downey, 1994). When the legacy of rejection is internalized, it leads the individual to expect rejection and to be concerned with its occurrence. Thus, individuals come to anxiously expect rejection. It is this expectation of rejection, and the concern with it what lies at the core of the RS dynamic.

Support for our idea that expectations of rejection originate in early experiences comes from both the attachment literature and from research on clinical disorders of interpersonal relating and functioning. Specifically, rejection sensitivity—when measured in clinical interviews as an intense, negative emotional reaction following a perceived rejection—is considered one of the core symptoms of extreme social avoidance and extreme social preoccupation. Extreme social avoidance characterizes social phobia and avoidant personality disorder, while extreme social preoccupation is characteristic of dependent depression, dependent personality disorder, and borderline personality disorder (Feldman & Downey, 1994). Research has shown that atypical or dependent depressives and social phobics are more likely than a normal person to have experienced parental rejection as children (Blatt & Zuroff, 1992; Liebowitz, Gorman, Fyer, & Klein, 1985; Parker, 1979; Parker & Hadzi-Pavlovic, 1992; Stravynski, Elie, & Franche, 1989). The behavior of individuals diagnosed with these disorders parallels that of children who are insecurely attached.

Two forms of insecure attachment styles parallel the disorders of interpersonal functioning outlined above. Individuals that were identified as anxious-avoidant, insecurely attached children are more likely to display social avoidance like that of social phobics as adults. Anxious-avoidant, insecurely attached children grow up to be adults who are distressed by intimacy and find trust difficult (Hazan & Shaver, 1987). Similarly, the social preoccupation of dependent and atypical depressives has many parallels in the behavior of children who were anxious-ambivalently, insecurely attached. As children, anxious-ambivalent individuals make continuous demands for reassurance from caretakers, but these are often accompanied by displays of hostility (Ainsworth, Blehar, Waters, & Wall, 1978). Adults who were anxious-ambivalent children tend to be plagued by concerns about the possibility of rejection and are preoccupied with avoiding it (Hazan & Shaver, 1987).

In a large survey study of college students, we learned that respondents who reported witnessing higher levels of family violence or discord during childhood were more likely to have an insecure attachment style as adults (Feldman & Downey, 1994). Participants who had anxious-avoidant or anxious ambivalent attachment styles also had significantly higher scores on the RSQ relative to participants who were securely attached. Respondents' RSQ scores mediated the impact of exposure to family violence on adult attachment style. Domestic violence and discord are forms of rejection expressed in a covert or overt fashion and as such, exposure to violence at home predicted higher levels of rejection sensitivity, which in turn predicted an insecure adult attachment style. In these analyses, RS accounts for nearly 50% of the variance in adult attachment for which exposure to violence accounted in regression models that did not include rejection sensitivity as a predictor. While this study was strictly correlational, it did provide support for our account of the origins of RS and for the impact of this processing dynamic on the patterns of behavior that people display as adults in interpersonal situations.

Peer Rejection as Predictor of Rejection Sensitivity

Recently, we have explored the origins of the RS dynamic in children by considering the impact of another source of acceptance and rejection, the peer group (Downey, Bonica, London, & Paltin, 1997). Work by other researchers had found a link between peer rejection and increases in internalizing (Burks, Dodge, & Price, 1995; Hodges & Perry, 1999; Rubin, LeMare, & Lollis, 1990) and externalizing problems in adolescents (Coie, Lochman, Terry, & Hyman, 1992; Coie, Terry, Lenox, & Lochman, 1995; DeRosier, Kupersmidt, & Patterson, 1994; Haselager, Cillessen, Van Lieshout, Riksen-Waraven, Marianne, & Hartup, 2002; Kupersmidt & Coie, 1990; Kupersmidt & Patterson, 1991). However, less empirical evidence from longitudinal studies was available to document the causal role of peer rejection in shaping the social-cognitive processes underlying these behavioral maladjustments (cf., Dodge et al., 2003; Panak & Garber, 1992). We believed that rejection sensitivity was a good candidate for the role of a mediator of the link between peer rejection and troubled behavior. Through a 2-wave, 4-month study of middle-school students, we tested the hypothesis that rejection by peers would lead to higher self-reported levels of rejection sensitivity.

Participants in Downey et al. (1997) were 6th-grade students attending a public grade school in a large city in the northeastern United States. During the first wave of data collection, participants completed the CRSQ and a peer nomination measure that would serve to measure each child's sociometric status. A week later, all participants completed the CRSQ once again, as well as measures of social avoidance and loneliness. Four months later, in the second wave of the study, participants once again completed the CSRQ and the measures of social avoidance and loneliness.

The peer nominations measure asked each child to report the names of the three children in their class they liked the best, and the name of the three children they liked the least. With this information, two social preference scores were obtained for each child: an index of how liked and an index of how disliked the child was. In a regression analysis, these indexes had unique predictive value when each child's RS scores were the predicted variable. The likeability score alone predicted a reduction in anxious expectations of rejection from time 1 to time 2, even when controlling for the index of how much peers disliked each child. We have interpreted these findings as a clear indication that children's experiences of rejection with their peers can contribute to the increase of their rejection sensitivity over time.

Work tracing the origins of rejection sensitivity has allowed us to see a clear association between the development of the RS dynamic and experiences of rejection from caretakers and peers. In the following section, we summarize some key findings from what has been the main part of the body of research about RS.

THE IMPACT OF RS ON PERSONAL AND INTERPERSONAL FUNCTIONING AFTER REJECTION

As we have conceptualized the RS dynamic, it serves as a defensive motivational system that impacts behavior and psychological functioning in many ways. Part of the research conducted over the past 10 years has looked at the way RS influences adjustment in children and adults by directing, to different extents, long-term and short-term affective responses to rejection.

RS and Internalizing Problems in Children and Adolescents

As part of our study on the impact of peer rejection in the development of the RS dynamic, (Downey et al., 1997) we explored the hypothesis that RS could predict children's maladjustment. In the study, rejection sensitivity clearly predicted troubled affect in children. Anxious expectations of rejection at the onset of the project were associated with increases in scores in social avoidance scales at time of the second data collection, 4 months later. Both angry and anxious expectations of rejection at the start of the study predicted loneliness 4 months later. Children who anxiously expected rejection were more likely to become socially avoidant and experience loneliness because they had little contact with others. Children who angrily expected rejection were more likely respond to cues of rejection in a hostile manner, eliciting rejection.

We believe that the RS dynamic of children is maintained into adulthood, and as such, it impacts psychological and social functioning in adults, much like attachment researchers have theorized that an individual's attachment style as a child will shape adult attachment style (Hazan & Shaver, 1987). The behavioral pattern of high RS children perpetuates the RS dynamic by eliciting rejection or minimizing positive social interactions that may lead to acceptance. High RS children who anxiously expect rejection are socially withdrawn, and high RS children who angrily expect rejection are aggressive toward their peers. Those who anxiously expect rejection and avoid social contact will not experience acceptance or learn to interact with peers and significant others, while those who angrily expect rejection will continue to elicit the feared outcome, expanding the gamut of their rejection experiences, thus strengthening their angry expectations.

RS and Internalizing Problems in Adults

Given the theorized causal role of personal loss on the onset of depression (Brown & Harris, 1978; Bowlby, 1980), we have explored the possibility that RS may be one of the links between rejection and depression (Ayduk, Downey, & Kim, 2001). We reasoned that interpersonal loss should lead to depressive symptoms to the extent that the said loss conveys a rejection message. We theorized that individuals who expect rejection and are highly concerned with its occurrence are more likely to become depressed after a rejection experience. Expecting rejection alone, without concern about its occurrence (and vice versa) should not be sufficient to elicit depressive symptoms. This vulnerability to post-rejection depression is captured in RS itself.

Women are at a higher risk for depression than are men (Kessler & Zhao, 1999) and find interpersonal difficulties to be more distressful than do men (Rudolph & Hammen, 1999). Hence, when looking at the impact of RS on depression, we looked at college age women. Two weeks prior to arriving at their college, participants in our study completed the RSQ and various other measures, including the Beck Depression Inventory (BDI), and Levy and Davis' (1988) Adult Attachment Questionnaire. At the end of their school year, participants completed the same measures and, in addition completed a questionnaire that served to generate their dating history over the past year, including information about break-ups and about who had initiated those break-ups (Ayduk et al., 2001).

Because we predicted that RS would lead to depression after an interpersonal loss that is perceived as a rejection, we compared the impact of RS on depressive symptoms among participants who had recently experienced a breakup and among those who had not. Furthermore, we were interested in showing that after a partner initiated the breakup, individuals who were higher in RS would report more depressive symptomatology relative to individuals low in RS. A partner-initiated breakup should be interpreted as a rejection by all people whereas a mutually-initiated or self-initiated rejection would not, due in large part to the greater degree of control the individual exercises over those situations.

As expected, RS predicted higher scores on the BDI at the end of the school year for participants who had experienced a partner-initiated breakup during the 6 months preceding the end of the school year. The experience of a partner-initiated breakup alone was not a predictor of depression, but the interaction of rejection sensitivity and having experienced a romantic rejection was a statistically significant predictor. For those women whose partners had initiated a breakup, RS did predict more depressive symptomatology. By contrast, RS had no statistically reliable effect on the BDI scores of participants who had not experienced any breakups or on the BDI scores of participants who had initiated the breakup in some manner.

In order to ensure that RS is not a general vulnerability to depression following stress, we looked at RS as a predictor of depression after an academic setback (Ayduk et al., 2001) by comparing young women who had not met their own expectations of academic success to those who had met or exceeded them. RS did not predict depressive symptomatology for either group, a fact consistent with our assumption that high RS individuals react in intensely negative ways to rejection because it represents failure to attain a goal (avoid rejection and gain acceptance) in an important domain, that of interpersonal relations. When the relevant goal is not in the highly valued domain of interpersonal relations, RS does not predict the impact of failure to meet the goal.

We have found that RS can also predict depressive symptoms in men (Romero-Canyas, Downey & Cavanaugh, 2003). Unlike high RS women, high RS men seem to develop more depressive symptomatology when they experience a lower social status, or feel devalued by peers, a fact that is consistent with work by other researchers on sex differences in collective identity (Baumeister & Sommer, 1997; Brewer & Gardner, 1996; Gabriel & Gardner, 1999). Hence, we find that on a college campus where the political atmosphere is predominantly liberal, conservative men who are highly rejection sensitive report feeling devalued and disliked by their peers. These same men obtain higher scores in the depressive symptoms scale of the SCL-90. We find no relation between RS and depressive symptoms in men from the same sample who consider themselves to be liberal. For women, political orientation does not interact with RS to predict their feelings of trust or belonging at the university, or their scores on the depressive symptoms scale of the SCL.

We have conducted research suggesting that RS can also impact social avoidance in adult males, just as it does in children. In a study of dating violence, anxious expectations of rejection predict different outcomes depending on the level of involvement of the individual in the maintenance and pursuit of romantic relationships (Downey, Feldman, & Ayduk, 2000). For young men who were romantically involved with someone and who valued being in a romantic relationship, RS predicted a greater probability of engaging in some sort of violent behavior against their partner. Anxious expectations of rejection did not predict social anxiety, or any other sign of social withdrawal in men who valued involvement in their relationship.

For men who reported that being in a romantic relationship was not important to them, RS did not predict violence against a romantic partner (all participants were dating someone at the time of the study). For these men who do not value romantic relationships, anxious expectations of rejection predicted higher levels of social anxiety, a finding that mirrors those we have obtained with children. More importantly, for these men, RS predicted having a smaller number of close friends, relative to their low RS peers who were not invested in romantic relationships. Finally, high RS, un-invested men also reported a smaller number of significant, past, dating relationships.

It seems that for young men, anxious expectations of rejection are highly correlated with socially avoidant coping strategies, just as in children, and, in many ways, as is the case for women with many symptoms of depression. These finding are consistent with our hypothesis that anxious expectations of rejection interact with other personality (e.g., need for romantic involvement) and environmental factors (e.g., rejection cues) and dictate different defensive strategies such as social avoidance. These social withdrawal strategies are long-term responses to the rejection experience that do not occur in one discrete instance, but rather over an extended period of time. While the affective states that result from social withdrawal are not likely to be permanent or reach clinical levels, they may become the established response pattern to stressful social situations. Most of these maladaptive strategies probably lead to the social outcome that rejection sensitive individuals fear the most: rejection and absence of acceptance.

Much of our work over the past 10 years has looked at a different set of sequelae to rejection and cues of possible rejection, the immediate, behavioral, and affective responses to rejection. We have studied these responses not only in terms of when and how they are elicited from the high RS individual, but also in terms of the impact that they have on those around highly rejection sensitive people. As we will present in the following section, these immediate, short-term responses are just as likely to lead to the feared outcome as the long-term responses. Furthermore, we have evidence that these short-term responses are very likely to elicit rejection from the socially desirable target, and thus perpetuate the rejection sensitive individual's expectations of rejection, and paradoxically, their reliance on the maladaptive coping strategies that RS activates.

RS AS A PREDICTOR OF HOSTILE AND DISTRESSED RESPONSES TO REJECTION

Early in the research on RS, we detected a link between rejection and hostile intentions on the part HRS individuals toward those who they believe have rejected or could reject them (Downey & Feldman, 1996; Feldman & Downey, 1994). This is consistent with research on the experience of rejection in general, which has documented a robust link between the experience of rejection and aggression against others (Twenge, Baumeister, Tice, & Stucke, 2001). We have investigated the impact of RS on the rejection-aggression link extensively, and have documented it in both adults and children.

RS as a Predictor of Hostility in Children

Building on the work of other researchers (Dodge, 1980), we set out to show that children's expectations about the behavior of their peers toward them could impact their responses to perceived cues of rejection and acceptance. We presented a group of children with two situations in which a teacher or a group of peers treated them in an ambiguous manner that could be interpreted as rejecting (Downey et al., 1998). We found that RS predicted a greater endorsement of hostile responses to the rejection. In the case of the teacher, an example item was "I would feel like hitting someone or something" or "Next time when the teacher wants me to be quiet in class, I won't."

We tested the link between RS and hostile affect in an experimental study. An experimenter came to the middle school and interviewed each child individually in a private classroom. After a few minutes, the experimenter mentioned that it would be useful to continue the interview with another child, and asked the participant to choose a friend from class to join them. A research assistant went to get the child's friend, and returned a few minutes later. The research assistant reported to half of the children that the child's chosen peer did not want to join them. The other half of the children were told that the teacher could not let their friend leave the classroom at the moment. For those children who were led to believe that their friend had refused to help, RS predicted an increase in levels of emotional distress.

We also looked at RS as a predictor of aggression against and from peers at school. A year after completing the CRSQ, children completed a questionnaire that allowed them to report incidents of aggression in which they were either the victim or the aggressor. RS at time 1 was strongly associated with reporting more incidents of aggression and victimization. Likewise, RS as measured at time 1 predicted the probability of conflict with adults and peers when we used official school data as the index of conflict.

RS and Hostile Responses to a Perceived Rejection

Downey and Feldman (1996) showed that high RS adult participants in a laboratory study felt more rejected after an interaction with a friendly confederate ended without explanation. Through experiments such as this, and from diary studies (that we will describe below) we came to realize that the distress experienced by highly rejection sensitive individuals after what they interpret as a rejection is noticeable to others and can take many forms. One reaction that was particularly salient was a display of hostility immediately after a rejection experience, much like the hostile intent manifested by children (Downey et al., 1998). While both boys and girls reported this impulse toward aggression, in adults, the rejection-aggression linked seemed more salient in women than in men (Ayduk, Downey, Testa, Yen, & Shoda, 1999).

We set out to explore the possibility that a link between thoughts of rejection and thoughts of aggression exists in the cognitive-affective networks that are activated in women when they think of rejection. To this end we conducted a study of the automaticity of the link between thoughts of aggression and rejection using a sequential priming-pronunciation paradigm (Ayduk et al., 1999). Using this paradigm, we tested the idea that rejection words would facilitate pronunciation of aggression and hostility-related words in highly rejection sensitive women.

As we expected, high RS women responded to hostility words following rejection words significantly faster than did low RS women. RS did not impact response time to rejection words following hostility words, thus showing that the link between rejection and hostility is unidirectional. Non-rejection negative words or neutral words did not facilitate pronunciation of hostility words for high or low RS women. We have interpreted this pattern of findings as indicative of the fact that thoughts of hostility are not more chronically accessible to high RS women, but rather, that they are made more accessible when the high RS person is primed with thoughts of rejection.

Recently, we have replicated these findings with college age men (Ayduk & Downey, 2003). Consistent with research about young men's concerns with social status (Gabriel & Gardner, 1999), college age men are quicker to respond to hostility words when these are preceded by a rejection word that implies rejection from individuals and groups (e.g., banish, ditch). Hence, we know that thoughts of rejection prime thoughts of hostility in men and in women. Knowing this, we set out to show that the hostile thoughts activated by RS can translate into hostile behavior. Through a variety of studies we explored the link between RS and indirect, retaliatory hostility as expressed in the form of the evaluation participants make of those who have rejected them.

In one study (Ayduk et al., 1999), women were brought into the laboratory and told that they would be interacting with an opposite sex individual over the Internet. Participants were asked to write a biographical sketch and received a bio-sketch of the individual with whom they would be interacting, purportedly, in a few minutes. After the exchange of biographical information, participants in the experimental condition were told that the second participant did not want to continue being a part of the study. Those in the control condition were told that there had been some equipment failure and that the experiment would have to end at that moment. All participants were then given the opportunity to evaluate the fictitious other participant. As we expected, for women in the experimental condition, RS scores predicted a more negative evaluation of the partner while RS had no effect on the ratings made by participants in the control condition.

When we used this very same paradigm with male participants, RS did not predict retaliatory hostility. Given our findings, and anecdotal suggestions from participants, we decided to create a new situation that would make the rejection public (Ayduk & Downey, 2004). We conducted a study with a paradigm that was almost identical to the one described above, but implemented an additional manipulation. At the onset of the study, participants were told another same sex participant would be watching them through a video circuit. A camera was set up in the lab to make the cover story believable. While this manipulation did not impact the behavior of women in any way, it did impact men's behavior. For male participants in the condition in which the fictitious partner left the study and a second participant was watching the proceedings, RS predicted a less positive evaluation of the ambiguously rejecting partner. In the control condition, the addition of the camera did not modify the behavior of male participants. Thus, consistent with our findings about the impact of social devaluation on high RS men, we find that after a public rejection, RS predicts defensive, reactive hostility as it does for women after a private rejection by the other member of a dyad.

Our work on RS and violence in romantic relationships (Downey et al., 2000) also showed us that RS predicts aggression in men under the threat of rejection. High RS male college students who are highly invested in their relationships are more likely to report in survey studies that they would engage in dating violence. Rejection sensitivity did not predict more violence in male college students who were involved in relationships but did not regard being in a relationship as important to them.

Through a series of diary studies we have examined the rejection-hostility link in the natural context of people's relationships (Ayduk et al., 1999; Downey et al., 1998; Ayduk & Downey, 2004). In all of these studies both members of heterosexual couples completed a daily diary study for at least two weeks. Every day, as part of the daily diary, participants were asked to make ratings of how they had felt that day. Every day participants also reported whether or not they had experienced some sort of conflict with their partner. Overall RS does not predict probability of reporting conflict in these studies. However, we found that RS does predict probability of conflict on days after days when participants feel higher levels of rejection (Ayduk et al., 1999; Ayduk & Downey, 2003).

The Great Paradox Inherent in RS: The Self-Fulfilling Prophecy

Our study of the emergence of hostility after rejection has led us to observe that high RS people, overtly concerned as they are with rejection, are more likely to elicit rejection from significant others. As outlined above, some rejection sensitive people withdraw socially in an effort to avoid rejection, but in so doing they also avoid opportunities for acceptance. Other high RS individuals respond with hostility and negative affect to cues of rejection, a reaction that is likely to elicit rejection.

In diary studies we have looked at RS as a predictor of breakup for romantic couples. In one study (Downey et al., 1998) we found that a year after completing a daily diary study, 44% of the participating couples that had included a high RS woman had separated, whereas only 15% of the couples that included a low RS woman had done so. Of those couples that included a high RS man, 42% had broken up a year after the diary study, and only 15% of the couples that included a high RS man had broken up.

In this study, the RS score of one member of the couple affected the second member's ratings of dissatisfaction with the relationship on days preceded by conflict. We believed that RS would predict more dissatisfaction after conflict, and found that this was the case. Partners of high RS women reported significantly higher levels of relationship dissatisfaction after a conflict relative to partners of low RS women. We found no such pattern for days that were not preceded by conflict (or for partners of men in general).

These data also revealed that low and high RS individuals differed in the extent to which they were aware of their partner's affective response to the conflict. High RS women perceived their partners to be less accepting on days preceded by conflict, while low RS women did not. These findings suggest that the partners' reactions were evident in their behavior to some degree on days preceded by conflict. This idea is supported by the finding that partners' dissatisfaction partially mediated the effect of RS on women's feelings of rejection on days preceded by conflict, so that the more dissatisfied the partners were, the more rejected the women felt.

Spurred by these findings, we sought to study the mediating role of partners' feelings in a controlled environment. We conducted a laboratory experiment (Downey et al., 1998) in which both members of a couple engaged in a discussion about a topic from a pre-selected list of topics we had pilot-tested among college students. The videotaped interactions were coded by independent raters who were trained to use the Marital Interaction Coding System-IV (MICS-IV; Weiss & Summers, 1983) and who looked for signs of negative affect and of negative behavior toward the partner.

We found that for partners of men, having a high RS partner did not predict negative mood after the discussion. For partners of women, partner's RS predicted greater levels of anger after the discussion, even when controlling for pre-conflict anger. Rejection sensitivity also predicted more negative behavior during the discussion for women, even when controlling for their partner's initial mood (Downey et al., 1998). Hence, high RS women were more likely than low RS women to assume a negative mindset or motivation on the part of their partner, use a hostile tone of voice, deny responsibility for a problem, express disgust or displeasure, demean or mock their partner, and show dysphoric affect (depression, sadness, or a whiny voice). After we introduced the coders' ratings of women's negative behaviors toward their partners as a mediator of the impact of women's RS on their partners' post-conflict anger, we found that the ratings of negative behavior account for 54% of the effect of women's RS on their partner's negative affect after the discussion.

These findings provide support for our proposal that the behavioral and affective responses of highly rejection sensitive individuals to the threat of rejection (e.g., a discussion or conflict) tend to elicit negative affect from those around them. In turn, this negative affect may impel the recipient of these maladaptive strategies to withdraw and realize the high RS individuals' fears of being rejected.

Given our findings about high RS men's responses to conflict in relationships (Downey et al., 2000), we were not surprised by the gender differences that have emerged in some of the studies. Our work suggests that for college age men (the group of men most commonly used in our work) conflicts in relationships evoke responses similar to those of women if the young men are invested in the relationship to a great degree, or if the rejection results in a loss of social status or a humiliation (Ayduk & Downey, 2004). Some of our most recent work, which we outline below, supports this idea that the focus of young men's rejection concerns is the larger social group.

The two studies described above and those described previously all looked at the link between RS and negative affective responses, or socially avoidant behaviors. The negative response of high RS individuals to cues of rejection engenders a correspondingly negative response in their romantic partners or significant others. In turn these negative responses are perceived as rejection and strengthen the expectations of rejection held by the rejection sensitive individual.

Hostility and anger, however, are not the only behaviors that may elicit a negative response from others. Sometimes, positive and typically benign behaviors, when manifested in a socially inappropriate time and place, may elicit rejection. The link between these behaviors and rejection sensitivity has recently become part of the scope of our work.

RS AND EFFORTS TO SECURE ACCEPTANCE

Within the last couple of years, we have begun to explore a different set of behaviors that rejection sensitive individuals manifest when threatened with rejection. These behaviors are not, on the surface, as negative as those described in the preceding sections of this chapter. However, these responses may be equally maladaptive for the individual and, possibly, as likely to elicit rejection and hostility from significant others and desirable social targets. These behaviors are generally benign acts—such as buying a gift or doing a favor for someone—but high RS individuals manifest them in an exaggerated and inappropriate manner and time. We believe that high RS individuals deploy these strategies, ingratiation behaviors, when they are faced with situations and social encounters in which they have come to expect rejection (and which some high RS individuals would rather avoid, but may not be able to). Ingratiation behaviors are especially likely to appear when the threat of rejection is concomitant with the possibility of securing acceptance from the person from whom rejection is expected or from other members of a plural social unit, like a group of peers or friends.

This line of work stemmed from the study of RS as a predictor of adolescent girls' problems in romantic relationships (Purdie & Downey, 2000). In a survey study of 154 minority girls from disadvantaged backgrounds, we learned that higher levels of rejection sensitivity predicted greater feelings of jealousy about romantic partners, expressed as preoccupation for what the partner was doing when not with the respondent. We reasoned that the constant concern about their boyfriends' whereabouts manifested by high RS girls could be interpreted not only as a sign of jealousy but also of need to monitor the significant other and keep him close. If that was the case, high RS girls should also be more willing to engage in behaviors that they believe would keep their boyfriends close and secure acceptance. We found that, indeed, high RS girls reported being more willing to do anything to keep their boyfriends, even if that meant doing something they thought was wrong (Purdie & Downey, 2000).

Inspired by this work, we set out to see if RS would predict other-directed behavior in situations laden with the simultaneous possibility of rejection and acceptance. We wanted to carry out this exploration by putting people in a situation in which even high RS individuals that are generally socially avoidant would be forced to interact with the social target. We conducted our studies looking at participants' efforts to gain acceptance from novel social targets that were unknown to the participant until the time of the study. Our rationale was that as they approached a novel social target all people should see that the possibility of acceptance and rejection coexist in that first encounter. The prior history that accompanies an established relationship would not interfere with the participants' efforts to gain acceptance. The first behavior we studied was self-presentation, how the participants presented themselves to the new social target.

RS and Self-Presentation in Anticipation of Rejection

In the first of our studies on the role of RS on efforts to secure acceptance, we brought participants into the lab and had them complete a battery of measures that included a series of questions about their attitudes about politics, religion, arts, and sports, as well as their involvement with campus activities in these domains. The experimenters then told them that we would be assigning them to an Internet group based on their responses to the questionnaire and that they would then have a chance to create an online profile to introduce themselves to the group members. During a second session, participants would purportedly get to see the responses the other group members made to their profiles.

While participants completed a battery of measures, an experimenter pretended to assign the participant to an Internet group and opened a Web-site containing the profiles of six individuals. Each profile included a short narrative written by real participants in past studies, as well as a series of numerical self-ratings that the group members have purportedly made about their beliefs and attitudes. In essence, each profile mirrored the first questionnaire the participant had completed at the start of the experiment.

Once participants had completed the second questionnaire packet, they were asked to sit at the computer and read the profiles of the group members. After the last profile came up, participants found a Web page that allowed them to create their own profile by writing an introduction and completing an online version of the attitudes questionnaire they had completed earlier. After they had filled out the online form, the experimenter handed participants a brief questionnaire and explained that there would be no second session of the experiment.

We used this paradigm to see if RS would predict changes in the ratings that participants made of themselves along various dimensions as a function of how different from the group participants were. We focused on the differences between the private ratings participants made in their questionnaire packet and the ratings they made in the public profile that group members would see. We found that all participants shifted toward or away from the group mean in accordance of campus stereotypes. In the small, liberal arts environment of our campus, having interest in the arts and humanities is highly valued, while being athletic is associated with the stereotype of the "jock," and thus carries with it some negative connotations. In accordance with these stereotypes, participants who rated themselves less artistic than their Internet group tended to shift toward the group mean. RS had a powerful impact on this shift and magnified it. Likewise, we predicted that for athleticism, those participants who were much more athletic than the group would decrease their public ratings and shift toward the group mean, presenting themselves as less athletic than they did initially. This was the case only for high RS individuals, and the impact of RS was particularly strong for high RS women.

We used this same paradigm to look at whether high RS individuals would shift their ratings along a dimension that was particularly important to them, one that could also be a reason for rejection because it carries some stigma (Romero-Canyas, Downey, Pelayo, & Bashan, 2004). We decided to look at whether RS would predict changes in self-ratings of political conservatism when the participant was placed in a group of highly liberal individuals as opposed to a situation in which the participant was placed in a highly conservative group. Past work (Romero-Canyas et al., 2003) had shown that RS predicted depressive symptoms among conservative men, as well as feelings of alienation and stigmatization; hence, we knew that high RS, conservative men believe that being conservative would be likely to elicit rejection. We anticipated that these feelings would be particularly salient when we conducted the study—at the onset of President George W. Bush's efforts to depose Iraq's Saddam Hussein, a time when the campus was particularly anti-conservative.

Participants in this study were brought into the lab and received the same cover story as all other participants, but they were randomly assigned to a highly liberal group or a highly conservative group. As we expected, highly conservative, high RS men who were placed in the liberal group decreased their self-ratings of conservatism at the time of their public presentation to the group. We also found a similar trend for conservative women. By contrast, we did not find that liberal individuals changed their ratings of conservatism significantly in the highly conservative condition.

Encouraged by these findings, we decided to look at the efforts high RS individuals would make after an initial, rejecting encounter to gain acceptance from a social target. Again, we looked at a group situation, assuming that if participants did not know how many members there were in the group, rejection by some of them would not lead them to discard the possibility of gaining acceptance from other members of the social group.

RS as a Predictor of Ingratiation Efforts
Following Rejection Experiences

Our laboratory has looked at the efforts high RS individuals make after rejection to obviate that rejection and to secure acceptance. We believe that high RS individuals may do this by engaging in ingratiating behaviors. Other rejection researchers have found that after rejection experiences, people often manifest prosocial behaviors if they are given the opportunity to win back acceptance and replenish their belonging needs (Sommer, Williams, Ciarocco, & Baumeister, 2001; Sommer & Rubin, this volume).

Our first study exploring ingratiation utilized a paradigm similar to the one we used in the study of self-presentation. This time, however, participants did not read about their Internet groups in advance. Rather, they sent out an e-mail to the members of their group through an e-mail account set up for them by the experimenter. Participants sent out their introduction without any knowledge about the group members other than the fact that the group was "compatible" with them. Participants returned to the lab a day later to read the responses other group members had made to their introduction and to complete a series of questionnaires. The e-mail groups were not real, but were simulated by an automatic responder that sent out automatic messages and by experimenters using a pre-established template. All participants received four e-mails, one from each of four characters. We randomly assigned participants to one of three conditions, in each of which the purported members of the group sent the same e-mail messages, except for minor modifications, intended to create the three conditions. In the acceptance condition, all four messages were warm and welcoming. Two of the messages were automatic, and two were tailored to the participant by including mention of something the participant liked to do. Hence, if the participant said she enjoyed reading poetry and dancing, one character said that he enjoyed poetry as well, and another said that she liked dancing, too. Similarly, in the harsh rejection condition, all four messages were cold, rude and rejecting. One character would say that he hated some activity the participant liked, and a second character would say he hated another activity or like of the participant. The final condition was one in which the group was ambivalent about the participant. There were no personalized messages in this condition, but all characters were rather lukewarm and questioned the match between the group and the participant.

During the second experimental session participants read responses they received from the group and sent out a response to the group. They then filled out a questionnaire packet in which we assessed their ingratiation intentions. We measured these intentions by asking participants how likely they would be to carry out a series of tasks for the group, including organizing a live meeting of the group, cooking dinner, and sorting and archiving past messages exchanged by group members. The questionnaire also asked participants to report how much money they would be willing to donate to a possible group meeting, and to make ratings about their mood, their feelings toward the group, and their interest in meeting the group.

In the acceptance condition, participants' RS scores predicted more willingness to carry out tasks for the group and to make a larger donation, as well as more positive feelings toward the group. However, in the ambivalent, mildly rejecting condition, RS predicted less willingness to ingratiate, a smaller donation, and more negative feelings toward the group. When we compare the harsh rejection condition to the other condition, we find some interesting gender differences. After rejection, RS predicts a response from women that is consistent with our past work (Ayduk et al., 1999). Hence, following rejection RS predicts less ingratiation intentions, a smaller donation, and more negative feelings toward the group for women. Consistent with work on the importance of collective identity and status for men (Brewer & Gardner, 1996; Gabriel & Gardner, 1999), being denigrated by some group members elicits efforts to secure acceptance from the other group members, even though the participant has not encountered them. Thus, RS predicts the opposite for men as it does for women. After the rejection from some group members, RS predicts more willingness to ingratiate and to make a large monetary contribution to the live meeting of the group, more interest in that meeting and more positive feelings toward the group.

In a more recent study we have found that RS also predicts ingratiating behaviors toward the experimenter after a rejection. In a replication of the above study we added a new component. At the end of the experiment, before debriefing, the experimenter accidentally knocks off a container of thumbtacks as he exits the room to get the participants' payment. We measured the length of time that elapses from the moment the container falls until the participant begins to pick up the tacks. We also count the number of tacks that are collected by each participant.

In the ambiguous condition, RS is unrelated to picking the tacks. In the harsh rejection condition RS does predict the onset of pick up of the thumbtacks and the number of tacks that are collected. So, high RS men and women both begin to pick up the tacks more quickly, sometimes even before the experimenter has left the room. High RS participants are also more likely to collect all the tacks, even though they end up hurting their fingers.

The findings from these experiments are consistent with our past findings of RS as leading to social rejection. Their willingness to transform themselves into a different person to gain acceptance, and their apparently servile behavior after a rejection experience may elicit mistrust and suspicion from the social target from whom the high RS individual seeks acceptance. These findings are also consistent of with our view of RS as a defensive motivational system that prepares the individual to function in their social environment but which has gone awry because of early experiences of rejection.

RS AS A DEFENSIVE MOTIVATIONAL SYSTEM

In recent years we have begun to think of RS as a defensive motivational system sensitive to the social environment, but because it has resulted from a history of rejection, the system functions in a way that generates a maladaptive response. Our work suggests that high RS individuals seem incapable of assessing the socially appropriate response to the cues of rejection that they perceive around them. Perhaps because they are overtly anxious about the possibility of the realization of their fears, high RS individuals cannot allow themselves the time to assess the socially appropriate response, or the most adaptive and least harmful response. Instead, high RS individuals act on an automatic impulse. Thus, some high RS individuals shun others to avoid rejection while others confront the potential rejecter in a "fight or flight" response. Similarly, other high RS individuals counteract the negative social experience by making efforts to obviate the rejection and engage in what can be deemed as tend-and-befriend (Taylor, Klein, Lewis, Gruenewald, Gurung, & Updegraff, 2000) behaviors, like ingratiation.

While we have shown that RS tends to lead to maladaptive behavior, we also have hints that under certain situations, the RS dynamic can lead to adaptive behaviors that are beneficial to the individual. Specifically, we have found that when women who are high in RS are asked to recall a rejection they experienced and are then given the opportunity to perform on a cognitive task, they actually perform better on the task than if asked to recall an acceptance or nothing at all. This is not true of women low in RS (Halim & Downey, 2004). Although these findings are preliminary, they have led us to speculate that for rejection sensitive women, the opportunity to engage in and do well in another task may be particularly appealing as a way out of thinking about rejection. Doing well on the task may also provide an opportunity for gaining the positive regard of others (in this case the experimenter). Thus, when high RS individuals are consciously aware of their rejection concerns they may be able to actively and consciously distract when the possibility for engaging in tasks that may provide alternative sources of acceptance or gratification are available, a fact consistent with work on rejection experiences in general (Sommer & Rubin, this volume). We would suggest that this ability to pursue alternative sources of acceptance or personal gratification illustrates how RS is distinct from low self-esteem. High RS individuals are motivated by a desire to gain acceptance or avoid rejection and when such opportunities present themselves they will act energetically to pursue them. An essential component of global low self-esteem is negative evaluation of the self and of one's abilities to achieve one's goals. It is can be construed as a simple evaluative framework for interpreting the world: "I'm no good and others agree and treat me accordingly. If their behavior indicates otherwise they are being insincere." By contrast we view RS as a defensive motivational system that becomes activated quickly and automatically when cues of rejection are present leading to actions to defend against the threat of rejection.

What evidence is there that supports the view that RS operates as a defensive motivational system? In addition to the behavioral data outlined above, we have recently found evidence in support of this assumption in a startle paradigm study showing that in the face of rejection-relevant cues individuals high in RS showed heightened potentiation of the startle response, a robust autonomic nervous system indicator of activation in the defensive motivational system (Lang, Bradley, & Cuthbert, 1990; see Dawson, Schell, & Bohmelt, 1999). Research on both animals and humans suggests that when the DMS is activated by the potential of danger, there is an amplification of physiological responses to newly encountered threat-congruent cues, and an attenuation of physiological response to threat-incongruent cues. That is, the organism is oriented to detect cues that are congruent with a state of threat and to act when confirmatory cues are detected (see Lang, et al., 2000). When the appetitive system is activated there should be a relative dampening of physiological responses to threatening cues. The rationale underlying this paradigm is that when an organism is already in a high-arousal, negatively valenced state, independently evoked defensive responses such as the eye-blink response to an unexpected loud noise are augmented (Lang et al., 1990; 2000). For example, when individuals are viewing a picture depicting a gun pointing toward them, they show exaggerated startle (indexed by the magnitude of their eye-blink response) when disturbed by an unexpected loud noise. The eye-blink is a reflexive defensive response that follows unexpected and averse stimuli. Both the picture and the noise are unpleasant and both evoke defensive responses. The magnitude of the startle response to the loud noise is potentiated, however, because the individual is already in a defensive state due to viewing the unpleasant, arousing picture. Conversely, when viewing a positively arousing pictorial stimulus, independently evoked defensive responses are attenuated because the individual is in an appetitive state. Thus, startle reflex magnitude changes systematically with the valence of the psychological context (Lang et al., 1990).

Previous studies have used the startle probe paradigm to infer individual differences in the extent to which DMS is activated in a particular psychological context. For example, people with a specific phobia are more responsive than nonphobics to a startle probe such as a noise burst that is presented in the presence of a phobia-relevant stimulus, but not to the same probe when it is presented in the presence of a phobia-irrelevant negative stimulus (e.g., Hamm, Cuthbert, Globisch, & Vaitl, 1999).

Capitalizing on this research, we used the startle probe paradigm to examine individual differences in DMS activation in the presence of rejection cues as a function of RS (Downey, Mougios, Ayduk, London, & Shoda, 2004). We hypothesized that the operation of the RS dynamic entails a context-dependent activation of the DMS, and thus expected HRS people, relative to those low in RS, to show a greater relative increase in eye-blink magnitude following a startle probe presented in a rejection-relevant context (e.g., when viewing pictures depicting rejecting themes).

We expected no differences between high and low RS people in the magnitude of startle response in a negative but rejection-irrelevant context.

In contrast to rejection, we hypothesized that RS would *not* covary systematically with reactions to acceptance. Thus, we expected that high and low RS people would *not* differ in their eye-blink magnitude following a startle probe presented in an acceptance-relevant context (e.g., when viewing pictures depicting acceptance themes) compared to a positively valenced but acceptance-irrelevant context.

Based on extensive pilot work, we used pictures by Edward Hopper to depict rejection and by Renoir to depict acceptance. As controls, we identified artists whose work was characterized by non-representational depictions of positive (Joan Miró) and negative themes (Mark Rothko). Consistent with predictions, when viewing art depicting rejection themes by Hopper, people high in RS showed an amplified eye-blink following a loud noise, relative to their eye-blink response when viewing the other types of art work. Those low in RS did not. This finding indicates that when HRS individuals are viewing rejection-related stimuli they show heightened DMS activation. We found no evidence that acceptance cues (Auguste Renoir) elicit a positive, appetitive motivational state in HRS individuals to a greater extent than in LRS individuals. These findings support our view that acceptance and rejection are not of equivalent importance for HRS individuals and that RS system develops specifically to protect the self against the threat of rejection. Work is underway to link peripheral evidence of DMS activation with more direct evidence of DMS activation using neuroimaging techniques. It is also important to link evidence of DMS activation in response to rejection stimuli with behavior in HRS individuals. For example, estimates of individual differences in reactivity to rejection stimuli obtained in studies like the present one could be used to predict behavior in real life situations deemed likely to activate rejection concerns. Such a study design exemplifies a way of linking biological with cognitive-affective and contextual influences to further the understanding of self-defeating and socially harmful responses to rejection.

CONCLUSION

Our goal in this chapter has been to show the ways in which heightened sensitivity to rejection develops and can influence the individual's relations to significant others and social groups and, through this, the individual's well-being. Our approach is guided by the view that RS develops to defend the self against rejection while maintaining social connection. Drawing on research on the neurobiology of emotion (Cacioppo & Gardner, 1999; Lang, Bradley, & Cuthbert, 1990; LeDoux, 1996), we propose that situations where high RS individuals expect rejection (e.g., conflict) activate the DMS, a generic affectively-based system evolved to guide rapid and intense responses to threats of danger. Where rejection is the danger, activation of this system should orient and prepare the individual to detect signs of interpersonal negativity and to use prior expectations to determine whether the danger is directed to the self when negativity is detected. At the same time, DSM activation should motivate vigorous efforts to prevent the occurrence of rejection. Because the desired outcome is to maintain connection with the threat source—a significant other—the fight-or-flight responses typically associated with activation of the DMS are not preferred options initially. Thus, we would expect that rejection prevention efforts should take the form of highly-regulated efforts to accommodate the partner, even at the expense of important personal goals. Failure of prevention efforts and the detection of the feared rejection should trigger hostile and depressive overreactions that ultimately undermine relationships, thus fulfilling rejection expectations.

REFERENCES

Ainsworth, M., Blehar, M., Waters, E., & Wall, S. (1978). *Patterns of attachment: A psychological study of the strange situation.* Hillsdale, NJ: Erlbaum.

Ayduk, O., & Downey, G. (2003). [Rejection elicits hostility in highly rejection sensitive men. Columbia University]. Unpublished data.

Ayduk, O., & Downey, G. (2004). Unpublished data.

Ayduk, O., Downey, G., & Kim, M. (2001). Rejection sensitivity and depressive symptoms in women. *Personality & Social Psychology Bulletin, 27* (7), 868–877.

Ayduk, O., Downey, G., Testa, A., Yen, Y., & Shoda, Y. (1999). Does rejection elicit hostility in rejection sensitive women? *Social Cognition, 17,* 245–271.

Ayduk, O., Mendoza-Denton, R., Mischel, W., Downey, G., Peake, P. L., K., & Rodriguez, M. (2000). Regulating the interpersonal self: Strategic self-regulation for coping with rejection sensitivity. *Journal of Personality & Social Psychology, 79*(5), 776–792.

Bandura, A. (1986). *Social foundations of thought and action.* Englewood Cliffs, NJ: Prentice-Hall.

Baumeister, R. F., & Sommer, K.L., (1997). What do men want? Gender differences and two spheres of belongingness: Comment on Cross and Madson. *Psychological Bulletin, 122,* 38–44.

Baumeister, R. F., & Leary, M. R. (1995). The need to belong: desire for interpersonal attachments as a fundamental human motivation. *Psychological Bulletin, 117,* 497–529.

Blatt, S. J., & Zuroff, D. C. (1992). Interpersonal relatedness and self-definition: Two prototypes for depression. *Clinical Psychology Review, 12,* 527–562,

Bowlby, J. (1980). *Attachment and loss: Vol. 3. Loss, sadness, and depression.* New York: Basic Books.

Brewer, M. B., & Gardner, W. (1996). Who is this "we"? Levels of collective identity and self representation. *Journal of Personality and Social Psychology, 71,* 83–93.

Brown, G. W., & Harris, T. (1978). Social origins of depression: a reply. *Psychological Medicine, 8,* 577–588.

Burks, V. S., Dodge, K.A., & Price, J.M. (1995). Models of internalizing outcomes of early rejection. *Development and Psychopathology, 7*(4), 683–695.

Cacioppo, J. T., & Gardner, W. L. (1999). Emotions. *Annual Review of Psychology, 50,* 191–214.

Coie, J., Lochman, J., Terry, R., & Hyman, C. (1992). Predicting early adolescent disorder from childhood aggression and peer rejection. *Journal of Consulting and Clinical Psychology, 60*(5), 783–792.

Coie, J., Terry, R., Lenox, K., & Lochman, J. (1995). Childhood peer rejection and aggression as predictors of stable patterns of adolescent disorder. *Development and Psychopathology, 7,* 697–713.

Dawson, M. E., Schell, M. E., & Bohmelt, A. H.

(Eds.) (1999). *Startle modification: Implications for neuroscience, cognitive science, and clinical science.* New York: Cambridge University Press.

DeRosier, M., Kupersmidt, J., & Patterson, C. (1994). Children's academic and behavioral adjustment as a function of the chronicity and proximity of peer rejection. *Child Development, 65*(6), 1799–1813.

Dodge, K. A. (1980). Social cognition and children's aggressive behavior. *Child Development, 51,* 162–170.

Dodge, K. A., Lansfrod, J. E., Burks, V. S., Bates, J. E., Pettit, G. S., Fontaine, R., & Price, J. M. (2003). Peer rejection and social information-processing factors in the development of aggressive behavior problems in children. *Child Development, 74*(2), 374–393.

Downey, G., Bonica, C., London, B. E., & Paltin, I. (1997). Social causes and consequences of rejection sensitivity. Submitted for publication.

Downey, G., & Feldman, S. (1996). Implications of rejection sensitivity for intimate relationships. *Journal of Personality & Social Psychology, 70*(6), 1327–1343.

Downey, G., Feldman, S., & Ayduk, O. (2000). Rejection sensitivity and male violence in romantic relationships. *Personal Relationships, 7,* 45–61.

Downey, G., Lebolt, A., Rincon, C., & Freitas, A. L. (1998). Rejection sensitivity and children's interpersonal difficulties. *Child Development, 69,* 1074–1091.

Downey, G., Freitas, A. L., Michaelis, B., & Khouri, H. (1998). The self-fulfilling prophecy in close relationships: Rejection sensitivity and rejection by romantic partners. *Journal of Personality & Social Psychology, 75,* 545–560.

Downey, G., Mougios, V., Ayduk, O., London, B., & Shoda, Y. (2004). Rejection sensitivity and the defensive motivational system: Insights from the startle response to rejection cues. *Psychological Science, 15,* 668-673.

Feldman, S., & Downey, G. (1994). Rejection sensitivity as a mediator of the impact of childhood exposure to family violence on adult attachment behavior. *Development and Psychopathology, 6,* 231–247.

Gabriel, S., & Gardner, W.L. (1999). Are there 'his' and 'hers' types of interdependence? The implications of gender differences in collective versus relational interdependence for affect, behavior,

and cognition. *Journal of Personality and Social Psychology, 77,* 642–655.

Halim, N., & Downey, G. (2004). *Rejection's silver lining: rejection's positive effects on performance in rejection sensitive individuals.* Poster presented at the Fifth Annual Meeting of the Society for Personality and Social Psychology. Austin, Texas.

Hamm, A., Cuthbert, B., Globisch, J., & Vaitl, D. (1999). Fear and the startle reflex: Blink modulation and autonomic response patterns in animal and mutilation fearful subjects. *Psychophysiology, 34,* 97–107.

Haselager, G., Cillessen, A., Van Lieshout, C., Riksen-Walraven, J., Marianne A., & Hartup, W. (2002). Heterogeneity among peer-rejected boys across middle childhood: Developmental pathways of social behavior. *Developmental Psychology, 38*(3), 446–456.

Hazan, C., & Shaver, P. (1987). Romantic love conceptualized as an attachment process. *Journal of Personality and Social Psychology, 52,* 511–524.

Hodges, E. V., & Perry, D. G. (1999). Personal and interpersonal antecedents and consequences of victimization by peers. *Journal of Personality and Social Psychology, 76*(4), 677–685.

Kessler, R. C., & Zhao, S. (1999). The prevalence of mental illness. In A. V. Horwitz & T. L. Scheid (Eds.), *A handbook for the study of mental health: Social contexts, theories, and systems* (pp. 55–78). New York: Cambridge University Press.

Kupersmidt, J., & Coie, J. (1990). Preadolescent peer status, aggression, and school adjustment as predictors of externalizing problems in adolescence. *Child Development, 61*(5), 1350–1362.

Kupersmidt, J., & Patterson, C. (1991). Childhood peer rejection, aggression, withdrawal, and perceived competence as predictors of self-reported behavior problems in preadolescence. *Journal of Abnormal Child Psychology, 19*(4), 427–449.

Lang, P. J., Bradley, M. M., & Cuthbert, B. N. (1990). Emotion, attention, and the startle reflex. *Psychology Review, 97,* 377–395.

Lang, P., Davis, M., Ohman, A. (2000). Fear and anxiety: Animal models and human cognitive psychophysiology. *Journal of Affective Disorders, 61,* 137–159.

LeDoux, J. (1996). *The emotional brain.* New York: Touchstone.

Levy, M., & Davis, K. (1988). Love styles and attachment styles compared: Their relations to each other and to various relationship characteristics. *Journal of Social and Personal Relationships, 5,* 439–471.

Liebowitz, M. R., Gorman, J. M., Fyer, A. J., & Klein, D. F. (1985). Social phobia. Review of a neglected anxiety disorder. *Archives of General Psychiatry, 42,* 729–736.

Panak, W. F., & Garber, J. (1992). Role of aggression, rejection, and attributions in the prediction of depression in children. *Development & Psychopathology, 4,* 145–165.

Parker, G. (1979). Parental characteristics in relation to depressive disorders. *British Journal of Psychiatry, 134,* 138–147.

Parker, G., & Hadzi-Pavlovic, D. (1992). Parental representations of melancholic and non-melancholic depressives: Examining for specificity to depressive type and for evidence of additive effects. *Psychological Medicine, 22,* 657–665.

Purdie, V., & Downey, G. (2000). Rejection sensitivity and adolescent girls' vulnerability to relationship-centered difficulties. *Child Maltreatment, 5,* 338–349.

Romero-Canyas, R., Downey, G., & Cavanaugh, T. J. (2003). *Feelings of alienation among college men: the impact of rejection sensitivity and political beliefs.* Columbia University. Unpublished data.

Romero-Canyas, R., Downey, G., Pelayo, R., & Bashan, U. (2004). *The threat of rejection triggers social accommodation in rejection sensitive men.* Poster presented at the Fifth Annual Meeting of the Society for Personality and Social Psychology. Austin, Texas.

Rubin, K. H., LeMare, L. J. & Lollis, S. (1990). Social withdrawal in childhood: Developmental pathways to peer rejection. In S. R. Asher & J. D. Coie (Eds.), *Peer rejection in childhood. Cambridge studies in social and emotional development* (pp. 217–249). New York: Cambridge University Press.

Rudolph, K. D., & Hammen, C. (1999). Age and gender as determinants of stress exposure, generation, and reactions in youngsters: A transactional perspective. *Child Development, 70,* 660–677,

Stravynski, A., Elie, R., & Franche, R. L. (1989). Perception of early parenting by patients diagnosed avoidant personality disorder: A test of the overprotection hypothesis. *Acta Psychiatrica Scandinavica, 80,* 415–420.

Sommer, K. L., Williams, K. D., Ciarocco, N. J., & Baumeister, R. F. (2001). When silence speaks louder than words: Explorations into the intrapsychic and interpersonal consequences of social ostracism. *Basic & Applied Social Psychology, 23,* 225–243.

Taylor, S. E., Klein, L. C., Lewis, B. P., Gruenewald, T. L., Gurung, R. A. R.; Updegraff, J. A. (2000). Biobehavioral responses to stress in females: Tend-and-befriend, not fight-or-flight. *Psychological Review, 107,* 411–429.

Twenge, J. M., Baumeister, R. F., Tice, D. M., & Stucke, T. S. (2001). If you can't join them, beat them: effects of social exclusion on aggressive behavior. *Journal of Personality and Social Psychology, 81,* 1058–1069.

Weiss, R. L., Summers, K. (1983). Marital Interaction Coding System III. In E. Filsinger (Ed.), *Marriage and family assessment* (pp. 35–115). Beverly Hills, CA: Sage.

9

The Rejected and the Bullied

Lessons About Social Misfits from Developmental Psychology

JAANA JUVONEN
ELISHEVA F. GROSS

A Decade of Studying the Outcast: Comparing Developmental
and Social Research
The Outcast as a Social Misfit
The Aversive Consequences of Being Rejected or Bullied
Lessons Learned: Proposed Model of Peer Rejection

The study of social outcasts has a long tradition in developmental psychology, in part because of the surprisingly potent long-term consequences of being rejected or bullied (Downey & Romero-Canyas, this volume). Rejected and bullied children are at risk for a range of subsequent problems, including school dropout, compromised mental health, and criminality (Coie, Dodge, & Kupersmidt, 1990; Parker & Asher, 1987). More recently, this topic has received renewed attention in light of media accounts of infamous school shootings in the United States. Many of the youngsters who hurt and killed their schoolmates and teachers were allegedly rejected and bullied by their peers (see also Gaertner & Iuzzini; and Twenge, this volume).

The goal of this chapter is to provide insights from developmental research on the complex array of intrapersonal and interpersonal difficulties that both lead to

Draft of Presentation at the 7th Annual Sydney Symposium of Social Psychology: "The Social Outcast: Ostracism, Social Exclusion, Rejection, and Bullying." Address Correspondence to: Jaana Juvonen, Department of Psychology, University of California, Los Angeles, Los Angeles, CA 90095-1521. E-mail: juvonen@psych.ucla.edu

and result from peer rejection. Contrary to the traditional developmental approach that focuses on behavioral subgroups of rejected children, we aim to provide a broad conceptual analysis of social outcasts. After a brief comparison of the last decade of relevant research published in developmental and social psychology's leading journals, we present developmental evidence that rejection serves a *social function* for the group. Next, we examine the *personal consequences* of rejection. We will argue that both individual differences and social-contextual moderators affect whether and how children experience rejection. We end the chapter by proposing a general conceptual model of the intrapersonal and group-level processes by which chronic peer rejection places youth at risk for long-term maladaptive outcomes.

In our developmental analysis of rejection, we focus on rejection by *peers* for both theoretical and practical reasons. From a theoretical perspective, same or similar age peers provide a unique developmental context. In contrast to relationships with adults, peer relationships are presumably more symmetrical or balanced in terms of power. In addition, peer relationships, and friendships in particular, provide opportunities for "social practice" in interpersonal behaviors that are critical to both current and future relationship development and maintenance. These behaviors include cooperation, negotiation, compromise, conflict resolution, and the provision and seeking of social support (Hartup, 1996). It is therefore imperative to understand what happens to rejected children who are deprived of normative opportunities for social practice.

As anyone who has been picked last for kickball, endured ridicule or nasty rumors from ostensible friends, or sprinted home to avoid the neighborhood bully will attest, there are numerous ways to experience peer rejection (see also Leary, this volume). Following Asher, Rose, and Gabriel (2001), who undertook the onerous task of counting those ways (and counted 32), we employ the term "peer rejection" inclusively. It should be noted, however, that this is not typical of developmental psychologists, who normally differentiate bullying or victimization by peers from peer rejection. In developmental research, rejection is commonly defined as peers' social avoidance of, dislike of, or reluctance to affiliate with an individual child. In contrast, bullying is conceptualized as an active form of hostility toward a target (rather than mere avoidance or dislike) that is characterized by an imbalance of power (Olweus, 1978), such as a strong person intimidating a weaker one. In the present review, we include bullying within the broad category of peer rejection because we presume that from the perspective of the target, the *experiences* of being rejected or bullied are more similar than different. We also propose that although the manifestations of rejection (avoidance) and bullying (hostility) vary, the action of non-inclusion or exclusion serves similar *functions* for the group (i.e., the rejectors).

But how do developmental psychologists study peer rejection and bullying? We now turn to a brief comparison between developmental and social psychological research.

A DECADE OF STUDYING THE OUTCAST: COMPARING DEVELOPMENTAL AND SOCIAL RESEARCH

We conducted an analysis of relevant studies published between 1993 and 2003 in the two leading journals in developmental psychology (*Child Development* and *Developmental Psychology*) and social psychology (*Journal of Personality and Social Psychology* and *Personality and Social Psychology Bulletin*), respectively. Based on a search using six key words (*rejection, exclusion, ostracism, harassment, victimization,* and *bullying*), a total of 145 articles were identified (49% were published in the social psychology journals). Each of 13 methodological characteristics were coded independent of the others; that is, an article could include both experimental and non-experimental data, or rejection by both strangers and familiar others. This method is a short-hand way to represent the two fields and, as such, has limitations. Nevertheless, this quick comparison reveals striking differences in conceptualizations and methodological approaches across the two areas of psychology.

Our review (summarized in Table 9.1) showed that one of the most notable differences between the social and developmental studies pertains to duration of

Table 9.1 Comparison of Characteristics of Social
and Developmental Investigations, 1993–2003

Characteristic	Percent of Articles in Developmental Psychology Journals (n = 74)	Percent of Articles in Social Psychology Journals (n = 71)	χ^2
Duration of Rejection			
Chronic	89%	45%	29.56**
Discrete	26%	75%	36.76**
Source of Rejection			
Strangers	4%	48%	33.81**
Familiar others	96%	55%	33.29**‡
Individual	16%	73%	52.59**‡
Group	89%	34%	47.38**‡
Assessment of Rejected Status			
Other-report	78%	18%	52.32**
Self-report	19%	51%	16.20**
Rejection involving no direct interpersonal interaction with source	1%	18%	12.33**
Experimental manipulation or behavioral coding only	12%	44%	16.24**
Research Design			
Experimental	20%	62%	26.11**
Non-experimental	81%	49%	16.20**
Longitudinal	45%	21%	8.89*

Notes: Unless otherwise noted, χ^2 statistics reflect Fisher's Exact test comparing articles with and without each characteristic in the two fields; comparisons that include a third category "unspecified," used a standard two-tailed χ^2 test, and are noted by "‡"; * = $p < .01$; ** = $p < .001$.

rejection: 89% of the developmental studies, compared to 45% of the social psychology articles, investigated rejection as a repeated experience or chronic problem. Also, 96% of the developmental studies versus 54% of the social psychological studies examined rejection by familiar others, as opposed to strangers, who were the specified source of rejection in 48% of social and just 4% of developmental investigations. Compared to 78% of the developmental studies, 18% of social psychological studies assessed rejection based on others' perceptions. The most typical developmental assessment of rejection consists of using sociometric methods: children name classmates with whom they do not want to affiliate (i.e., play or "hang out"), and the number of nominations received captures the consensus of the group toward one of its members (see Cillessen & Bukowski, 2000, for a comprehensive review of these methods). Finally, the vast majority (81%) of the relevant studies on social outcasts published in the developmental journals were non-experimental, whereas those published in social psychology journals are fairly evenly split between experimental (51%) and non-experimental (49%).

How might the developmental body of research, which consists mainly of *correlational* research conducted in natural environments and examining *chronic rejection* by *familiar peers,* then complement social psychological research on rejection? We contend that developmental research allows us to make inferences about the unfolding of rejection, the group function it may serve, and the conditions under which rejection is associated with acute distress as well as long-term negative outcomes, such as mental health problems and criminality. We begin our review of the developmental body of research by asking: why are some children rejected from their social groups?

THE OUTCAST AS A SOCIAL MISFIT

Although virtually everyone experiences peer rejection or bullying at some point in their childhood or adolescence, repeated rejection and chronic bullying are neither random nor universal experiences. Numerous studies indicate that *aggressive* and *socially withdrawn* youth are most likely to be cast out from the group (see Coie et al., 1990; McDougall, Hymel, Vaillancourt, & Mercer, 2001, for comprehensive reviews).

What can account for children and adolescents' intolerance for aggression and social withdrawal among their peers? The associations between peer rejection and both aggression and social withdrawal indicate that these behaviors may be among the most salient deviations from group behavioral norms across childhood and adolescence. Aggression and shyness (cf. social withdrawal) were among the behavioral descriptions most frequently mentioned by first- through 11-grade students when Coie and Pennington (1976) asked children to describe someone who is "different from other kids." Similar results were obtained in a study with 12-year-old Finnish children (Juvonen, 1991). Younger, Gentile, and Burgess (1993) have likewise shown that both aggression and social withdrawal are perceived as deviant in middle childhood.

There is a small body of developmental research specifically testing the deviance-rejection hypothesis. These studies suggest that determinants of rejection are not necessarily invariant across all groups; rather, they differ depending on the prevailing group norms. Wright, Giammarino, and Parad (1986) were the first to formally propose and test a norm-based model of rejection. They examined associations between individual behavior and peer status in groups of 10-year-old boys at a summer camp for children with behavioral difficulties. They found that aggression and withdrawal each predicted peer rejection only in groups in which the behavior was non-normative (i.e., the group mean for the behavior was relatively low). In groups displaying low levels of aggressive behavior (e.g., verbal threats, hitting), aggressive individuals were rejected. In contrast, in high-aggression groups, social withdrawal was the non-normative and less accepted behavior, whereas aggressive behavior was unrelated to peer status. Recently, similar group effects have been found in both experimental (Boivin, Dodge & Coie, 1995) and large-scale studies of classroom contexts (Stormshak, Bierman, Bruschi, Dodge, & Coie, 1999).

In sum, rejection can be conceptualized as a socializing force within the peer group: to the extent that rejection represents an aversive response of the peer group to social norm violation, it functions to preserve individual adherence to those norms (see Hogg, this volume; Ouwerkerk, Van Lange, Gallucci, & Kerr, this volume). In other words, it appears that aggressive and withdrawn behaviors that are often considered invariant behavioral predictors of peer rejection may be more accurately and parsimoniously conceptualized as behaviors that most frequently invite exclusion and hostility from the group to the extent that they deviate from group norms. Group effects on the predictors of rejection and victimization including aggression and withdrawal have been found for groups defined by age, social network, and assignment (e.g., classroom or novel play groups).

Although one of the group functions of rejection may be to mark, and presumably limit, group deviance, a critical question remains to be addressed: What is the *effect* of peer rejection on the deviant individual? If, as we propose, rejection and bullying serve to deter deviance from group norms, then these group behaviors should be experienced as aversive by targets, in a manner analogous to the painful burn experienced by a child who is learning that hot stoves should be avoided.

THE AVERSIVE CONSEQUENCES OF BEING REJECTED OR BULLIED

In light of the mainly correlational body of developmental research on peer rejection, it is often debatable whether what are conceptualized as "consequences" of exclusion are in fact mere correlates or antecedents of rejection and bullying (see Parker & Asher, 1987). Tests of causal models that span relatively long time periods may be most effective in distinguishing consequences from correlates and antecedents; we therefore focus here on a few key longitudinal studies.

Direct Effects of Rejection on Social Distress

In a study capitalizing on transition to a new school, Vernberg, Abwender, Ewell, and Beery (1992) examined the longitudinal associations between bullying experiences and social anxiety. They found that socially anxious young teens were no more likely than their non-anxious peers to experience bullying in the new school, but teens who were bullied were at increased risk for social avoidance and distress one month into the school-year. Furthermore, Kiesner (2002) found that the less liked young teens were by their classmates, the more likely they were to display symptoms of depression 2 years later, even when earlier levels of depression were controlled for.

If social withdrawal is conceptualized as a behavioral manifestation of distress, then there is additional evidence for the prediction that rejection produces social pain (Eisenberger & Lieberman; MacDonald, Kingsbury, & Shaw; Williams & Zadro, this volume). In a study examining the emergence of bullying in novel play groups, Schwartz et al. (1993) found that non-assertive boys, who emerged as victims of peer maltreatment across multiple play sessions, became increasing withdrawn as the group's behavior became more targeted, negative, and coercive toward them. The most victimized boys spent less and less time in social play as they received increasing negative responses from their peers. Similarly, in one of the first studies of contrived play groups, Dodge (1983) found that boys who were neglected (i.e., not liked or disliked) by their peers displayed high levels of withdrawn behavior only *after* receiving repeated rebuffs from their peers. To return to the analogy of the child at a hot stove, these findings convey that the child who experiences pain in response to the burn of the stove's heat is likely to subsequently avoid the stove altogether.

The research reviewed above indicates that rejection and bullying place youth at increased risk for emotional as well as behavioral difficulties (see also Juvonen & Graham, 2001). However, in real life, these associations are decidedly more complex, because, as we will show below, the consequences of rejection vary depending on certain social contextual conditions and individual differences in the sensitivity to social cues, attributional inferences, and expectations.

The Moderating Effects of Social Context

Developmental researchers have begun to examine a variety of social moderators of the impact of rejection and bullying on feelings of distress. For example, having even just one friend appears to mitigate the social pain of peer victimization: Bullied youth with a friend tend to display lower levels of internalizing problems than those who are victimized and friendless (Hodges, Malone, & Perry, 1997; Hodges,

Boivin, Vitaro, & Bukowski, 1999). In one longitudinal study of Canadian third-through seventh-graders (Hodges et al., 1999), children who experienced bullying but had a friend reported neither elevated behavioral problems nor increased distress. In contrast, the behavioral problems of bullied children with no protective friendships worsened over time (see also Cacioppo & Hawkly, this volume).

Our recent research on daily encounters with bullying illustrates more subtle social moderators of children's responses to victimization (Nishina & Juvonen, in press). We proposed that youth interpret their experience of being bullied not in a social vacuum but in comparison to others. Hence, in addition to obtaining data on personal experiences of bullying, we also asked youth to describe bullying incidents that happened to others. We then examined fluctuations in daily affect among young teens as a function of their reported incidents of bullying. As expected, we found that *witnessing others* being bullied ameliorated some of the acute effects of being bullied oneself. On days when youth reported both experiencing and witnessing bullying, their feelings of anxiety were increased, whereas their reports of humiliation were reduced, compared to days when they experienced but did not witness bullying. Hence, social comparisons may simultaneously ease and exacerbate different manifestations of social pain.

In our most recent work on bullying, we examined the moderating role of classroom environment on the psychological responses of victims (Bellmore, Witkow, Graham, & Juvonen, 2004). Extending the person-group misfit hypothesis (e.g., Stormshak et al., 1999), we hypothesized that victimization is most strongly associated with emotional and social pain when the classroom is orderly as opposed to disorderly. In other words, the victim's plight is worse when local norms disfavor disruption and peer maltreatment (e.g., Leadbeater, Hoglund, & Woods, 2003). In disorderly classrooms, all students (bullied or not) experienced relatively high levels of social anxiety, whereas in the orderly classrooms, it was only bullied students who reported higher rates of social anxiety. Paradoxically, this may mean that classroom environments that are most protective for the majority of students (i.e., when bullying is rare) may be most risky for the few who do experience bullying.

Underlying Social Cognitive Processes

To better understand the moderating effects of social comparisons (e.g., witnessing victimization) and contexts (e.g., classroom level of disorder), it is helpful to examine the social cognitive processes that may be involved in these episodes. That is, how do victims of bullying construe their plights? Our research shows that compared to their non-bullied classmates, youth who view themselves as frequently harassed by their peers are more likely to blame themselves for being bullied (Graham & Juvonen, 1998). Furthermore, our research shows that characterological self-blame partly mediates the relation between self-perceptions of being a frequent victim of bullying and emotional distress (i.e., social anxiety and loneliness). In light of our earlier findings, we suspect that youth are most likely to blame themselves when there is little bullying in their classroom and when they do not notice others being bullied. Such self-blaming tendencies then partly account for bullied children's reported distress and depression.

Research on children's self-perceptions or their awareness of their plight also further helps us understand the rejection–distress linkage. Research by Panak & Garber (1992) has shown that sociometrically rejected children (i.e., those whose peers avoid or dislike them) who were aware of their low status were more depressed than sociometrically rejected children who were unaware of their low status. Consistent with these findings, our studies also indicate that children who view themselves as victimized by their peers but who do not have a victim reputation are more likely to feel emotionally distressed than those who have a reputation of a victim but who do not see themselves as such (Graham & Juvonen, 1998). Hence, self-perceptions of one's social plight are critical in determining whether rejected youth experience social distress (see also Williams & Zadro, this volume).

Expectations of rejected youth also play a role in maintaining (or changing) their social experiences. Using novel play group methodology, Rabiner and Coie (1989) showed that the mere manipulation of expectations of the sociometrically rejected children improved their social status within the new play groups consisting of unfamiliar non-rejected peers. Sociometrically rejected children who received a positive expectancy induction (i.e., they were told after the first play session that their new playmates liked them) were better liked than rejected children who received no expectancy induction. Although it remains unclear how positive expectations "worked" to produce more favorable reactions, these findings nevertheless indicate that expectations on the part of the rejected children play a part in maintaining or changing others' reactions toward them.

Expectations and attributional biases of peers (or rejectors) also contribute to the perpetuation of peer rejection. For example, Hymel (1986) found that rejected children acquire social reputations that function as cognitive schemas biasing the reactions toward the rejected. Whereas liked peers were given the benefit of doubt for negative actions, disliked peers were perceived to have intentionally performed negative behaviors and were rarely credited for positive actions (see also Hymel, Wagner, & Butler, 1990 for a review). Such expectations or what Hymel calls "affective biases" make it more likely that the same children continue to get excluded and ostracized. Taken together, Rabiner and Coie's (1989) and Hymel and colleagues' (1990) findings suggest that social cognitive processes of both the rejected and rejectors may conspire to perpetuate a child's status as outcast.

Increased Sensitivity and Bidirectional Associations

There is evidence suggesting that once rejected children experience distress, they are even more likely to be sensitive to social threat cues (cf. Downey & Romero-Canyas, this volume). Based on interpretations of videotaped peer interactions, Bell-Dolan (1995) found that compared to their non-anxious peers, anxious children were more likely to misinterpret non-hostile interactions as hostile. In addition, anxious youth (girls in particular) were more likely to rely on maladaptive reactions in response to perceived hostility. Hence, increased sensitivity to threat is likely to maintain (and possibly exacerbate) the distress experienced, and the social ineffectiveness displayed by the most vulnerable youth.

Social-cognitive mechanisms explaining the associations between rejection and distress are also likely to be cyclical. In a 1-year longitudinal study of bullying among young teens (Nishina, Juvonen, & Witkow, 2005), we found that psychological indicators of social pain—depression, social anxiety, and loneliness—may both contribute to and be triggered by bullying experiences (cf. Hodges et al., 1999). Similarly, Egan and Perry (1998) found that low self-regard predicted increased risk of being bullied and that bullying experiences also predicted negative self-views across a 1-year interval. These data suggest that psychologically vulnerable youth are easy targets who, when bullied, become even more vulnerable. We propose that this is because rejection experiences give rise to social-cognitive biases (i.e., sensitivity to threat cues, attributions, self-perceptions, expectations of and by others) that can maintain the social plight and the distress experienced by the target of rejection (see Pickett & Gardner, this volume). But there are exceptions. We turn next to cases in which chronic rejection does not appear to cause emotional distress, but is nevertheless linked with negative long-term outcomes, such as antisocial behavior.

Immunity from Social Pain: The Case of Aggressive Outcasts

Social-cognitive processes may advance our understanding of not only what accounts for the social pain experienced by rejected youth, but also why some children appear *not* to be hurt by peer rejection. A number of explanations have been advanced to account for the absence of direct adverse psychological effects of peer rejection on aggressive children and adolescents. One explanation that has received considerable attention is that aggressive-rejected youth display a variety of self-protective (although interpersonally problematic) social cognitive biases. Numerous studies have documented aggressive children and adolescents' tendencies to display self-serving biases in evaluations of their own competencies and in their responsibility (or lack thereof) for problematic peer experiences (Dodge & Crick, 1990; Orobio de Castro, Veerman, Koops, Bosch, & Monshouwer, 2002; White, Rubin, & Graczyk, 2002).

In a recent meta-analysis of research on aggressive behavior and hostile attributions, Orobio de Castro and colleagues (2002) found strong evidence for the tendency of aggressive children to perceive a peer's ambiguously threatening behavior as intentionally provocative. This attributional bias may help to explain the aggressive child's lack of emotional distress, inasmuch as blame directed at others is associated with anger and hostility (see Weiner, 1995) rather than with social anxiety or depression (Graham, Hudley, & Williams, 1992).

Other types of biases in social information processing may also account for the lack of distress following peer rejection. Schippell, Vasey, Cravens-Brown, and

Bretveld (2003) found attentional biases among adolescents identified as reactively aggressive—such youth displayed suppressed attention to rejection, ridicule, and failure cues. Hence, the apparent protection enjoyed by aggressive-rejected youth may be in part explained by individual differences in social cognitive processing, including but not limited to attributional and attentional biases (see Dodge & Crick, 1990; Crick & Dodge, 1994 for a discussion of additional processing biases and deficiencies in aggressive youth; also Sommer & Rubin, this volume).

Given our chief concern in the present review is to examine the role of the peer group in the individual's experience of rejection, we now move from the well-charted realm of individual difference explanations to more recent explorations of social-contextual factors that may protect the feelings of aggressive youth. The first social contextual explanation we address is rooted in the fact that a peer rating of rejection is an indicator of peer sentiment, but not necessarily peer *treatment* of the individual. The harsh treatment and ostracism one would expect disliked individuals to experience may be reserved for targets not expected to retaliate. A rejected child's aggressiveness appears to be a critical factor in the degree to which he or she receives negative peer feedback regarding his or her unacceptable behavior. When 10- to 13-year-old children documented their acute, everyday peer experiences, withdrawn-rejected boys were significantly more likely than their aggressive-rejected counterparts to report negative peer treatment (Sandstrom & Cillessen, 2003). Hence, the peer context experienced by aggressive-rejected children may be a "kinder" one than might be expected on the basis of their sociometric status. If peer rejection serves to enforce group norms regarding interpersonal behavior, then the absence of negative, rejecting behaviors from peers toward aggressive children may constitute a breakdown of the norm enforcement process. The absence of negative feedback from peers may protect aggressive-rejected children from social distress, but at the same time they may also have little impetus to modify their behavior.

Another protective factor in aggressive-rejected children's social experience has been observed upon closer examination of their peer relationships. Although aggressive youth may be rejected by their normative peer group, they are no less likely than their non-aggressive peers to be socially connected—to have a best friend, for example, or to be perceived as a central group member—but the peers with whom aggressive youth associate are typically more aggressive than the peers of non-aggressive youth (Cairns, Cairns, Neckerman, Gest, & Gariepy, 1988). Patterson, Capaldi, and Bank (1991) suggest that rejection limits aggressive children's options for healthy peer relationships, permitting them only to associate with and befriend similarly aggressive and rejected peers. Moreover, because affiliation among deviant peers facilitates "deviance training," whereby anti-social youth encourage one another's problematic behavior (Dishion, Spracklen, Andrews, & Patterson, 1996), it is not surprising that anti-social (including aggressive) youth who repeatedly affiliate with similar others are at greater risk for subsequent criminal behavior (Dishion, McCord, & Poulin, 1999).

LESSONS LEARNED: PROPOSED MODEL OF PEER REJECTION

We began by noting that developmental psychologists have long been concerned with how and why repeated rejection experiences affect development in the long term. Having discussed the complex mechanisms that have been shown to mediate these long-term effects at both person- and group-levels, we propose in Figure 9.1 a general model of rejection's impact on social development.

We first suggest that rejection is initially triggered by a lack of fit between the child and the group (path #1). The subsequent processes involve both the target (the individual child) and source (the normative peer group) of the initial rejection. The upper section of path model depicts the personal or intrapsychological processes following the experiences of rejection; the lower part depicts the group level processes that capture the thoughts and actions of the rejectors.

Consistent with social-cognitive information processing models (e.g., Dodge & Crick, 1990; Crick & Dodge, 1994), we propose that rejection elicits negative expectancies and social-cognitive (attentional as well as attributional) biases in both the rejected and their rejectors. These social-cognitive biases, in turn, account for the subsequent behavioral reactions. Focusing first on the lower level of the figure, rejected children acquire social reputations (Hymel, 1986) that function as cognitive schemas biasing the reactions against the rejected (path #2). Such affective biases then, in turn, make it more likely that these same children continue to get excluded and ostracized (path #3).

At the intrapsychological level, rejection experiences can foster different types of social-cognitive biases (path #4) depending on individual differences that promote the very behaviors that elicited rejection in the first place. In the case of most children, and submissive and socially withdrawn children in particular, tendency to blame oneself, specifically characterological self-blame, increases feelings of depression, anxiety, and depression, which, in turn, promote avoidance or withdrawal from peer interactions (see also, Williams & Zadro, this volume). In the case of aggressive children, inferences of hostile intent of the actions by others further promote anger and retaliation. Hence, the social-cognitive biases are likely to promote the very behavior patterns (e.g., social withdrawal and aggression) that elicited the rejection in the first place (path #5) (see also, Catanese & Tice; Twenge, this volume). Research on the experimental manipulation of interpersonal expectations of rejected children (Rabiner & Coie, 1989) suggests that negative expectations might also maintain their rejected status (path #6).

Repeated rejection on the part of the peer group, in turn, is likely to accentuate the initial behavioral responses that elicited rejection in the first place. However, such a pathway is likely to be bi-directional (path #7), inasmuch as increased social withdrawal and aggression are associated with prolonged experiences of rejection. Repeated rejection by normative peer group, in turn, restricts children's opportunities for normative peer interactions (path #8). Also, accentuated eliciting behaviors are bidirectionally linked to restricted opportunities to affiliate with

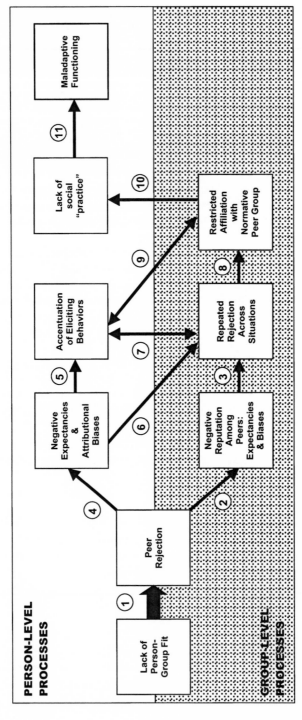

FIGURE 9.1 Proposed developmental model of intrapersonal and interpersonal consequences of peer rejection.

normative peer group (path #9). We reviewed evidence showing how increased withdrawal means that children end up playing alone and that ceasing to interact restricts their opportunities to engage in normative peer interactions. In the case of aggressive youth, we documented that their opportunities are restricted in the sense that they seek the company of other aggressive children.

Restricted opportunities to affiliate with the normative peer group result in lack of "social practice" for the rejected children (path #10), which, in turn, predicts maladaptive functioning of these youth (path #11). Socially withdrawn youth are at risk for internalizing problems, such as depression, anxiety, and low self-esteem, whereas aggressive youth are at risk for antisocial behaviors (McDougall et al., 2001).

In summary, the proposed developmental model depicts an array of interpersonal and intrapersonal processes that appear to propel the social outcast toward increased deviance and maladaptive functioning among normative peers, although not necessarily away from all relationships (e.g., in the case of aggressive youth). The set of predictions and associations depicted in this model reflect our review of existing developmental research. It is certainly possible that other sets of linkages can be added to this basic model; future research is needed to complete this already complex picture.

Contributions of Developmental Psychology to Social Psychological Research on Rejection

How does the developmental research reviewed within this chapter help us understand rejection? We think that there are at least three ways that developmental research complements social psychological research on rejection.

1. Examination of antecedents of rejection allows us to make inferences about the group or social *function* of exclusion. The social function hypothesis (cf. Brewer, this volume; Ouwerkerk, et al., this volume) allows us to make predictions about the effects of rejection. For example, we argued that one of the group functions of peer rejection in childhood is to foster group norms by punishing individuals who deviate from those norms. Consistent with this hypothesis then, we maintained that in order for rejection to be effective, it should hurt. Theoretically, the hurt feelings should prohibit children from further deviating from the group norms. Because developmental psychologists have mainly studied chronic rejection we know more about when rejection fails to change deviant behavior. Hence, we know about cases in which exclusion maintains or exacerbates the difficulties that brought about the rejection in the first place.

2. The exploration of a broad array of the correlates of rejection in naturalistic settings enriches our understanding of the association between rejection experience and social pain with the identification of both individual and

social contextual *moderators*. Particularly intriguing is the power of the social context, in which the presence of even a single friend, or the observation of others being bullied, can significantly ameliorate or exacerbate the social pain of rejection.

3. The study of both individual differences and social contextual moderators, in turn, enable us to specify general *mediating mechanisms* that can explain how and why rejection can increase the risk for maladaptive outcomes in the long term. For example, we documented how aggressive and non-aggressive (particularly socially withdrawn) youth differ in terms of sensitivity to social cues, self-perceptions of their social standing, and attributions under perceived threat. Identification of general mediating mechanisms enables us then to predict different long-term developmental outcomes within one model—independent of individual differences.

In conclusion, the research reviewed here underscores the complex interplay of intrapersonal and interpersonal factors that cause children to become—and too often, remain—rejected by their peers. Contextual effects, and in particular the degree of similarity or fit between individuals and their peers, have already begun to explain questions such as why sometimes aggressive children are rejected but other times not, or why victims of bullying might feel more distressed in some situations than others. We believe that examination of such complex person-environment interactions helps us better understand the chain of events associated with rejection as well as the varied long-term trajectories of social outcasts.

REFERENCES

Asher, S. R., Rose, A. J., & Gabriel, S.W. (2001). Peer rejection in everyday life. In, Mark R. Leary (Ed.), *Interpersonal rejection* (pp. 105–142). London: Oxford Press.

Bell-Dolan, D. J. (1995). Social cue interpretation of anxious children. *Journal of Clinical Child Psychology, 24,* 2–10.

Bellmore, A., Witkow, M., Graham, S., & Juvonen, J. (2004).. Beyond the individual: The impact of ethnic context and classroom behavioral norms on victims' adjustment. *Developmental Psychology, 40,* 1159-1172.

Boivin, M., Dodge, K. A., & Coie, J. D. (1995). Individual-group behavioral similarity and peer status in experimental play groups of boys: The social misfit revisited. *Journal of Personality and Social Psychology, 69,* 269–279.

Cairns, R. B., Cairns, B. D., Neckerman, H. J., Gest, S. D., & Gariepy, J. L. (1988). Social networks and aggressive behavior: Peer support or peer rejection? *Developmental Psychology, 24,* 815–823.

Cillessen, A. H. N. & Bukowski, W. M. (Eds.). (2000). Recent advances in the measurement of acceptance and rejection in the peer system. *New Directions for Child and Adolescent Development, 88.* San Francisco: Jossey-Bass.

Coie, J. D., Dodge, K. A., & Kupersmidt, J. B. (1990). Peer group behavior and social status. In S. R. Asher & J. D. Coie (Eds.), *Peer rejection in childhood. Cambridge studies in social and emotional development* (pp. 17–59). New York: Cambridge University Press.

Coie, J. D., & Pennington, B. F. (1976). Children's perceptions of deviance and disorder. *Child Development, 47,* 407–413

Crick, N. R., & Dodge, K. A. (1994). A review and reformulation of social information-processing mechanisms in children's social adjustment. *Psychological Bulletin, 115,* 74–101.

Dishion, T. J., McCord, J., & Poulin, F. (1999). When interventions harm: Peer groups and problem behavior. *American Psychologist, 54,* 755–764.

Dishion, T. J., Spracklen, K. M., Andrews, D. W., & Patterson, G. R. (1996). Deviancy training in male adolescent friendships. *Behavior Therapy, 27,* 373–390.

Dodge, K.A. (1983). Behavioral antecedents of peer social status. *Child Development, 54,* 1386–1399.

Dodge, K. A., & Crick, N. R. (1990). Social information-processing bases of aggressive behavior in children. *Personality and Social Psychology Bulletin. Special Issue: Illustrating the value of basic research, 16,* 8–22.

Egan, S. K., & Perry, D. G. (1998). Does low self-regard invite victimization? *Developmental Psychology, 34,* 299–309.

Graham, S., Hudley, C., & Williams, E. (1992). Attributional and emotional determinants of aggression among African American and Latino early adolescents. *Developmental Psychology, 31*(28), 731–740.

Graham, S., & Juvonen, J. (1998). Self-blame and peer victimization in middle school: An attributional analysis. *Developmental Psychology, 34,* 587–599.

Hartup, W. W. (1996). The company they keep: Friendships and their developmental significance. *Child Development, 67,* 1–13.

Hodges, E. V. E., Boivin, M., Vitaro, F., & Bukowski, W. M. (1999). The power of friendship: Protection against an escalating cycle of peer victimization. *Developmental Psychology, 35,* 94–101.

Hodges, E. V. E., Malone, M. J., & Perry, D. G. (1997). Individual risk and social risk as interacting determinants of victimization in the peer group. *Developmental Psychology, 33,* 1032–1039.

Hymel, S. (1986). Interpretations of peer behavior: Affective bias in childhood and adolescence. *Child Development, 57,* 431–445.

Hymel, S., Wagner, E., & Butler, L. J. (1990). Reputational bias: View from the peer group. In S. R. Asher & J. D. Coie (Eds.), *Peer rejection in childhood. Cambridge studies in social and emotional development* (pp. 60–76). New York: Cambridge University Press.

Juvonen, J. (1991). Deviance, perceived responsibility, and negative peer reactions. *Developmental Psychology, 27,* 672–681.

Juvonen, J., & Graham, S. (Eds.). (2001). *Peer harassment in school: The plight of the vulnerable and victimized.* New York: Guilford Press

Kiesner, J. (2002). Depressive symptoms in early adolescence: Their relations with classroom problem behavior and peer status. *Journal of Research on Adolescence, 12,* 463–478.

Leadbeater, B., Hoglund, W., & Woods, T. (2003). Changing contents? The effects of a primary prevention program on classroom levels of peer relational and physical victimization. *Journal of Community Psychology, 31,* 397–418.

McDougall, P., Hymel, S., Vaillancourt, T., & Mercer, L. (2001). The consequences of childhood peer rejection. In M. Leary (Ed.), *Interpersonal rejection* (pp. 213–247). London: Oxford University Press.

Nishina, A., & Juvonen, J. (in press). Daily reports of witnessing and experiencing peer harassment in middle school. *Child Development.*

Nishina, A., Juvonen, J., & Witkow, M. (2005). Sticks and stones may break my bones, but names will make me sick: The consequences of peer harassment. *Journal of Clinical Child and Adolescent Psychology, 34,* 37–48.

Olweus, D. (1978). *Aggression in the schools: Bullies and whipping boys.* Oxford, England: Hemisphere.

Orobio de Castro, B., Veerman, J. W., Koops, W., Bosch, J. D., & Monshouwer, H. J. (2002). Hostile attribution of intent and aggressive behavior: A meta-analysis. *Child Development, 73,* 916–934.

Panak, W. F., & Garber, J. (1992). Role of aggression, rejection, and attributions in the prediction of depression in children. *Development and Psychopathology, 7,* 145–165.

Parker, J. G., & Asher, S. R. (1987). Peer relations and later personal adjustment: Are low-accepted children at risk? *Psychological Bulletin, 102,* 357–389.

Patterson, G. R., Capaldi, D., & Bank, L. (1991). An early starter model for predicting delinquency. In Debra J. Pepler. & Kenneth H. Rubin, (Eds.), *The development and treatment of childhood aggression* (pp. 139–168). Hillsdale, NJ: Lawrence Erlbaum Associates.

Rabiner, D., & Coie, J. (1989). Effect of expectancy inductions on rejected children's acceptance by unfamiliar peers. *Developmental Psychology, 25,* 450–457.

Sandstrom, M. J., & Cillessen, A. H. N. (2003). Sociometric status and children's peer experiences: Use of the daily diary method. *Merrill-Palmer Quarterly, 49,* 427–452.

Schippell, P. L., Vasey, M.W., Cravens-Brown, L. M., and Bretveld, R. A. (2003). Suppressed attention to rejection, ridicule, and failure cues: A unique correlate of reactive but not proactive aggression in youth. *Journal of Clinical Child & Adolescent Psychology, 32,* 40–55.

Schwartz, D., Dodge, K. A., & Coie, J. D. (1993). The emergence of chronic peer vicitimization in boys' play groups. *Child Development, 64,* 1755–1772.

Stormshak, E. A., Bierman, K. L., Bruschi, C., Dodge, K. A., & Coie, J. D. (1999). The relation between behavior problems and peer preference in different classroom contexts. *Child Development, 70,* 169–182.

Vernberg, E. M., Abwender, D. A., Ewell, K. K., & Beery, S. H. (1992). Social anxiety and peer relationships in early adolescence: A prospective analysis. *Journal of Clinical Child Psychology, 21,* 189–196.

Weiner, B. (1995). *Judgments of responsibility: A foundation for a theory of social conduct.* New York: Guilford Press.

White, K. J., Rubin, E. C., & Graczyk, P. A. (2002). Aggressive children's perceptions of behaviorally similar peers: The influence of one's own behavioral characteristics on perceptions of deviant peers. *Journal of Social and Personal Relationships, 19,* 755–775.

Wright, J. C., Giammarino, M., & Parad, H. W. (1986). Social status in small groups: Individual-group similarity and the social "misfit." *Journal of Personality & Social Psychology, 50,* 523–536.

Younger, A., Gentile, C., & Burgess, K. (1993). Children's perceptions of social withdrawal: Changes across age. In K. H. Rubin & J. B. Asendorpf (Eds.), *Social withdrawal, inhibition, and shyness in childhood* (pp. 215–235). Hillsdale, NJ: Lawrence Erlbaum Associates.

10

Role of Social Expectancies in Cognitive and Behavioral Responses to Social Rejection

KRISTIN L. SOMMER
YONATA S. RUBIN

*T*he desire to form and sustain meaningful social connections is an indelible feature of the human psyche. Social rejection represents an acute threat to relational bonds, leading those who are rejected to experience low self-esteem, hurt, anxiety, and a host of other negative emotions (e.g., Baumeister & Leary, 1995; Bowlby, 1969, 1982, 1973; Leary, 1990; Leary, Koch, & Hechenbleikner, 2001). Several theorists have argued that these negative emotions

---

Draft prepared for Sydney Symposium, March 16–18, 2004. Address correspondence to: Krisin Sommer, Department of Psychology, Baruch College, CUNY, 55 Lexington Ave., Box B-8215, New York, NY 10010. Email: Kristin_Sommer@baruch.cuny.edu.

serve as warning signals of low relational value, which in turn motivate rejected people to behave in ways that obviate the potential for future rejection and increase the likelihood of acceptance (Baumeister & Tice, 1990; Leary, 2004; Williams, 2001). Proximity-seeking and relationship-enhancing behaviors allow rejected people to replenish a sense of belongingness within social groups and affirm their desirability to others.

Indeed, the research presented in the current volume provides incontrovertible evidence that rejection leads to profound changes in behavior. The theoretical link between innate attachment needs and responses to rejection has been complicated, however, by a series of findings indicating that people do not always behave in ways that objectively increase their chances of acceptance (see Twenge, Catanese & Tice, this volume). Specifically, while some evidence suggests that rejection leads people to behave in ways that improve their standing in social groups (Williams, Cheung, & Choi, 2000; Williams & Sommer, 1997), other research shows that coping responses thwart rather than enhance one's potential for future relationships (Twenge, Catanese, & Baumeister, 2002). The notion that people need attachments and will do anything necessary to strengthen these attachments seems insufficient when trying to explain the varied, sometimes interpersonally destructive responses to being rejected.

We began this chapter by giving greater consideration to what exactly rejection does to a person. The most immediate outcome, perhaps, is to weaken or sever one's relationship with the rejector. In such instances, emotional and physical ties with the rejector are broken, and damage to these bonds alone may leave the rejected person feeling anxious and lonely. Another possible outcome of social rejection is to jeopardize one's overall feelings of desirability to others. Thus, even if the core relationship were somehow to remain intact, the rejected person may begin to question whether he or she possesses the traits and characteristics that make him or her valuable as a relationship partner.

In the present chapter, we suggest that threats to felt desirability lead people to question their potential for future inclusion. Expectations of future inclusion (whether positive or negative), in turn, predict the cognitive and behavioral strategies that people employ to cope with the rejection. Specifically, when people believe that others will like and accept them, they will respond to rejection by reinforcing and strengthening their relationships with others. However, if they believe that others will not like and accept them, they will withdraw from and devalue their relationships with others. As support for the role of social expectancies, we review evidence showing that responses to rejection often depend on trait self-esteem, which reflects chronic assumptions regarding one's desirability to others. Later in the chapter, we present new research that tests directly the role of social expectancies in coping responses to rejection. Finally, we discuss how the emotional detachment and interpersonally-destructive behaviors of rejected people may be motivated by efforts to protect the self from additional harm.

FELT DESIRABILITY

Forming and maintaining relationships is a fundamental part of human nature. An understandable and common reaction to being rejected is to feel unworthy of others' love and affection. Rejected individuals may come to believe that they lack the physical beauty, intelligence, social skills, or other traits that make them valuable or desirable as relationship partners. In some cases, these concerns may extend beyond the broken relationship to contaminate perceptions about how they are viewed by others in general. In other words, any event that arouses concerns about or feelings of rejection within the context of a specific relationship has the potential to change the way people think about and behave toward outside relationship partners.

Threats to felt desirability may be thought of as threats to self-esteem, insomuch as self-esteem reflects our perceptions of how others view us (Leary, Tambor, Terdal, & Downs, 1995). Leary and colleagues (1995; Leary, Haupt, Strausser, & Chokel, 1998) have argued convincingly that self-esteem is a proxy for perceived acceptance. That is, people do not desire self-esteem for its own sake; rather, self-esteem decreases and increases as a function of our perceived relational value. Within the framework of sociometer theory, then, humans should care about having desirable traits and characteristics only to the extent that these attributes connect them to other people. In strong support of this notion, several studies have shown that long- or short-term feelings of rejection or ostracism are associated with low self-esteem and self-esteem feelings (Leary et al., 1995; 1998; Sommer, Williams, Ciarocco, & Baumeister, 2001; Williams et al., 2000).

Temporary or chronic assumptions about one's ability to secure social acceptance may be key to understanding how people cope with rejection. When a rejected person believes that, despite his or her best efforts, acceptance-driven behaviors will only result in additional rejection, coping responses may take the form of relational distancing and devaluation. When a person believes that, despite the rejection, he or she is indeed worthy and likely of being accepted, coping responses will take the form of proximity seeking and relationship enhancement.

What are some of the situations and traits that give rise to positive and negative social expectancies? Thus far, the literature has been largely silent on the question of situational predictors, and so we defer our discussion of this issue until later in the chapter. Relatively more evidence has accumulated regarding dispositional predictors of social expectancies. One of these, rejection sensitivity, is discussed in detail elsewhere in this volume (Downey, this volume). Another, trait self-esteem, is described in the pages that follow.

TRAIT SELF-ESTEEM AND SOCIAL EXPECTANCIES

Leary (2004) has argued that self-esteem is an internal gauge or monitor of perceived relational value, increasing when people feel accepted by others and decreasing when people do not. As support for this view, studies have shown that trait self-esteem is strongly, positively correlated with general feelings of social acceptance (e.g., Leary et al., 1995; 1988; Sommer et al., 2001) and that perceived social rejection or ostracism leads to a drop in state (temporary) self-esteem (Leary et al., 1995; Williams et al., 2000). Though theoretically interpersonal rejection should be equally threatening both to people high and low in self-esteem, the former group should be better able to resist the conclusion that they are generally unworthy of others' high regard.

The research generally supports this conclusion. Nezlek, Kowalski, Leary, Blevins, and Holgate (1997) exposed participants to inclusion or exclusion from their groups and then asked them to report temporary feelings of self-esteem. They found that the lower participants' trait self-esteem, the worse they felt following exclusion. Trait self-esteem remained unrelated to self-esteem feelings following inclusion. Thus, high self-esteem individuals' strong confidence in others' general liking for them seemed to buffer the negative impact of group exclusion.

More recently, Sommer and Baumeister (2002) subliminally primed high and low self-esteem participants with words related to acceptance, rejection, or other acts of misfortune. Participants were then asked to report whether each of several positive and negative traits described them. The results showed that participants low in trait self-esteem responded to rejection (compared to other primes) by endorsing a greater percentage of negative trait adjectives and lower percentage of positive trait adjectives. Those high in self-esteem did the complete opposite, endorsing fewer negative and more positive trait adjectives. In other words, people with low self-esteem automatically adopted a negative self-concept in the face of subliminal rejection threat, whereas those high in self-esteem adopted a relatively positive self-concept.

In a follow-up study, Sommer and Baumeister (2002) examined whether rejection primes would lead to changes in performance motivation. They hypothesized that people with high self-esteem would not only be resistant to downward self-evaluation in the face of threat but actively work hard to override the negative implications of rejection. Those low in self-esteem, conversely, would give up on tasks on which they might fail. Participants were primed with thoughts of acceptance, rejection, or other acts of misfortune by way of a sentence unscramble task. They were then asked to work on a difficult (actually unsolvable) anagram task and to let the experimenter know when they wanted to stop. The experimenter surreptitiously timed how long participants worked on the task. Results showed that, following acceptance and misfortune primes, low and high self-esteem participants persisted about the same amount of time. Following the rejection primes, however, high self-esteem participants nearly doubled their efforts, working twice as long on the anagrams, whereas low self-esteem participants quit significantly sooner. In a final experiment, participants were told to solve as many (solvable) anagrams within three minutes. Paralleling the findings for persistence, people high in self-esteem solved slightly more anagrams following the rejection primes, whereas those low in self-esteem solved significantly fewer.

These findings suggest that high self-esteem provides a resource for overcoming (unconscious) thoughts of rejection. People who believe that others like and accept them respond to subtle rejection cues by rating themselves even more positively and by working hard so as to prove that they are really good. Those who question others' liking of them seem to internalize the implications of rejection and quickly withdraw from difficult tasks that threaten to expose their negative qualities (and possibly result in additional rejection). These widely different coping responses to rejection threat seem to parallel high and low self-esteem individuals' responses to other types of threats, such as poor test performance (e.g., Baumeister & Tice, 1985; Sommer, 2001). It is important to note that performance-based threats may also imply social rejection, because low ability or intelligence signifies that one may not be desirable as a relationship partner (Leary, 2004).

The impact of rejection on performance motivation was also examined in a recent study on linguistic ostracism (Dotan, Rubin, & Sommer, 2004). We defined linguistic ostracism as a situation in which two or more people speak in a language that others who are present do not understand. In this study, participants were randomly assigned to be linguistically-ostracized or included by two other participants, actually confederates working for the experimenter. In the linguistic ostracism condition, the confederates spoke to the participant in English but spoke to one another intermittently in Russian. In the linguistic inclusion condition, the confederates spoke to everyone in English. Subsequently, participants were separated from their groups and asked to work on a brainstorming task. Half were told that their efforts would be combined with those of the other group members and that their group's total performance would be evaluated. Participants in this condition understood that they would reconvene with their group members and that everyone would know what each member had contributed to the group product. The other participants were told that their work would be evaluated individually and that they would not reconvene with their group members.

Prior to the onset of the study, we measured participants' trait self-esteem and social self-efficacy, that is, their confidence in their abilities to make friends. These two variables were significantly correlated ($r = .45$). Our findings showed that following linguistic inclusion, people low and high in self-esteem worked about equally hard on the brainstorming task. Following linguistic ostracism, however, high self-esteem participants worked harder on behalf of their groups, whereas low self-esteem participants contributed somewhat less. Social self-efficacy, which more directly taps individual differences in social expectancies, was an even stronger predictor of high performance motivation following linguistic ostracism. Importantly, these patterns were not found when people believed their performance would be evaluated individually, suggesting that strong performance efforts among people high in self-esteem (or social self-efficacy) were motivated by an attempt to elicit favorable evaluations from their group members.

TRAIT SELF-ESTEEM AND PERCEIVED REJECTION
WITHIN CLOSE RELATIONSHIPS

We turn now to an examination of how trait self-esteem influences behaviors within close relationships. Close relationships are those in which people presumably feel most valued, and thus these relationships should provide an ideal channel through which to enhance feelings of worthiness and desirability to others. One might expect that people who are concerned about rejection from their romantic partners will draw closer to these partners and remind themselves of their partners' love for them. However, a series of studies by Sandra Murray and colleagues have shown that people engage in these relationship-affirming behaviors only when they trust in their partners' ongoing regard for them. People who generally question their partners' regard for them respond to rejection threat by distancing themselves from their partners.

In the most recent of these studies, Murray, Bellavia, Rose, and Griffin (2003) assessed the extent to which people felt chronically, positively regarded by their partners. They then asked them to provide daily reports of their partners' ill-mannered behaviors and of their own feelings and behaviors. The results of this diary study showed that people who felt less regarded by their partners at the onset of the study responded to their partners' moody behaviors with increased hurt, felt rejection, and greater negative (rejecting) behaviors toward their partners. Those who initially felt positively regarded, however, responded to these occasional slights by drawing closer to their partners. The authors concluded that people who feel poorly regarded by their partners retaliate against their partners to protect themselves from additional hurt. Those who have greater trust in their partners' regard avoid these "tit for tat" defensive strategies and focus instead on affirming their relationships.

Other studies have shown that trait self-esteem is a reliable predictor of whether people use their close relationships as a resource for coping with threat. For example, Murray and colleagues have shown that when people are reminded of their faults or prior transgressions (Murray, Holmes, MacDonald, & Ellsworth, 1998) or led to believe that their partners perceive a problem in their relationships (Murray, Rose, Bellavia, Holmes, & Kusche, 2002), those with low self-esteem derogate their partners and downplay the importance of their relationships, whereas those high in self-esteem praise their partners and affirm their commitment to their relationships. As Murray et al. (2002) noted, the tendency of low self-esteem people to overreact to their partners' occasional criticism led them to needlessly weaken their attachments with their partners. In these and other studies (e.g., Murray, Holmes, & Griffin, 2000), Murray and colleagues demonstrated that the links between trait self-esteem and relationship enhancement processes were mediated by perceived acceptance. Specifically, the lower participants' self-esteem, the less they believe that their partners loved and accepted them for who they were, and these negative expectancies, in turn, led them to defensively devalue their partners and their relationships. Their findings are consistent with other studies linking low self-esteem with a greater use of neglect (e.g., ignoring the partner) during relationship conflict (Rusbult, Morrow, & Johnson, 1987; Rusbult, Verette, Whitney, Slovik, & Lipkus, 1991), greater use of defensive ostracism (i.e., ostracism to divert attention from one's weaknesses or faults) (Sommer, Williams, Ciarocco, & Baumeister, 2001), and lower levels of forgiveness (Mauger, Perry, Freeman, & Grove, 1992).

The extensive work by Murray and colleagues shows that people high in self-esteem respond to concerns about rejection by strengthening their attachment with their partners. We emphasize the word *concern*, here, because it seems vital to one's interpretation of these findings. Participants in this research were never faced with incontrovertible evidence of their partners' aversion to them. Rather, the magnitude of rejection implied in experimental manipulations of remembered transgressions, for example (Murray et al., 1998), was largely in the mind of the beholder, allowing individual differences in perceived regard to color people's interpretations of their partners' views of them.

Further, while people high in self-esteem may look to their romantic partners as evidence of their own virtues, they may have greater difficulties gaining reassurance from those with whom they are less close. In these cases, a hefty dose of rejection may overwhelm even the most confident of people, leading them to doubt themselves and their abilities to be accepted outside of the rejecting relationship.

Several laboratory studies of rejection by strangers have shown that people become hostile and destructive toward those who have rejected them. For example, Bourgeois and Leary (2001) led participants to believe they were chosen either first or last by the captain of a laboratory team. Later, they were provided the opportunity to evaluate the team captain. Results showed that participants who were chosen last rated the captain less positively and expressed lower interest in having him as a friend compared to those who were chosen first. Other research has similarly shown that ostracized or rejected people dislike and avoid their rejectors (Geller, Goodstein, Silver, & Sternberg, 1974) and express hostility and lack of interest in working with rejecting groups (Pepitone & Wilpizeski, 1960).

Finally, there is reason to believe people high compared to low in self-esteem will be particularly likely to derogate and distance themselves from rejecting partners. These people expect to be treated favorably by others, and they probably perceive a greater number of alternatives to their current relationships (Rusbult et al., 1987; 1991). For these reasons, people high in self-esteem may be especially unwilling to tolerate rejection. In partial support of this, Rusbult et al. (1987) found that high self-esteem was associated with greater exit behaviors (e.g., actively criticizing the partner or leaving the relationship) in response to relational dissatisfaction. Similarly, Sommer et al. (2001) found that people with high self-esteem were more likely than those with low self-esteem to report terminating their relationships with people who had ostracized them. These data suggest that, when confronted with clear evidence of rejection, high self-esteem individuals are equally if not more likely than those low in self-esteem to behave in interpersonally destructive ways.

NEGATIVE EXPECTANCIES AND RELATIONAL DEVALUATION

So far, we have relied largely on the self-esteem literature to make our case for the role of expectancies in coping responses to social rejection. Recently, we sought to measure and test directly the mediating role of social expectancies in responses to rejection (Sommer, Benkendorf, & Kirkland, 2004). Our goal was to determine whether the link between rejection and behaviors toward outside (nonrejecting) relationship partners could be explained by changes in the extent to which rejected people thought they were (or would be) accepted by these partners.

Participants previously unacquainted with one another arrived to the study in groups of four. They completed a trait self-esteem scale and then wrote a short essay. We told participants that they would be exchanging and rating each other's essays later in the experiment. As part of an ostensibly unrelated task, we randomly paired two participants and asked them to spend 10 minutes engaging in an intimacy-building exercise. This exercise had previously been shown to increase feelings of closeness and liking among strangers (Sedikides, Campbell, & Reeder, 1999). After completing the exercise, participants were then paired with a second person (who had completed the intimacy building task with someone else) and instructed to repeat the process. This time they believed that they would be recording and exchanging their impressions of one another. Unbeknownst to the participants, we replaced their actual impressions with bogus ratings that varied by condition. In the acceptance condition, participants believed that the second partner liked them and wanted to be friends with them in the future, whereas those in the rejection condition believed that their partner did not like them and did not want to be friends with them.

Participants were then asked to evaluate the essay that ostensibly had been written by their first (intimate) partner or a stranger (the fourth person in the experiment with whom they had not met or interacted). In reality, all participants rated the same essay written by the experimenters. Prior to rating these essays, participants were asked to indicate how much they thought the essay writer liked them and how much they believed he or she wanted to be friends with them in the future. Together, these items provided a measure of social expectancies. We also asked participants to rate how important it was to them that the essay writer liked them and how much they cared about their future relationship with this person. These items provided a measure of concern for the relationship. Finally, participants rated the quality of the essays along several dimensions, such as creativity of solution, writing style, and quality of solution proposed. These ratings were summed to provide an overall measure of essay evaluation.

Did participants' social expectancies vary across feedback conditions? The answer is yes. Rejected participants reported that both their previous (intimate) relationship partners and strangers would not like them or want to be friends with them in the future. These effects did not depend on participants' levels of self-esteem. In other words, social rejection caused participants to develop negative social expectancies regardless of whether they felt generally accepted by others (i.e., had high self-esteem).

These negative expectancies, in turn, caused rejected participants to report decreased concern for their relationships. When we controlled statistically for social expectancies, the link between rejection and decreased concern for the relationship was completely eliminated. It appeared, then, that people defensively devalued their relationships with both previous, intimate partners and those they had never met, and all because they believed they would be rejected.

Finally, we found that rejected participants were more likely than accepted participants to return negative ratings of others' essays. This occurred regardless of whether they were evaluating the essays of their previous, intimate partners or those of complete strangers. When we controlled for social expectancies, the effect of rejection on essay ratings was largely reduced (although not completely eliminated). Put another way, expectations of impending rejection caused rejected participants to derogate others. Once again, trait self-esteem played no role in these findings.

Our findings fit well with previous research on rejection sensitivity by Downey and colleagues (see Downey, this volume). This research shows that high anxiety about rejection coupled with strong expectations of rejection predict increased hostility and aggression among children (Downey, Lebolt, Rincon, & Freitas, 1998) and adults (e.g., Downey & Feldman, 1996; Downey, Feldman, & Ayduk, 2000). Our recent findings seem to suggest that a single, acute rejection makes people rejection-sensitive, propelling a series of coping behaviors that parallel those of people dispositionally high in rejection sensitivity. Particularly noteworthy was the finding that rejection led people to anticipate rejection from those outside of the rejecting relationship, including both strangers and those with whom they had already developed some intimacy. These findings underscore the important role of rejection in broader interpersonal functioning.

SITUATIONAL DETERMINANTS OF EXPECTANCIES

Are negative social expectancies impervious to change? At least some research suggests that the answer is "no." In the only known experimental manipulation of social expectancies, Rabiner and Coie (1989) recruited third grade males of low and high sociometric status (i.e., unpopular and popular boys) and gave half a positive expectancy induction. Specifically, experimental participants were introduced briefly to two other male children ("hosts") enrolled in a different school, and then informed a week later that the children had really liked them and were hoping to play with them again. Control participants underwent the same procedure but were given no expectancy induction. All children were then left alone to play with their hosts. Play sessions were videotaped.

Host children interacted with one participant who had received the expectancy induction and one who had not. They were then asked to report which child "most kids would rather have in this kind of group" and which one they "would prefer to be friends with."

Rabiner and Coie (1989) found that the positive expectancy induction had a significant impact on the impressions that unpopular children made on their hosts. Among 20 hosts, 12 showed a clear preference (on both measures) for the experimental (positive expectancy) children; 3 preferred the control child, and 5 failed to show a clear preference. Of the 18 hosts who interacted with popular children, 3 preferred the experimental child, 4 preferred the control child, and 11 showed no preference. Thus, hosts did not distinguish between the popular children who did and did not receive the expectancy induction. Despite the clear effectiveness of the expectancy induction on rejected (unpopular) boys' impressions on their hosts, content analyses of their videotaped interactions failed to detect differences in their behavior.

Using an almost identical procedure, Rabiner and Coie (1989) tested the same positive expectancy induction with unpopular females. Popular females were not examined. Of the 16 hosts, 8 expressed a clear preference for the experimental child, 3 chose the control child, and 5 insisted they could not decide. Though these differences were not significant, they were in the predicted direction. Further, analyses of videotaped behaviors indicated that rejected girls who received the expectancy induction approached their hosts significantly more "competently" (e.g., with a greater amount of prosocial than antisocial behavior) and exhibited more cooperative engagement in their hosts' activities than those who did not receive the positive expectancy induction.

The authors concluded that rejected children may possess knowledge of the behaviors appropriate for social situations but choose not to display them because they believe they will ultimately fail at being accepted. Interventions that improve expectancies, however, will lead rejected children to abandon strategies that minimize embarrassment and adopt prosocial strategies that are more risky but provide a greater payoff. Currently, the effects of positive expectancy inductions among adults are not known, but we anticipate that such "interventions" may be equally effective in overriding the negative social expectancies that people spontaneously develop in response to a single rejection experience (Sommer et al., 2004).

NEGATIVE SOCIAL EXPECTANCIES AND SELF-PROTECTION

It has been demonstrated that people who anticipate rejection from others behave in ways that objectively decrease their chances for acceptance, such as devaluing their relationships and derogating their partners. In this sense, negative social expectancies are self-fulfilling (see also Downey, Twenge, and Catanese and Tice, this volume). One cannot easily reconcile these findings with the innate need for social connections without considering what other functions these behaviors may serve.

To address this question, we turn to the early attachment work by Bowlby (1969; 1982). Bowlby identified a sequence of coping behaviors that infants and children display in response to the absence of an attachment figure. The first is protest and proximity seeking, wherein the child does everything possible to bring the person closer. Next, when efforts to re-establish contact are unsuccessful, the child enters a state of deep depression and despair. Finally, after prolonged absence of the attachment figure, the child becomes self-reliant and emotionally detached from others. This final stage of coping is viewed as the most defensive in nature because it allows the child to avoid additional feelings of separation anxiety and distress.

These coping stages—from attachment seeking to attachment avoidance—also seem to parallel the myriad social behaviors exhibited by rejected people. Thus, we suggest that coping responses to rejection may follow this same general pattern (see also Hazan & Shaver, 1994; and Williams and Zadro, this volume). Based on the attachment framework, we may further predict that weak or ambiguous rejection (i.e., threatened attachment) will increase anxiety but leave social expectancies relatively intact, especially among those who generally trust in others' regard for them (e.g., those high in self-esteem). In such cases, people will cope with the rejection by drawing closer to others and seeking felt security within close relationships. As rejection becomes increasingly salient, however, it overwhelms dispositionally-based expectancies and causes people to become sullen, withdrawn, and to develop a marked apathy for those around them. Finally, when there is no apparent hope for replenishing felt belongingness, people detach emotionally from others.

Bowlby (1982) suggested that emotional detachment may be adaptive by way of allowing people to redirect their efforts to forming new attachments. To our knowledge, no research has demonstrated whether detachment behaviors leave people in a better state emotionally to pursue alternative relationships. Feelings of self-reliance and social indifference could make proximity-seeking behaviors seem less risky, although they would probably also make them less likely.

Finally, though attachment theory provides little insight into why rejected individuals become interpersonally-destructive (e.g., derogating and distancing), we believe that the constellation of antisocial behaviors seen in the literature may assist in the process of emotional detachment. By rejecting others before others have had the opportunity to reject them, people can generate alternative, nonthreatening attributions for their treatment and also stave off the feelings of worthlessness and anxiety that accompany feelings of being unwanted. From a cognitive and emotional standpoint, then, antisocial behaviors may protect the self from future harm.

SUMMARY

Theory and reason would suggest that people respond to rejection by behaving in ways that increase their opportunities for acceptance (Baumeister & Tice, 1990). However, several studies have now demonstrated that rejected people often behave in ways that damage rather than strengthen interpersonal bonds. The key to predicting how people cope with rejection may lie with their expectations of future acceptance. Positive social expectancies lead people to draw closer to others, whereas negative expectancies lead them to distance themselves from others.

Trait self-esteem reflects chronic perceptions of one's value to others (Leary et al., 1995) and typically predicts how people cope with rejection threat. People high in self-esteem respond by affirming their close relationships and excelling on difficult tasks so as to show they are indeed worthy of others' high regard. People low in self-esteem respond by distancing themselves from relationship partners and giving up on difficult tasks. In the face of clear rejection, however, both high and low self-esteem individuals derogate their rejectors and develop negative expectancies about their potential for inclusion within new relationships. Relationally destructive behaviors may help rejected individuals to detach emotionally from others, thereby thwarting the pain and anxiety of perceived, impending rejection.

REFERENCES

Baumeister, R. F., & Leary, M. R. (1995). The need to belong: Desire for interpersonal attachments as a fundamental human motivation. *Psychological Bulletin, 117*, 497–529.

Baumeister, R. F., & Tice, D. M. (1985). Self-esteem and responses to success and failure: Subsequent performance and intrinsic motivation. *Journal of Personality, 53*, 450–467.

Baumeister, R. F., & Tice, D. M. (1990). Anxiety and social exclusion.. *Journal of Social and Clinical Psychology, 9*, 165–195.

Bourgeois, K. S., & Leary, M. R. (2001). Coping with rejection: Derogating those who choose us last. *Motivation and Emotion, 25*, 101–111.

Bowlby, J. (1969). *Attachment and loss: Vol. 1. Attachment.* New York: Basic Books.

Bowlby, J. (1982). *Attachment and loss: Vol. 1. Attachment* (2nd edition). New York: Basic Books.

Bowlby, J. (1973). *Attachment and loss: Vol. 2. Separation. Anxiety and anger.* New York: Basic Books.

Dotan, O., Rubin, Y., & Sommer, K. L. (April, 2004). *Impact of language diversity on team-member's self-feelings, team-perceptions, and individual-performance.* Presented at the annual conference of the Society for Industrial and Organizational Psychology, Chicago, IL.

Downey, G., & Feldman, S. I. (1996). Implications of rejection sensitivity for intimate relationships. *Journal of Personality and Social Psychology, 70*, 1327–1343.

Downey, G., Feldman, S., & Ayduk, O. (2000). Rejection sensitivity and male violence in romantic relationships. *Personal Relationships, 7*, 45–61.

Downey, G., Lebolt, A., Rincon, C., & Freitas, A. L. (1998). Rejection sensitivity and children's interpersonal difficulties. *Child Development, 69*, 1072–1089.

Geller, D. M., Goodstein, L., Silver, M. & Sternberg, W. C. (1974). On being ignored: The effects of violation of implicit rules of social interaction. *Sociometry, 37*, 541–556

Hazan, C., & Shaver, P. R. (1994). Attachment as an organizational framework for research on close relationships. *Psychological Inquiry, 5*, 1–22.

Leary, M. R. (1990). Responses to social exclusion: Social anxiety, jealousy, loneliness, depression, and low self-esteem. *Journal of Social and Clinical Psychology, 9*, 221–229.

Leary, M. R. (2004). The sociometer, self-esteem, and the regulation of interpersonal behavior (pp. 373–391). In R. F. Baumeister & K. D. Vohs (Eds.), *Handbook of self-regulation: Research, theory, and applications*. New York: Guilford Press.

Leary, M. R., Haupt., A. L., Strausser, K. S., & Chokel, J. T. (1998). Calibrating the sociometer: The relationship between interpersonal appraisals and state self-esteem. *Journal of Personality and Social Psychology, 74*, 1290–1299.

Leary, M. R., Koch, E. J., & Hechenbleikner, N. R. (2001). Emotional responses to interpersonal rejection (pp. 145–166). In M. Leary (Ed.), *Interpersonal rejection*. New York: Oxford University Press.

Leary, M. R., Tambor, E. S., Terdal, S K., & Downs, D. L. (1995). Self-esteem as an interpersonal monitor: The sociometer hypothesis. *Journal of Personality and Social Psychology, 68*, 518–530.

Mauger, P. A., Perry, J. E., Freeman, T., & Grove, D. C. (1992). The measurement of forgiveness: Preliminary research. *Journal of Psychology and Christianity, 11 (Special Issue: Grace and Forgiveness), 170–180.

Murray, S. L., Holmes, J. G., Griffin, D. W. (2000). Self-esteem and the quest for felt security: How perceived regard regulates attachment processes. *Journal of Personality and Social Psychology, 78*, 478–498.

Murray, S. L., Bellavia, G. M., Rose, P., & Griffin, D. W. (2003). Once hurt, twice hurtful: How perceived regard regulates daily marital interactions. *Journal of Personality and Social Psychology, 84*, 126–147.

Murray, S. L., Holmes, J. G., MacDonald, G., & Ellsworth, P. C. (1998). Through the looking glass darkly? When self-doubts turn into relationship insecurities. *Journal of Personality and Social Psychology, 75*, 1459–1480.

Murray, S. L., Rose, P., Bellavia, G. M., Holmes, J. G., & Kusche, A. G. (2002). When rejection stings: How self-esteem constrains relationship-enhancement processes. *Journal of Personality and Social Psychology, 83*, 556–573.

Nezlek, J. B., Kowalski, R. M., Leary, M. R., Blevins, T., & Holgate, S. (1997) Personality moderators of reactions to interpersonal rejection: Depression and trait self-esteem. *Personality and Social Psychology Bulletin, 23*, 1235–1244.

Pepitone, A., & Wilpizeski, C. (1960). Some consequences of experimental rejection. *Journal of Abnormal and Social Psychology, 60*, 359–364.

Rabiner, D., & Coie, J. (1989). Effects of expectancy inductions on rejected children's acceptance by unfamiliar peers. *Developmental Psychology, 25*, 450–457.

Rusbult, C. E., Morrow, G. D. & Johnson, D. J. (1987). Self-esteem and problem solving behavior in close relationships. *British Journal of Social Psychology, 26*, 293–303.

Rusbult, C. E., Verette, J., Whitney, G. A., Slovik, L. F., & Lipkus, I. (1991). Accommodation processes in close relationships: Theory and preliminary empirical evidence. *Journal of Personality and Social Psychology, 60*, 53–78.

Sedikides, C., Campbell, W. K., & Reeder, G. D. (1999). The Relationship Closeness Induction Task. *Representative Research in Social Psychology, 23*, 1–4.

Sommer, K. L. (2001). Interpersonal rejection, self-esteem, and ego-defensive strategies. (pp. 167–188). In M. Leary (Ed.), *Interpersonal rejection*. New York: Oxford University Press.

Sommer, K. L., & Baumeister, R. F. (2002). Self-evaluation, persistence, and performance following implicit rejection: The role of trait self-esteem. *Personality and Social Psychology Bulletin, 28*, 926–938.

Sommer, K. L., Benkendorf, D., & Kirkland, K. L. (2004). *Rejection, self-esteem, and interpersonal behavior within intimate and nonintimate relationships*. Unpublished manuscript.

Sommer, K. L., Williams, K. D., Ciarocco, N. J., & Baumeister, R. F. (2001). When silence speaks louder than words: Explorations into the interpersonal and intrapsychic consequences of social ostracism. *Basic and Applied Social Psychology, 23*, 225–243.

Twenge, J. M., Catanese, K. R., & Baumeister, R. F. (2002). Social exclusion causes self-defeating behavior. *Journal of Personality and Social Psychology, 83*, 606–615.

Williams, K. D. (2001). *Ostracism: The power of silence*. New York, NY: Guilford Press.

Williams, K. D., Cheung, C. K. T., & Choi, W. (2000). Cyberostracism: Effects of being ignored over the Internet. *Journal of Personality and Social Psychology, 79*, 748–762

Williams, K. D, & Sommer, K. L. (1997). Social ostracism by coworkers: Does rejection lead to loafing or compensation? *Personality and Social Psychology Bulletin, 23*, 693–706.

11

Coping With Rejection
Core Social Motives Across Cultures

SUSAN T. FISKE
MARIKO YAMAMOTO

Core Social Motives
Motives and Rejection: Evidence
Conclusion

*P*eople are right to dread rejection. Social isolates feel bad, suffering anxiety and depression in the moment, and a general lack of well-being over the long-term (Baumeister, 1991; Baumeister & Tice, 1990; Leary, 1990; Nezlek, Kowalski, Leary, Blevins, & Holgate, 1997; Williams, Cheung, & Choi, 2000; and in this volume, see Williams & Zadro; Eisenberger & Lieberman; MacDonald, Kingsbury, & Shaw). Social isolates damage their immune systems and threaten their cardio-vascular health (House, Landis, & Umberson, 1988; Kiecolt-Glaser, McGuire, Robles, & Glaser, 2002; see Cacioppo & Hawkley , this volume). Social isolates die sooner (Berkman, 1995; Berkman et al., 2000; Berkman & Syme, 1979; Berscheid & Reis, 1998). Throughout human history, being banished from the group has amounted to a death sentence.

Not surprisingly, then, people care deeply about social rejection and acceptance. Being accepted by other people represents a core concern: the motive to belong (e.g., Fiske, 2004; Leary & Baumeister, 2000; Pickett & Gardner, this volume). People want to connect with other people in their own group, arguably in order to survive and thrive. The core motive to belong defines ingroup (own group) and outgroup (all other groups). Ingroup *belonging* matters because the

---

Address correspondence to: Susan T. Fiske, Professor, Department of Psychology, Princeton University. E-mail: sfiske@princeton.edu

ingroup by definition shares one's goals, which facilitates other core social motives, for example, socially shared *understanding*, a sense of *controlling* one's outcomes, *enhancing* the self, and *trusting* close others (Fiske, 2004). The outgroup by definition does not share the ingroup's goals, being at best indifferent and at worst hostile, so it is viewed as threatening and elicits negative affect (Fiske & Ruscher, 1993). This approach to social behavior highlights the importance of knowing who is with "us" and who is against "us," in the service of furthering shared goals.

The approach has elements in common with other emphatically social adaptationist perspectives on social cognition (e.g., Kurzban & Leary, 2001; Neuberg, Smith & Asher, 2000), but it focuses less specifically on reproductive strategies and more on social surviving and thriving within a group (Brewer, 1997; Caporael, 1997; Hogg, this volume). This approach also fits with a pragmatic, goal-based analysis of social behavior (Fiske, 1992). Social perception, expectations, and norms provide the foundation for social survival within one's group. When people respond to another social entity, whether a group or an individual, they do so in the service of core social motives, especially belonging.

As this book makes clear, everyone hates interpersonal rejection, reflecting the importance of belonging across individuals and cultures. Nevertheless, cultures differ in the ways they manage the possibility of rejection, differentially enacting the other core social motives, as our research is beginning to explore. We take Japan and the United States as our comparative cases to illustrate these points.

CORE SOCIAL MOTIVES

Belonging Securely versus Belonging Widely

We assume that a few core motives can help explain people's reactions in both cultures to the threat of rejection and to actual rejection. We have used five motives drawn from personality and social psychology's most common themes over their history (Stevens & Fiske, 1995). The core motive of belonging, most violated by rejection, is posited to be universal, but it is enacted differently depending on culture.

Several theories contrast Eastern and Western views, with relevance for belonging. Cultural self theory (Markus & Kitayama, 1991) contrasts Eastern interdependent selves, focused on relational motives to maintain harmony, with Western independent selves, focused on self-enhancing motives to keep autonomy. Basic trust theory (Yamagishi & Yamagishi, 1994) contrasts Japanese caution with American trust, respectively requiring a long confirmation and preference for acquaintances versus a short confirmation and openness to strangers. We address each of these in a more specific context soon, but in the context of belonging motives, they form the basis of our hypothesis that Japanese will be characterized by *belonging securely* and selectively, expecting relationships to be life-long units, and showing cautious neutrality toward strangers. In contrast, Americans will be characterized by *belonging widely* and loosely, expecting relationships to have more flexible autonomy and showing immediate positivity toward strangers. These cultural variations in belonging underlie variations in the other core social motives that operate in the service of this fundamental, universal motive for belonging: shared understanding, effective control, self enhancement, and trusting.

Understanding Relationships versus Persons

People are demonstrably motivated to develop a socially shared understanding of each other and their environment (Fiske, 2002, 2004). A shared information framework allows people to function in groups and in any kind of relationship. It informs their assessment of their own rejection and acceptance. This understanding is likely to operate along particular dimensions that facilitate belonging, and these dimensions will be, we suggest, pancultural. But people's strategies for understanding will also show some cultural variation, consistent with Western emphasis on autonomy and unvarnished honesty or with Eastern emphasis on interdependence and social harmony. Japanese focus relatively more on socially shared understanding of secure relationships, whereas Americans relatively emphasize the individual self and other, in wide, loose relationships.

Controlling as a Group or Individual

Being rejected violates one's feeling of control (Williams et al., 2000). People are highly motivated to know the contingencies between their own actions and their outcomes (Fiske, 2002, 2004). Feelings of control reflect feeling effective in one's environment. Feeling efficacious promotes both individual health and group life, so people try to restore lost control, but cultures and individuals vary on this motive.

Previous research on interdependence showed that Westerners attend to those who control their outcomes, reflecting a basic motive for a sense of personal control (Dépret & Fiske, 1999; Erber & Fiske, 1984; Neuberg & Fiske, 1987; Ruscher & Fiske, 1990; Stevens & Fiske, 2000). Americans, at least, search for information that will restore a sense of personal prediction and control when their outcomes depend on another person. Similarly, when their sense of control is threatened generally, they search for information about others in their environment (Pittman & Pittman, 1980).

Cultural differences in control reflect a greater emphasis on social harmony, whereby the individual cedes control to ingroup others, seeking to create and maintain collective compatibility. For example, a scale of harmony control (Morling & Fiske, 1997) included items such as feeling secure in friends taking care of oneself, getting one's own needs met by meeting the needs of others, and going along with intangible forces larger than the self. As one cultural contrast, for example, Latinos (collectivists) score higher than Anglos (individualists). One would predict that Japanese would tend to score higher than Americans, and this will be the subject of a future study. In the current context, we predict that Japanese control would be ceded to the secure ingroup more than American feelings of control by the efficacious self, who then freely participates in a variety of relationships.

Enhancing Relationship versus Self

The self plays a special role in people's lives. Westerners tend to enhance themselves relative to other people or relative to other people's view of them (Kwan et al., 2004). Easterners tend to be more modest, and view the self more in the context of group memberships (Markus & Kitayama, 1991). Some have posited that Easterners view the self with a special sympathy, despite its admitted flaws (Heine, Lehman, Markus, & Kitayama, 1999). The Eastern self may be improved, although the task is difficult and success is not guaranteed. This contrast appears in American self-confidence about belonging widely and loosely versus Japanese caution about belonging securely.

Trusting Selectively versus Widely

Americans generally have positive expectations about other people, as a baseline (Fiske, 2002, 2004). This is one reason that rejection rankles as much as it does. Americans, in general, trust other people not to create unprovoked negative outcomes for themselves. In Japan, trust operates more narrowly, within the ingroup, and only then based on the assurance of knowing the other person's incentive contingencies (Yamagishi, 1998). As a result of the more narrow trusting motive and the embedding of self in a network, caution should be more evident in our Japanese data on belonging and rejection.

MOTIVES AND REJECTION: EVIDENCE

This chapter reports five kinds of preliminary comparative data: (a) societal stereotypes reflecting rejection between groups, (b) reported norms about rejection among friends, (c) a scenario study about potential rejection, (d) a study of expected interaction and potential rejection, and (e) a study of actual interaction and actual rejection. In each case, we find cultural similarities as well as differences reflecting the motive to belong more securely or more loosely.

Societal Stereotypes: Rejection Between Groups

Background When people encounter another social entity (individual or group), they want to know belonging immediately—whether the other is friend or foe. That is, they first want to know the other's intent, for good or ill. If the other's intent is benign, the other is ingroup or a close ally and less likely to be rejecting (see also Gaertner & Iuzzini, this volume). But intentions are meaningless without capability, so people also must learn whether the other is able or unable to enact them.

If the core motive of belonging matters so much, then people's central concern when trying to understand another person or group will be the other person's group membership. The Continuum Model (CM) argues that such social category-based responses are rapid and primary, coming before more individuated, person-specific responses (e.g., Fiske & Neuberg, 1990; Fiske, Lin, & Neuberg, 1999).

Current work more closely examines the nature of those social categories. We proceed from the premise that the crucial categories essentially answer: friend or foe? And then: able or unable? That is, when people encounter strangers, they first want to know the strangers' intentions (good or ill) and their ability to enact them (capability). If the intentions are good, then the social other's goals are at least compatible, and the other is ingroup or a close ally. Otherwise, the other entity is unsafe. And whether the goals are compatible or not, people want to know whether the other entity actually matters (if capable) or not (if incapable).

The Stereotype Content Model (SCM; Fiske, Xu, Cuddy, & Glick, 1999; Fiske, Cuddy, Glick, & Xu, 2002) proposes that societal groups are universally perceived along two primary dimensions, *warmth* and *competence*. The two proposed primary dimensions of general stereotype content—warmth (e.g., friendly, good-natured, and sincere) and competence (e.g., capable, confident, and skillful)—respectively answer the friend-foe and able-unable questions. They have received copious support from several areas of psychology. These dimensions emerge in classic person perception studies (Asch, 1946; Rosenberg, Nelson, & Vivekananthan, 1968). And in more recent person perception research, these two dimensions account for more than 80% of the variance in global impressions of individuals (Wojciszke, Baryla, & Mikiewicz, 2003; Wojciszke, Bazinska, & Jaworski, 1998). Similar twin dimensions appear in work on social-value orientations (e.g., self- and other-profitability, Peeters, 1983; Peeters, 1992, 1995), in construals of others' behaviors (Wojciszke, 1994), and in voters' ratings of political candidates in the United States (Kinder & Sears, 1985) and Poland (Wojciszke & Klusek, 1996). Related dimensions also describe national stereotypes (e.g., competence and morality, Alexander, Brewer, & Hermann, 1999; Phalet & Poppe, 1997; Poppe, 2001; Poppe & Linssen, 1999) and surface in numerous in-depth analyses of prejudices toward specific social groups (e.g., Glick, 2002; Glick, Diebold, Bailey Werner, & Zhu, 1997; Glick & Fiske, 1996, 1997; Hurh & Kim, 1989; Kitano & Sue, 1973; Helmreich, Spence, & Wilhelm, 1981). People in many circumstances want to know who is with them (acceptance) or against them (rejection) and what they can do about it.

Cultural Similarities in Group Stereotypes   We have recently found that these dimensions also generalize across cultures (Cuddy, Fiske, Kwan, Glick, et al., 2005). In several European and three Asian cultures, using their own societal groups, we find substantially the same patterns, supporting the contention that the dimensions represent universal human concerns about societal groups. The pancultural model was tested in studies comprising 12 international samples. If the SCM describes universal human principles of human motives for belonging, they should not be limited to American perceivers or groups in an individualistic, multicultural context. As expected, across culturally varied perceivers and target groups: (a) perceived warmth and competence reliably differentiate group stereotypes; (b) many outgroups receive evaluatively-mixed stereotypes, high on one dimension but low on the other; and (c) higher-status groups are stereotyped as competent, while competitive groups are stereotyped as lacking warmth. These studies suggest pancultural principles: People are deeply concerned with information of acceptance and rejection, namely the other groups' warmth (intent for good or ill) and ability to act on it (competence).

Cultural Differences in Group Stereotypes   In the context of an overall similar space for societal groups, defined by with-us warmth and can-do ability, or their opposites, some cultural variants do appear. Ingroups and societal reference groups uniformly dominate the high-warmth/high-competence cluster in Western samples. We, our allies, and our societal reference groups are good; others are less good or all bad. However, in samples from Japan (gathered by Yamamoto & Tin Tin Htun), Korea (Kim), and Hong Kong (Kwan & Bond), the ingroups, allies, and societal reference groups all migrate to the modest center of the space, consistent with the idea of more positive self views in the West than the East (Cuddy et al., 2005). Outgroup derogation does not require ingroup favoritism. More relevant here, secure belonging does not require overt ingroup favoritism, but the overall space for societal groups remains defined by parameters of acceptance and rejection characterized by warmth and the ability to enact it.

Reported Norms: Rejection among Friends

Moving from the societal to the interpersonal level, another comparative study, currently in progress, also highlights Japanese focus on belonging securely and American focus on belonging widely. We (Miyamoto, Yamamoto, et al., 2004) are developing a scale on how people prefer to relate to others, for example friends of a friend, to contrast an orientation toward autonomy (friendships as one-on-one, independent, potentially temporary) or toward unit-relations (friendships as embedded in larger networks, interdependent, life-long). Both the autonomous and unit orientations express people's approaches to relationships, in which the American context focuses on independent actors coming together and the Japanese context focuses on people coming together within a network of relationships (see also Fitness, this volume, for a discussion of interpersonal rejection within families).

The contrast between autonomy and interdependence fits the broader literature in cultural psychology on bases of well-being (Kitayama, Markus, & Kurokawa, 2000) and on individualism-collectivism or independence-interdependence generally (A. P. Fiske, Kitayama, Markus, & Nisbett, 1998). The implications for experiences of rejection are that in the American instance, it violates a relationship between two individuals, but in the Japanese context, it violates an entire network of relationships. In effect, the stakes are raised by diffusing control across two networks (each partner's network), not just between two people. As the next section indicates, the social network encourages people to be cautious (cf. Adams & Plaut, 2003).

Scenario Study: Potential Rejection

In another comparative study (Yamamoto, Miyamoto, Fiske, & Wright, 2004), participants (70 U.S. students, 70 Japanese students) read a hypothetical scenario involving a chance encounter with the friend of a friend. They answered a series of open-ended questions designed to tap their meta-expectations about the relationship.

Cultural Similarities   Shared norms of belonging require everyone to greet the other person and to strike a balance between presuming too much intimacy and avoiding open rejection or hostility. The ways of enacting these norms, however, differ in communicating more caution outside of a secure established relationship (Japanese) and more indiscriminant openness to any friend of a friend (American).

Cultural Differences   For Americans, the normal response to the friend of a friend entails smiling and chatting, with a favorable attitude. They report that it would be rude not to address the person, and some report that they would respond on behalf of their friend or to get to know the other person. For some, it would not be normal to be too negative (look displeased, have a cold attitude, act aggressive) but also not to be inappropriate (too intimate or unsuitable). They tend to explain any potentially abnormal behavior by the other person as dispositional, either temporary (busy, distracted) or long-term (just that kind of person).

For the Japanese, the normal response includes more caution, less presumption: introducing oneself and discussing the mutual friend, more so than the Americans. In a similar vein, but more formally, some Japanese might also bow or inquire as to whether they had met previously. A few Japanese express relatively negative expectancies: ignoring, leaving immediately, avoiding eye contact, not talking, and having a negative attitude. Some report that the interaction would be awkward, that they might have nothing to say, or the person might not remember them. Like the Americans, the Japanese strike a balance between avoiding open negativity and inappropriate intimacy. They are relatively more concerned with presuming intimacy (too friendly, too self-disclosing), although some think that ignoring the person would be abnormal. They tend to explain any potentially abnormal behavior by the other person as resulting from relational breakdown (does not remember me or conversely too sociable) or temporary, uncontrollable causes (not feeling well). Overall, apart from the minimal social requirements of greeting the other person, their expected response was cautious, minimizing contact and waiting to see what the other person would do. They were reserved, noncommittal, and awkward. Similarly, they expected that the other person would not be either too friendly or too rude. That is, rejection is definitely unexpected, reflecting a degree of openness to belonging, but not as much optimism as Americans.

Thus, both cultural samples expect civility without presumption or hostility, with Americans more favorable but blaming the other for any breakdown, and with Japanese more cautious but mutually so.

Expected Interaction: Potential Rejection

In a fourth comparative study (Miyamoto, Yamamoto, Fiske, & Miki, 2004), Japanese (n = 70) and American (n = 74) students were recruited to test computer game software with a stranger. In the course of this study (otherwise irrelevant for current purposes), they reported their motives in the expected interaction and mutual evaluation. Factor analyses indicated three dimensions. Understanding reflected an equivalent desire to get to know their partner and vice versa. And everyone wanted to be seen positively and to exchange accurate evaluations.

The Americans were somewhat more likely to endorse self-enhancing expectations (hoping for especially positive evaluations of their own creativity and personality). The Japanese were especially more likely to expect accuracy, rate a partner highly, and build a unit relationship, presumably because they have to work with each other (unlike the previous studies).

Thus, given the prospect of required interaction, Americans self-enhance and Japanese orient to the relationship.

Actual Interaction: Actual Rejection

As indicated, we believe that the human motive to belong is essentially universal. People all suffer under social rejection, as various contributors to this symposium have shown in their respective programs of research. Our own empirical foray illustrates the cultural similarity of the actual rejection experience, regardless of whether the culture is individualist or collectivist, but some variations exist.

Background   We conducted a comparative experiment with a three-factor between-subjects experimental design. Participants (57 U.S. and 97 Japanese undergraduates) experienced distinct feedback (positive or negative evaluation) in the context of research on intimacy processes, which would require them to interact with a randomly assigned new acquaintance. All procedures used table top computers and a pre-programmed partner. In a "preliminary step," they exchanged brief videotaped greetings. On a questionnaire, participants then described themselves, and they evaluated their partners' speech, their potential compatibility, and their preliminary impression of their partner. Using this newly exchanged information, participants then had to decide whether to accept the other as a partner for the intimacy processes session. To decide, they searched through answers from their partner's preliminary questionnaire. After searching information, participants answered some additional questions before the debriefing.

In learning how to search their partner's responses via computer, they immediately saw their partner's evaluation of their introductory speech. Half of the participants were randomly assigned to encounter negative feedback and half positive, as one of the independent variables. In the negative condition, participants learned that their partner's evaluation was, on a 5-point scale, "2. Not very good" and described thus: "I thought you did not express yourself well. I did not think you had any intention of making me understand you. I couldn't tell what kind of person you are from your speech." In the positive condition, they learned their evaluation was "4. Quite good" and described thus: "I thought that you expressed yourself well. I thought that you were trying to make me understand you. I could tell you what kind of person you are from your speech." Recall that this information would be diagnostic for predicting whether their partner was likely to accept or reject them as a partner for the second part of the study on intimacy processes.

The manipulation check showed that the manipulation of feedback was successful. The participants in the positive condition gave higher scores to a question about their partner's evaluation of their speech, and the participants in the negative condition gave lower scores. This happened identically in both countries; no one denied the feedback (and potential rejection).

Cultural Similarities in Belonging   Under negative feedback, all participants reported feeling bad, and under positive feedback, all reported feeling good. Moreover, under negative feedback, half subsequently rejected their negative partners. None of the positive-feedback partners did. These results imply that negative social feedback commonly makes people—Japanese or American—feel bad. Reciprocity of rejection also commonly occurs in both countries.

Cultural Differences in Belonging   In our comparative study, factor analyses separated impression items into three factors: warmth, competence, and compatibility. Consistent with the idea of generalized trust in others, American participants showed positive impressions of their partner on all three factors before they received positive or negative feedback. Consistent with the idea of less trust and more caution, the Japanese participants showed a lower score in compatibility even before they received feedback. This result implies that the Japanese are cautious about whether or not they will be accepted by (and accept) their partners.

For the American participants, negative feedback lowered the impressions of their partners on all three aspects of impression; these results fit the idea of initially optimistic Americans nevertheless responding to what they perceive as objective feedback. These results imply that Americans have a positivity bias toward a new acquaintance but that the positive impression of the person will change if the person reacts negatively.

For the Japanese participants, on the other hand, the negative feedback made only the warmth impressions worse; the compatibility and competence scores stayed about the same under negative feedback. The Japanese seemed not to make a quick decision but instead kept their attitude toward a new acquaintance neutral. That is why the impression of compatibility started low and stayed neutral even under negative feedback.

As noted, the participants could search for information related to their partner's impression of them. American participants tried to confirm both positive and negative feedback, as if seeking a clear understanding of the nature of the rejection. The Japanese showed quite a different tendency, namely that they seem to confirm the evaluation they received *only* when it was negative. Participants in the two countries thus showed different search strategies when they were rejected or received negative feedback.

In a similar vein, the Americans seemed to emphasize an unvarnished form of honesty, taking the feedback at face value. Americans accepted the feedback as a valid expression of the other person's autonomous opinion. The positive feedback was accepted as positive, and the negative feedback was accepted as negative. In contrast, the Japanese could not accept the feedback as necessarily valid, whether it was negative or positive. They evaluated the feedback as neutral. The Japanese judged the negative evaluator as more serious than the positive one, searched for information related to potential compatibility, and seemed to confirm that they were rejected by their partner through searching for items about mutual compatibility. These results supported our hypothesis that Americans believed the feedback as a valid expression of their partner's own attitude, and the Japanese thought that their partner did not necessarily reveal a valid expression of attitude.

The data from our comparative study reinforce the idea that the self is special in both countries: Upon receiving feedback, all participants focused on information about self. Both American and Japanese participants in both feedback conditions searched for more information about their partners' judgments of them (that is, self-related information).

The motives in both cases concern evaluations of self, but the Americans apparently operated in the context of objective understanding, as described earlier. (The feedback was so unambiguous that they could not easily deny it and simply self-enhance.) The Japanese also searched for self-relevant information, but the self in context of relationships. Although both looked at the partner's evaluations of them, the Americans and the Japanese used different strategies for searching self-related information. Americans showed more interest in the evaluation of their own speech, consistent with their focus on autonomous understanding. On the other hand, the Japanese showed more interest in mutual compatibility, especially in the positive feedback conditions. Americans showed much less interest in compatibility compared to the Japanese. This result confirms our hypothesis that the Japanese put more focus on the self within the interpersonal relationship than Americans do.

CONCLUSION

Our comparative results suggest that people in the two cultures sometimes have different motives and meta-expectations about interpersonal relationships. Americans' sense of wide, loose belonging apparently fits autonomous understanding, with people being direct and speaking the truth. They view relationships as a matter of individual choice and control, show self-confidence and self-enhancement, and trust optimistically until proven otherwise.

The Japanese apparently have slightly different motives and meta-expectations. They prioritize social harmony, relation-oriented motives, and do not mind saying different things in different situations. Thus, they did not think feedback was necessarily true, even if their partner evaluated them positively. To the Japanese, to say positive words means only that they want to show that they are not actively refusing the other person or that they are just being flattering. Understanding, control, self-enhancement, and trust all operate in the context of interpersonal compatibility.

Our ongoing research continues to explore cross cultural comparisons on belonging widely or securely, with implications for people's well-being in the face of acceptance and rejection.

REFERENCES

Adams, G., & Plaut, V. C. The cultural grounding of personal relationship: Friendship in North American and West African worlds. *Personal Relationships, 10,* 333–347.

Alexander, M. G., Brewer, M. B., & Hermann, R. K. (1999). Images and affect: A functional analysis of out-group stereotypes. *Journal of Personality and Social Psychology, 77,* 78–93.

Asch, S. E. (1946). Forming impressions of personality. *Journal of Abnormal and Social Psychology, 41,* 1230–1240.

Baumeister, R. F. (1991). *Meanings of life.* New York: Guilford Press.

Baumeister, R. F., & Leary, M. R. (1995) The need to belong: Desire for interpersonal attachments as a fundamental human motivation. *Psychological Bulletin, 117,* 497–529.

Baumeister, R. F., & Tice, D. M. (1990). Anxiety and social exclusion. *Journal of Social and Clinical Psychology, 9,* 165–195.

Berkman, L. F. (1995). The role of social relations in health promotion. *Psychosomatic Medicine, 57,* 245–254.

Berkman, L. F. & Syme, S. L. (1979). Social networks, host resistance, and morality. *American Journal of Epidemiology, 109,* 186–204.

Berkman, L. F., Glass, T., Brissette, I., & Seeman, T. E. (2000). From social integration to health: Durkheim in the new millennium. *Social Science and Medicine, 51,* 843–857.

Berscheid, E., & Reis, H. T. (1998). Attraction and close relationships. In D. T. Gilbert, S. T. Fiske, & G. Lindzey (Eds.), *Handbook of social psychology: Vol. 2* (4th ed., pp. 193–281). New York: McGraw-Hill.

Brewer, M. B. (1997). On the social origins of human nature. In C. McGarty & S. A. Haslam (Eds.), *The message of social psychology* (pp. 54–62). Cambridge, MA: Blackwell.

Caporael, L. R. (1997). The evolution of truly social cognition: The core configurations model. *Review of Personality and Social Psychology, 1,* 276–298.

Cuddy, A. J. C., Fiske, S. T., Kwan, V. S. Y., Glick, P., et al. (2005). *Toward pancultural principles of stereotyping.* Unpublished manuscript. Princeton University.

Dépret, E. F., & Fiske, S. T. (1999). Perceiving the

powerful: Intriguing individuals versus threatening groups. *Journal of Experimental Social Psychology, 35,* 461–480.

Erber, R., & Fiske, S. T. (1984). Outcome dependency and attention to inconsistent information. *Journal of Personality and Social Psychology, 47,* 709–726.

Fiske, S. T. (1992). Thinking is for doing: Portraits of social cognition from daguerreotype to laserphoto. *Journal of Personality and Social Psychology, 63,* 877–889.

Fiske, S. T. (2002). Five core social motives, plus or minus five. In S. J. Spencer, S. Fein, M. P. Zanna, & J. Olson (Eds.), *Motivated social perception: The Ontario Symposium: Vol 9* (pp. 233–246). Mahwah, NJ: Erlbaum.

Fiske, S. T. (2004). *Social beings: A core motives approach to social psychology.* New York: Wiley.

Fiske, S. T., & Neuberg, S. L. (1990). A continuum of impression formation, from category-based to individuating processes: Influences of information and motivation on attention and interpretation. In M. P. Zanna (Ed.), *Advances in experimental social psychology: Vol. 23* (pp. 1–74). New York: Academic Press.

Fiske, S. T., & Ruscher, J. B. (1993). Negative interdependence and prejudice: Whence the affect? In D. M. Mackie & D. L. Hamilton (Eds.), *Affect, cognition, and stereotyping: Interactive processes in group perception* (pp. 239–268). San Diego CA: Academic Press.

Fiske, S. T., Lin, M. H., & Neuberg, S. L. (1999). The Continuum Model: Ten years later. In S. Chaiken & Y. Trope (Eds.), *Dual process theories in social psychology* (pp. 231–254). New York: Guilford Press.

Fiske, S. T., Xu, J., Cuddy, A. J. C., & Glick, P. S. (1999). (Dis)respecting versus (dis)liking: Status and interdependence predict ambivalent stereotypes of competence and warmth. *Journal of Social Issues, 55,* 473–489.

Fiske, S. T., Cuddy, A. J., Glick, P., & Xu, J. (2002). A model of (often mixed) stereotype content: Competence and warmth respectively follow from perceived status and competition. *Journal of Personality and Social Psychology, 82,* 878–902.

Fiske, A. P., Kitayama, S., Markus, H. R., & Nisbett, R. E. (1998). The cultural matrix of social psychology. In D. T. Gilbert, S. T. Fiske, & G. Lindzey (Eds.), *Handbook of social psychology: Vol. 2* (4th ed., pp. 915–981). New York: McGraw-Hill.

Glick, P. (2002). Sacrificial lambs dressed in wolves' clothing: Envious prejudice, ideology, and the scapegoating of Jews. In L. S. Newman & R. Erber (Eds.), *Understanding genocide: The social psychology of the Holocaust* (pp. 113–142). London: Oxford University Press.

Glick, P., & Fiske, S. T. (1996). The ambivalent sexism inventory: Differentiating hostile and benevolent sexism. *Journal of Personality and Social Psychology, 70,* 491–512.

Glick, P., Diebold, J., Bailey-Werner, B., & Zhu, L. (1997). The two faces of Adam: Ambivalent sexism and polarized attitudes toward women. *Personality and Social Psychology Bulletin, 23,* 1323–1334.

Heine, S. J., Lehman, D. R., Markus, H. R., & Kitayama, S. (1999). Is there a universal need for positive self-regard? *Psychological Review, 106,* 766–794.

Helmreich, R. L., Spence, J. T., & Wilhelm, J. A. (1981). A psychometric analysis of the Personal Attributes Questionnaire. *Sex Roles, 7,* 1097–1108.

House, J. S., Landis, K. R., & Umberson, D. (1988). Social relationships and health. *Science, 241,* 540–545.

Hurh, W. M., & Kim, K. C. (1989). The "success" image of Asian Americans: Its validity and its practical and theoretical implications. *Ethnic and Racial Studies, 12,* 512–538.

Kiecolt-Glaser, J. K., McGuire, L., Robles, T. F., & Glaser, R. (2002). Emotions, morbidity, and mortality: New perspectives from psychoneuroimmunology. In S. T. Fiske, D. L. Shacter, & C. Zahn-Waxler (Eds.), *Annual review of psychology: Vol. 53,* (pp. 83–107). Palo Alto, CA: Annual Reviews.

Kinder, D. R., & Sears, D. O. (1981). Prejudice and politics: Symbolic racism versus racial threats to the good life. *Journal of Personality and Social Psychology, 40,* 414–431.

Kitano, H. H. L., & Sue, S. (1973). The model minorities. *Journal of Social Issues, 29,* 1–9.

Kitayama, S., Markus, H. R., & Kurokawa, M. (2000). Culture, emotion, and well-being: Good feelings in Japan and the United States. *Cognition and Emotion, 14,* 93–124.

Kurzban, R., & Leary, M. R. (2001). Evolutionary origins of stigmatization: The functions of social exclusion. *Psychological Bulletin, 127,* 187–208.

Kwan, V. S. Y., John, O. P., Kenny, D. A., Bond, M. H., & Robins, R. W. (2004). Reconceptualizing individual differences in self enhancement bias: An interpersonal approach. *Psychological Review, 111*, 94–110.

Leary, M. R. (1990). Responses to social exclusion: Social anxiety, jealousy, loneliness, depression, and low self-esteem. *Journal of Social and Clinical Psychology, 9*, 221–229.

Leary, M. R., & Baumeister, R. F. (2000). The nature and function of self-esteem: Sociometer theory. In M. P. Zanna (Ed.), *Advances in experimental social psychology: Vol. 32* (pp. 1–62). New York: Academic Press.

Markus, H. R., & Kitayama, S. (1991). Culture and the self: Implications for cognition, emotion, and motivation. *Psychological Review, 98*, 224–253.

Miyamoto, S., Yamamoto, M., Fiske, S., & Miki, H. (2004). Unpublished data, Tsukuba University.

Morling, B., & Fiske, S. T. (1999). Defining and measuring harmony control. *Journal of Research in Personality, 33*, 379–414.

Neuberg, S. L., & Fiske, S. T. (1987). Motivational influences on impression formation: Outcome dependency, accuracy-driven attention, and individuating processes. *Journal of Personality and Social Psychology, 53*, 431–444.

Neuberg, S. L., Smith, D. M., & Asher, T. (2000). Why people stigmatize: Toward a biocultural framework. In T. F. Heatherton, R. E. Kleck, M. R. Hebl, & J. G. Hull (Eds.), *The social psychology of stigma* (pp. 31–61). New York: Guilford Press.

Nezlek, J. B., Kowalski, R. M., Leary, M. R., Blevins, T., & Holgate, S. (1997). Personality moderators of reactions to interpersonal rejection: Depression and trait self-esteem. *Personality and Social Psychology Bulletin, 23*, 1235–1244.

Peeters, G. (1983). Relational and informational patterns in social cognition. In W. Doise & S. Moscovici (Eds.), *Current issues in European social psychology* (pp. 201–237). Cambridge, UK: Maison des Sciences de l'Homme and Cambridge University Press.

Peeters, G. (1992). Evaluative meanings of adjectives in vitro and in context: Some theoretical implications and practical consequences of positive-negative asymmetry and behavioral-adaptive concepts of evaluation. *Psychologica Belgica, 32*, 211–231.

Peeters, G. (1995). What's negative about hatred and positive about love? On negation in cogni-tion, affect, and behavior. In H. C. M. de Swart & L. J. M. Bergman (Eds.), *Perspectives on negation* (pp. 123–133). Tilburg, NL: Tilburg University Press.

Phalet, K., & Poppe, E. (1997). Competence and morality dimensions of national and ethnic stereotypes: A study in six eastern-European countries. *European Journal of Social Psychology, 27*, 703–723.

Pittman, T. S., & Pittman, N. L. (1980). Deprivation of control and the attribution pro-cess. *Journal of Personality and Social Psychology, 39*, 377–389.

Poppe, E. (2001). Effects of changes in GNP and perceived group characteristics on national and ethnic stereotypes in central and eastern Europe. *Journal of Applied Social Psychology, 31*, 1689–1708.

Poppe, E., & Linssen, H. (1999). In-group favou-ritism and the reflection of realistic dimensions of difference between national states in Central and Eastern European nationality stereotypes. *British Journal of Social Psychology, 38*, 85–102.

Rosenberg, S., Nelson, C., & Vivekananthan, P. S. (1968). A multidimensional approach to the structure of personality impressions. *Journal of Personality and Social Psychology, 9*, 283–294

Ruscher, J. B., & Fiske, S. T. (1990). Interpersonal competition can cause individuating processes. *Journal of Personality and Social Psychology, 58*, 832–843.

Stevens, L. E., & Fiske, S. T. (1995). Motivation and cognition in social life: A social survival perspective. *Social Cognition, 13*, 189–214.

Stevens, L. E., & Fiske, S. T. (2000). Motivated impressions of a powerholder: Accuracy under task dependency and misperception under evaluation dependency. *Personality and Social Psychology Bulletin, 26*, 907–922.

Williams, K. D., Cheung, C. K. T., & Choi, W. (2000). CyberOstracism: Effects of being ignored over the internet. *Journal of Personality and Social Psychology, 79*, 748–762.

Wojciszke, B. (1994). Multiple meanings of behav-ior: Construing actions in terms of competence or morality. *Journal of Personality and Social Psychology, 67*, 222–232.

Wojciszke, B., & Klusek, B. (1996). Moral and competence-related traits in political perception. *Polish Psychological Bulletin, 27*, 319–325.

Wojciszke, B., Baryla, W., & Mikiewicz, A. (2003). *Two dimensions of interpersonal attitudes: Liking is based on self-interest, respect is based on status.* Unpublished manuscript. Polish Academy of Science.

Wojciszke, B., Bazinska, R., & Jaworski, M. (1998). On the dominance of moral categories in impression formation. *Personality and Social Psychology Bulletin, 24*, 1251–1263.

Wright, R., & Fiske, S. T. (2004). Unpublished data. Princeton University.

Yamagishi, T. (1998). *The structure of trust: An evolutionary game of mind and society.* Tokyo: Tokyo University Press.

Yamagishi, T., & Yamagishi, M. (1994). Trust and commitment in the United States and Japan. *Motivation and Emotion, 18,* 129–166.

Yamamoto, M., & Miyamoto, S. (2004). Unpublished data. Tsukuba University.

PART IV

INFLUENCES OF REJECTION ON EMOTION, PERCEPTION, AND COGNITION

12

When Does Social Rejection Lead to Aggression?

The Influences of Situations, Narcissism, Emotion, and Replenishing Connections

JEAN M. TWENGE

WHEN DOES SOCIAL REJECTION CAUSE AGGRESSION?

The Influences of Situations, Narcissism, Emotion, and Replenishing Connections

Justin, a seventh-grader, goes to school one day to find that his best friend Mike will no longer talk to him. He learns that Mike has decided to become friends with a more popular group of boys, and that Mike will be seen as less "cool" in the eyes of the popular crowd if he talks to Justin. So Justin has lost a friend. How will Justin react to this social rejection?

Address correspondence to: Jean M. Twenge, Department of Psychology, San Diego State University, 5500 Campanile Drive, San Diego, CA 92126-4611. E-mail: jtwenge@mail.sdsu.edu.

Both research and real-world incidents suggest that Justin is likely to react with aggression. A careful study of the school shooting incidents during the late 1990s found that almost all of the perpetrators experienced repeated social rejection (Leary, Kowalski, Smith, & Phillips, 2003). Many other incidents of physical and verbal aggression also result from social rejection. The Surgeon General's Report on Youth Violence (2001) found that social rejection (conceptualized as "weak social ties") was the most significant risk factor for adolescent violence—stronger than gang membership, poverty, or drug use. Adults who are socially isolated display similar behavior; single men are more likely to commit crimes than married men, even when age is controlled (Sampson & Laub, 1990).

Recently, several lab studies have demonstrated a causal link between social rejection and aggression that goes beyond the correlational data noted above. Twenge, Baumeister, Tice, and Stucke (2001) randomly assigned participants to experience rejection or acceptance. Rejected participants blasted a higher level of unpleasant white noise, even against an innocent target unconnected to the rejection (see also Catanese & Tice, this volume). Buckley, Winkel, and Leary (2004) randomly assigned participants to be rejected or accepted by an unseen peer; rejected participants assigned the peer more unpleasant tapes to hear and expressed more hostility (see also Leary, this volume, and Gaertner & Iuzzini, this volume). Warburton, Williams, and Cairns (2003) covaried ostracism (vs. inclusion) and level of control in an unpleasant situation. Ostracized participants who had no control were highly aggressive toward a peer who did not like spicy foods, assigning them to eat four times as much hot sauce as those in the other conditions assigned (see also Williams & Zadro, this volume). In a quasi-experimental study, Kirkpatrick, Waugh, Valencia, and Webster (2002) found that participants with low social self-esteem (who felt excluded in real life) also allocated more hot sauce to a spice-hating peer.

However, it seems unlikely that social rejection leads to aggression under all circumstances. Going back to the example of Justin, whether he reacts with aggression will depend on situational factors, his personality, his opportunities for other friendships, and his emotional resources (among many possible factors). Rejection cannot invariably lead to aggression: Ostracism and rejection are so common in daily life (Williams, 2001) that we would be aggressing against each other constantly if we always responded aggressively. Many children and adults experience rejection, yet only some of them become aggressive or violent. In other words, there must be moderators of the effect, and/or mediating variables that can prevent aggression after rejection. The Warburton et al. (2003) study, for example, showed that ostracized participants who had control over an unpleasant situation were not any more aggressive than included participants (see Williams & Zadro, this volume). My co-authors and I found that rejected participants were not aggressive toward a friendly partner who had issued praise (Twenge et al., 2001, Experiment 3); in contrast, rejected participants were highly aggressive toward someone who had insulted them (Experiments 1 and 2). Perhaps there are some situations and personalities that do not promote aggression after social rejection, and others that do.

WHEN REJECTION MAY LEAD TO AGGRESSION

Moderators and preventative mediators seem especially likely given the theory behind belongingness and ostracism. Baumeister and Leary (1995) argue that humans are motivated to belong to social groups. People who find themselves socially rejected should quickly take steps to correct this situation, seeking ways to rejoin the group and re-establish relationships. Several empirical studies have found that rejected and ostracized individuals responded by acting more pro-social (Williams, Cheung, & Choi, 2000; Williams & Sommer, 1997) and being more receptive to social clues (Gardner, Pickett, & Brewer, 2000; see also Gardner, Pickett, & Knowles, this volume, and Pickett & Gardner, this volume). This makes sense: If people are inherently motivated to belong, rejection should cause them to seek belongingness elsewhere. Yet, as noted above, a growing number of laboratory studies find that social rejection leads to aggression against others—an action that is likely to drive others away rather than bring them closer.

How can these two sets of results be reconciled? In our previous work (Twenge et al., 2001), we theorized that social rejection eliminated the usual strictures against aggressive behavior, because people were acting impulsively and no longer saw the need to act in socially acceptable ways. These experiments examined aggression against anonymous people who were presented as lone actors (e.g., "someone making up an experiment"). In the context of a reaction time game on the computer, participants were able to blast unpleasant white noise at unseen targets; they did not expect to interact with in person. The targets of aggression in these experiments were not potential friends, instead were unfriendly, unavailable for future interaction, or both. The motivation to belong may still be present, but may only manifest itself when an interaction partner could provide some degree of social acceptance.

Personality variables may also moderate the effect. Bushman and Baumeister (1998) found that narcissism predicted aggressive reactions after receiving an insult from another participant. Self-esteem did not predict aggression after narcissism was controlled. Narcissists may be more aggressive because they admit to lower levels of empathy toward others (Watson, Grisham, Trotter, & Biderman, 1984). Although narcissists do not value relationships highly (Campbell, Rudich, & Sedikides, 2002), they may react to social rejection with aggression because people are not giving them the respect they believe they deserve. Thus, narcissists should be more angry and aggressive after a social rejection.

Preventative mediators may also play a role. The motivational theory of belongingness suggests that rejected people will seek out opportunities to fulfill their need to belong. For example, see Pickett & Gardner's (this volume) excellent flow chart "Regulatory Model of Belonging Need." In this model, the lack of belonging activates the social monitoring system, which then leads to further attempts at social interaction. If excluded participants are given the chance to again fulfill their belongingness needs, they may seize this opportunity and subsequently might not be aggressive. Thus, replenishing connectedness might reduce aggression after rejection.

Given the tremendous amount of aggression and violence that results from social rejection (e.g., Office of the Surgeon General, 2001), it seems very important to determine the situations that elicit aggression after rejection and to identify the circumstances that can prevent such incidents. Will socially rejected people always (or usually) act aggressively? Which situations lower the risk of aggression after rejection, and which do not? Do some personality traits predict who will respond to rejection with aggression? Can aggression after rejection be prevented by improving mood or providing opportunities for social interaction? In this chapter, I will review research that has addressed moderators and mediators of the rejection-aggression link, including situational and target effects, narcissism as a moderator, and replenishing connectedness.

SITUATIONAL AND TARGET EFFECTS

The danger of aggression exists across many different situations. The studies reviewed above demonstrate that social rejection often leads to aggression. But when is aggression most likely to occur? In the first series of studies, we examined the situations that lead to aggression after social rejection (Twenge, Cacho, & Lyche, 2003). In the first experiment, participants met a group of their peers and talked with them for 15 minutes. They then nominated the two people they wanted to work with next. We randomly assigned participants to hear that either everyone chose them or no one chose them. They were then told they would play a computer game in which they set the intensity and the duration of white noise that their game partner would hear. The higher levels of noise are very unpleasant, so this is a common measure of behavioral aggression (Bartholow & Anderson, 2002; Bushman & Baumeister, 1998). Participants were told that their game partner was someone making up an experiment, and thus not one of the people they met in the group. Half of the participants heard that they would meet their game partner later and would work with them on another task; the other half heard that they would not meet their game partner. This created a 2 (rejected vs. accepted) X 2 (anticipated interaction vs. none) design. We predicted that rejected participants who expected to interact with their game partners would not be aggressive, as they would perceive their partners as potential sources of acceptance.

The results supported the prediction. When participants did not expect to interact with their game partners, rejected participants were more aggressive than accepted participants (replicating previous research). However, rejected participants who expected to interact with their game partners were not aggressive; in fact, they were significantly less aggressive than accepted participants who anticipated interaction. Thus, expecting to interact with a target can prevent aggression after social rejection.

In the second experiment (based on Janet C. Cacho's [2002] masters thesis), we manipulated acceptance and rejection and varied the identity of the target (the recipient of the aggression in the noise-blasting game). Some participants heard that the target was from another group of students who had been talking in a room "down the hall" and were given no other information. Others heard that the target had been rejected by the other group (no one had chosen the target). A third group heard that the target had been accepted by the other group (everyone had chosen the target). Participants then played the noise-blasting game with the target. We expected several different factors to affect aggressive behavior across these situations. In previous experiments (e.g., Buckley et al., 2004; Twenge et al., 2001) the target has been described as "someone making up an experiment," a lone actor unconnected with any other group. Rejected participants might behave less aggressively toward someone who belonged to another group. Having been rejected by their own group, rejected people might see this person as a representative from another group they might be more accepted in. The results supported this prediction, as rejected and accepted participants were equally nonaggressive toward a neutral member of another group.

Other participants heard that the target had been accepted or rejected by another group. A number of factors might influence behavior in this situation. The attraction paradigm (Byrne, 1997) posits that people will like those who are similar to them. In other words, people display an ingroup bias (e.g., Tajfel & Turner, 1986). Even small indicators of similarity, such as sharing a birthday or a social security number digit, elicit greater cooperation and favoritism (Miller, Downs, & Prentice, 1998; Tajfel & Billig, 1974; Wilder, 1981). Externally assigned conditions have the same effect; groups formed by flipping a coin still exhibited ingroup bias (Billig & Tajfel, 1973). The affiliation paradigm and ingroup bias suggest that accepted people should be least aggressive toward other accepted people (most similar to themselves) and most aggressive toward rejected people (least similar to themselves). Similarly, rejected people should be least aggressive toward rejected people (most similar to themselves) and most aggressive toward accepted people (least similar to themselves).

The results were consistent with the similarity hypothesis in three out of the four conditions involving a rejected or accepted target. Accepted participants were most aggressive toward rejected targets, less toward neutral targets, and still less toward accepted targets. In addition, rejected participants were most aggressive toward accepted targets. However, there was one notable exception to the similarity hypothesis: Rejected participants were also highly aggressive toward rejected targets. These results can be explained by downward comparison (e.g., Wills, 1981) and social identity threat (e.g., Branscombe et al., 1999). Rejected participants paired with a rejected target may have felt unfairly categorized into a "rejected group" and may have responded with aggression in an attempt to disidentify themselves from the low status group. Rejected participants had no desire to belong to the ingroup of rejected people and did not see the rejected target as someone they wanted to affiliate with. They responded to the threat inherent in rejection by denigrating another rejected person, thus distancing themselves from the ingroup of rejected people. In addition, rejected participants may have resented being paired with another rejected person and chose to lash out in aggression.

These studies demonstrate the situational moderators of the rejection-aggression link. Some situations prevent aggression after rejection: expecting to interact with the target, and hearing that the target belongs to another group. Other situations, however, lead to high levels of aggression: expecting the target to remain anonymous, interacting with a dissimilar target, and interacting with a rejected target.

These results can be applied to real-world social situations, particularly to children's playgroups. Rejected children will be least likely to be aggressive toward children they will interact with again. They should also be less aggressive toward a child from another social group. However, rejected children should not be grouped with other rejected children or with popular children; both pairings are likely to lead to increased aggression.

Notably, even accepted participants showed above-average aggression toward rejected targets. This demonstrates another unfortunate outcome of rejection: Not only are rejected people more likely to perpetrate aggression, but they are also more likely to be victims of aggression. This is consistent with correlational research, which shows that rejected children are victimized more often (e.g., Crick & Grotpeter, 1996; Hanish & Guerra, 2000). As rejected children are more likely to be both the instigator and the victims of aggression, their play partners need to be chosen carefully.

NARCISSISM AS A MODERATOR

In the months before the Columbine shootings, perpetrators Eric Harris and Dylan Klebold made a series of videotapes of themselves. On first reading the *Time* magazine article about the tapes (Gibbs & Roche, 1999), I was struck by the similarity between their statements and several of the items on the Narcissistic Personality Inventory (Raskin & Terry, 1988), the most common measure of narcissism. For example, Eric Harris said, "I could convince them that I'm going to climb Mount Everest, or I have a twin brother growing out of my back. I can make you believe anything," which bears a close resemblance to NPI item #35, "I can make anyone believe anything I want them to." After picking up a gun and making a shooting noise, Harris then said, "Isn't it fun to get the respect that we're going to deserve?" This statement is strikingly similar to "I insist upon getting the respect that is due me." In addition, both Harris and Klebold talked about the rejection they had repeatedly experienced at the hands of their peers.

Thus, the combination of rejection by peers and a narcissistic, grandiose view of the self seemed to be two motivating factors behind the shootings at Columbine, and possibly other acts of violence.

Keith Campbell and I addressed this possibility in a series of four studies (Twenge & Campbell, 2003). Participants in the first study completed the NPI, the Rosenberg Self-Esteem Scale (Rosenberg, 1965), and the revised Janis-Field Feelings of Inadequacy Scale (JFFIS) (Fleming & Courtney, 1984; Janis & Field, 1959). Participants then wrote about a time when they were socially rejected and described the mood they experienced after the rejection by responding to a long list of mood words. Narcissists reported more anger after rejection and fewer internalized negative emotions such as sadness, guilt, and anxiety. Self-esteem was not correlated with anger when narcissism was controlled.

In the second study, participants completed the NPI and then experienced rejection or acceptance by the group (using the method described in the previous series of studies). As predicted, narcissists reported feeling more angry after experiencing rejection. However, narcissism was not correlated with anger when participants had been socially accepted. Narcissists are not angrier across all situations, but they are angry after rejection.

We then examined behavioral aggression using the noise-blast game described in the previous studies. Participants experienced rejection by a group of peers and then (they thought) played the noise-blast game with a group member. Narcissism was significantly correlated with aggressive behavior, whereas self-esteem was not. Narcissists blast a higher level of noise against someone who rejected them.

In the last study, participants experienced either social rejection or acceptance by the group. This time, however, they were told that they would play the game with a new person—someone who was making up the experiment—and not a member of the group that accepted or rejected them. Narcissists were significantly more aggressive even toward this innocent third party. However, they were not more aggressive after being socially accepted. Once again, self-esteem was not correlated with aggressive behavior after rejection, but narcissism was.

These studies show that narcissists respond to a social rejection with anger and aggression. This is similar Bushman and Baumeister's (1998) studies on aggression after an insult, with one exception: In contrast to our findings in the last study, they did not find that narcissists were more aggressive toward an innocent third party. Apparently, social rejection facilitates indirect aggression from narcissists, at least against individuals who might be viewed as members of the rejecting group, even if this group is as broad as "students from the same university."

These findings are particularly compelling given narcissists' reported lack of concern for interpersonal relatedness (e.g., Campbell, 1999; Campbell, Rudich, & Sedikides, 2002). Narcissists' apparent independence, however, may veil a deep need for social acceptance—or perhaps for social dominance. This need may only be evident in the aftermath of social rejection. Rejected narcissists are not serene or unperturbed by relational dissolution. Rather, they become angry and violent toward rejecters and third parties alike.

Indeed, this may be a reasonable, albeit partial, depiction of the events at Columbine. Although we can only speculate, it may be that two individuals with inflated self-opinions became angry in the face of perceived social rejection. Certainly, there were other variables that influenced this attack (e.g., accessibility of firearms). Narcissism and perceived social rejection, however, appear to be at least two of the central causes.

REPLENISHING BELONGINGNESS

The research discussed thus far examined the moderators of the rejection-aggression link, showing that some situations and some personalities are more likely to demonstrate the effect. However, people do not have much control over the situation accompanying the rejection, and it is very difficult to change one's personality. So how can aggression be prevented? How can people actively try to reduce aggression after rejection?

In a series of three experiments, we examined emotion and replenishing connections as possible conduits to lowering aggression after rejection (Twenge, Zhang, Catanese, & Baumeister, 2003). In previous studies, the opportunity to aggress followed almost immediately after the social rejection. We wondered if an intervening, positive task might mitigate aggression. Specifically, we hypothesized that rejected participants would seize the opportunity to replenish their need to belong. This follows from the motivational theory of belongingness (Baumeister & Leary, 1995; Gardner, Pickett, & Brewer, 2000), which predicts that rejected people will seek out ways to fulfill their social needs. As Pickett & Gardner (this volume) and Gardner et al. (this volume) note, low belongingness should activate the social monitoring system, and people should attempt further social interaction. This may satisfy belonging needs and eliminate the usual negative consequences of exclusion. We also wondered if a mood boost might have the same effect: If rejected people had a positive affective experience, they might no longer be aggressive.

In the first experiment, we used the same manipulation of acceptance or rejection described previously: Participants met a group of their peers and then heard that either everyone or no one chose them. In addition, half of the participants had the positive experience of receiving a bag of candy and verbal thanks from the experimenter. The other half received only a written receipt for their course credit. This created a 2 (acceptance vs. rejection) X 2 (positive vs. neutral interaction) design. Participants then played the noise-blasting game against a new person. When participants received only the written receipt, the results followed the usual pattern: Rejected participants were significantly more aggressive than were accepted participants. However, rejected participants who received candy and thanks were not aggressive. Thus, a positive interaction with the experimenter eliminated the aggression that usually follows after social rejection.

This result could be interpreted in two ways: Either the social nature of the interaction helped eliminate aggression, or receiving the candy and thanks improved mood, which then eliminated the aggression. However, there were no significant differences in mood on the PANAS measure, and mood did not mediate the effect.

The second experiment used a mood induction method that was not social—watching videos designed to have neutral, positive, or negative mood valence. Participants first experienced a social exclusion manipulation (also see Baumeister & DeWall, this volume). Some participants heard, ostensibly on the basis of a personality test, that they were likely to be alone later in life (future alone condition); others heard that they would be accident prone in the future (a negative outcome unrelated to relationships: future misfortune); and a third group received no future prediction (no feedback). Participants were then exposed to a standard mood induction: watching videotapes designed to induce specific mood states (e.g., Gross & Levenson, 1995; Hemenover, 2003; Muraven, Tice, & Baumeister, 1998). This created a 3 (future alone, future misfortune, no feedback) X 3 (positive, negative, or neutral tape) design. Participants then played the noise-blasting game. The results showed a main effect for exclusion condition (the future alone group was more aggressive), but no effect for the mood induction and no interaction. Thus, a mood induction that was not social was not enough to eliminate aggression after rejection.

The last experiment tested the effect of writing about a social relationship. Participants heard either that they would be alone later in life or that they would be accident prone. They then wrote for 2 minutes on one of three topics: their most recent meal (a control), their favorite celebrity, or their favorite family member (the technique of writing about a celebrity is modified from Gardner et al. [this volume]). This was a 2 (future alone or future misfortune) X 3 (writing task) design. As expected, those who wrote about a recent meal showed the usual effect: future alone participants were more aggressive. Among those who wrote about a family member or a celebrity, future alone participants were not more aggressive. Writing about a family member may help participants remember that they have social connections, thus eliminating the aggression usually seen after rejection. The result for writing about a celebrity shows that recalling even a tenuous social connection can help; many people feel that they know their favorite celebrity even if they have never met in person. On the other hand, mood did not play a role—participants who wrote about their favorite celebrity reported a significantly more negative mood, but they were no more aggressive.

These experiments suggest that replenishing connections can reduce aggression after social rejection, but improving mood cannot. Rejected participants who watched mood-inducing videotapes that were not social showed no reduction in aggressive behavior. Rejected participants who wrote about their favorite celebrity were not aggressive, yet they reported higher levels of negative mood compared to the other groups.

The only explanation that ties all of the results together is that social interaction—real or recalled, experimentally manipulated or spontaneously generated, small or smaller. The last observation is particularly interesting: Even small and seemingly insignificant social interactions such as recalling social ties or having a friendly interaction with the experimenter were enough to reduce aggression. Remembering social connections can eliminate aggression after social rejection.

This is encouraging news for teachers, parents, and others who seek to reduce aggression. After a child experiences rejection, parents can remind children of their other friends and the other people who love them. People who have just experienced a romantic breakup can seek out their friends. This advice is not as obvious as it might sound, as many people respond to rejection by spending more time alone. They believe that they need time to "center" themselves, or to think about what might have led to the rejection. As Susan Nolen-Hoeksema's work shows, however, ruminating over problems is more likely to lead to depression rather than insight (e.g., Nolen-Hoeksema, 1990).

CONCLUSIONS

These studies offer encouraging news: Aggression after social rejection is not inevitable. Some situations and personalities promote aggression, whereas others can eliminate it. To return to the example of 12-year-old Justin, we would predict that Justin will be more aggressive toward other children if: he does not expect to interact with the children around him, the children are very popular or unpopular, he has a narcissistic personality, he does not have any other positive social interactions, and he does not actively recall his close social ties.

Future research should examine other possible moderators and preventative mediators of the effect. Personality variables other than narcissism may also predict levels of aggression after rejection (e.g., rejection sensitivity, loneliness, extraversion, and agreeableness). The mood question is also not fully settled. Although these manipulations show that mood inductions do not lead to decreased aggression after rejection, other mood inductions might reduce the effect. In addition, some researchers find significant increases in negative mood after rejection (e.g., Buckley et al., 2004; Leary, this volume; Williams & Zadro, this volume). This seems to be a particularly important question to address: Are rejected participants who report neutral moods using mood regulation or defensiveness? Is this regulation conscious or unconscious? Answering these questions might also provide additional routes to reducing aggression after rejection.

These experiments are consistent with the motivational theory of belongingness (e.g., Baumeister & Leary, 1995). Interacting with an anonymous or a low-status person without any reminder of other social relationships provides little opportunity to fulfill belongingness needs, and thus leads to aggression. Interacting with a future task partner or remembering other relationships provides more opportunity for fulfilling belongingness needs, and thus leads to more pro-social behavior. Narcissists, people who do not seek relationships or value empathy, are more aggressive after rejection. Overall, the results show that aggression after social rejection is situational and determined by the motivation to belong. It is most likely to occur when opportunities for affiliation are low, and least likely to occur when opportunities for affiliation are high.

REFERENCES

Bartholow, B. D., & Anderson, C. A. (2002). Effects of violent video games on aggressive behavior: Potential sex differences. *Journal of Experimental Social Psychology, 38*, 283–290.

Baumeister, R. F., & Leary, M. R. (1995). The need to belong: Desire for the interpersonal attachments as a fundamental human motivation. *Psychological Bulletin, 117*, 497–529.

Billig, M., & Tajfel, H. (1973). Social categorization and similarity in intergroup behaviour. *European Journal of Social Psychology, 3*, 27–52.

Branscombe, N. R., Ellemers, N., Spears, R., & Doosie, B. (1999). The context and content of social identity threat. In N. Ellemers, R. Spears, & B. Doosie (Eds.), Social identity: Context, commitment, content (pp. 35–58). Oxford: Blackwell.

Buckley, K., Winkel, R., & Leary, M. (2004). Reactions to acceptance and rejection: Effects of level and sequence of relational evaluation. *Journal of Experimental Social Psychology, 40*, 14–28.

Bushman, B. J., & Baumeister, R. F. (1998). Threatened egotism, narcissism, self-esteem, and direct and displaced aggression: Does self-love or self-hate lead to violence? *Journal of Personality and Social Psychology, 75*, 219–229.

Byrne, D. (1997). An overview (and underview) of research and theory within the attraction paradigm. *Journal of Social and Personality Relationships, 14*(3), 417–431.

Cacho, J. C. (2002). *The effects of social rejection and target group status on aggressive behavior.* Unpublished master's thesis, San Diego State University, San Diego, CA.

Campbell, W. K. (1999). Narcissism and romantic attraction. *Journal of Personality and Social Psychology, 77*, 1254–1270.

Campbell, W. K., Rudich, E., & Sedikides, C. (2002). Narcissism, self-esteem, and the positivity of self-views: Two portraits of self-love. *Personality and Social Psychology Bulletin, 28*, 358–368.

Crick, N. R., & Grotpeter, J. K. (1996). Children's treatment by peers: Victims of relational and overt aggression. *Development & Psychopathology, 8*, 367–380.

Fleming, J. S., & Courtney, B. E. (1984). The dimensionality of self-esteem II: Hierarchical facet model for revised measurement scales. *Journal of Personality and Social Psychology, 46*, 404–421.

Gardner, W. L., Pickett, C. L., & Brewer, M. B. (2000). Social exclusion and selective memory: How the need to belong influences memory for social events. *Personality and Social Psychology Bulletin, 26*, 486–496.

Gibbs, N., & Roche, T. (1999). The Columbine tapes. *Time*, December 20, 1999.

Gross, J. J, & Levenson, R.W. (1995). Emotion elicitation using films. *Cognition and Emotion, 9*, 87–108.

Hanish, L. D., & Guerra, N. G. (2000). Predictors of peer victimization among urban youth. *Social Development, 9*, 521–543.

Hemenover, S. H. (2003). Individual differences in rate of affect change: Studies in affective chronometry. *Journal of Personality and Social Psychology, 85*, 121–131.

Janis, I. L., & Field, P. B. (1959). Sex differences in factors related to persuasibility. In C. I. Hovland & I. L. Janis (Eds.), *Personality and persuasibility* (pp. 55–68, 300–302). New Haven, CT: Yale University Press.

Kirkpatrick, L. A., Waugh, C. E., Valencia, A., & Webster, G. D. (2002). The functional domain specificity of self-esteem and the differential prediction of aggression. *Journal of Personality and Social Psychology, 82*, 756–767.

Leary, M. R., Kowalski, R. M., Smith, L., & Phillips, S. (2003). Teasing, rejection, and violence: Case studies of the school shootings. *Aggressive Behavior, 29*, 202–214.

Miller, D. T., Downs, J. S., & Prentice, D. A. (1998). Minimal conditions for the creation of a unit relationship: The social bond between birthdaymates. *European Journal of Social Psychology, 28*, 475–481.

Muraven, M., Tice, D. M., & Baumeister, R. F. (1998). Self-control as limited resource:

Regulatory depletion patterns. *Journal of Personality and Social Psychology, 74,* 774–789.

Nolen-Hoeksema, S. (1990). *Sex differences in depression.* Stanford, CA: Stanford University Press.

Office of the Surgeon General. (2001). *Youth violence: A report of the surgeon general.* U.S. Department of Health and Human Services. http://www.mentalhealth.org/youthviolence/default.asp

Raskin, R. N., & Terry, H. (1988). A principle components analysis of the Narcissistic Personality Inventory and further evidence of its construct validity. *Journal of Personality and Social Psychology, 54,* 890–902.

Rosenberg, M. (1965). *Society and the adolescent self-image.* Princeton, NJ: Princeton University Press.

Sampson, R. J., & Laub, J. H. (1990). Crime and deviance over the life course: The salience of adult social bonds. *American Sociological Review, 55,* 609–627.

Tajfel, H., & Billig, M. (1974). Familiarity and categorization in intergroup behavior. *Journal of Experimental Social Psychology, 10,* 159–170.

Tajfel, H., & Turner, J. C. (1986). The social identity theory of intergroup behavior. In W. Austin & S. Worchel (Eds.), *The social psychology of intergroup relations* (pp. 7–24). Monterey, CA: Brooks/Cole.

Twenge, J. M., Baumeister, R. F., Tice, D. M., & Stucke, T. S. (2001). If you can't join them, beat them: Effects of social exclusion on aggressive behavior. *Journal of Personality and Social Psychology, 81,* 1058–1069.

Twenge, J. M., & Campbell, W. K. (2003). "Isn't it fun to get the respect that we're going to deserve?" Narcissism, social rejection, and aggression. *Personality and Social Psychology Bulletin, 29,* 261–272.

Twenge, J. M., Catanese, K. R., & Baumeister, R.

F. (2003). Social exclusion and the deconstructed state: Time perception, meaninglessness, lethargy, lack of emotion, and self-awareness. *Journal of Personality and Social Psychology, 85,* 409–423.

Twenge, J. M., Cacho, J., & Lyche, L. F. (2003). *The effect of target status and affiliation on aggression avger social rejection.* Unpublished manuscript.

Twenge, J. M., Zhang, L., Catanese, K. R., Dolan-Pascoe, B. & Baumeister, R. F. (2003). *Replenishing connectedness: Current or remembered social interaction eliminates aggression after social exclusion.* Unpublished manuscript.

Warburton, W., Williams, K. D., & Cairns, D. (2003, April). *Effects of ostracism and loss of control on aggression.* Paper presented at the 32nd Annual Meeting of the Society of Australasian Social Psychology, Bondi Beach, Australia.

Watson, P. J., Grisham, S. O., Trotter, M. V., & Biderman, M. D. (1984). Narcissism and empathy: Validity evidence for the narcissistic personality inventory. *Journal of Personality Assessment, 45,* 159–162.

Wilder, D. A. (1981). Perceiving persons as a group: Categorization and intergroup relations In D. L. Hamilton (Ed.), *Cognitive processes in stereotyping and intergroup behavior.* Hillsdale, NJ: Lawrence Erlbaum.

Williams, K. D. (2001). *Ostracism: The power of silence.* New York: Guilford Press.

Williams, K. D., Cheung, C. K. T., & Choi, W. (2000). Cyberostracism: Effects of being ignored over the Internet. *Journal of Personality and Social Psychology, 79,* 748–762.

Williams, K. D., & Sommer, K. L. (1997). Social ostracism by coworkers: Does rejection lead to loafing or compensation? *Personality and Social Psychology Bulletin, 23,* 693–706.

Wills, T. A. (1981). Downward comparison principles in social psychology. *Psychological Bulletin, 90,* 245–271.

13

The Social Monitoring System

Enhanced Sensitivity to Social Cues as an Adaptive Response to Social Exclusion

CYNTHIA L. PICKETT
WENDI L. GARDNER

> *The Archdiocese of Philadelphia recently approved a rare petition from a man to be an official hermit under the Catholic Church's canons. Richard Withers, 46, has vowed to do all the things a priest does except that he spends almost all of his time away from people, in contemplation (based on "an almost unremitting desire to be alone with God"). Brother Withers has a paying job (which he works at in silence) one day a week and exchanges e-mail with other hermits.*
>
> Chuck Shepherd's *News of the Weird*
> *New York Times*, Oct. 30, 2001

Address Correspondence to: Cynthia Pickett, Department of Psychology, University of California at Davis, Davis, CA 95616, USA. E-mail: cpickett@ucdavis.edu

INTRODUCTION

A fundamental aspect of human existence is the desire for social inclusion and acceptance from others. Attesting to the relative importance of belonging in human functioning, Maslow (1970) considered only two other needs to be prepotent to belonging: basic physiological needs (e.g., hunger and thirst) and safety needs. Indeed, as exemplified by the *News of the Weird* story quoted above, even those individuals who claim to desire solitude and isolation from other humans still appear to seek out social connections.

In their review of the need to belong as a basic human motivation, Baumeister and Leary (1995) summarize a variety of evidence that supports the assertion that humans are driven to seek belongingness and that they suffer both physically and psychologically when belongingness needs go unsatisfied. In terms of physical health, social isolation and lack of social support have been associated with increased risk of heart attack (Case, Moss, Case, McDermott, & Eberly, 1992); poorer blood pressure regulation (Uchino, Cacioppo, & Kiecolt-Glaser, 1996); and poorer sleep efficiency (Cacioppo, Hawkley, Berntson, Ernst, Gibbs, Stickgold, & Hobson, 2002). The mental health consequences are also quite severe. Social exclusion has been linked to anxiety (Baumeister & Tice, 1990), negative affect (Marcus & Askari, 1999; Williams, Cheung, & Choi, 2000), and depressed self-esteem (Leary, 1990; Leary, Tambor, Terdal, & Downs, 1995). When social isolation occurs over long periods of time, loneliness (Jones, 1990; Jones & Carver, 1991; Peplau & Perlman, 1982) and depression (Leary, 1990) may result.

Despite the obvious benefits of social connectedness, one of the barriers to its achievement is social exclusion and rejection by others. Most societies, including non-human societies (Lancaster, 1986; Raleigh & McGuire, 1986), engage in routine rejection of some of their group members. This rejection is often the result of an individual failing to conform to some social norm or rule and can take the form of mild social rejection (e.g., a snub) to complete exclusion and ostracism (e.g., Williams, 2001; Williams & Zadro, this volume). Although it is clear that many negative emotional and behavioral consequences can result from social exclusion and rejection, what is not well understood are the specific ways that individuals deal with daily rejection experiences and how they avoid prolonged social exclusion. Most individuals encounter some form of mild rejection in their daily lives—e.g., being turned down for a date or being left out of a conversation. While these experiences may result in temporary feelings of dejection, many individuals are able to bounce back from these episodes and regain inclusion and belonging. But what are the processes and mechanisms that contribute to individuals' ability to recover from and avoid rejection?

The goal of this chapter is to provide a potential answer to this question by describing a model for the regulation of belonging needs (see Figure 13.1). This chapter begins with a description of the components of the model and the model's relation to other known processes involved in detecting and responding to social exclusion. This is then followed by a summary of the evidence collected to date in our lab that bears upon various aspects of the model.

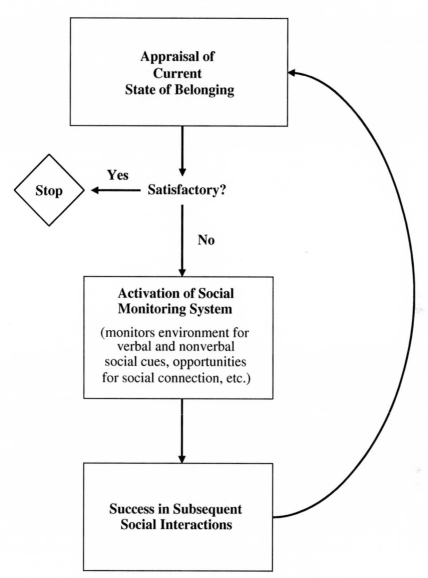

FIGURE 13.1 Regulatory Model of Belonging Need

THE REGULATION OF BELONGING NEED

Optimal human functioning requires the regulation of our basic needs (e.g., food, water, sleep). Within any regulatory system, there must be mechanisms that allow for the assessment of current needs, some type of signal when the needs are unmet, and integrative mechanisms that then monitor the environment and guide behavior in a goal-directed fashion. For example, our bodies typically need 8 hours of sleep per night. Sleep is regulated, in part, by a homeostatic mechanism that tracks our sleep accumulation, signals to the body when a sleep debt arises (via increased sleepiness and irritability), and guides the body toward engaging in greater sleep as a means of returning the system to equilibrium (via the ability to fall asleep more quickly the next night and sleep more deeply) (Dement & Vaughan, 1999). Similar to the regulation of other basic needs, the regulation of belonging needs can be conceived as occurring via an analogous series of psychological and physiological mechanisms.

Our proposed model for the regulation of belonging needs (see Figure 13.1) begins with the idea that in order to ensure that humans maintain a stable and acceptable level of social inclusion, mechanisms need to be in place to assess and monitor levels of belonging need and inclusionary status. Leary (1999; Leary et al., 1995) has argued persuasively that self-esteem may in fact serve this function. According to Leary's sociometer theory, self-esteem can be thought of as a type of psychological gauge that monitors the quality of people's social relationships. When an individual's relational value is low, this is reflected in reduced feelings of self-worth (i.e., lower self-esteem; Leary, Haupt, Strausser, & Chokel, 1998). According to the present model, when the sociometer or other assessment mechanisms indicate that one's state of belonging is satisfactory, the regulatory system is in a state of equilibrium and there is no need for the system to become further engaged. However, when an individual's state of belonging is unsatisfactory, the next process in the regulatory system becomes activated.

Similar to how hunger leads individuals to notice and quickly process information related to food (Atkinson & McClelland, 1948), a belongingness deficit is predicted to lead individuals to monitor social information that may provide cues to belonging and inclusion. This information may be self-related (e.g., noticing that a friend seems eager to end a conversation) or other-related (e.g., noticing the response that another person receives from others). The social monitoring system (SMS) is considered to be adaptive in that it allows individuals to notice the cues that may signal an impending rejection (and perhaps ward off the rejection) and also notice the interpersonal techniques that lead to greater belonging and inclusion. Because much of the work of interpersonal communication is done in a fairly subtle fashion (see Fichten, Tagalakis, Judd, Wright, & Amsel, 1993; Folkes, 1982), individuals need to be sensitive to a range of verbal and nonverbal social cues. For example, detecting whether a conversation partner is bored often requires taking into account whether the partner is looking away or tapping her feet. To the extent that a perceiver is attentive to this information and vigilant, he or she can decipher the cues and realize that a change (e.g., changing the topic) needs to be made to avoid being rejected by the partner. In sum, we conceive of the SMS as providing the integrative mechanism for the regulation of belonging needs. At the most basic level, the purpose of the SMS is to attune individuals to information that will help them navigate the social environment more successfully.

The hypothesis that heightened belonging need will result in increased social monitoring is related to some extent to work on rejection sensitivity by Downey and her colleagues (e.g., Downey & Feldman, 1996; Romero-Canyas & Downey, this volume). Downey's research indicates that individuals who are dispositionally inclined to anxiously expect rejection tend to readily perceive intentional rejection in the ambiguous behavior of others and react intensely to this perceived rejection. One way of interpreting rejection sensitivity is as a maladaptive outcome of the more general social monitoring system. When operating functionally, the social monitoring system should temporarily heighten sensitivity to both positive and negative social information. It is adaptive for individuals to notice both the signals that indicate belonging and acceptance and the cues that indicate possible rejection. Thus, for individuals whose social monitoring system is functioning normally, increased interpersonal sensitivity following a rejection should ultimately lead to the ability to secure and maintain social inclusion. However, like other self-regulatory systems that have the potential to go awry, it is possible for the social monitoring mechanism to occasionally result in non-optimal outcomes.

The final stage of the regulatory model is further attempts at social interaction. Although researchers have demonstrated antisocial tendencies in response to rejection and anticipated social exclusion (e.g., Twenge, Baumeister, Tice & Stucke, 2001), it is generally expected that despite temporary feelings of anger and hostility, individuals will seek out opportunities for belongingness need satisfaction. Prior activation of the SMS should not only attune individuals to opportunities for social inclusion, but should also aid in achieving that inclusion via enhanced interpersonal sensitivity. A feedback loop is incorporated into the self-regulatory model representing the idea that information regarding the success of these subsequent social interactions is hypothesized to feed back to the sociometer which is then updated with the new information.

Caveats

The model depicted by Figure 13.1 is only one of many potential systems that may work to regulate belongingness. In addition, the present model assumes that individuals will generally have the opportunity to engage in future social interaction subsequent to experiencing heightened belonging need. This, however, is not always the case. Individuals may find themselves temporarily isolated from their normal sources of social support. When this occurs individuals may need to seek other methods for fulfilling their unmet need. Potential methods for doing so are described in the following chapter (Gardner, Pickett, & Knowles, this volume).

PREDICTED FUNCTIONS OF THE SOCIAL MONITORING SYSTEM

According to our conceptualization of the social monitoring system, heightened belonging need should lead to enhanced sensitivity to social cues and social information. To date, our tests of the SMS have focused on two types of sensitivity—biased recall of social versus non-social information and interpersonal sensitivity. Individuals with heightened belonging need are hypothesized to scan their environment for information related to social connections and relationships. Thus, we predicted that when belonging need is high, individuals will exhibit biases in the type of information that they encode and recall. We have also examined the relationship between belonging need and interpersonal sensitivity. In this research, we have chosen to use a broad definition of interpersonal sensitivity that encompasses "... the ability to sense, perceive accurately, and respond appropriately to one's personal, interpersonal, and social environment." (Bernieri, 2001, p. 3). Because interpersonal sensitivity can aid in achieving greater social inclusion, we predicted that greater belonging need would also be associated with heightened interpersonal sensitivity.

The prediction that levels of interpersonal sensitivity will covary with individuals' state of belonging need (which presumably fluctuates to some degree over time and situations) assumes that interpersonal sensitivity is not a static or fixed ability. Although some stable individual differences in interpersonal sensitivity do appear to exist (e.g., Hall, 1978), it is also generally acknowledged that motivation, practice, and social context can affect levels of sensitivity (e.g., Marangoni, Garcia, Ickes, & Teng, 1995). In general, it is our assumption that natural variation in levels of social sensitivity exist such that some individuals are chronically more sensitive than others. However, we also believe that both conscious and nonconscious motivations can affect sensitivity levels (e.g., Simpson, Ickes, & Blackstone, 1995). Thus, we predicted that within their own individual range of ability, individuals would exhibit greater sensitivity when their need to belong is higher.

Because interpersonal sensitivity is a complex construct involving a range of different skills (i.e., attending to social cues, decoding the meaning of those cues, and responding appropriately), individual ability levels may constrain performance even when motivation is high. A recently rejected person may be motivated to be more sensitive to an interaction partner's thoughts and feelings, but may lack the training, practice, or requisite skills to do so. Because both motivation and ability affect performance on social sensitivity tasks, it is necessary to take into account the level of skill required by a particular measure of social sensitivity in order to predict the relationship between belonging need and sensitivity. When the sensitivity measure is relatively easy (e.g., simply attending to social information or vocal tone), temporary or situational manipulations of belonging need may be sufficient to produce greater sensitivity. However, when the task is more complex and skill-dependent (e.g., inferring an individual's thoughts or feelings), then only individuals who engage in chronic attempts at social sensitivity (i.e., individuals dispositionally high in belonging need) may exhibit enhanced task performance. Thus, although we generally predict that heightened belonging need should result in increased social sensitivity, we also acknowledge that this relationship may be attenuated when the sensitivity task is difficult.

In testing our predictions regarding the social monitoring system, we distinguished between two sources of belonging need—chronic and situational. Chronically high belonging need may result when an individual craves higher levels of social contact and inclusion than the social situation affords. This is the state captured by the construct of loneliness (Peplau & Perlman, 1982; see also Cacioppo & Hawkley, this volume). Lonely individuals perceive a deficiency in their social relationships (Russell, Cutrona, Rose, & Yurko, 1984) and may experience long periods of unmet belonging need (Baumeister & Leary, 1995). Because lonely individuals experience a chronic lack of belonging, one might predict that these individuals would exhibit enhanced social sensitivity in attempt to satisfy their unmet need. Although we will summarize evidence supportive of this prediction, it should be noted that loneliness is associated with objective and subjective measures of social isolation and poorer interaction quality (e.g., Jones, Hobbs, & Hockenbury, 1982). Given the association between loneliness and general social skill deficits (e.g., DiTommaso, Brannen-McNulty, Ross, & Burgess, 2003; Jones et al., 1982), it is likely that lonely individuals may be motivated to exhibit greater social sensitivity as a means of improving their social relationships (and, in fact, may do so on some tasks), but that their skill level may constrain their performance on many measures of sensitivity.

Apart from loneliness, chronically activated belonging need may stem from dispositionally high needs for social acceptance and inclusion (Leary, Kelly, Cottrell, & Schreindorfer, 2005). According to Leary et al. (2001), some individuals appear to have especially strong needs for acceptance such that they seek out large numbers of social relationships, experience strong negative reactions to exclusion, and worry about their level of social regard. Leary et al. (2001) developed a scale to measure individual differences in belonging need (the Need to Belong Scale (NTBS)) and found that this measure was uncorrelated with measures of perceived social support and acceptance, loneliness, and alienation. It appears that individuals high in the need to belong simply desire and worry about social acceptance irrespective of the status of their current social ties. Given the nature of the need to belong construct, we predicted that scores on the NTBS would be positively associated with interpersonal sensitivity. Unlike lonely individuals, high need to belong individuals should be both motivated and able to exhibit enhanced sensitivity as a means of achieving greater social inclusion.

In addition to chronic sources of belonging need, we also examined situational threats to belongingness. When people are not chosen for a team or are excluded from a conversation, they are presumed to experience a deficit in their level of belongingness need satisfaction and should be motivated to reduce that deficit (Baumeister & Leary, 1995). To do so, individuals are expected to engage in behaviors aimed at improving their level of social inclusion (e.g., Lakin & Chartrand, this volume). Therefore, we predicted that situational threats to belongingness would temporarily heighten individuals' need to belong and would also lead to greater subsequent sensitivity to social information and verbal and nonverbal social cues.

EMPIRICAL EVIDENCE

Chronic Sources of Belonging Need

As a first attempt at studying the relationship between loneliness and enhanced social sensitivity, we measured individual differences in loneliness using the UCLA Loneliness Scale (Russell, Peplau, & Cutrona, 1980) among two samples of college students. Participants in one study (Gardner, Pickett, Jefferis, & Knowles, in press) were subsequently exposed to a social memory task. In this task, participants were told that they would be reading about 4 days in the life of an undergraduate student (matched in gender to each participant) and that they would see a series of entries for each day, much like a diary. These entries were of five different types: positive and negative information related to interpersonal or collective relationships (social information), positive and negative individual information related to individual performance (non-social information), and neutral filler information—i.e., non-valenced individual information. For example, participants read "My roommate and I went out on the town tonight and had a really great time together" (positive social information), and "I got a haircut that I absolutely can't stand; it's incredibly ugly" (negative non-social information). After reading all of the diary entries, participants completed a filler task, and then were given a surprise recall task and were told to list all of the diary events that they could remember. As predicted, lonely participants remembered a greater proportion of information related to interpersonal or collective social ties compared to non-lonely participants. In addition, this effect was not qualified by valence of the information. Thus, this initial study suggests that loneliness (a state of unmet belonging need) is associated with better recall of socially-relevant information (regardless of valence) and provides evidence that lonely individuals may engage in greater social monitoring.

It should be noted, however, that recalling information about another person presented semantically via computer is not socially threatening and does not require any special perceptual skills. It may be the case that when a social perception task enhances social anxiety, loneliness may be unrelated to social sensitivity or even negatively related to sensitivity. To examine this idea, loneliness was measured in a second sample, and participants' performance at decoding facial expressions was tested. The Diagnostic Analysis of Nonverbal Behavior 2 (DANVA-2) (Nowicki & Duke, 1994) was used as our measure of participants' ability to detect nonverbal social cues. The DANVA-2 consists of 24 male and female faces depicting four emotions (anger, fear, happiness, and sadness) of high and low intensity. The faces were presented individually for a 1-second duration, and participants were asked to judge the emotional expression conveyed by the face presented. Results revealed a significant negative correlation ($r = -30$) between loneliness and performance on the DANVA-2. Higher levels of loneliness were associated with less accurate facial expression detection.

These data are in line with other studies (e.g., DiTommaso et al., 2003; Jones et al., 1982) that indicate that loneliness is associated with poor social skills. What this suggests for our model of the social monitoring system is that unmet belonging need may indeed lead to greater attention to cues related to social acceptance and belonging (i.e., greater social monitoring), but that it is not necessarily the case that the result of this process will be enhanced social sensitivity (i.e., correct decoding of the cues). Because lonely individuals come in to the lab with existing social skill deficits, it is impossible in a correlational design to examine how the experience of loneliness per se affects levels of interpersonal sensitivity. The goal of our experimental work has been to get around these issues by experimentally manipulating feelings of belongingness.

In conjunction with this line of research on loneliness, we have also conducted a series of studies (Pickett, Gardner, & Knowles, 2004) aimed at examining how individual differences in the need to belong (Leary et al., 2001) relate to various measures of social sensitivity. In a first study, we had participants complete a facial expression identification task (similar to the DANVA-2) where they had to indicate the facial expressions of a series of faces presented individually for 1 second. Participants also completed a vocal tone identification task where they listened to a series of words spoken in a positive and negative tone of voice and were asked to press a button to indicate the valence of the vocal tone. We predicted that individuals higher in the need to belong would exhibit better performance at these tasks. In support of this prediction, regression analyses revealed significant positive associations between scores on the NTBS and accuracy on the facial expression and vocal tone identification tasks.

In this first study, social sensitivity was examined using two fairly simple tasks—i.e., identifying vocal tone and static emotional facial expressions. However, during daily social interactions, one reason that individuals attend to social cues is so that they can decipher other people's state of mind. To mimic the type of social sensitivity challenges that individuals are likely to encounter in their natural social environment, a second study was conducted that included an empathic accuracy task (Gesn & Ickes, 1999; Klein & Hodges, 2001). As noted by Gesn and Ickes (1999), accurate decoding of a target's thoughts and feelings in an empathic accuracy task requires that perceivers attend to both verbal and nonverbal cues arriving through visual and auditory channels and combine these cues to infer the target's state of mind. Because of the complexity of the empathic accuracy task, we felt that it would provide a strong test of the relationship between belonging needs and social sensitivity.

The task itself involved watching a 5-minute videotape of a female college student describing her plans for graduate school and her performance on the GRE. The woman on the video—the target—had recorded her thoughts and feelings at 4 different intervals. While participants watched the video, the experimenter stopped the tape at the intervals at which the target woman had recorded a thought or feeling and asked participants to write down what they thought the woman was thinking or feeling at that moment. Blind coders then rated participants' inferences for the extent to which the inferred thought or feeling matched the actual thought or feeling that the woman in the video reported having.

An additional goal of this second study was to disentangle attention to social cues from the correct decoding of those cues. To do so, we altered the vocal tone identification task used in the first study so that it assessed attention to vocal tone as opposed to accurate identification. Using the logic of a Stroop task, it is possible to construct the task so that participants are required to indicate the valence of the word content while ignoring the vocal tone in which they hear the word (see Ishii, Reyes, & Kitayama, 2003). To the extent that individuals attend to vocal tone, they should be faster at indicating the semantic meaning of the word when the vocal tone is congruent with the semantic meaning of the word (e.g., *sly* spoken in a negative tone of voice) than when the tone is incongruent with the semantic meaning (e.g., *sly* spoken in a positive tone of voice). We predicted that higher need to belong scores would be associated with a bigger difference between the congruent and incongruent trials in this task (vocal Stroop task) indicating that participants higher in the need to belong attended more to vocal tone.

In line with our expectations, NTBS scores were positively associated with empathic accuracy and attention to vocal tone supporting the contention that the desire for greater social inclusion is related to enhanced social sensitivity. The results of our program of research involving individual differences in loneliness and the need to belong are consistent with our theoretical model of the social monitoring system. Individuals who experience chronically high belonging need should monitor their environment for social information to a greater extent than those with lower levels of need. Furthermore, we hypothesized the increased social sensitivity—attending to social cues and accurately decoding them—would also be related to greater belonging need. However, in order to cast a wider nomological net and to establish a causal link between belonging need and social sensitivity, we are engaged in another line of research designed to examine the effect of situational manipulations of social exclusion on levels of social monitoring and sensitivity.

Situational Threats to Belonging Need

Our first attempt at providing empirical evidence for a causal relationship between belonging need and social monitoring involved two studies reported in Gardner, Pickett, and Brewer (2000). In both studies, we had participants engage in what they thought was an Internet chat session. In actuality, participants' Internet conversations were rigged and participants were randomly assigned to one of three experimental conditions. One third of the study participants experienced acceptance during the Internet conversation, while another third experienced a dyadic rejection—being excluded from a dyadic relationship—whereas a final third experienced a group rejection—being rejected by an entire group. At the end of the Internet session, participants were asked to complete a social memory task—the same task described earlier in the study by Gardner et al. (in press). As expected, after a rejection experience (either dyadic or group) participants recalled a smaller proportion of the non-social, individual activities and a larger proportion of the social (interpersonal or collective) activities. These findings are consistent with the idea that rejection can trigger enhanced monitoring and retention of social information.

In another study (Pickett et al., 2004; Study 2), we sought to provide further evidence that experimental manipulations of social exclusion result in greater attention and sensitivity to social cues. In this study, participants were randomly assigned to one of three reliving conditions (rejection, failure-control and neutral-control). In the rejection-reliving condition, participants were asked to write about a time in which they felt intensely rejected in some way. In the failure-control condition, participants wrote about a time in which they felt intense failure in an intellectual domain. Finally, participants in the neutral-control condition wrote about their walk (or drive) to campus that morning. The failure recall condition was included as a negative control that was predicted to elicit similar levels of negative affect as the rejection condition while not manipulating feelings of social exclusion. There were two primary dependent measures in this study—the vocal Stroop task and the empathic accuracy task described previously.

Results of the reliving manipulation on the two measures of interpersonal sensitivity provided partial support for our hypotheses. As predicted, participants asked to relive a rejection experience exhibited significantly greater attention to vocal tone than did participants in the neutral-control and failure-control conditions as evidenced by a larger difference in their response times for the congruent and incongruent vocal tone trials. Unexpectedly, however, participants' performance on the empathic accuracy task revealed the opposite pattern. Participants who were asked to recount a rejection experience were *less* empathically accurate than were participants in the two control reliving conditions.

What might account for this pattern of data? One clue to a possible explanation is that the vocal Stroop task and the empathic accuracy task differ markedly in the set of skills required by the two tasks. Perceiving that one has not achieved a desired level of belonging may lead individuals to attend more to social cues (as evidenced by the vocal Stroop task data). However, it may only be with practice and feedback that individuals are able to achieve accuracy in decoding the meaning of these cues. Thus, a potential interpretation of the data pattern is that participants in the rejection-reliving condition did indeed attend more to the verbal and nonverbal cues emitted by the target, but lacked the skills to accurately decode the additional information. This is analogous to a novice air traffic controller attempting to read a radar screen. Instead of improving the controller's accuracy, more information on the radar screen might, in fact, reduce his ability to arrive upon a correct interpretation of the data. The finding that need to belong scores were positively associated with better performance on the empathic accuracy task might reflect the fact that high NTB individuals are expected to routinely attend to and decode social cues. Hence, we would expect chronic belonging needs to be associated with greater empathic accuracy. It may be unrealistic though to assume that the same effects will hold after situational rejection. Accuracy in decoding the meaning of this information may require development through repeated attempts to understand social cues.

The potential disjoint between attention and accuracy may be particularly likely to emerge in cases with complex social cues requiring integration, or when a task involves making broader cue-based inferences. In these cases, attention to the cues themselves may have little impact on overall accuracy and, in fact, may impair accuracy to the extent that attending to multiple cues creates confusion or multiple erroneous inferences. Hence, we would expect both situational manipulations of rejection and chronic belonging needs to result in increased accuracy at detecting and decoding social cues when the social sensitivity tasks are relatively simple and easy. When the social sensitivity tasks are complex and require practice, then only chronic belonging needs may be related to accuracy. Future research will need to address the conditions under which situational manipulations of rejection lead to better versus worse perceptual accuracy.

CONCLUSIONS

Data from several lines of research have provided encouraging initial support for the operation of a social monitoring system within a larger system for regulating belonging needs. An important ultimate goal of this project is to link activation of the SMS to individuals' subsequent levels of experienced social rejection and exclusion and the quality of their social interactions. Those individuals who fail to show temporary increases in social monitoring following a rejection episode may experience greater levels of social exclusion in their daily lives and may report lower levels of global social acceptance and belonging. Our research to date represents initial steps in this line of study and has the potential to elucidate a critical mechanism through which social acceptance and belonging are maintained.

REFERENCES

Atkinson, J. W., & McClelland, D. C. (1948). The effect of different intensities of the hunger drive on thematic apperception. *Journal of Experimental Psychology, 38,* 643–658.

Baumeister, R. F., & Leary, M. R. (1995). The need to belong: Desire for interpersonal attachments as a fundamental human motivation. *Psychological Bulletin, 117,* 497–529.

Baumeister, R. F., & Tice, D. M. (1990). Anxiety and social exclusion. *Journal of Social and Clinical Psychology, 9,* 165–195.

Bernieri, F. J. (2001). Toward a taxonomy of interpersonal sensitivity. *Interpersonal sensitivity:*

Theory and measurement (pp. 3–20). Mahwah, NJ: Lawrence Erlbaum Associates.

Cacioppo, J. T., Hawkley, L. C., Berntson, G. G., Ernst, J. M., Gibbs, A. C., Stickgold, R., & Hobson, J. A. (2002). Lonely days invade the nights: Social modulation of sleep efficiency. *Psychological Science, 13,* 385–388.

Case, R. B., Moss, A. J., Case, N., McDermott, M., & Eberly, S. (1992). Living alone after myocardial infarction: A prospective, population–based study of the elderly. *Journal of the American Medical Association, 267,* 515–519.

Dement, W. C., & Vaughan, C. (1999). *The*

Promise of sleep. New York: Dell Publishing.

DiTommaso, E., Brannen-McNulty, C., Ross, L., & Burgess, M. (2003). Attachment styles, social skills and loneliness in young adults. *Personality and Individual Differences, 35,* 303–312.

Downey, G., & Feldman, S. (1996). Implications of rejection sensitivity for intimate relationships. *Journal of Personality and Social Psychology, 70,* 1327–1343.

Fichten, C. S., Tagalakis, V., Judd, D., Wright, J., & Amsel, R. (1992). Verbal and nonverbal communication cues in daily conversations and dating. *Journal of Social Psychology, 132,* 751–769.

Folkes, V. S. (1982). Communicating the reasons for social rejection. *Journal of Experimental Social Psychology, 18,* 235–252.

Gardner, W. L., Pickett, C. L., Jefferis, V., & Knowles, M. L. (in press). On the outside looking in: Loneliness and social monitoring. *Personality and Social Psychology Bulletin.*

Gardner, W. L., Pickett, C. L., & Brewer, M. B. (2000). Social exclusion and selective memory: How the need to belong influences memory for social events. *Personality and Social Psychology Bulletin, 26,* 486–496.

Gesn, P. R., & Ickes, W. (1999). The development of meaning contexts for empathic accuracy: Channel and sequence effects. *Journal of Personality and Social Psychology, 77,* 746–761.

Hall, J. A. (1978). Gender effects in decoding nonverbal cues. *Psychological Bulletin, 85,* 845–857.

Ishii, K., Reyes, J. A., & Kitayama, S. (2003). Spontaneous attention to word content versus emotional tone: Differences among three cultures. *Psychological Science, 14,* 39–46.

Jones, W. H. (1990). Loneliness and social exclusion. *Journal of Social and Clinical Psychology, 9,* 214–220.

Jones, W. H., & Carver, M. D. (1991). The experience of loneliness: Adjustment and coping implications. In C. R. Snyder & D. R. Forsyth (Eds.), *Handbook of social and clinical psychology: The health perspective* (pp. 395–415). New York: Pergamon.

Jones, W. H., Hobbs, S. A., & Hockenbury, D. (1982). Loneliness and social skill deficits. *Journal of Personality and Social Psychology, 42,* 682–689.

Klein, K. J. K., & Hodges, S. D. (2001). Gender differences, motivation, and empathic accuracy: When it pays to understand. *Personality and*

Social Psychology Bulletin, 27,* 720–730.

Lancaster, J. B. (1986). Primate social behavior and ostracism. *Ethology and Sociobiology, 7,* 215–225.

Leary, M. R. (1990). Responses to social exclusion: Social anxiety, jealousy, loneliness, depression, and low self-esteem. *Journal of Social and Clinical Psychology, 9,* 221–229.

Leary, M. R. (1999). Making sense of self-esteem. *Current Directions in Psychological Science, 8,* 32–35.

Leary, M. R., Haupt, A. L., Strausser, K. S., & Chokel, J. T. (1998). Calibrating the sociometer: The relationship between interpersonal appraisals and state self-esteem. *Journal of Personality and Social Psychology, 74,* 1290–1299.

Leary, M. R., Kelly, K. M., Cottrell, C. A., & Schreindorfer, L. S. (2005). *Individual differences in the need to belong: Mapping the nomological network.* Unpublished manuscript, Wake Forest University, Winston-Salem, NC.

Leary, M. R., Tambor, E. S., Terdal, S. K., & Downs, D. L. (1995). Self-esteem as an interpersonal social monitor: The sociometer hypothesis. *Journal of Personality and Social Psychology, 68,* 518–530.

Marangoni, C., Garcia, S., Ickes, W., & Teng, G. (1995). Empathic accuracy in a clinically relevant setting. *Journal of Personality and Social Psychology, 68,* 854–869.

Marcus, D. K., & Askari, N. H. (1999). Dysphoria and interpersonal rejection: A social relations analysis. *Journal of Social and Clinical Psychology, 18,* 370–384.

Maslow, A. H. (1970). *Motivation and personality* (2nd ed.). New York: Harper & Row.

Nowicki, S., & Duke, M. P. (1994) Individual differences in the nonverbal communication of affect: The Diagnostic Analysis of Nonverbal Accuracy Scale. *Journal of Nonverbal Behavior, 18,* 9–35.

Peplau, L. A., & Perlman, D. (1982). *Loneliness: A sourcebook of current theory, research, and therapy.* New York: Wiley-Interscience.

Pickett, C. L., Gardner, W. L., & Knowles, M. (2004). Getting a cue: The need to belong and enhanced sensitivity to social cues. *Personality and Social Psychology Bulletin, 30,* 1095–1107.

Raleigh, M. J., & McGuire, M. T. (1986). Animal analogues of ostracism: Biological mechanisms and social consequences. *Ethology and Sociobiology, 7,* 201–214.

Russell, D., Cutrona, C., Rose, J., & Yurko, K. (1984). Social and emotional loneliness: An examination of Weiss's typology of loneliness. *Journal of Personality and Social Psychology, 46,* 1313–1321.

Russell, D., Peplau, L. A., & Cutrona, C. E. (1980). The revised UCLA Loneliness Scale: Concurrent and discriminant validity evidence. *Journal of Personality and Social Psychology, 39,* 472–480.

Simpson, J. A., Ickes, W., & Blackstone, T. (1995). When the head protects the heart: Empathic accuracy in dating relationships. *Journal of Personality and Social Psychology, 69,* 629–641.

Twenge, J. M., Baumeister, R. F., Tice, D. M., & Stucke, T. S. (2001). If you can't join them, beat them: Effects of social exclusion on aggressive behavior. *Journal of Personality and Social Psychology, 81,* 1058–1069.

Uchino, B. N., Cacioppo, J. T., & Kiecolt–Glaser, J. K. (1996). The relationship between social support and physiological processes: A review with emphasis on underlying mechanisms and implications for health. *Psychological Bulletin, 119,* 488–531.

Williams, K. D. (2001). *Ostracism: The power of silence.* New York: Guilford Publications.

Williams, K. D., Cheung, C. K. T., & Choi, W. (2000). CyberOstracism: Effects of being ignored over the Internet. *Journal of Personality and Social Psychology, 79,* 748–762.

14

Social Snacking and Shielding

Using Social Symbols, Selves, and Surrogates in the Service of Belonging Needs

WENDI L. GARDNER
CYNTHIA L. PICKETT
MEGAN KNOWLES

INTRODUCTION

*I*n the movie *Cast Away* (Rapke & Zemeckis, 2000), hapless FedEx worker Chuck Noland overcame the combined threat of physical and social starvation after being stranded alone on a remote island. Chuck devised ingenious strategies that allowed him to survive both types of challenges for 4 years. In addition to spearing fish, catching rainwater, and finding shelter to provide for his physical needs, Chuck found that conversations with a snapshot of his girlfriend Kelly and the companionship of a volleyball that he named Wilson both proved useful in staving off the despair of social isolation.

Address correspondence to: Wendi Gardner, Department of Psychology, Northwestern University, Evanston, IL 60208, USA. E-mail: wgardner@northwestern.edu

Although few of us will ever be marooned on a deserted island, we nevertheless all share the need for daily social sustenance and face challenges to belonging. Rejection, ostracism, or temporary separation from loved ones can all threaten our subjective sense of social connection (see Leary, this volume; Williams & Zadro, this volume). Like Chuck, we appear adept in using indirect strategies to gain and sustain a sense of belonging even when direct social connection is difficult, risky, or impossible. The current chapter speculates on the forms such social fallbacks take and presents suggestive evidence of their use and effectiveness in meeting the mundane social hardships of daily life. We propose that using tangible social symbols, affirmation of the social self, and even attachment to social surrogates like Wilson, the volleyball, all have a place within the broad portfolio of coping strategies that serve successful belonging regulation.

BELONGING REGULATION

In Maslow's (1954) classic hierarchy of needs, the need to belong, to feel accepted by and connected to others, maintained a privileged position—it's importance exceeded only by survival needs such as food, shelter, and safety. However, despite robust and repeated confirmation of the importance of belonging needs (e.g., Baumeister & Leary, 1995; Bowlby, 1969; Maslow, 1954; Schachter, 1959), it was not until the last decade or so that social psychologists began to explicitly pursue the mechanisms of belonging regulation, defined here as the processes that afford adaptive monitoring and responding to changes in inclusionary status. We have begun to develop and explore such a model (see Pickett & Gardner, this volume), attempting to integrate our own and others' work in an attempt to understand when and how challenges to belonging are met. A greater understanding of these processes seems needed, given the breadth and magnitude of negative consequences suffered as a result of unmet belonging needs.

In addition to the hurt feelings (Baumeister & Tice, 1990; Eisenberger & Lieberman, this volume; Leary, 1990) and lowered sense of self-worth (Leary, Tambor, Terdal, & Downs, 1995; Leary, 1999) that may result from exclusion or rejection, more insidious and unexpected effects have been documented both in and outside the lab. In laboratory experiments, rejected individuals behave more aggressively (see Twenge, this volume; Tice, this volume) and less intelligently (see Baumeister & DeWall, this volume), resulting in a wide variety of self-defeating behavior (Twenge, Catanese, & Baumeister, 2003).

Outside of the lab environment, a high level of rejection sensitivity serves as a vulnerability factor for a host of psychological difficulties, including depression (Ayduk, Downey & Kim, 2001; Downey, Feldman, & Ayduk, 2000), hostility violence (Ayduk, Downey, Testa, Yen, & Shoda, 1999), and general social stress (Downey & Feldman, 1996; see Romero-Canyas & Downey, this volume). In addition, loneliness and social isolation have been consistently associated with poor sleep quality, cardiovascular disease, immune system problems, increases in blood pressure, and other somatic maladies (Cacioppo et al., 2002; Cacioppo & Hawkley, this volume; DeLongis, Folkman, & Lazarus,1988; Kiecolt-Glaser et al., 1984; Lynch, 1979; Stroud, Tanofsky-Kraff, Wilfley, & Salovey, 2000). Indeed, the negative impact of isolation on health rivals more widely acknowledged killers such as smoking and diabetes (House, Landis, & Umberson, 1988).

The profusion of negative effects suffered as a result of unmet belonging needs compels a deeper understanding of belonging regulation. The strategies deployed to regulate these needs have been a focus of multiple recent lines of research (many reflected in chapters in this volume, e.g., Pickett & Gardner; Sommer & Rubin; Twenge; Williams & Zadro). Pickett and Gardner (this volume) outline a potential model of the stages of belonging regulation and focuses in depth upon the assessment and monitoring stages. The current chapter will briefly review the model and then continue from the point at which the last chapter concluded: The discussion of both direct and indirect social strategies that may be deployed in the service of belonging needs.

Assessment and Monitoring

Given the importance of social sustenance among primary human needs, we have consistently seen the processes essential to physiological regulation systems as appropriate blueprints for belonging regulation (e.g., Gardner, Pickett, & Brewer, 2000; Gardner, 2001; Pickett, Gardner, & Knowles, 2004). Within the system regulating hunger, for example, there are mechanisms that allow for the assessment of current needs (e.g., blood sugar levels and food needs), some type of signal when the needs are unmet (e.g., the state of feeling hungry), and mechanisms that then monitor the environment and guide information processing in a goal directed fashion (e.g., the increased notice of restaurant signs on the highway when one is hungry). We believe similar stages characterize belonging regulation. As can be seen in Figure 14.1, the sociometer (e.g., Leary et al., 1995; Leary, 1999) provides a cornerstone of the model by providing the means through which the assessment and signaling of belonging needs can occur.

In the model, the workings of the sociometer supply the first inputs into the belonging regulation system. Through the continuous monitoring and adjustment of internal proxies for subjective inclusion (e.g., affect and self-esteem), the sociometer provides the mechanism for the initial assessment stage in the belonging regulation process.

When subjective inclusion is low, the activation of what we have termed the Social Monitoring System (SMS) takes place. The SMS monitors the external environment, heightening attention to social aspects of the environment whenever a threat to belonging is perceived. The primary purpose of the SMS is to attune individuals to information that will help them navigate the social environment more successfully.

In support of the existence and functionality of the SMS, we have found that rejected individuals and/or those with a chronically high "need to belong" (Leary,

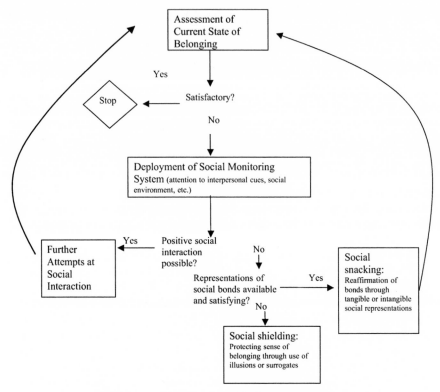

FIGURE 14.1 An Extended Model of Belonging Regulation

Kelly, & Schreindorfer, 2001) seem particularly attentive to aspects of the social environment that could assist them in understanding the social networks or intentions of others. For example, after a laboratory rejection experience, individuals exhibit preferential recall for information concerning the social relations and group memberships of others (Gardner et al., 2000). Moreover, individuals chronically high in the need to belong show enhanced accuracy at interpreting subtle social cues such as facial expressions and vocal tones when compared to their low need to belong counterparts, as well as a heightened level of interpersonal sensitivity after a rejection experience (Pickett et al., 2004).

Importantly, the advantages of engaging the SMS seem constrained to social information processing. No differences between those with high and low belonging needs were found for information unrelated to social bonds, nor were differences found for nonsocial problem solving, suggesting the effects did not result from arousal, heightened motivation to perform, or greater eagerness to please the experimenter. Finally, these effects remained (and sometimes were strengthened) when negative mood was covaried out of the analyses, lending still greater support to Baumeister and colleagues' notion that many rejection effects are not mere consequences of the affective responses to exclusion (Baumeister & DeWall, this volume; Twenge et al., 2003).

The SMS guides attention to all forms of social information and cues to inclusion as well as exclusion. Although the tuning of the SMS can potentially go awry in cases such as rejection sensitivity (Downey & Feldman, 1996; Romero-Canyas & Downey, this volume) and chronic loneliness (Cacioppo & Hawkley, this volume), we believe that the SMS is a generally adaptive system. Through engaging information gathering processes that might ease social interactions in the future, the SMS helps to initiate positive and direct reconnection with others (for greater detail, see Pickett & Gardner, this volume).

The Pursuit of Satisfying Social Interactions

The most efficient and thus preferred response to low levels of belonging will presumably be social acceptance and reconnection. Thus, to the extent that social opportunities are available, behavioral strategies that promote reconnection should be efficiently deployed. In fact, several recent avenues of research now point to belonging-related shifts in both automatic and controlled affiliative behaviors (see Lakin & Chartrand, this volume; Ouwerkerk, vanLange, Gallucci, & Kerr, this volume; Williams & Sommer, 1997; Williams & Zadro, this volume).

One growing body of evidence points to the success of behavioral mimicry as an affiliation strategy. Mimicry has been shown to increase whenever affiliation goals are activated (e.g., Lakin & Chartrand, 2003) and enhances interpersonal rapport (e.g., Chartrand & Bargh, 1999; Lakin, Jefferis, Cheng, & Chartrand, 2003). Given that affiliation goals and heightened belonging needs presumably occur in parallel, mimicry would be an adaptive response to rejection. Indeed, recent evidence showed that individuals who had previously experienced a laboratory rejection mimicked interaction partners, particularly when there was a relatively good chance for repairing bonds (e.g., when they were ingroup members, Lakin, Chartrand & Arkin, 2004). The absence of awareness or conscious intention on the part of the mimicker implies that these adaptive affiliative processes are marshaled automatically in the presence of a reconnection opportunity.

In addition to these relatively effortless processes of attention to and mimicry of the social cues and behaviors of others, other research has documented equally adaptive effortful behavioral compensation strategies that also appear to be directed at regaining social inclusion. In the model of ostracism developed by Williams (1997; 2001) one relatively immediate response to ostracism was proposed to be behaviors enacted in order to directly repair broken social bonds. For example, Williams and Sommer (1997) found that women who were left out of a ball-toss game worked harder on a subsequent group task, perhaps as a hopeful attempt at ingratiation. Similarly, Williams, Cheung, and Choi (2000) revealed a heightened tendency for those excluded from cyberball (an Internet ball-toss game) to conform to the opinions of others. Finally, recent work by Oewerkerk and colleagues (this volume) may suggest that enhanced cooperation in a social dilemma may also serve as a potential affiliative strategy evoked when inclusionary status is threatened.

All of the above strategies, whether demonstrating automatic and low level perceptual biases or more complex and strategic ingratiating behaviors, clearly require the opportunity for potential acceptance by another human being. As such, they may be viewed as direct social strategies however subtle their manifestations may be. Yet, because belonging needs are sometimes triggered in the absence of such direct social opportunities, direct strategies cannot represent the sole channels for belonging satiation.

HOW DO YOU PURSUE BELONGING WHEN MAROONED ON A DESERTED ISLAND?

We opened this chapter with the example of Chuck the unfortunate castaway on an uninhabited island far from home. Obviously, even if the assessment and monitoring stages of the belonging regulatory system were working perfectly, in a case like Chuck's (and in the milder situational isolation common in daily life), the seeking and smoothing of future social interactions would be woefully insufficient in addressing his belonging needs. Fortunately, other avenues for belonging regulation may exist. In the lower right hand side of Figure 14.1, we introduce other strategies that may provide temporary substitutes for direct interaction. We refer to these sets of more indirect social strategies as "social snacking" and "social shielding."

Social Snacking

When hungry, we want a meal. However, when we do not have the proper time or resources to create a meal, we are often willing to settle for a snack. Similarly, we propose that there may be "social snacks" that provide temporary stopgaps for social hunger when a "social meal" (e.g., interaction with an accepting other) is unavailable. Given that we have yet to run into anything approximating a social "vending machine" through which belonging is handily distributed, these snacks need to be self-supplied. What might serve as a social snack? We have proposed that any reminder of a social bond—be it a photo, an old love letter, a wedding ring, or other tangible reminder of being connected and accepted—can serve the function of a social snack, and that these symbolic reminders can (at least temporarily) fulfill belonging needs (Gardner, 2001). Anyone who has ever tucked a child into bed with the t-shirt of an absent parent will acknowledge the comforting power of physical reminders of loved ones. Even in adulthood, studies have provided evidence that socially symbolic objects (e.g., a souvenir bought on a honeymoon, a child's scribbled valentine to a parent) can provide a powerful sense of connection for individuals ranging in age from young newlyweds (Arriaga, Goodfriend, & Lohman, 2004) to the elderly (Sherman, 1991).

Through multiple studies, we have generated and tested the types of tangible reminders or symbolic social behaviors that could serve as common social snacks (Gardner, Jefferis, & Knowles, 2004). Undergraduates report rereading e-mails, daydreaming of loved ones, and looking at photos of friends, family, and romantic partners in times when they do not have time for real social contact, or times when they are feeling lonely. Moreover, these types of symbolic social behaviors are preferred to similar and equally enjoyable non-social behaviors (e.g., surfing the Web, daydreaming of fun activities, and looking through magazines) in times of social need. When we polled students about the likelihood of engaging in these behaviors on any given day, the social and nonsocial were roughly equivalent in frequency. However, the symbolic social behaviors were significantly and positively correlated with the need to belong, and in a subsequent study, were more likely after students were asked to imagine studying alone all day. Finally, in a study in which rejection was experimentally manipulated, participants who were not included in a group task because other members did not like them endorsed more of the symbolically social items on a social snacking scale than participants who were not included because their creativity levels were too low.

A Picture's Social Worth

Of all of the potential social snacking behaviors, looking at photos of loved ones was the one most frequently reported (indeed, it was endorsed as a potential strategy by almost 100% of every sample we asked). Recall that throughout Chuck's ordeal, a photo of his girlfriend sustained him, and after returning home (and finding her married) he stated, "I'm so sad that I don't have Kelly. But I'm so grateful that she was with me on that island." We do keep loved ones with us through photographs. National surveys have shown that over 85% of adults have photographs or mementos of loved ones on their desks at work or in their wallets, and that these reminders can enhance worker well-being, feelings of social support, and overall productivity (Gifford, 1997; Harris, 1991; Wells, 2000). Photographs serve as potent reminders of social bonds.

Research supports the social power of photographs. Photographs have been used in family therapy, both as a basis for analysis and as reminders for family bonds (Sedgwick, 1979; Kaslow & Friedman, 1980). Photos have been successfully used by neonatal nurses with mothers for whom touch and other close contact with the infant is extremely limited or unavailable due to illness or prematurity. In several studies, when a photo of the infant was sent home with the mother, it increased her sense of bonding with the infant (Minton, 1983; Huckabay, 1987; 1999). Indeed, the ability of a photograph to affirm a social bond is so well-ingrained that recent research has shown that simply being given a photo of the self with a stranger is enough to induce reciprocal feelings of affinity (Burgess, Enzle, & Murray, 2000).

In our own research, we too have found that photos appear to serve as useful reminders of social bonds. We asked undergraduates to bring in a photograph of an off-campus friend or a liked celebrity to the lab for what they thought would be a study of memory and visualization. The experimenter went around the room at the beginning of the session and checked to ensure that the participants brought the photos that they were told would be needed for the second half of the experiment, then left the photos on the participants' desks. The participants then were randomly assigned to vividly relive and write about a rejection experience or a failure experience. Blind coding of the reliving essays showed that all essays were extremely (and equivalently) negative, regardless of the type of photo on the desk. However, whereas participants who relived a failure experience suffered an equal drop in mood regardless of the type of picture on the desk, participants who relived a rejection experience suffered a large drop in mood if a picture of a celebrity had been left on their desk, but almost no change in mood if the picture of a friend had been left on the desk. Moreover, after writing an essay about the qualities of the person in the photograph that they liked and admired, rejected participants exposed to the photo of their friend continued to improve their mood, whereas those exposed to the photo of the celebrity did not. Photo type again made no difference in the relived failure condition. Although no participants reported suspicion that the picture and responses to either essay might be related (perhaps implying that the pictures were not consciously used) the differences in affective responses were clear.

The Use of Intangible Social Representations

Of course, photos are not the only way to remind oneself of social bonds. Recent work by McGowan (2002) and Twenge, Zhang, Catanese, Dolan-Pascoe, and Baumeister (2003) demonstrates that feelings of connection and belonging can be replenished simply by remembering a positive social relationship or interaction, even one in the distant past. Impressively, the research by Twenge et al. (2003) shows that this type of positive social representation was sufficient to reduce the robust tendency rejected participants have toward aggression. Thus, not all social snacks appear to require a tangible reminder. In recent research, we also have been exploring the more intangible forms of social representations that can be used in times of increased belonging needs. Specifically, we have been investigating the extent to which social connections represented as part of an individual's self-construal could provide a social snack in an emergency situation.

Robust cultural, individual and situational differences have been documented in the extent to which self-definitions explicitly include close relationships with others and important group memberships (e.g., Brewer & Gardner, 1996; Cross, Bacon, & Morris, 2000; Gardner, Gabriel & Lee, 1999; Markus & Kitayama, 1991; Singelis, 1994). These interdependent self-construals appear to come with several costs to the self, including a general reduction of self-enhancement and self-esteem (Gardner, Gabriel, & Hochschild, 2003; Heine, Lehman, Markus, & Kitayama, 1999), a greater focus on avoiding losses (Elliot, Chirkov, Kim, & Sheldon, 2002; Lee, Aaker, & Gardner, 2000), and a heightened awareness of the expectations and standards of others (Pennington, Gardner & Bessenoff, 2004). However, with burdens come benefits, one of which may be an added resource of social representations that can be used to fulfill belonging needs. When one's social connections are represented as part of the self, it is possible that these may then be available as an affirmational resource, an intangible but effective social snack.

To investigate this possibility, my colleagues and I have compared the responses to rejection suffered by individuals who have this resource highly accessible available with those who do not (Gardner, Knowles, & Jefferis, 2004). In an initial study, we simply allowed individuals to list their self-construal after reliving either a rejection or failure experience. Participants who listed more relational and collective self-construals fared better on mood measures than those who listed more independent attributes, even though those independent attributes were highly positive (e.g., intelligent, athletic). Differences as a function of self-construal only emerged after the rejection task; no differences were found after reliving a failure.

In other studies, individuals chronically high in interdependence were found to be buffered from both rejection induced cognitive deficits, and rejection induced aggression. For example, participants high or low in interdependence as measured by Singelis' (1994) self-construal scale were left out of a cyberball game (Williams et al., 2000) that was played between two analytical problem solving tests. Although previous research by Baumeister and colleagues (2002) had shown a reduction in intelligent thought to be one of the negative outcomes of rejection, only individuals low in interdependence showed a significant drop in accuracy after being left out of the cyberball game. Individuals high in interdependence showed no such reduction, implying that perhaps they had successfully replenished belonging through the activation of stored social connections.

In more direct tests of the role of interdependent self-construal in these effects, we examined implicit activation of interdependent self-construals in response to rejection, and showed these mediated the protective effect of chronic interdependence. We also blocked or encouraged participants to activate stored social representations through the priming of either the independent or interdependent self (e.g., Gardner et al., 1999) and found that, as expected, those who were blocked from activating interdependent self-construals showed a greater reduction in both mood and self-esteem after reliving rejection. Again, the protective value of stored social connections appeared limited to the rejection condition; the two priming conditions did not differ after reliving a failure experience. In summary, it appears as if social representations stored as part of the self-construal may also be used as social snacks to replenish belonging when needed (Gardner, Knowles, & Jefferis, 2004).

The accumulated evidence for social snacking appears consistent and supportive. In times of heightened belonging needs individuals report using symbolic reminders of their social bonds, and appear to benefit from them. Social snacks may take the form of symbolic social behaviors such as rereading emails, tangible social symbols such as photographs or mementos, or intangible social representations such as memories and daydreams, or social representations stored as part of the self. All appear successful in reaffirming and replenishing a subjective sense of connection, and thus may potentially act as social reserves to be drawn upon when direct social interaction is thwarted or impossible.

Social Shielding with Surrogates

The strategy of using photographs or other representational reminders of real social bonds to temporarily assuage belonging needs possesses the triple benefit of being intuitively plausible, societally evident, and empirically supported. Similarly, the notion of defensively activating positive social memories or social connections within the self may also seem relatively plausible in the context of the large body of evidence for self-protective strategies of all kinds. It seems a much more dubious endeavor to propose an attachment to imaginary relationships with unresponsive social figures such as Wilson, the volleyball, could serve as a shield from belonging distress. Yet it was in his attachment to Wilson that the character of Chuck Noland was rendered so poignantly and desperately human, or at the very least, poignantly primate.

Perhaps the most dramatic demonstration of the power of belonging needs and the lengths we might go to fulfill them was the classic study of Harlow's motherless infant monkeys (Harlow, 1958). Some snippets of chicken wire, a few buttons shaped like ears on a wooden ball, and a small scrap of terrycloth provided just enough for an infant monkey to cling to, take comfort in, and connect with. Although it is true that monkeys "raised" by a terrycloth mother did not fare as well as those with responsive and real monkey mothers, what is often forgotten about these studies is that the terrycloth raised monkeys were significantly (and substantially) better off than monkeys with no attachment figures at all. Terrycloth raised monkeys gained weight and grew into adulthood at a rate more similar to mothered monkeys than their orphan counterparts. Like the monkeys raised with real, flesh and blood mothers, those raised with terrycloth mothers would cower in a corner when their surrogate mother was absent, however, they would comfortably explore their environment when their mother was present. In other words, even a mother made of wire and cloth provided a secure base for these monkeys. Harlow concluded at the end of these studies that they demonstrated the necessity of feeling loved to a primate's ability to survive and thrive. My co-authors and I would take a slightly different tack; we believe these studies are perhaps the most dramatic showcase possible of the necessity of *loving*. We primates appear built to love, to bond, to feel attached and connected. And, in the absence of suitable and reciprocal human targets, we too are all undoubtedly capable of clinging to the psychological equivalent of a terrycloth mother.

How might that manifest? Anecdotally, a colleague and good friend of the authors' once confessed that in her first lonely years as an assistant professor, she became concerned, some would say obsessed, with a pair of houseplants. She reported thinking of them at work, talking to them at home, and genuinely looking forward to her daily "interactions" with them. She also reported that when she moved to a more sociable department and made more friends, her plants were cheerfully relegated back to their role as oft-neglected living room decor. Empirical evidence for a similar phenomenon may be seen in the literature concerning "parasocial attachments" (Auter, 1992; Cole & Leets, 1999; Finn & Gorr, 2001; Horton & Wohl, 1956). Parasocial attachments are defined as attachments to television personae, such as news anchors or fictional characters on sitcoms or soap operas. These attachments are (obviously) non-reciprocal, yet go far beyond mere interest in a show or a character. Horton and Wohl (1956) defined them as a compensatory strategy providing "the socially and psychologically isolated with a chance to enjoy the elixir of sociability" (p. 222). Indeed, items on the parasocial attachment scale (Rubin, Perse, & Powell, 1985) not only reflect an enhanced interest in TV characters and shows such as "If there were a story about my favorite TV character in a newspaper or magazine, I would read it," but also reflect a sense of connection such as "I like hearing the voice of my favorite TV character in my home," and "My favorite TV character keeps me company when his or her program is on television."

A few studies have empirically investigated the potential link between parasocial attachments and gratification of social needs. Finn and Gorr (2001) examined individual differences in motivations for television viewing and found that shyness was positively correlated with a social compensation motive; but they did not measure parasocial attachment directly. Cole and Leets (1999) investigated the moderation of parasocial attachment by attachment styles and found that anxious-ambivalent individuals showed the highest parasocial attachment scores. Given the conflicting high desire for social connection coupled with the greater fear of rejection that characterizes those with anxious-ambivalent attachments, these researchers proposed that they might turn to parasocial attachments as a less risky strategy for relationship formation.

We have recently begun exploring the phenomena of parasocial attachments and their potential use as a social shield. We first wished simply to investigate whether the strength of these attachments, particularly the sense of connection with the parasocial relationship, would be related to the need to belong. In repeated surveys of hundreds of college students, we have consistently found that the "interest" and "connection" subscales load on different factors, and that the connection (but not interest) subscale significantly correlates with the need to belong. However, this is not a result of individuals with a chronically high need to belong generally watching more television, as hours watched per week and NTB were uncorrelated (and indeed, were in a slight negative direction).

Additionally, when examining the type of character that could serve as targets for parasocial connection, the realism of the attachment target (e.g., human vs. animated character) mattered less for individuals higher in the need to belong. In exploratory analyses, we found that (as might be expected) participants who named a human character as their favorite TV character endorsed more parasocial connection than those who named an animated character. However, an interaction emerged revealing that whereas individuals both high and low in the need to belong may experience parasocial connection with human television characters, only individuals high in the need to belong can form such relationships with completely unrealistic animated characters.

Whether parasocial relationships of any kind are capable of successfully shielding from rejection distress is a question for future research. An intriguing study by Kanazawa (2002) revealed the possibility that parasocial relationships may be subjectively experienced as friends. Arguing that evolution did not prepare us to distinguish humans on television from genuine social interaction, he hypothesized that people who watch sitcoms and other forms of television in which they are repeatedly exposed to the same characters should perceive themselves as having more friends. In the General Social Survey, this appeared to be true. Women who watched a greater number of social television shows (e.g., those that depicted on-going social relationships among the characters) reported greater satisfaction with friendship quality, as if they had actually socialized more often However, whether this type of parasocial friendship is sufficient to shield a socially isolated or lonely individual, or whether it serves to supplement existing friendships among more socially attuned individuals, remains unknown.

CONCLUSIONS

When social interaction is temporarily unavailable, people appear to turn to indirect social strategies to satisfy belonging needs. We refer to these behaviors as social snacking because they seem to be the temporary stopgaps to be used between opportunities for true social sustenance. Some may be tangible symbols such as photos, and others may rely on representational reminders of social connections that may even be represented as part of the self-concept. Finally, some people may even fallback on "imaginary friends," parasocial relationships that provide the mere illusion of connection. Like actual snacks, we suspect none are ultimately as satisfying or as healthy as true positive and accepting interaction. However, all may be helpful in shielding one from the stings of isolation or rejection, at least temporarily.

For Chuck Noland, the threats to physical survival were ultimately easier to confront than the psychological challenges faced by a life alone. Although fallback strategies like social snacking and shielding may have protected him from complete social starvation, in the end, they were insufficient to sustain him. To fully escape his sense of isolation required Chuck to build a raft and risk a long and treacherous voyage home. For the lonely, rejection sensitive, or isolated individual, the journey back to social connection must sometimes feel as daunting. Given the numerous and severe consequences of unmet belonging needs, fully understanding the strategies of belonging regulation and the ways in which they go awry seems imperative. It is hoped that the study of social snacking and social shielding, the belonging strategies of last resort, may ultimately contribute to this venture.

REFERENCES

Arriaga, X. B., Goodfriend, W., & Lohmann, A. (2004). Beyond the individual: Concomitants of closeness in the social and physical environment. In D. Mashek & A. Aron (Eds.), *Handbook on relationship closeness* (pp. 287–303). Lawrence, NJ: Erlbaum.

Auter, P. J. (1992). TV that talks back: An experimental validation of a parasocial interaction scale. *Journal of Broadcasting and Electronic Media, 36,* 173–181.

Ayduk, O., Downey, G., & Kim, M. (2001). Rejection sensitivity and depressive symptoms in women. *Personality & Social Psychology Bulletin, 27*(7), 868–877.

Ayduk, O., Downey, G., Testa, A., Yen, Y., & Shoda, Y. (1999). Does rejection elicit hostility in rejection sensitive women? *Social Cognition, 17,* 245–271.

Baumeister, R. F., & Leary, M. R. (1995). The need to belong: Desire for interpersonal attachments as a fundamental human motivation. *Psychological Bulletin, 117,* 497–529.

Baumeister, R. F., & Tice, D. M. (1990). Anxiety and social exclusion. *Journal of Social and Clinical Psychology, 9,* 165–195.

Baumeister, R. F., Twenge, J. M., & Nuss, C. K. (2002). Effects of social exclusion on cognitive processes: Anticiapted aloneness reduces intelligent thought. *Journal of Personality & Social Psychology, 83,* 817–827.

Bowlby, J. (1969). *Attachment and loss: Volume 1. Attachment.* London: Hogarth.

Brewer, M. B., & Gardner, W. L. (1996). Who is this 'we'? Levels of collective identity and self representations. *Journal of Personality and Social Psychology, 71,* 83–93.

Burgess, M., Enzle, M., & Murray, M.(2000). The social psychological power of photography: Can the image freezing machine make something out of nothing? *European Journal of Social Psychology, 30,* 613–630.

Cacioppo, J. T., Hawkley, L. C., Berntson, G. G., Ernst, J. M., Gibbs, A. C., Stickgold, R., & Hobson, J. A. (2002). Lonely days invade the nights: Social modulation of sleep efficiency. *Psychological Science, 13,* 385–388.

Chartrand, T. L., & Bargh, J. A. (1999). The chameleon effect: The perception-behavior link and social interaction. *Journal of Personality and Social Psychology, 76,* 893–910.

Cole, T., & Leets, L. (1999). Attachment styles and intimate television viewing. Insecurely forming relationships in a parasocial way. *Journal of Social and Personal Relationships, 16,* 495–511.

Cross, S. E., Bacon, P., & Morris, M. (2000). The relational- interdependent self-construal and relationships. *Journal of Personality and Social Psychology, 78,* 791–808.

DeLongis, A.,Folkman, S., & Lazarus, R. S. (1988). The impact of daily stress on health and mood: Psychological and social resources as mediators. *Journal of Personality and Social Psychology, 54*(3), 486–495.

Downey, G., & Feldman, S. (1996). Implications of rejection sensitivity for intimate relationships. *Journal of Personality & Social Psychology, 70,* 1327–1343.

Downey, G., Feldman, S., & Ayduk, O. (2000). Rejection sensitivity and male violence in romantic relationships. *Personal Relationships, 7,* 45–61.

Eisenberger, N. I., Lieberman, M. D., & Williams, K. D. (2003). Does rejection hurt? An fMRI study of social exclusion. *Science, 302,* 290–292.

Elliot, A. J., Chirkov, V. I., Kim, Y., & Sheldon, K. M. (2002). A cross-cultural analysis of avoidance personal goals. *Psychological Science, 12,* 505–510.

Finn, S., & Gorr, M.B. (2001). Social isolation and social support as correlates of television viewing motivation. *Communications Research, 15,* 135–158.

Gardner, W. L. (2001). *Social hunger: Parallels between the search for nutritional and social sustenance.* Society for Personality and Social Psychology, San Antonio, TX.

Gardner, W. L., Gabriel, S., & Hochschild, L. (2002). When you and I are "we," you are no longer threatening: The role of self-expansion in social comparison processes. *Journal of Personality and Social Psychology,* 239–251.

Gardner, W. L., Gabriel, S., & Lee, A. (1999). 'I' value freedom, but 'we' value relationships: Self-construal priming mimics cultural differences in judgment. *Psychological Science, 10,* 321–326.

Gardner, W. L., Jefferis, V. E., & Knowles, M. L. (in press). Never alone: The interdependent self as a buffer from rejection. *Journal of Personality and Social Psychology.*

Gardner, W. L., Pickett, C. L., & Brewer. M. B. (2000). Social exclusion and selective memory: How the need to belong influences memory for social events. *Personality and Social Psychology Bulletin, 26,* 486–496.

Gifford, R. (1997). *Environmental Psychology: Principles and Practice* (2nd ed.). Boston: Allyn & Bacon.

Harlow, H. (1958). The nature of love. *American Psychologist, 13,* 573–685.

Harris, D. (1991). What do office workers place on their desks and in their offices? *Salmagundi, 92,* 202–210.

Heine, S. J., Lehman, D. R., Markus, H. R., & Kitayama, S. (1999). Is there a universal need for positive self-regard? *Psychological Review, 4,* 766–794.

Horton, D., & Wohl, R. (1956). Mass communication and parasocial interaction. Psychiatry: *Journal for the Study of Interpersonal Processes, 19,* 215–229.

House, J. S., Landis, K. R., & Umberson, D. (1988). Social relationships and health. *Science, 241,* 540–545.

Huckabay, L. (1987). The effect on bonding of giving a mother her premature baby's picture. *Scholarly Inquiry for Nursing Practice, 1,* 115–129.

Huckabay, L. (1999). Impact of research a decade later: The use of pictures in a neonatal intensive care unit as a mode of nursing intervention to enhance maternal bonding. *Scholarly Inquiry for Nursing Practice, 13,* 367–373.

Kanazawa, S. (2002). Bowling with our imaginary friends. *Evolution and Human Behavior, 23,* 167–171.

Kaslow, F., & Friedman, J. (1980). Utilization of family photos and movies in family therapy. *Advances in Family Psychiatry, 2,* 257–266.

Kiecolt-Glaser, J. K., Garner, W., Speicher, C., Penn, G. M., Holliday, J., & Glaser, R. (1984). Psychosocial modifiers of immunocompetence in medical students. *Psychosomatic Medicine, 46,* 7–14.

Lakin, J. L., & Chartrand, T. L. (2003). Using nonconscious behavioral mimicry to create affiliation and rapport. *Psychological Science, 14,* 334–339.

Lakin, J. L., Chartrand, T. L., & Arkin, R. M. (2004). *Exclusion and nonconscious behavioral mimicry: Mimicking others to resolve threatened belongingness needs.* Manuscript submitted for publication.

Lakin, J. L., Jefferis, V. E., Cheng, C. M., & Chartrand, T. L. (2003). The Chameleon Effect as social glue: Evidence for the evolutionary significance of nonconscious mimicry. *Journal of Nonverbal Behavior, 27,* 145–162.

Leary, M. R. (1990). Responses to social exclusion: Social anxiety, jealousy, loneliness, depression, and low self-esteem. *Journal of Social and Clinical Psychology, 9,* 221–229.

Leary, M. R. (1999). Making sense of self-esteem. *Current Directions in Psychological Science, 8,* 32–35.

Leary, M. R., Kelly, K. M., & Schreindorfer, L. S. (2001). *Individual differences in the need to belong.* Unpublished manuscript, Wake Forest University, Winston-Salem, NC.

Leary, M. R., Tambor, E. S., Terdal, S. K., & Downs, D. L. (1995). Self-esteem as an interpersonal social monitor: The sociometer hypothesis. *Journal of Personality and Social Psychology, 68,* 518–530.

Lee, A. Y., Aaker, J., & Gardner, W. L. (2000). The pleasures and pains of distinct self-construals: The role of interdependence in regulatory focus. *Journal of Personality and Social Psychology, 78,* 1122–1134.

Lynch, J. J. (1979). *The broken heart: The medical consequences of loneliness.* New York: Basic Books.

Markus, H. R., & Kitayama, S. (1991). Culture

and the self: Implications for cognition, emotion, and motivation. *Psychological Review, 98,* 224–253.

Maslow, A. (1954). *Motivation and personality.* New York: Harper

McGowan, S. (2002). Mental representations in stressful situations: The calming and distressing effects of significant others. *Journal of Experimental Social Psychology, 38,* 152–161.

Minton, C (1983). Use of photographs in perinatal social work. *Health & Social Work, 8,* 123–125.

Pennington, G.L., Gardner, W.L., & Bessenoff, G. (2004). *Regulating to others' standards: The role of the interdependent self.* Manuscript under review.

Pickett, C. L., Gardner, W. L., & Knowles, M. L. (2004). Getting a cue: The need to belong and enhanced sensitivity to social cues. *Personality and Social Psychology Bulletin, 30,* 1095–1107.

Rapke, J., & Zemeckis, R. (2000). *Cast Away.* Twentieth Century Fox

Rubin, A. M., Perse, E., & Powell, R. (1985). Loneliness, parasocial interaction, and local news viewing. *Human Communications Research, 12,* 155–180.

Schachter, S. (1959). *The psychology of affiliation.* Palo Alto, CA: Stanford Press.

Sedgwick, R. (1979). The use of photographs and family memorabilia in the study of family interaction. *Corrective and Social Psychiatry, 25,* 137–141.

Sherman, E. (1991). Reminiscenntia: Cherished objects as memorabilia in late life reminiscence. *International Journal of Aging and Human Development, 33,* 89–102.

Singelis, T. M. (1994). The measurement of independent and interdependent self-construals. *Personality & Social Psychology Bulletin, 20,* 580–591.

Stroud, L. R., Tanofsky-Kraff, M., Wilfley, D. E., & Salovey, P. (2000). The Yale interpersonal stressor (YIPS): Affective, physiological, and behavioral responses to a novel interpersonal rejection paradigm. *Annals of Behavioral Medicine, 22,* 204–213.

Twenge, J. M., Catanese, K. R., & Baumeister, R. F. (2003). Social exclusion causes self-defeating behavior. *Journal of Personality and Social Psychology, 83,* 606–615.

Twenge, J. M., Zhang,L., Catanese, K. R., Dolan-Pascoe, B., & Baumeister, R. F. (2003). *Replenishing connectedness: Current or remembered social interaction eliminates aggression after social exclusion.* Manuscript under review.

Wells, M. (2000). Office clutter or meaningful personal displays: The role of office personalization in employee and organizational well-being. *Journal of Environmental Psychology, 20,* 239–255.

Williams, K. D. (1997). Social ostracism. In R. Kowalski (Ed.), *Aversive interpersonal behaviors* (pp. 133–170). New York: Plenum Press.

Williams, K. D. (2001). *Ostracism: The power of silence.* New York: Guilford Press.

Williams, K. D., Cheung, C. K. T., & Choi, W. (2000). Cyberostracism: Effects of being ignored over the Internet. *Journal of Personality & Social Psychology, 79,* 748–762.

Williams, K. D., & Sommer, K. L. (1997). Social ostracism by coworkers: Does rejection lead to loafing or compensation? *Personality and Social Psychology Bulletin, 23,* 693–706.

15

All Animals Are Equal but Some Animals Are More Equal than Others

Social Identity and Marginal Membership

MICHAEL A. HOGG

The quote in the title of this chapter, "All animals are equal but some animals are more equal than others," is from George Orwell's 1945 satirical novel *Animal Farm*. In this novel, Orwell's lifelong mistrust of autocratic governments was focused on Stalin's Soviet Union; in particular the contradiction between an ideology of egalitarianism (everyone is equal), and the reality of sharp internal differentiation based on status, power and influence (everyone is not equal). The novel was an attack on what Orwell saw as the hypocrisy of Soviet

Some of the research reported in this chapter was made possible by grant support to Michael Hogg from the Australian Research Council. Address correspondence to: Michael A. Hogg, School of Psychology, University of Queensland Brisbane, QLD 4072, Australia. E-mail: mike@psy.uq.edu.au

communism, which he believed was actually a reincarnation of Tsarist Russia (inequality, privilege, and exclusion) merely under the guise of socialism (equality, tolerance, and inclusion).

Animal Farm captures well the general paradox that is the starting point of this chapter. On the one hand groups accentuate commonalties among members and are about fairness, equality, and inclusion, but on the other hand they are intolerant of diversity, contain sharp divisions that identify some members as marginal and of less worth than others, and engage in social exclusion.

One way, proposed here, to resolve this paradox of group life is to argue that groups organize themselves around prescriptive norms that are cognitively represented as prototypes. Because these prototypes define the group and thus one's self-concept as a group member they are highly salient. Members are acutely attentive to the prototype, and the extent to which they and fellow members fit the prototype. Group life is oriented toward and influenced by the prototype itself and the extent to which self and others fit the prototype. The consequence is a dynamic of conformity to the prototype and deference to prototypical members, coupled with an array of reactions to non-prototypical marginal members, ranging from socialization to rejection. Inclusion and exclusion are inextricable facets of group life.

In this chapter I develop and expand this argument to describe a social identity analysis of the behavior of marginal group members, and their treatment by the rest of the group. The focus is on group not interpersonal processes, and on functional and phenomenological aspects of marginal status in groups. The aim is to provide an integrative framework showing how social identity processes can marginalize and exclude people from group membership—which is somewhat different to the more familiar social identity emphasis on ingroup inclusion and intergroup differentiation.

In addition, this chapter is somewhat different to most of the chapters in this book that focus on the interpersonal dimension of exclusion and marginalization (e.g., Leary's chapter), because it focuses on the group context (but also see Juvonen and Gross's chapter on rejection and bullying in school settings, Fitness's chapter on the family context of rejection, and the chapters by Gardner, Knowles and Pickett, and by Pickett and Gardner, which deal with belonging as a broader social process).

GROUPS, PROTOTYPES, AND GROUP MEMBERSHIP

Groups differ in a multitude of ways—size, longevity, entitativity, function, interdependence, and so forth (e.g., Deaux, Reid, Mizrahi, & Ethier, 1995; Lickel, Hamilton, Wieczorkowska, Lewis, Sherman, & Uhles, 2000; Prentice, Miller and Lightdale (1994). Typically, slightly different definitions of "group" are associated with research on different types of group. In this chapter I adopt a social identity definition of and perspective on groups (Hogg, 2003, in press-a; Hogg & Abrams,

1988; Tajfel & Turner, 1986; Turner, Hogg, Oakes, Reicher, & Wetherell, 1987). A group is three or more people who share a definition and evaluation of who they are—they have a common social identity. This definition has wide generality and applies to almost all groups one can think of—ranging from small, short-lived, interactive task oriented groups to large, enduring, highly dispersed and non-interactive social categories. Social identity is not the only property of group life and group membership, but it may be the most fundamental.

Groups are social categories. They contain members who belong by virtue of possessing attributes that are associated with the category, and therefore allow them to be categorized as members. The attributes of a category can be represented in different ways (e.g., as an exemplar, Smith & Zárate, 1992), however, the social identity approach considers them to be cognitively represented as a prototype—a fuzzy set of attributes (beliefs, attitudes, feelings, and behaviors) that simultaneously capture similarities among group members and differences between members of one group and members of another group.

Prototypes obey the meta-contrast principle—they accentuate perceived intragroup similarities and intergroup differences and thus imbue groups with greater entitativity (also see Gaertner & Iuzzini, this volume, for a discussion of entitativity and rejection). Because prototypes are influenced by both who is in the group and what the relevant outgroup is, they can vary as a function of the intergroup context. Group prototypes can be considered the individual cognitive representation of group norms (e.g., Turner, 1991), and typically within a group there is significant agreement on the prototype or norm. Groups tend to lose cohesion and to disintegrate if members disagree too much over what the group's attributes are.

The essence of the social identity analysis is that group membership is a matter of identifying with the group and thus categorizing oneself and others in terms of the group prototype. Self-categorization applies the prototype to oneself and thus transforms the way one views oneself and the way one perceives, thinks, feels and behaves in that context.

PROTOTYPICALITY AND GROUP STRUCTURE

When group membership is salient, people are depersonalized in terms of the relevant group prototype. Other people are viewed through the lens of the prototype, and one's own self-conception, cognition, affect, and conduct are governed by the ingroup prototype (Oakes, Haslam & Turner, 1994). The prototype defines and prescribes people in group contexts—it is the essence of group life. Not surprisingly, people in groups pay close attention to the prototype, to information that delineates the prototype, and to people who provide information about the prototype (cf. Reicher's, 1984, 2001, analysis of crowd behavior). People also know, and strive to know, with some precision how well they themselves match the prototype, how well others match the prototype, and how prototypical others think one is (e.g., Haslam, Oakes, McGarty, Turner, & Onorato, 1995).

Perceived prototypicality locates one within the fabric of the group—it positions people relative to the prototype and therefore relative to one another. And because the prototype governs group life, prototypicality becomes a critical influence on how people perceive one another within the group, how they treat and feel about one another, and how they interact with one another. Indeed, much of what happens within groups can be characterized as a dialogue or discourse about prototypes and prototypicality—about "who we are" (Hogg & Tindale, 2005). Through what they say and what they do, people identify, consolidate or change the group norm, and position themselves and others relative to that norm.

Groups are structured by perceived prototypicality; there is a prototypicality gradient with some people being viewed as more prototypical than others. Groups are certainly not flat and internally homogeneous. They are differentiated in many different ways—for example, in terms of people's generic and specific roles within the group (e.g., Moreland & Levine, 2003; Ridgeway, 2001). Prototypicality is not the only way in which a group is internally structured, but it certainly is a fundamental component of group structure.

Prototype-based internal group structure is dynamic not static. It hinges on the nature of the prototype, and the group prototype, as we have seen, reflects the social comparative context–dynamic ingroup members cognitively present, the salient outgroup, and the group's context-dependent goals and purposes. To the extent that the comparative context remains the same then the prototype remains the same and prototype-based structure remains the same. So, for example, a political group whose manifesto remains the same and whose outgroup remains the same will have an invariant prototype and apparently fixed group structure with the same individuals being prototypically central and prototypically marginal.

To illustrate context dependent prototype-based structure let us use a simple example, adapted from Hogg (2001a). Consider a 21-point attitude scale with seven ingroup members occupying attitudinal positions 8 through 14, seven outgroup members occupying positions 15 through 21, and no one occupying positions 1 through 7. The subjectively salient comparative frame is represented by all positions occupied by ingroup and outgroup members; unoccupied positions are not relevant to social comparison in that context. The ingroup prototypicality of each ingroup member can be calculated as a metacontrast ratio (MCR)—for each ingroup position the MCR is the mean absolute difference between the position and each outgroup position, divided by the mean absolute difference between the position and each other ingroup position. Figure 15.1 shows the MCRs for each ingroup member. Figure 15.2 shows MCRs for the same ingroup members, occupying positions 8 through 14, but now with the salient outgroup occupying positions 1 through 7.

What emerges from comparison of Figure 15.1 (right outgroup) and Figure 15.2 (left outgroup) is: (1) The prototype is polarized from the scale midpoint of

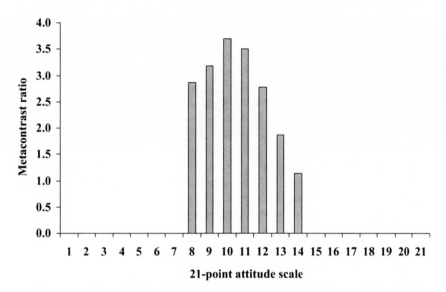

FIGURE 15.1 Metacontrast ratios (MCRs) for seven ingroup members occupying positions 8 through 14 on a 21-point attitude scale with the salient outgroup to the right, occupying positions 15 through 21.

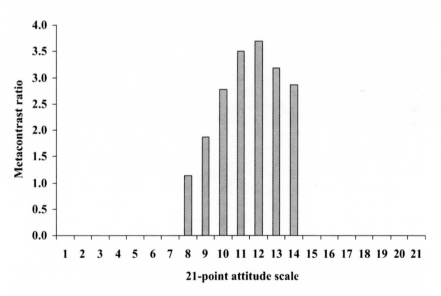

FIGURE 15.2 Metacontrast ratios (MCRs) for seven ingroup members occupying positions 8 through 14 on a 21-point attitude scale with the salient outgroup to the left, occupying positions 1 through 7.

11 to reflect the salient intergroup comparative context—the most prototypical ingroup position shifts from 10 to 12. (2) The person who occupies position 8 is less prototypical when the outgroup is on the left than the right (MCRs = 1.14 and 2.86, respectively). (3) The person who occupies position 14 is less prototypical when the outgroup is on the right than the left (MCRs = 1.14 and 2.86). (4) When the outgroup is on right (Figure 15.1) the person occupying position 14 is less prototypical/more marginal than the person occupying position 8, and vice versa when the outgroup is on the left (Figure 15.2).

Relative prototypicality casts some people as central members who fit the prototype closely, and others as marginal members who deviate significantly from the prototype. In this sense, perceived deviance and centrality in salient groups with which people identify strongly, are a function of metacontrast-based perceptions of prototypicality. Furthermore marginal members vary in their prototypicality depending on whether their marginal position is close to or remote from the salient outgroup.

SOME CORRELATES OF RELATIVE PROTOTYPICALITY

Perceptions of relative prototypicality structure a group into highly prototypical central members and less prototypical peripheral members. In recent years the social identity analysis of prototypically central members has largely been the social identity analysis of leadership (Hogg, 2001b; Hogg & van Knippenberg, 2003; van Knippenberg & Hogg, 2003). The social identity analysis of prototypically marginal members has been the study of deviance (e.g., Hogg, Fielding, & Darley, 2005; Marques, Abrams, Pàez, & Hogg, 2001; Marques & Paez, 1994), and the theory of subjective group dynamics (e.g., Marques, Abrams, Paez, & Martinez-Taboada, 1998; Marques, Abrams, & Serôdio, 2001). From a social identity perspective, degree of prototypicality is associated with an array of outcomes.

Social Attraction

In salient groups, patterns of social evaluation and liking are depersonalized—idiosyncratic personal attraction is transformed into prototype based depersonalized social attraction (Hogg, 1993). People are positively evaluated and liked to the extent that they embody the group prototype—more prototypical members are liked more than less prototypical members. Furthermore, since members of salient groups largely agree on the prototype, social attraction is consensual—members agree on who is prototypical and who is not, and thus agree on who they like more and who they like less, as group members. A "popularity" and evaluative status hierarchy is instantiated within the group. Prototypically central members are popular and imbued with status, whereas prototypically peripheral members are less popular and have less status.

Normative Behavior and Perceived Influence

By definition, prototypical members are perceived to embody group norms more than peripheral members (Turner, 1991). One consequence of this is that because social identity related social influence and conformity processes within the group (e.g., Abrams & Hogg, 1990; Turner & Oakes, 1989) cause members to strive to be more normative, members' behavior appears to become more like that of highly prototypical members. This gives the appearance of differential influence, which makes peripheral members appear to be more influenced, and central members to be the source of that influence (Hogg, 2001b).

Another aspect of differential influence flows from differential liking based on depersonalized social attraction. Prototypical members are liked more than peripheral members. Research on attraction shows that if you like someone you are more likely to agree with them and to comply with their requests and suggestions (e.g., Berscheid & Reis, 1998). In this way, prototypical members actually do have more influence than do marginal members—they can more easily gain compliance with their suggestions and ideas.

Trust and Innovation

Prototypicality influences trust within groups—highly prototypical core members are trusted more by the group than are marginal members (Hogg, in press-b; Tyler, 1997; van Knippenberg & Hogg, 2003). Core members are considered to be more strongly identified with the group than are peripheral members. Core members embody the group to a greater extent, and their self-concept and fate is considered to be more strongly tied to the group. Members, therefore, assume that core members are less likely to act in ways that will harm the group and thus the group's members—they are trusted to have the group's best interest at heart. Marginal members are trusted less, and they may even be viewed suspiciously as potential traitors or members who will undermine the group in various ways. The membership credentials of core members are not in dispute, whereas the credentials of peripheral members are under close scrutiny—marginal members have to work hard at being accepted as trusted members, core members do not.

One important consequence of prototypicality-based trust is that the group extends greater latitude of acceptable behavior to core members than it does to peripheral members. Core members can, paradoxically, diverge from group norms much more than can marginal members (e.g., Sherif & Sherif, 1964)—this is precisely because, within limits, whatever core members do is assumed to be in the best interest of the group. Marginal members need to adhere closely to group norms in order to demonstrate their identification with the group and to build trust in the minds of fellow members—normative divergence is viewed with suspicion or hostility by the group. Core members can therefore be more innovative and idiosyncratic and play a greater role in transforming group norms than can marginal members—this is another basis for more effective leadership of salient groups by prototypical members (e.g., Platow & van Knippenberg, 2001; cf. Hollander's, 1958, notion of idiosyncrasy credit).

Attribution and Essentialism

The group prototype and associated member prototypicality are key indices of group life. They inform one how to behave as a group member and what behaviors to expect from fellow members. They structure interaction and perception, create social structure within the group, and locate self and others within that structure. People therefore attend very closely to all information that relates to the prototype. Although the outgroup can convey information about the ingroup prototype, generally the ingroup is a more direct and immediate source of reliable information—people pay more attention to the ingroup (e.g., Yzerbyt, Castano, Leyens, & Paladino, 2000). Within the ingroup, highly prototypical members are also more immediately informative than more marginal members (e.g., Reicher, 1984, 2001).

In a social cognitive sense, then, within a salient group prototypical members are likely to be figural against the background of the group—they attract disproportionate attention and sponsor associated cognitive processing. One consequence of this is that there is an enhanced tendency to make internal/dispositional attributions for prototypical members' behavior. The fundamental attribution error (Ross, 1977), correspondence bias (Gilbert & Malone, 1995), or essentialism (Haslam, Rothschild, & Ernst, 1998; Medin & Ortony, 1989) is more pronounced for people who are perceptually distinctive (e.g., figural against a background) or cognitively salient (e.g., Taylor & Fiske, 1978). This process will be enhanced over time if the comparative context remains stable, and prototypicality thus remains fixed.

Because prototypical members seem to have disproportionate influence over the group, are socially liked, and are trusted, their behavior is represented as reflecting an internal disposition or essence to behave in this way—a charismatic leadership personality is constructed (Hogg, 2001b; also see Haslam & Platow, 2001). That prototypical members attract attention, and fellow members seek to make personality attributions for their behavior has support from research by Fiske and her colleagues (e.g., Fiske & Dépret, 1996; Goodwin, Gubin, Fiske, & Yzerbyt, 2000).

It is not so well established that attribution processes operate on marginal members in the same way. However, it is plausible to speculate that they do. Although highly prototypical core members are a direct source of prototype information, marginal members are also likely to attract attention because they tell one what the group is not and also because they may pose a threat to the group's normative integrity or even its existence. To the extent that marginal members are distinctive and stand out as a focus of attention, then their behavior is likely to be internally attributed. The fact that they are, for example, marginally normative, disliked, unpopular, and distrusted by the group, will be seen to reflect the type of people they are rather than their social position in a particular comparative context. They will be viewed as deviants and outcasts rather than people who simply have different opinions and behave in different ways within the group. Diversity is translated into deviance and pathology.

Indeed, leaders (who can be considered highly prototypical members) frequently deliberately and strategically engage in a rhetoric that identifies marginal members and goes on to pillory and pathologize them as deviants (e.g., Reicher & Hopkins, 1996, 2001).

Uncertainty and Identification

A key motivation for social identity processes is subjective uncertainty reduction, particularly self-conceptual uncertainty reduction (Hogg, 2000, 2001c). Social categorization provides a very effective solution to a sense of self-conceptual uncertainty, because it ties self-definition, behavior and perception to prescriptive and descriptive prototypes. Prototypes define who we are and who others are, how we should behave and how others will behave, and how we should interact with members of our own group and of other groups. Thus, prototypes reduce social and self-conceptual uncertainty.

The greater the self-conceptual uncertainty the more that people strive to belong, and, in particular, the more they strive to belong to groups that are highly distinctive and have a simple, consensual, and prescriptive prototype (Hogg, 2004). Typically these groups are ones that are orthodox with a rigid and steep hierarchical leadership structure (Hogg & Reid, 2001). These are groups where leaders have enormous power and influence, and where, because a premium is placed on loyalty and conformity, marginal members suffer particularly harshly.

Generally, conditions that motivate enhanced uncertainty reduction are likely to produce more orthodox groups, with the consequence of more sharply polarized responses to central and marginal members. Such conditions would include threats to the group's entitativity or distinctiveness, as opposed to threats to the group's valence or social standing (Hogg, Fielding, & Darley, 2005; Reid & Hogg, 2003).

Uncertainty may also be affected directly by relative prototypicality within the group. Quite simply, the less prototypical a person is the more self-conceptually uncertain he or she will feel. Marginal members have less influence over the group and its destiny, and their membership status is continually called into question and under scrutiny by the group. This further adds to the burden of uncertainty.

Differential uncertainty may not only cause core and peripheral members to behave differently due to differential uncertainty reduction motivation, but it may also introduce conflict over certainty. Marris (1996) has argued that certainty is a highly valued, but zero-sum, resource within society and that there is a power struggle for greater certainty. If we extrapolate this analysis to groups as a whole, then differential uncertainty, which may be enhanced under group entitativity and distinctiveness threat, may sponsor intragroup competition or even conflict between those with more and those with less group membership-based certainty,

THE EXPERIENCE OF PROTOTYPICALLY MARGINAL MEMBERSHIP

Based on the processes we have just discussed we can describe how prototypically marginal members may be treated by the group, and how marginal members may feel and behave.

Consequences of Being Prototypically Marginal

Due to the social attraction process, marginal members tend to be consensually disliked by the group—they are socially unpopular and have low evaluative status within the group. This phenomenon has been explored by Marques and his colleagues (e.g., Marques & Pàez, 1994; also see Marques, Abrams, Pàez, & Hogg, 2001). Dubbed the "black sheep effect," they not only find evaluative rejection of prototypically marginal ingroup members, but also that a person holding a position that is on the ingroup-outgroup boundary is more disliked and rejected if he or she is an ingroup member than an outgroup member. Marginal members tend to feel affectively rejected by the group (see Fitness, this volume, on rejection in family contexts).

Marginal members have significantly less influence over the group than do prototypical members. They find it difficult to gain compliance with their ideas, to be innovative, or to take an effective leadership role in the group. The group expects them to conform, provides them with very little latitude to diverge from group norms, and is intolerant of deviation or non-conformity. The group may initially try to socialize marginal members to conform to group norms (e.g., Schachter, 1959; also see Levine & Moreland, 1994) but, given the group's intolerance of deviation, if this does not quickly show effects the group will soon lose patience.

Marginal members are likely to feel disenfranchised and relatively impotent. They feel they have no effective voice in the group. This feeling of lack of recognition is accompanied by a sense of being distrusted by the group and of not being fully accepted as members by the group. The group seems suspicious, and their behavior is under scrutiny for evidence to confirm their membership credentials.

Attribution processes associated with the group's explanation of marginal membership and deviant behavior construct a view of the marginal member as having an underlying deviant and possibly untrustworthy personality. Such an enduring and essentialist label makes it difficult for marginal members to change the way they behave or the way they are viewed by the group. A deviant label is difficult to escape, and it may become a self-fulfilling prophecy.

Marginal members are more uncertain about their membership status and social identity in the group than are more central members. This raised sense of self-conceptual uncertainty may cause marginal members to strive hard to be tightly conformist, endorse a rigid internal hierarchy, promote and idolize powerful leadership, and generally engage in zealotry (e.g., Hogg 2004). Ironically, marginal members may be the most fiercely intolerant of normative diversity. Not all marginal members will behave in this way—some may dissociate themselves from the group and gradually dis-identify.

The intriguing possibility exists that core members may strategically try to make marginal members as uncertain as possible about their membership status in order to elicit over-conformity, leader worship, zealotry, and so forth. If "certainty" is power, then those central members who have less membership uncertainty are likely to try to widen the uncertainty gulf between themselves and marginal members (cf. Marris, 1996).

Group level threats, perhaps grounded in intergroup relations, may threaten the distinctiveness and entitativity of the group as a whole or the social status or valence of the group as a whole. The consequences for marginal members depend on the nature of the threat, and on whether the marginal member's position is close to or remote from the salient outgroup (Fielding, Hogg, & Annandale, in press; Hogg, Fielding, & Darley, 2005; Hogg & Hornsey, in press; Reid & Hogg, 2005)—see Figures 15.1 and 15.2, and associated discussion of prototypicality.

Where the group's entitativity is under threat, all marginal members will be unfavorably reacted to by the group. The group is motivated to consolidate itself around a clearly prescriptive and consensual prototype—marginal members do not contribute to consensuality. Prototypically marginal members will be particularly vulnerable to affective rejection, distrust, and possibly ejection from the group. Group leaders may take an active role in identifying and vilifying marginal members and in mobilizing the group to treat them as outcasts.

Where the group's valence or social status is under threat, marginal members who are positioned away from the outgroup (position 8 in Figure 15.1 and position 14 in figure 15.2) will not be treated as harshly as those who are positioned close to the outgroup (position 14 in Figure 15.1 and position 8 in figure 15.2). They might even be treated favorably. The reason for this is that the former marginal members allow the group to distance itself evaluatively from the negatively valued outgroup—the group can claim as its own the evaluative advantage of having a positive deviant (e.g., an over-achiever) in the group.

Responding to Being Prototypically Marginal

Marginal members are distrusted and disliked by the group. They may even be vilified and persecuted by the group—perhaps at the behest of the group's leadership. Their membership credentials are constantly under surveillance, and they may feel uncertain about their membership and place in the group. They have little influence over the group, the group extends to them little latitude for acceptable behavior, and they feel pressure to be highly conformist and subservient. The group may even treat them as if the correlates of marginal prototypically are reflections of personality deficit. Life on the fringe of the group is not pleasant.

Not surprisingly, marginal members may decide to leave the group physically and psychologically, and perhaps gain membership in another group. If this works, the problem is solved. However, there are many hurdles to effective "exit" (e.g., Ellemers, 1993; Hirschmann, 1970; Hogg & Abrams, 1988; Tajfel & Turner, 1986). Although the group may treat marginal members with suspicion and dislike and apparently desire them to leave, marginal members can play an important function in group life. They help define the group prototype by representing what the group is not. They also act as a common scapegoat for the group's problems and failings, and therefore help unite the rest of the group. Groups can depend heavily on marginal members. When confronted with the stark reality of their exit, the group will often do a great deal to try to retain them—but retain them as marginal members. One way the group could do this is by nourishing membership uncertainty with vague promises of future core membership.

Another obstacle to exit is uncertainty itself. Although life on the fringe of the group is not very pleasant it may, under some circumstances, be thought to be preferable to the self-conceptual uncertainty of not belonging and of having to forge new group ties and a new social identity (Hogg, 2000). Resistance to dis-identification and exit may be accompanied by a "false consciousness" that justifies the status quo by minimizing its perceived personal harm and amplifying perceived obstacles to exit (e.g., Jost & Hunyadi, 2002; Jost & Kramer, 2003). This false-consciousness may be encouraged and facilitated by the group, if the group chooses to retain a marginal member for the reasons given above.

Problems associated with exit are not necessarily "false." Intergroup boundaries are rarely as permeable as one believes, and psychological entry to a new group can be genuinely difficult and may simply replace marginal status in one group with marginal status in another. Indeed, if you do successfully leave one group then that group may well treat you as a genuine traitor and outsider, and the new group you are trying to join may, understandably, be very suspicious about your motives and intentions. Exit under conditions of low intergroup permeability may leave one with a truly marginal identity—belonging to neither group (e.g., Breakwell, 1986).

So, for many reasons, marginal members may remain within the group or be reluctant to depart—leaving them with the challenge of trying to improve their status within the group. As individuals, attempts to change the group's prototype so that they are more centrally located are unlikely to be effective. This leaves them with effectively three options. The first is simply to quietly and consistently conform so that over a period of time, which could be years, their membership credentials and prototypicality are finally acknowledged—they gradually come to be seen by the group as prototypical and highly identified and trusted members.

This is a long process and if marginal status is particularly harmful it may simply not be possible to endure.

The second option is to gain a redefinition of self within the group. The self is multifaceted—we have many identities tied to many groups. In any context we can be categorized in many different ways—by gender, by profession, by religion, by nationality, by work group, and so forth. In any group context there are many cross cutting or nested categorizations. For example members of an organization could be categorized as members of the organization, members of nested work groups, or cross cutting gender or ethnic categories. The consequences of marginal membership in the organization may be muted if one can get the organization to recognize that outside the organization one is a core member of a prestigious group such as doctors. One way to cope with marginal membership is to recruit cross cutting categorizations that cast one in a more favorable light (e.g., Brewer, von Hippel, & Gooden, 1999; Crisp, Ensari, Hewstone, & Miller, 2003).

A related way to relocate oneself within the group is described by status characteristics theory (e.g., Berger, Fisek, Norman, & Zelditch, 1977; Ridgeway, 2001). There are two main sources of status within a group. One, called specific status characteristics, derives directly from how well one is perceived to fulfill the group's functions. The other, called diffuse status characteristics, derives from one's membership of other groups that have high social standing in society (e.g., doctors). From the perspective of the analysis provided in this chapter, prototypical marginality is a low specific status characteristic. Members in this position who have a high diffuse status characteristic might try to draw attention to that. This option is, of course, not open to marginal members who do not possess high diffuse status characteristics, for example societal minorities.

The third option for improving status within the group is collective action. In life, people can often achieve more collectively than alone. This is also true of marginal members—they can band together into a small subgroup to try to protect themselves, to promote themselves, or to transform the group so that they are no longer prototypically marginal. As individuals this can be difficult to achieve, but as an active minority it can be easier. Research on minority influence (e.g., Moscovici, 1980; Mugny, 1982; Nemeth, 1986; see Martin & Hewstone, 2003) suggests that if a number of marginal members band together to form a subgroup they can be quite effective in changing the majority group norm or prototype. To do this they need to adopt minority influence tactics such as promulgating a diachronically and synchronically consistent message. Effective use of minority influence tactics can produce latent social influence over the majority, leading ultimately to sudden conversion of the majority to the minority's position. In this way the minority can redefine the group so that the minority is no longer marginal, or so that the group comes to value diversity of positions as normative of the group.

Marginal members organized as an active minority may be better placed to criticize what the group stands for and how it treats its members (cf., Hornsey, Oppes, & Svensson, 2002), or they may form a schism that recruits outsiders and helps them directly confront and change what the group stands for (e.g., Sani & Reicher, 1999).

PROCESSES AND CONDITIONS THAT MAY FAVOR DEVIANCE AND DIVERSITY

The discussion so far has rested on the rather gloomy assumption that deviance, and therefore diversity, is bad for a group. The group either tries to socialize marginal members or, if that fails, persecutes and rejects them as undesirable social outcasts. Marginal members themselves try to leave groups that cast them as outcasts, or to engage in conformist behaviors to gradually be accepted as normative core members.

However, diversity may actually be desirable for groups. In support of the discussion above, there is evidence that dissent created by minorities within groups can be beneficial, largely through its impact on creativity and innovation (e.g., Nemeth & Staw, 1989; Nemeth & Wachtler, 1983), and internal criticism of a group's culture or operations can play a crucial role in reinvigorating groups and laying the groundwork for positive change (e.g., Hornsey & Imani, 2004; Hornsey, Oppes, & Svensson, 2002). There is also evidence that task-oriented groups that embrace diverse views and diverse subgroups function better than groups that are homogeneous in terms of attitudes, positions, and demographic characteristics. An effective way to combat groupthink is to ensure attitudinal diversity within a decision making group (e.g., Postmes, Spears, & Cihangir, 2001; Stasser, Stewart, & Wittenbaum, 1995), and many organizations benefit from demographic diversity (e.g., Brewer, 1996). Generally, there is evidence that unshared information can have a distinct advantage for overall group functioning (e.g., Larson, Foster-Fishman, & Keys, 1994; for reviews see Tindale, Kameda, & Hinsz, 2003; Wittenbaum & Stasser, 1996).

Generally, groups automatically react negatively to marginal membership and thus diversity—even though diversity is often beneficial to group life. The key question is how can groups make a rational decision about whether to include or exclude marginal members? This may be part of a larger question to do with how, if at all, it is possible for deviance or diversity to become part of the solution to group composition rather than an obstacle to effective group composition (Hogg & Hornsey, in press). For marginal members to be fully embraced and for diversity to be celebrated, the group needs to have diversity as a key component of its prototype—the group needs to define itself as embracing and benefiting from internal diversity (cf., Niedenthal & Bieke, 1997; Roccas & Brewer, 2002; Wright, Aron, & Tropp, 2002). How a group arrives at this outcome is less easy to specify.

One obvious circumstance is when the group's task is defined in terms of diversity—for example a decision-making group that is explicitly set up to discover new ideas resting on diverse views. Another condition, alluded to above, is when a group is under valence or status threat. Positive deviants, marginal members whose marginality positions them far from a salient outgroup, contribute positively to the group's valence and will be included. However, this is likely to be transitory and instrumental, and to not reflect a true transformation of the group prototype to include diversity.

Generally speaking initiatives to celebrate diversity and to exercise inclusion are most likely to come from marginalized members themselves. And for this to be effective they need to organize into active minorities.

CONCLUDING COMMENTS

In this chapter I have presented an integrative social identity analysis of the causes, consequences, and experiences of marginal membership in groups. The key point is that groups are very rarely homogeneous—they are almost always internally structured in terms of group prototypicality so that some members are prototypically central and others are prototypically marginal.

The operation of basic social identity processes of categorization, depersonalization, social influence, and social attraction generates very different group experiences for central and marginal members. These experiences hinge mainly on the fact that central members are more normative members and are trusted more as members, they are more socially attractive and popular in group terms, they are more certain about their membership status, they are more influential in the group and are allowed to be more innovative, and their positive attributes are likely to be attributed internally to charisma or good character.

In contrast, marginal members are distrusted and disliked by the group. They may be vilified and persecuted—perhaps on the initiative of the group's leadership. Their membership credentials are under constant surveillance, and they feel uncertain about their membership and their place in the group. They have little influence over the group, are allowed little latitude for acceptable behavior, and feel pressured to be conformist and subservient. These negative attributes are likely to be attributed internally to character deficit or a deviant personality.

Marginal members may try to gain full acceptance, but this can be an uphill struggle because marginal members serve an important function for the group. They help define the group prototype by representing what the group is not, and they act as a scapegoat for the group's problems and shortcomings, and thus unite the rest of the group. Groups can depend heavily on marginal members. When confronted with the prospect of their exit, the group will often work hard to retain them—but retain them as marginal members—perhaps with vague promises of future core membership, which actually increases marginal members' membership uncertainty, and thus core members' power over them.

However, attempting to leave the group can leave marginal members with an even more marginal identity, and an even greater sense of self-conceptual uncertainty. Instead, they can try to renegotiate their role or status within the group, or they can band together as an active minority to try to change the nature of the group and the group's prototype so that their own position is more central.

This is not an empirical chapter—evidence for, and research on, many of the processes and phenomena, can be found in some of the literature cited. The main aim was to provide an integrative framework showing how social identity processes can marginalize and exclude people from group membership—a perspective that is somewhat different to the more familiar social identity emphasis on ingroup inclusion and intergroup differentiation. Hopefully, this framework will provide an impetus for research on prototypicality-based marginality, perhaps with a particular emphasis on the experience of being marginalized within a group and on what people do to cope with marginal status (cf. stigma: Crocker, Major, & Steele, 1998; Major & Schmader, 1998).

REFERENCES

Abrams, D., & Hogg, M. A. (1990). Social identification, self-categorization and social influence. *European Review of Social Psychology, 1*, 195–228.

Berger, J., Fisek, M. H., Norman, R. Z., & Zelditch, M., Jr. (1977). *Status characteristics and social interaction.* New York: Elsevier.

Berscheid, E., & Reis, H. T. (1998). Attraction and close relationships. In D. T. Gilbert, S. T. Fiske, & G. Lindzey (Eds.), *The handbook of social psychology: Vol. 2* (4th ed., pp. 193–281). New York: McGraw-Hill.

Breakwell, G. (1986). *Coping with threatened identities.* London: Methuen.

Brewer, M. B. (1996). Managing diversity: The role of social identities. In S. Jackson & M. Ruderman (Eds.), *Diversity in work teams* (pp. 47–68). Washington, DC: American Psychological Association.

Brewer, M. B., von Hippel, W., & Gooden, M. P. (1999). Diversity and organizational identity: The problem of entrée after entry. In D. A. Prentice & D. T. Miller (Eds.), *Cultural divides: Understanding and overcoming group conflict* (pp. 337–363). New York: Russell Sage Foundation.

Crisp, R. J., Ensari, N., Hewstone, M., & Miller, N. (2003). A dual-route model of crossed categorization effects. In W. Stroebe & M. Hewstone (Eds.), *European Review of Social Psychology: Vol. 13* (pp. 35–74). New York: Psychology Press.

Crocker, J., Major, B., & Steele, C. (1998). Social stigma. In D. T. Gilbert, S. T. Fiske, & G. Lindzey (Eds.), *The handbook of social psychology: Vol. 2* (4th ed., pp. 504–53). New York: McGraw-Hill.

Deaux, K., Reid, A., Mizrahi, K., & Ethier, K. A. (1995). Parameters of social identity. *Journal of Personality and Social Psychology, 68,* 280–291.

Ellemers, N. (1993). The influence of socio-structural variables on identity management strategies. *European Review of Social Psychology, 4,* 27–57.

Fielding, K. S., Hogg, M. A., & Annandale, N. (in press). Reactions to positive deviance: Social identity and attribution dimensions. *Group Processes and Intergroup Relations.*

Fiske, S. T., & Dépret, E. (1996). Control, interdependence and power: Understanding social cognition in its social context. *European Review of Social Psychology, 7,* 31–61.

Gilbert, D. T., & Malone, P. S. (1995). The correspondence bias. *Psychological Bulletin, 117,* 21–38.

Goodwin, S. A., Gubin, A., Fiske, S. T., & Yzerbyt, V. Y. (2000). Power implicitly biases impression formation: Stereotyping subordinates by default and by design. *Group Processes and Intergroup Relationships, 3,* 227–256.

Haslam, N., Rothschild, L., & Ernst, D. (1998). Essentialist beliefs about social categories. *British Journal of Social Psychology, 39,* 113–127.

Haslam, S. A., Oakes, P. J., McGarty, C., Turner, J. C., & Onorato, S. (1995). Contextual changes in the prototypicality of extreme and moderate outgroup members. *European Journal of Social Psychology, 25*, 509–530.

Haslam, S. A., & Platow, M. J. (2001a). Your wish is our command: The role of shared social identity in translating a leader's vision into followers' action. In M. A. Hogg & D. J. Terry (Eds.), *Social identity processes in organizational contexts* (pp. 213–228). Philadelphia: Psychology Press.

Hirschmann, A. (1970). *Exit, voice, and loyalty: Responses to decline in firms, organizations, and states*. Cambridge: Harvard University Press

Hogg, M. A. (1993). Group cohesiveness: A critical review and some new directions. *European Review of Social Psychology, 4*, 85–111.

Hogg, M. A. (2000). Subjective uncertainty reduction through self-categorization: A motivational theory of social identity processes. *European Review of Social Psychology, 11*, 223–255.

Hogg, M. A. (2001a). Social identification, group prototypicality, and emergent leadership. In M. A. Hogg & D. J. Terry (Eds.), *Social identity processes in organizational contexts* (pp. 197–212). Philadelphia: Psychology Press.

Hogg, M. A. (2001b). A social identity theory of leadership. *Personality and Social Psychology Review, 5*, 184–200.

Hogg, M. A. (2001c). Self-categorization and subjective uncertainty resolution: Cognitive and motivational facets of social identity and group membership. In J. P. Forgas, K. D. Williams, & L. Wheeler (Eds.), *The social mind: Cognitive and motivational aspects of interpersonal behavior* (pp. 323–349). New York: Cambridge University Press.

Hogg, M. A. (2003). Social identity. In M. R. Leary & J. P. Tangney (Eds.), *Handbook of self and identity* (pp. 462–79). New York: Guilford Press.

Hogg, M. A. (2004). Uncertainty and extremism: Identification with high entitativity groups under conditions of uncertainty. In V. Yzerbyt, C. M. Judd, & O. Corneille (Eds.), *The psychology of group perception: Perceived variability, entitativity, and essentialism* (pp. 401–418). New York: Psychology Press.

Hogg, M. A. (in press-a). The social identity approach. In S. A. Wheelan (Ed.), *The handbook of group research and practice*. Thousand Oaks, CA: Sage.

Hogg, M. A. (in press-b). Social identity and the group context of trust: Managing risk and building trust through belonging. In M. Siegrist &

H. Gutscher (Eds.), *Trust, technology, and society: Studies in cooperative risk management*. London: Earthscan.

Hogg, M. A., & Abrams, D. (1988). *Social identifications: A social psychology of intergroup relations and group processes*. London: Routledge.

Hogg, M. A., Fielding, K. S., & Darley, J. (2005). Fringe dwellers: Processes of deviance and marginalization in groups. In D. Abrams, M. A. Hogg, & J. Marques (Eds.), *Social psychology of inclusion and exclusion* (pp. 191–210). New York: Psychology Press.

Hogg, M. A., & Hornsey, M. J. (in press). Self-concept threat and differentiation within groups. In R. J. Crisp & M. Hewstone (Eds.), *Multiple social categorization: Processes, models, and applications*. New York: Psychology Press.

Hogg, M. A., & Reid, S. A. (2001). Social identity, leadership, and power. In A. Y. Lee-Chai & J. A. Bargh (Eds.), *The use and abuse of power: Multiple perspectives on the causes of corruption* (pp. 159–180). Philadelphia: Psychology Press.

Hogg, M.A., & Tindale, R. S. (2005). Social identity, influence, and communication in small groups. In J. Harwood & H. Giles (Eds.), *Intergroup communication: Multiple perspectives* (pp. 141–164). New York: Peter Lang.

Hogg, M. A., & van Knippenberg, D. (2003). Social identity and leadership processes in groups. In M. P. Zanna (Ed.), *Advances in experimental social psychology: Vol. 35* (pp. 1–52). San Diego, CA: Academic Press.

Hollander, E. P. (1958). Conformity, status, and idiosyncrasy credit. *Psychological Review, 65*, 117–127.

Hornsey, M. J., & Imani, A. (2004). Criticising groups from the inside and the outside: An identity perspective on the intergroup sensitivity effect. *Personality and Social Psychology Bulletin, 30*, 365–383.

Hornsey, M. J., Oppes, T., & Svensson, A. (2002). It's OK if we say it, but you can't: Responses to intergroup and intragroup criticism. *European Journal of Social Psychology, 32*, 293–307.

Jost, J. T., & Hunyadi, O. (2002). The psychology of system justification and the palliative function of ideology. *European Review of Social Psychology, 13*, 111–153.

Jost, J. T., & Kramer, R. M. (2003). The system justification motive in intergroup relations. In D. M. Mackie & E. R. Smith (Eds.), *From prejudice to intergroup emotions: Differentiated reactions to social groups* (pp. 227–245). New York: Psychology Press.

Larson, J. R., Jr., Foster-Fishman, P. G., & Keys, C. B. (1994). Discussion of shared and unshared information in decision-making groups. *Journal of Personality and Social Psychology, 67,* 446–461.

Levine, J. M., & Moreland, R. L. (1994). Group socialization: Theory and research. *European Review of Social Psychology, 5,* 305–336.

Lickel, B., Hamilton, D. L., Wieczorkowska, G., Lewis, A., Sherman, S. J., & Uhles, A. N. (2000). Varieties of groups and the perception of group entitativity. *Journal of Personality and Social Psychology, 78*(2), 223–246.

Major, B., & Schmader, T. (1998). Coping with stigma through psychological disengagement. In J. K. Swim & C. Stangor (Eds.), *Prejudice: The target's perspective* (pp. 219–242). San Diego, CA: Academic Press.

Marques, J. M., Abrams, D., Pàez, D., & Hogg, M. A. (2001). Social categorization, social identification, and rejection of deviant group members. In M. A. Hogg & R. S. Tindale, (Eds.), *Blackwell handbook of social psychology: Group processes* (pp. 400–424). Oxford: Blackwell.

Marques, J. M., Abrams, D., Pàez, D., & Martinez-Taboada, C. (1998). The role of categorization and in-group norms in judgments of groups and their members. *Journal of Personality and Social Psychology, 75,* 976–988.

Marques, J. M., Abrams, D., & Seródio, R. (2001). Being better by being right: Subjective group dynamics and derogation of in-group deviants when generic norms are undermined. *Journal of Personality and Social Psychology, 81,* 436–47.

Marques, J. M., & Pàez, D. (1994). The 'black sheep effect': Social categorization, rejection of ingroup deviates and perception of group variability. *European Review of Social Psychology, 5,* 37–68.

Marris, P. (1996). *The politics of uncertainty: Attachment in private and public life.* London: Routledge.

Martin, R., & Hewstone, M. (2003). Social influence processes of control and change: Conformity, obedience to authority, and innovation. In M. A. Hogg & J. Cooper (Eds.), *The Sage handbook of social psychology* (pp. 347–366). London: Sage.

Medin, D. L., & Ortony, A. (1989). Psychological essentialism. In S. Vosnaidou & A. Ortony (Eds.), *Similarity and analogical reasoning* (pp.

179–195). Cambridge: Cambridge University Press.

Moreland, R. L., & Levine, J. M. (2003). Group composition: Explaining similarities and differences among group members. In M. A. Hogg & J. Cooper (Eds.), *The Sage handbook of social psychology* (pp. 367–380). London: Sage.

Moscovici, S. (1980). Toward a theory of conversion behavior. In L. Berkowitz (Ed.), *Advances in experimental social psychology: Vol. 13* (pp. 209–239). New York: Academic Press.

Mugny, G. (1982). *The power of minorities.* London: Academic Press.

Niedenthal, P. M., & Beike, D. R. (1997). Interrelated and isolated self-concepts. *Personality and Social Psychology Review, 1,* 106–128.

Nemeth, C., (1986). Differential contributions of majority and minority influence. *Psychological Review, 93,* 23–32.

Nemeth, C., & Staw, B. M. (1989). The tradeoffs of social control and innovation in groups and organizations. In L. Berkowitz (Ed.), *Advances in experimental social psychology: Vol. 22* (pp. 175–210). San Diego, CA: Academic Press.

Nemeth, C., & Wachtler, J. (1983). Creative problem solving as a result of majority vs. minority influence. *European Journal of Social Psychology, 13,* 45–55.

Oakes, P. J., Haslam, S. A., & Turner, J. C. (1994). *Stereotyping and social reality.* Oxford: Blackwell.

Platow, M. J., & van Knippenberg, D. (2001). A social identity analysis of leadership endorsement: The effects of leader ingroup prototypicality and distributive intergroup fairness. *Personality and Social Psychology Bulletin, 27,* 1508–1519.

Postmes, T., Spears, R., & Cihangir, S. (2001). Quality of decision making and group norms. *Journal of Personality and Social Psychology, 80,* 918–930.

Prentice, D. A., Miller, D., & Lightdale, J. R. (1994). Asymmetries in attachment to groups and to their members: Distinguishing between common-identity and common-bond groups. *Personality and Social Psychology Bulletin, 20,* 484–493.

Reicher, S. D. (1984). The St Pauls' riot: An explanation of the limits of crowd action in terms of a social identity model. *European Journal of Social Psychology, 14,* 1–21.

Reicher, S. D. (2001). The psychology of crowd dynamics. In M. A. Hogg & R. S. Tindale (Eds.),

Blackwell handbook of social psychology: Group processes (pp. 182–208). Oxford: Blackwell.

Reicher, S. D., & Hopkins, N. (1996). Self-category constructions in political rhetoric: An analysis of Thatcher's and Kinnock's speeches concerning the British miners' strike (1984–1985). *European Journal of Social Psychology, 26,* 353–371.

Reicher, S. D., & Hopkins, N. (2001). *Self and nation*. London: Sage.

Reid, S. A., & Hogg, M. A. (2003). Uncertainty reduction, self-enhancement and social identification. *Personality and Social Psychology Bulletin, 31,* 1–14..

Ridgeway, C. L. (2001). Social status and group structure. In M. A. Hogg & R. S. Tindale (Eds.), *Blackwell handbook of social psychology: Group processes* (pp. 352–375). Oxford: Blackwell.

Roccas, S., & Brewer, M. B. (2002). Social identity complexity. *Personality and Social Psychology Review, 6,* 88–109.

Ross, L. (1977). The intuitive psychologist and his shortcomings. In L. Berkowitz (Ed.), *Advances in experimental social psychology: Vol. 10* (pp. 174–220). New York: Academic Press.

Sani, F., & Reicher, S. D. (1999). Identity, argument and schisms: Two longitudinal studies of the split in the Church of England over the ordination of women to the priesthood. *Group Processes and Intergroup Relations, 2,* 279–00.

Schachter, S. (1959). *The psychology of affiliation*. Stanford, CA: Stanford University Press.

Sherif, M., & Sherif, C. W. (1964). *Reference groups*. New York: Harper & Row.

Smith, E. R., & Zárate, M. A. (1992). Exemplar-based model of social judgment. *Psychological Review, 99,* 3–21.

Stasser, G., Stewart, D. D., & Wittenbaum, G. (1995). Expert roles and information exchange during discussion : The importance of knowing who knows what. *Journal of Experimental Social Psychology, 31,* 244-265.

Taylor, S. E., & Fiske, S. T. (1978). Salience, attention, and attribution: Top of the head phenomena. In L. Berkowitz (Ed.), *Advances in experimental social psychology: Vol. 11* (pp.

249–288). New York: Academic Press.

Tajfel, H., & Turner, J. C. (1986). The social identity theory of intergroup behavior. In S. Worchel & W. Austin (Eds.), *Psychology of intergroup relations* (pp. 7–24). Chicago: Nelson-Hall.

Tindale, R. S., Kameda, T., & Hinsz, V. B. (2003). Group decision-making. In M. A. Hogg & J. Cooper (Eds.), *The Sage handbook of social psychology* (pp. 381–403). London: Sage.

Turner, J. C. (1991). *Social influence*. Milton Keynes, UK: Open University Press.

Turner, J. C., Hogg, M. A., Oakes, P. J., Reicher, S. D., & Wetherell, M. S. (1987). *Rediscovering the social group: A self-categorization theory*. Oxford: Blackwell.

Turner, J. C., & Oakes, P. J. (1989). Self-categorization and social influence. In P. B. Paulus (Ed.), *The psychology of group influence* (2nd ed., pp. 233–275). Hillsdale, NJ: Erlbaum.

Tyler, T. R. (1997). The psychology of legitimacy: A relational perspective on voluntary deference to authorities. *Personality and Social Psychology Review, 1,* 323–345.

van Knippenberg, D., & Hogg, M. A. (2003). A social identity model of leadership in organizations. In B. M. Staw & R. M. Kramer (Eds.), *Research in organizational behavior* (Vol. 25, pp. 243–295). Greenwich, CT: JAI Press.

Wittenbaum, G. M., & Stasser, G. (1996). Management of information in small groups. In J. L. Nye & A. M. Brower (Eds.), *What's social about social cognition* (pp. 3–28). Thousand Oaks, CA: Sage.

Wright, S. C., Aron, A., & Tropp, L. R. (2002). Including others (and groups) in the self: Self-expansion and intergroup relations. In J. P. Forgas & K. D. Williams (Eds.), *The social self: Cognitive, interpersonal, and intergroup perspectives* (pp. 343–363). New York: Psychology Press.

Yzerbyt, V., Castano, E., Leyens, J. -P., & Paladino, M. -P. (2000). The primacy of the ingroup: The interplay of entitativity and identification. *European Review of Social Psychology, 11,* 257–295.

16

Bye Bye, Black Sheep
The Causes and Consequences of Rejection in Family Relationships

JULIE FITNESS

Introduction
What Is a Family?
Family Rules and Rule Violations
Differential Family Treatment: Favored Children and Black Sheep
Consequences of Family Rejection
Conclusions

INTRODUCTION

*I*n a recent letter to a Sydney newspaper, a reader criticized a columnist for having asked why gay people would want to belong to an institution (the Catholic Church) that considered them depraved and evil. The answer, the reader claimed, was simple—these people have been born into the Church, it is their family. How would you feel, he asked, if you had been called evil and then rejected by your own *family*? The implication was clear: This would be an unspeakable act of betrayal, no other explanation was required.

According to Vangelisti (2004), the word "family" is laden with imagery. For some it brings to mind warm, happy memories; for others, it elicits "painful memories—visions of being left alone, feeling unwanted" (p. xiii). Whatever the associations for any one individual, there is no doubt that families are fundamental to human existence. They constitute the primary social group to which humans

---

Address correspondence to: Julie Fitness, Department of Psychology, Macquarie University, Sydney NSW 2109, Australia. E-mail: jfitness@psy.mq.edu.au

belong from birth; indeed, kinship has been described as "the primary organizing principle in human relations" (Daly, Salmon, & Wilson, 1997, p. 287). Surprisingly, however, social psychologists know very little about the ways in which different family members think, feel, and behave toward one another in different contexts, and of particular importance to the theme of this chapter, the whys and wherefores of rejection in family relationships (see Sommer & Rubin, this volume, for a discussion of rejection in close interpersonal relationships).

My aim in this chapter is to provide an integrative account of what we know and do not know about some of the most interesting aspects of rejection in families. Following a discussion of the nature of families and laypeople's implicit theories about the "rules"of appropriate family conduct, I will present the findings of two exploratory studies of unforgivable rule violations within family relationships—the kinds of transgressions considered by laypeople to be so serious as to warrant rejection from the family. I will then discuss a number of structural and dynamic features of families that may contribute to the rejection of particular family members, and present the results of a recent study on family favorites and black sheep. Finally, I will propose an agenda for future research.

WHAT IS A FAMILY?

The family exemplifies what has been referred to by Clark and colleagues as a prototypically communal, as opposed to exchange, relational context (see Clark, Fitness, & Brissette, 2001, for a review). Some of the most distinctive features of communal relationships are interdependence, sharing, giving without expectation of immediate reward, and a reluctance to keep a tally of who owes what to whom. Within communal relationships, people expect that relationship partners will meet their needs, just as they are expected to meet their partners' needs.

In line with the conceptualization of family as a network of communal relationships, both evolutionary psychologists and anthropologists have noted that humans are much more inclined to meet the needs of close family than of acquaintances. Similarly, humans are much more likely to express their needs to family members than to strangers (Buss, 1999). Evolutionary theorists have also speculated that, because of their shared interests in one another's welfare, family members should be more tolerant and forgiving of one another than they are of non-family members (Daly et al., 1997). Communication scholars, too, have argued that people may respond differently to hurtful behaviors from family members than from non-family members. For example, Vangelisti (1994) claimed that no matter how hurtful the behavior, family members have to forgive in order to maintain something more important than the individual—the family itself. As Robert Frost poetically put it, "home is the place that, when you have to go there, they have to take you in."

There is no doubt that family members do tolerate and support one another to a far greater extent than do acquaintances, colleagues, or even friends. There is, however, a huge body of popular literature, along with countless anecdotal accounts and court reports, about family relationships that have gone badly awry. Indeed, many family feuds and estrangements endure over generations. Clearly, and contrary to what we might expect on the basis of sentimental portrayals, the family is not always a haven of unconditional love and acceptance. But what are the causes of such breakdowns in family relationships? What behaviors are considered "beyond the pale" within families, and what are the likely consequences for family members if they enact such behaviors?

FAMILY RULES AND RULE VIOLATIONS

Family rules and rule violations may be explored from (at least) two theoretical perspectives. The first perspective takes a distal, evolutionary view of the origins and functions of relationship cognitions, motivations, and emotions. Daly et al. (1997), for example, have speculated that humans possess relationship-specific motivational and information processing devices designed to cope with "the peculiar demands of being a mother, a father, an offspring, a sibling, a grandparent, or a mate" (p. 266). Here, the focus of study is on the universal features and rules of family life, such as so-called "kin selection," or the propensity of humans (and other animals) to help kin in preference to non-genetically related individuals. From a more proximal but no less functional perspective, social cognitive psychologists are interested in laypeople's theories and beliefs about relationships and how such theories and beliefs shape their relational perceptions, judgments, memories, and behaviors. Again, some of these knowledge structures may be universally shared, suggesting evolutionary origins (e.g., help brothers and sisters first, before you help your friends). Others, however, may vary across generations, cultures, and even subcultures (e.g., grandparents should/should not offer advice to their adult offspring about how best to raise the grandchildren).

Clearly, the two levels of exploration and explanation are complementary, rather than mutually exclusive, and have the capacity to inform and enrich the other (see Fitness, Fletcher, & Overall, 2003). However, we know remarkably little about the features and rules associated with different family relationships (parents, children, and siblings) from either perspective. In particular, we have little data on the kinds of familial rule violations that are considered by laypeople (in Western cultures, at least) as too serious to forgive, and their consequences with regard to rejecting or otherwise punishing offending family members. The aim of the following studies was to explore some of these questions with a sample of Australian university students and community members.

Family Conflict Studies

In the first study of laypeople's beliefs about rules and rule violations in family relationships, 315 respondents (109 males and 208 females; M age = 26 years, *sd* = 10 years) completed a Family Conflict questionnaire (Fitness & Parker, 2003). Respondents were asked to describe the very worst thing that mothers and fathers could do to daughters and sons; that daughters and sons could do to mothers and fathers; and that brothers and sisters could do to one another. They were also asked to explain why the offenses were so serious—what rules they broke, and what the likely consequences would be.

Most Frequently Cited Offenses. Respondents wrote long and frequently impassioned accounts of familial offenses and violated rules. The most striking feature of their accounts, however, was the prominence given to the unforgivability of familial rejection and abandonment. Specifically, over 40% of respondents claimed that abandonment or desertion were the worst offenses that parents could commit against their children—only sexual abuse (by fathers) was reported as the worst offense by an equally large proportion of respondents (44%). Similarly, with respect to the most unforgivable thing a child could do to his or her parents, rejection was reported by over 25% of respondents, equaled only by a category of daughter behavior best described as "taboo sex" (i.e., promiscuity and inappropriate sexual behavior, including sleeping with her father's friends)—considered unforgivable for fathers by 27% of respondents—and a category of son behavior labeled "criminality" (including drug addiction)—considered unforgivable for both fathers and mothers by 32% of respondents. A small proportion of respondents (11%) also reported that a son's homosexuality would be the worst thing that could happen to a father.

With respect to siblings, the offense considered most unforgivable by 47% of respondents was betrayal, followed by deception (16%), and sexual abuse (8%). Betrayal may be conceptualized as a form of interpersonal rejection, in that it implies relational devaluation and a breach of trust (Fitness, 2001; Leary, this volume). Effectively, a relational partner decides to act in his or her own best interests, at the expense of the partner. Betrayal in the current context reflected this theme of relational devaluation and rejection. Offenses included sleeping with the sibling's romantic partner, failing to help a sibling in trouble, failing to stick up for a sibling under attack from outsiders, and working against a sibling's interests (e.g., defrauding him or her out of an inheritance). Deception, on the other hand, referred to telling lies and keeping secrets from siblings.

This study categorized offenses according to frequency of mention. In a second study, a new sample of participants rank ordered the offense categories with respect to their degree of unforgivability. Two hundred university students and their friends and relatives (75 males, 125 females, M age = 25 years) completed a short questionnaire which presented the different relationship combinations, the list of possible offenses, and instructions on ranking the unforgivability of offenses (from most unforgivable to least unforgivable) within each relationship type. The results were unequivocal, with offense rankings mirroring frequency of mention. Specifically, the offenses considered least forgivable for parents to commit against their children were abandonment and sexual abuse, and for children to commit against their parents were criminality (sons), taboo sex (daughters), and rejection (both sexes). Betrayal and sexual abuse were considered the most heinous offenses that siblings could commit against one another.

What Family Rules Were Broken?

With respect to parents' relationships with their children, the most important rules appear to be, do not desert or abandon your offspring, and if you are a father, do not have sex with your daughter. Both abandonment and sexual abuse break the rules about parents' primary duties to nurture and protect children, and abandonment in particular implies profound rejection (see also Leary, this volume; Juvonen & Gross, this volume). In his seminal work on attachment and loss, Bowlby (1973) described how the most violently angry and dysfunctional behaviors may be elicited in children and adolescents who are threatened with abandonment. Citing clinical observations by Stott (1950), he noted that some parents actually use the threat of abandonment (including suicide) as a means of disciplining and manipulating their children. As Bowlby noted, a child or adolescent threatened with abandonment may be terrified of expressing anger at the parent for threatening their security; a potent mix of anxiety and rage that in extreme cases may lead paradoxically to parental murder (once dead, they can no longer threaten to leave).

Despite the heinousness of parental abandonment, historical and cross-cultural data suggest that it is not, in fact, such an uncommon occurrence. Hrdy (2000), for example, cites some extraordinary figures on the rates of maternal abandonment of offspring (amounting to millions of infants) throughout history for an assortment of reasons, including lack of resources and infant non-viability. As Trivers (1974) noted in his seminal paper on parent–offspring conflict, children are a costly investment and mothers may not always be able or willing to invest in them. Children, however, need as much investment as they can get, and abandonment threatens their very survival.

The rules underpinning serious offspring offenses against parents were interesting in a variety of respects. Again, rejection was a major theme, with respondents describing the rejection of mothers by their children as particularly severe— "the hardest thing to forgive would be a daughter cutting herself off from her mother"; "telling his mother he didn't love her"; shutting her mother out of her life and not letting her see the grandchildren." The broken rules here related to what children owe their mothers for a lifetime of care and sacrifice; a mother's just reward is to "know her children and grandchildren are happy, and to be included in their lives."

With respect to taboo sex (daughters) and criminality (sons), respondents noted the costs to a family's reputation (considered to be particularly important to fathers). From an evolutionary perspective, it is also possible that both kinds of behaviors potentially limit a child's reproductive fitness. Female promiscuity, for example, may mean a daughter squanders her biologically-limited opportunities for producing high-quality offspring by, as one respondent explained, "going off with a loser." Criminality, too, (for middle-class parents, at least) severely reduces a son's status and the status of the whole family, so making it potentially harder for him (and possibly his siblings) to attract mates.

One other aspect of the results deserves mention. As noted previously, 11% of respondents claimed that homosexuality would be the worst thing a son could "do" to his father. Clearly, and despite what appears to be a growing acceptance of homosexuality in Western cultures, there is still a sizable proportion of people who find it difficult to accept, particularly in relation to their own children (see also Peplau & Beals, 2004). The nature and extent of the profound parental rejection that may be experienced by gay children is exemplified in an account provided by a gay respondent in the current research. Involved in a moderately serious car accident in a foreign country, the respondent rang his father from the hospital to tell him what had happened. His father immediately offered to jump on a plane and take him home, but his son reassured him that he was being cared for by his partner. It also seemed like an emotionally close and opportune moment to break the news to his father that his partner was a man, but the reaction was not favorable. After a minute's silence, his father replied, "I'd rather they'd rung me to say that you were dead."

Sexual abuse and betrayal were considered to be the worst offenses that siblings can commit against one another. Here, the broken rules were described in terms of the necessity for brothers and sisters to look out for, and not take advantage of, one another. Evolutionary theorists have noted that siblings are social allies because they share genes with one another, but they are also competitors for parental resources, including time, love, and attention (Daly et al., 1997; Fitness & Duffield, 2004). Given the risks of cheating that are intrinsic to a competitive relationship, it may make sense for siblings to emphasize their relatedness to one another, articulated as a rule that "we can depend on one another," especially in the face of external threats. Vangelisti and Caughlin (1997), too, have noted how families under threat (e.g., of having a "shameful" secret, such as a family member's mental illness, exposed) will band together to defend themselves against outsiders and to maintain their honor, or public face. Under these circumstances, family members who break ranks and disclose information to outsiders may be severely punished.

Consequences of Rule Violations.   Finally, the reported consequences of having broken unforgivable family rules were uniformly bleak and included likely rejection or expulsion from the family. But, as many respondents emphasized, the offenders brought such consequences on themselves through their behavior. In effect, offenders placed themselves outside the family; their behavior meant that they could not, by definition, belong to a *family* anymore.

In summary, these exploratory studies identified a number of beliefs that people hold about what is beyond forgiveness within different kinds of family relationships. Offenses involving explicit and/or implicit rejection of other family members predominated in respondents' accounts. The importance of family as an entity to which family members belong and owe allegiance was also clear, as was the notion that individuals may, through their own actions, forfeit their right to family membership. Such notions of belonging and family identity raise another important aspect of family rejection and exclusion: Specifically, does one actually have to commit an unforgivable offense before one is rejected from a family, or do some family members, simply by virtue of who they are, belong more than others? And if this is the case, what kinds of factors might contribute to such familial inclusion or exclusion?

DIFFERENTIAL FAMILY TREATMENT: FAVORED CHILDREN AND BLACK SHEEP

There is an implicit assumption (in Western society, at least) that parents aim to treat their children equally, yet children frequently perceive and complain about parental favoritism (Kowal, Kramer, Krull, & Crick, 2002; see Fiske & Yamamoto, this volume, for a general discussion of cross-cultural differences in reactions to rejection). Indeed, perceptions of parental favoritism—and its mirror image, disfavoritism—are widespread. Research shows that a sizable majority of siblings perceive signs of preferential treatment. Harris and Howard (1985), for example, found 50% of a sample of 600 high school students reported the existence of family favoritism. Similarly, Zervas and Sherman (1994) found 62% of 91 undergraduates believed their parents had a favored child. Klagsbrun (1992) found that 84% of 272 U.S. respondents perceived there had been parental favoritism in the family, with just under 50% reporting (with some guilt) that they had themselves been the favorite.

Given the assumption that parents love (or at least, treat) their children equally, how does it happen that some family members are favored while others are rejected and pushed to the edge of the family? A number of potentially important contributing factors have been suggested by evolutionary theorists. For example, and drawing again on Trivers' (1974) model of parent–offspring conflict, Rohde et al. (2003) argued that parental favoritism is potentially adaptive whenever offspring are not identical. The unpalatable fact is that some offspring are better investments than others, depending on factors such as the infant's sex, age, and health, the mother's age and health (and opportunities for future reproduction), and environmental factors such as availability of resources and support. Offspring who, for one reason or another, are perceived as a more risky investment (or perhaps as needing less investment than more vulnerable siblings) may indeed perceive that they are less welcome or included in the family than others (see also Burgess & Drais, 1999).

Other factors that may elicit differential treatment of children include the following:

Birth Order. Sulloway (1996) argued that offspring may increase their relative fitness (i.e., chances of surviving to pass on their genes) by occupying different family niches and effectively reducing inter-sibling competition for resources. Such niche partitioning leads to differences in the tendency to comply with family values, with middleborns considered more likely to rebel than responsible first-borns or indulged lastborns. Middleborns, then, should be more likely to perceive disfavoritism than firstborns or lastborns, and they may be as likely to reject their family as their family is to reject them for their rebelliousness.

There is some empirical evidence supporting the idea that middleborns differ from firstborns and lastborns in a number of respects (see Herrera, Zajonc, Wieczorkowska, & Cichomski, 2003, for a review). For example, Salmon (2003) found in a study of 245 Canadian students that middleborns expressed more positive views toward friends, and less positive opinions of family, than firstborns or lastborns. They were also less inclined to help the family in need than firstborns or lastborns.

Sex of Offspring. As noted by Hrdy (2000), there is an ancient and deep-rooted preference all over the world for sons versus daughters. Several cultures have (and some still do) practice female infanticide, either actively as in abandoning or murdering female infants, or passively by denying female babies access to the kinds of resources (including breast milk) that are provided to male babies. However, research also indicates that female infanticide has been considerably more common in elite, or resource-rich families, than in working-class, resource-poor families, who may actually prefer daughters to sons.

As Wright (1994) pointed out, there is an evolutionary logic to this. When times are tough, raising a fertile daughter who (despite being poor) is likely to attract a mate and produce (at least one) offspring is a safer strategy that raising a sickly, low-status male who cannot compete successfully with other males for mates and who may leave no offspring at all. High-status families, however, are better off investing in male offspring who will potentially be able to use their status and resources to father a number of offspring. For today's middle-class families, a preference for one sex or another may be more a function of personal likes and dislikes, and parenting history (e.g., having previously had a child or children of a particular sex).

Degree of Genetic Relatedness. Another potentially important factor contributing to differential care and potential rejection of family members derives from the principles of kin selection. Put simply, and as noted earlier, humans tend to invest more in genetically-related others than in non-related others. This implies that adopted and foster children may well feel less included and more rejected than biological children in a family. In line with this, Daly and Wilson (1998) have marshaled an impressive body of evidence demonstrating that stepchildren are at relatively greater risk for assault and murder by stepfathers than are fathers' biological offspring. Stepchildren are also more likely than biologically-related children to be killed by more violent and malicious means, as opposed to being killed in their sleep.

Related to this is the point that fathers can never be 100% certain that their children are biologically their own. Thus, it has been argued that the affection felt by fathers for particular children may be strongly influenced by those children's resemblance to themselves (resemblance being a cue for relatedness). In a recent study involving a hypothetical adoption task, Volk and Quinsey (2002) found that men did indeed respond most favorably to infants whose facial features most resembled their own, whereas women's preferences were based on signs of health and cuteness (cues to infant quality).

Family Dynamics—the Scapegoat. Clinicians with interests in family therapy have long been aware of the existence of family scapegoats, described by Dare (1993) as children who are treated "as though they are irretrievably bad and blamed for all the tension and strife in the family" (p. 31). Therapists argue that scapegoating allows families to maintain levels of solidarity and cohesiveness that they could not otherwise maintain (Vogel & Bell, 1960). However, such treatment is extremely painful for the family member who is object of scapegoating. Such a child tends to become full of rage and hatred, lacking in confidence, feeling hopeless about themselves, and living "miserably on the edge of the family" (Dare, 1993, p. 37). Furthermore, a scapegoated child, like the Biblical goat sent into exile carrying the ills of the tribe, is frequently threatened with eviction from the family, and may even be sent away, e.g., to boarding schools, reform schools, or foster families.

As might be expected from the previous discussion of genetic relatedness, clinical data suggest that stepchildren, adopted children, and foster children are all more vulnerable to being scapegoated, as are children with physical or intellectual disabilities and signs of difference, from other children in the family (Brody, Copeland, Sutton, Richardson, & Guyer, 1998). In addition, Dare (1993) notes that a single parent who holds a reservoir of hatred and anger toward a deserting partner may project that hostility onto the child in the family who most resembles that partner.

Study of Family Favorites and Black Sheep

As noted above, there are a number of factors that play potentially important roles in the differential treatment of children in families. An interesting question, then, concerns the extent to which such factors accord with laypeople's own experiences of favoritism and rejection. In a preliminary examination of this question, 70 university students (26 males and 44 females, M age = 27.5 years) completed a questionnaire in which they reported: (a) whether there had been a favorite in the family, and if so, how they knew, and why they thought that person had been the favorite; and (b) whether there had been a black sheep (defined for participants as "someone who was not approved of, or liked, or included as much as the others") in the family, and if so, how they knew, and why they thought that person had been the black sheep. They were also asked some questions about family upbringing and perceived family closeness.

Family Favorites.   In line with the findings from other, larger-scale studies, nearly 69% of respondents reported there was a family favorite, with 48% reporting it was themselves, 35% reporting a brother, and 17% reporting a sister. The most frequently reported reasons for favoritism were birth order (33%—first or last born—never the middle); sex (23%—being the only boy or girl in the family); goodness (21%—talent, attractiveness, likeability) and similarity to a parent (19%). Moreover, and in accord with Sulloway's (1996) birth-order theory, 58% of firstborns and 62% of lastborns believed they were the family favorites; however, only 31% of middleborns reported that they had favored status. Similarly, 38% of middleborns believed they were the black sheep of the family, compared to only 7% of firstborns and 18% of lastborns.

Black Sheep.   Remarkably, 80% of respondents reported that there was a black sheep in the family, with 21% claiming it was themselves, 13% naming a brother, 16% a sister, 25% an uncle, and 25% naming a cousin, in-law or distant relative. Reasons given for black sheep status differed, depending on who the target was. Unlike the findings for favorites, no one cited sex or birth order as a reason for black sheep status. In line with theories about genetic relatedness, however, three adopted respondents did explicitly blame biology for their outsider status. Moreover, perceived difference was the most frequently cited reason for black sheep status. In fact, 100% of those respondents who believed they were the black sheep claimed it was because of their difference to the rest of the family—they *looked* different (frequently reported), had different personalities, talents, or interests, and just did not fit into or feel they belonged to the family. The perception of difference was frequently reinforced by the comments and behaviors of parents and siblings. One respondent was pointedly given a t-shirt by her mother depicting a black sheep being ostracized by a flock of white sheep; she claims she took the hint and has had no contact with her family for many years.

Black sheep sisters were considered by 72% of respondents to have acquired their status via difference and failure to fit in—as one respondent explained, "Mum always made her out to be the sister we didn't love." Others (25%) claimed it was their sisters who had rejected the family by moving away, severing contact, and/or marrying undesirable partners. By contrast, black sheep brothers were considered by 71% of the sample to have earned their status via troublemaking: becoming involved in drugs and engaging in rebellious (and sometimes criminal) behavior.

Interestingly, the sizable proportions of black sheep uncles and other extended family members (99% of whom were male) were overwhelmingly described as not just different, but sexually or morally deviant. This category included homosexuals, hermits, alcoholics, gamblers, embezzlers, family deserters, and adulterers. Moreover, sometimes an entire side of a family was rejected by an entire other side for religious reasons or because of long-standing feuds and hatreds (the origins of which were not always known or understood by respondents).

Treatment of the Black Sheep.   The most frequently reported behaviors toward black sheep lay on a continuum ranging from total exclusion (51%) through coldness (9%) to chilly politeness (7%)—described by one respondent as."overt politeness that is cordially cool." Total exclusion from the family, with no effort made to maintain contact, was more typical of extended-family black sheep (especially uncles). As one respondent stated, "he never gets invited to family gatherings because he is so disapproved of." The second-most frequently reported behaviors toward black sheep involved active rejection (33%)—targeted criticism, sarcasm, and hostility—very much in line with clinical descriptions of scapegoating.

In summary, the findings of this study confirm that a sizable proportion of human beings do not enjoy the security and sense of belonging that families are supposed to provide. However, there was one interesting and unexpected finding that emerged in a section of the study designed to measure perceptions of family closeness. Specifically, the more contact respondents reported having had with their extended family as they grew up, the less likely they were to report there had been a black sheep ($r = -.47$) or a favorite ($r = -.29$) anywhere in the family. This finding suggests that having a large, available, and involved network of kin may provide a buffer against parental scapegoating of particular children. Perhaps, and to paraphrase Hillary Clinton, it really does take a village to raise a (healthy) child. This, in turn, raises an interesting question with respect to families in more collectivist cultures, where the complex webs of extended familial relationships may, likewise, buffer against parental rejection and exclusion. However, this may work both ways, with collectivists more threatened by rule violations that shame the family than individualists (see Triandis, 1994; see also Fiske & Yamamoto, this volume). Clearly, there is scope for more research on this question.

CONSEQUENCES OF FAMILY REJECTION

There is a fast-growing body of literature on the detrimental consequences of familial (and in particular, parental) rejection. As noted by several authors in this volume, the need to belong is fundamental to human beings, and the pain of not belonging may be severe (in this volume, see Baumeister & DeWall; Pickett & Gardner Leary; Williams & Zadro). Adult attachment researchers, for example, have identified an association between parental rejection during childhood and individuals' fearful-avoidant behavior in the context of adult relationships (Bartholomew & Horowitz, 1991). Strong links have also been found between parental rejection and depression in adolescents and adults (Robertson & Simons, 1998; Nolan, Flynn, & Garber, 2003).

Research also suggests that paternal rejection plays a uniquely important role in predicting later dysfunction. For example, Meesters, Muris, and Esselink

(1995) found that for both men and women, perceived paternal rejection was the strongest predictor of cynical hostility and distrust toward others. Similarly, in a recent study, Oliver and Whiffen (2003) found that perceived paternal rejection was directly associated with men's depression, and that the relationship between such rejection and depression was not mediated by attachment insecurity (as it was for maternal rejection). Being rejected by one's father, they claim, is depressogenic per se for sons. Furthermore, because childhood physical abuse was not predictive of men's depression over and beyond the variance shared with parental rejection, the authors concluded that physical abuse occurs as part of the larger context of parental rejection.

With respect to scapegoating and targeted rejection of a particular family member, there appear to be a number of negative outcomes. The effects of differential treatment have been shown to impact negatively on the disfavored child's sense of competence and self-worth (Dunn, Stocker, & Plomin, 1990), and on his or her attachment security and psychological adjustment (Sheehan & Noller, 2002). In a study of 127 males and females aged 17–30 years and 62 of their siblings (aged 18–32 years), Brody et al. (1998) found that participants who perceived themselves to be disfavored experienced more frequent shame and intense fear than their favored siblings. Moreover, these authors note that parental favoritism may lead to long-lasting bitterness between siblings, with disfavored offspring harboring feelings of "shame, resentment, envy and anger" (p. 270) that may lead to later depression.

Finally, Brody et al. (1998) pointed out that, if a child is disfavored, he or she receives relatively few parental rewards and so will exhibit fewer and fewer positive behaviors, and, in effect, will become less likable. As noted in this volume by Baumeister and DeWall, groups of people who feel rejected by society frequently exhibit the kinds of behaviors these researchers have observed in their laboratory studies, including self-defeating behaviors and impaired self-regulation. This begs the question regarding black sheep: To what extent were they rejected by their families because they were different (or deviant), and to what extent did they become different (or deviant) as a function of having been (or felt) rejected by their families? No doubt, there is a bi-directional relationship here. However, and as discussed earlier, there are also factors, such as birth order and degree of genetic relatedness that may push children toward the edge of their families from the beginning of their lives.

CONCLUSIONS

Clearly, there is an enormous amount of work still to be done in this fascinating and fast-moving field. The studies described in this chapter provide some interesting glimpses into people's beliefs about, and experiences of, familial rule violations and familial rejection, but they suffer from a number of limitations. Perhaps the most serious of these relate to the relatively small size of the samples, and the fact that the data were drawn from a culturally and socio-economically homogenous population. Answering questions about the universality and evolutionary origins of particular familial rules and their consequences for family belonging and exclusion will require cross-cultural (and cross-*sub*-cultural) data.

There is also a need in future research to be more specific about relational context. For example, the nature of unforgivable offenses between parents and children may change, depending on the relative ages of both—is taboo sex still a problem for elderly fathers in relation to middle-aged daughters? Similarly, reportedly unforgivable offenses may differ depending on the number, sex, and health of children already in the family, or degree of genetic relatedness, etc.

These are questions with considerable theoretical importance, but they have applied significance, too. As discussed in this chapter, the long-term consequences of familial rejection may be pronounced and severe. A better understanding of the causes, beliefs, and assumptions underlying such rejection can only enhance the health and happiness of humans in their first, and arguably most crucial, context of belonging: the family.

REFERENCES

Bartholomew, K., & Horowitz, L. (1991). Attachment style among young adults: A test of a four category model. *Journal of Personality and Social Psychology, 61*, 226–244.

Bowlby, J. (1973/1998). *Attachment and loss, Vol. 2: Separation*. London: Pimlico Press.

Brody, L., Copeland, A., Sutton, L., Richardson, D., & Guyer, M. (1998). Mommy and daddy like you best: Perceived family favoritism in relation to affect, adjustment, and family process. *Journal of Family Therapy, 20*, 269–291.

Burgess, R. L., & Drais, A. A. (1999). Beyond the "Cinderella effect": Life history theory and child maltreatment. *Human Nature, 10*, 373–398.

Buss, D. (1999). *Evolutionary psychology: The new science of the mind*. Needham Heights, MA: Allyn and Bacon.

Clark, M. S., Fitness, J., & Brissette, I. (2001). Understanding people's perceptions of relationships is crucial to understanding their emotional lives. In G. J. O. Fletcher & M. S. Clark (Eds.), *Blackwell handbook of social psychology: Interpersonal processes* (pp. 253–278). Malden, MA: Blackwell.

Daly, M., & Wilson, M. (1998). *The truth about Cinderella: A Darwinian view of parental love*. London: Orion Publishing

Daly, M., Salmon, C., & Wilson, M. (1997). Kinship: The conceptual hole in psychological studies of social cognition and close relationships. In J. Simpson & D. Kenrick (Eds.), *Evolutionary social psychology* (pp. 265–296).

Dare, C. (1993). The family scapegoat: An origin for hating. In V. Varma (Ed.), *How and why children hate* (pp. 31–45). London: Jessica Kingsley.

Dunn, J., Stocker, C., & Plomin, R. (1990). Nonshared experiences within the family: Correlates of behavioral problems in middle childhood. *Development and Psychopathology, 2*, 113–126.

Fitness, J. (2001). Betrayal, rejection, revenge, and forgiveness: An interpersonal script approach. In M. Leary (Ed.), *Interpersonal rejection* (pp. 73–104). New York: Oxford University Press.

Fitness, J., & Duffield, J. (2004). Emotion and communication in families. In A. Vangelisti (Ed.), *The handbook of family communication* (pp. 473–494). Mahwah, NJ: Lawrence Erlbaum.

Fitness, J., & Parker, V. (2003). *Breaking the rules: Exploring the causes and consequences of perceived rule violations by family members*. Paper presented at the 32nd Annual Meeting of the Society of Australasian Social Psychologists, Sydney.

Fitness, J., Fletcher, G. J. O., & Overall, N. (2003). Interpersonal attraction and intimate relationships. In M. Hogg & J. Cooper (Eds.), *The Sage handbook of social psychology* (pp. 258–278). Newbury Park, CA: Sage.

Harris, I. D., & Howard, K. I. (1985). Correlates of perceived parental favouritism. *Journal of Genetic Psychology, 146*, 45–56.

Herrera, N. C., Zajonc, R. B., Wieczorkowska, G., & Cichomski, B. (2003). Beliefs about birth rank and their reflections in reality. *Journal of Personality and Social Psychology, 85*, 142–150.

Hrdy, S. B. (2000). *Mother nature.* London: Vintage.

Klagsbrun, F. (1992). *Mixed feelings: Love, hate, rivalry, and reconciliation among brothers and sisters.* New York: Bantam Books.

Kowal, A., Kramer, L., Krull, J., & Crick, N. (2002). Children's perceptions of the fairness of parental preferential treatment and their socioemotional well-being. *Journal of Family Psychology, 16*, 297–306.

Meesters, C., Muris, P., & Esselink, T. (1995). Hostility and perceived parental rearing behaviour. *Personality and Individual Differences, 18*, 567–570.

Nolan, S., Flynn, C., & Garber, J. (2003). Prospective relations between rejection and depression in young adolescents. *Journal of Personality and Social Psychology, 85*, 745–755.

Oliver, L., & Whiffen, V. (2003). Perceptions of parents and partners and men's depressive symptoms. *Journal of Social and Personal Relationships, 20*, 621–635.

Peplau, A., & Beals, K. (2004). The family lives of lesbians and gay men. In A. Vangelisti (Ed.), *The handbook of family communication* (pp. 233–248). Mahwah, NJ: Lawrence Erlbaum.

Robertson, J., & Simons, R. (1998). Family factors, self-esteem, and adolescent depression. *Journal of Marriage and the Family, 51*, 125–138.

Rohde, P. A., Atzwanger, K., Butovskayad, M., Lampert, A., Mysterud, I., Sanchez-Andres, A., & Sulloway, F. J. (2003). Perceived parental favouritism, closeness to kin, and the rebel of the family: The effects of birth order and sex. *Evolution & Human Behavior, 24*, 261–276.

Salmon, C. (2003). Birth order and relationships: Family, friends, and sexual partners. *Human Nature, 14*, 73–88.

Sheehan, G., & Noller, P. (2002). Adolescents' perception of differential parenting: Links with attachment style and adolescent adjustment. *Personal Relationships, 9*, 173–190.

Stafford, L., & Dainton, M. (1994). The dark side of "normal" family interaction. In W. R. Cupach & B. H. Spitzberg (Eds.), *The dark side of interpersonal communication* (pp. 259–279). Hillsdale, NJ: Lawrence Erlbaum

Stott, D. H. (1950). *Delinquency and human nature.* Dunfermline, Fife: U.K., Carnegie Trust.

Sulloway, F. (1996). *Born to rebel: Birth order, family dynamics, and creative lives.* New York: Pantheon.

Triandis, H. (1994). *Culture and social behavior.* New York: McGraw Hill.

Trivers, R. (1974). Parent-offspring conflict. *American Zoologist, 14*, 249–264.

Vangelisti, A. (1994). Messages that hurt. In W. R. Cupach & B. H. Spitzberg (Eds.), *The dark side of interpersonal communication* (pp. 53-82). Hillsdale, NJ: Lawrence Erlbaum.

Vangelisti, A. (2004). Introduction. In A. Vangelisti (Ed.), *Handbook of family communication* (pp xiii–xx). Mahwah, NJ: Lawrence Erlbaum.

Vangelisti, A., & Caughlin, J. (1997). Revealing family secrets: The influence of topic, function, and relationships. *Journal of Social and Personal Relationships, 14*, 679–706.

Vogel, E. F., & Bell, N. W. (1960). The emotionally disturbed child as the family scapegoat. In: N. W. Bell & E. F. Vogel (Eds.), *A modern introduction to the family* (pp. 382–397). New York: Free Press.

Volk, A., & Quinsey, V. L. (2002). The influence of infant facial cues on adoption preferences. *Human Nature, 13*, 437–455.

Wright, R. (1994). *The moral animal.* New York: Pantheon Books.

Zervas, L. J., & Sherman, M. (1994). The relationship between perceived parental favoritism and self-esteem. *Journal of Genetic Psychology, 155*, 25–33.

PART *V*

EFFECTS OF SOCIAL
EXCLUSION ON
PRO- AND ANTI-SOCIAL
BEHAVIOR

17

Exclusion and Nonconscious Behavioral Mimicry

JESSICA L. LAKIN
TANYA L. CHARTRAND

H umans are clearly social animals (e.g., Aronson, 1999; Ehrlich, 2000). Our days would be incomplete without the many social interactions that typically fill them. We spend time with family, catch up on the latest gossip with friends, converse with colleagues, and acknowledge acquaintances and complete strangers. The most interesting thing to note about all of these types of events is that other "social animals" are always prominently involved. It is therefore not surprising that the need to belong and be accepted by family members, friends, peers, colleagues, acquaintances, and other important group members is strong, perhaps even fundamental (Baumeister & Leary, 1995). The reverse of this argument is also true—social exclusion and loneliness can be devastating (Cacioppo & Hawkley, this volume; Leary, 2001; Williams, 2001; Williams & Zadro, this volume).

Successful social interactions would have been (and probably still are) a significant component of physical survival (Buss & Kenrick, 1998; Johanson & Edgar, 1996). The environment of evolutionary adaptation was filled with obstacles and

---

Address correspondence to: Jessica L. Lakin, Psychology Department, Drew University, Madison, New Jersey, 07940, USA. E-mail: jlakin@drew.edu

dangers, and individuals relied on others to complete survival activities such as locating and securing food sources and shelter, defending against predators, finding mates, and raising offspring. The transition from sole living to group living would have made many of these activities easier (Lewin, 1993; Poirier & McKee, 1999), and as a result, group living may have become the most influential factor in an individual's ability to survive and reproduce (Brewer, 1997, this volume; Caporael & Brewer, 1991). Individuals who successfully cooperated with others and who maintained harmonious group relationships were included in the group (and thereby accomplished survival activities; de Waal, 1989); individuals who were unsuccessful at these pursuits were excluded by the group (and thereby unable to accomplish survival activities; Caporael, 1997, 2001a, 2001b).

THE SOCIAL PSYCHOLOGY OF EXCLUSION

Several social psychological literatures detail the importance of the needs to belong and to be included and the deleterious consequences of being ostracized or excluded. The chapters in the current volume discuss these literatures in depth, and therefore we will provide only a short review here.

Need to Belong

Baumeister and Leary (1995; see also Leary & Baumeister, 2000) argued that the need to belong, or the need to form and maintain strong, stable interpersonal relationships, is a fundamental human motivation. The need to belong seems to be present in all humans in all cultures (at least to some degree, see Fiske & Yamamoto, this volume). People easily form social bonds in a wide variety of situations, and are reluctant to break those bonds once they have been formed. At an affective level, increases in belongingness are related to positive affect, and decreases in belongingness are related to negative affect. The need to belong also affects cognition, as people devote a considerable amount of time to processing and understanding interpersonal information. At the behavioral level, the absence of meaningful personal relationships leads to an increase in affiliative behaviors, such as agreeing with another person's decision and engaging in behaviors, even negative behaviors, sanctioned by group members. Finally, people who are deprived of belongingness experience greater stress, more physical and mental health problems (e.g., sickness and psychopathology), and decreases in general well-being and happiness (Cacioppo & Hawkley, this volume).

Social Exclusion

The emotional, psychological, and behavioral consequences of not satisfying the need to belong are typically explored through the use of two different paradigms. One paradigm involves identifying people who claim to be lonely or have been excluded and then examining theoretically-related variables. Research using this paradigm has shown that anxiety, jealousy, depression, and hurt feelings occur because of actual or threatened exclusion from important social groups (Baumeister & Tice, 1990; Leary, 1990, Leary & MacDonald, 2003). Leary and his colleagues have utilized a slight variation of this paradigm to show that, consistent with the sociometer hypothesis (Leary & Baumeister, 2000; Leary, Tambor, Terdal, & Downs, 1995), trait self-esteem predicts the extent to which people feel that they are socially included or excluded. The more excluded people feel, the lower their self-esteem (Leary et al., 1995). These painful emotional consequences of exclusion are consistent with the recent finding that social exclusion activates the same areas of the brain that respond to physical pain (Eisenberger & Lieberman, this volume; Eisenberger, Lieberman, & Williams, 2003; MacDonald & Shaw, this volume).

A second paradigm used more frequently to study the consequences of social exclusion involves excluding participants from a relevant group and then examining the emotional, psychological, and behavioral consequences. Being excluded causes a decrease in state self-esteem, especially when the exclusion is a result of group choice rather than random factors (Leary, Cottrell, & Phillips, 2001; Leary et al., 1995). Being rejected or excluded also increases sensitivity to social information, perhaps by activating a social monitoring system which causes people to become more sensitive to social information and opportunities to develop social connections (Gardner, Pickett, & Knowles, this volume; Pickett & Gardner, this volume). Compared to people who have been accepted by a group, excluded people show an increase in memory for social information (Gardner, Pickett, & Brewer, 2000) and are more sensitive to emotional vocal tone and accurate on a facial emotion detection task (Pickett, Gardner, & Knowles, 2004).

The experimental paradigm has also revealed a number of behavioral consequences of actual or implied social exclusion. The mere threat of social exclusion may cause people to cooperate for the public good (Ouwerkerk, Van Lange, Gallucci, & Kerr, this volume). However, exclusion lowers performance on cognitively complex intellectual tasks, such as I.Q. tests and difficult questions from the Graduate Record Exam (but does not affect simple information processing performance, such as recalling nonsense syllables; Baumeister, Twenge, & Nuss, 2002). This finding is consistent with the idea that self-regulation is impaired after exclusion, which implies that *any* controlled process might be disrupted when belongingness is threatened (Baumeister & DeWall, this volume). In addition, exclusion causes people to behave more aggressively (Catanese & Tice, this volume; Gaertner & Iuzzini, this volume; Twenge, this volume; Twenge, Baumeister, Tice, & Stucke, 2001) and leads to derogation of the rejecters (Bourgeois & Leary, 2001). Finally, Twenge and her colleagues have also shown that threatened exclusion increases unintentionally self-defeating behaviors (Twenge, Catanese, & Baumeister, 2002) and may lead to a "deconstructed state," which is associated with a lack of strong emotion, lethargy, and escape from self-awareness (Twenge, Catanese, & Baumeister, 2003).

Ostracism

Models of ostracism (one type of social exclusion) also indicate the importance of being acknowledged and accepted by others (Williams, 1997, 2001; Williams & Zadro, this volume). Williams argues that being ostracized threatens four basic needs: belongingness, self-esteem, control, and meaningful existence (Sommer, Williams, Ciarocco, & Baumeister, 2001; Williams, Shore, & Grahe, 1998). To the extent that failure to fulfill these basic needs is aversive, people should actively try to accomplish them when they have been ostracized (Williams, 2001).

Empirical evidence is consistent with this argument. For the present purposes, evidence that participants engage in affiliative behaviors to address their threatened belongingness needs after being ostracized is the most relevant. Williams and Sommer (1997) demonstrated that ostracized female participants were more likely than non-ostracized females and ostracized and non-ostracized males to contribute to a group task, even when their contributions would not be individually identifiable. The authors argue that females are particularly concerned with maintaining group harmony, so when ostracized, they attempt to create this desired state by working extra hard and not engaging in social loafing. Conforming with the opinions of others might be another way to maintain group harmony. Williams, Cheung, and Choi (2000) found that participants who were ostracized while playing an online ball-tossing game were more likely to conform on a subsequent Asch line-judging task. The authors predicted that conformity would be most likely to occur in this condition, because agreeing with a group norm, even if it is incorrect, would be one strategy to affiliate with group members, thereby creating a smooth interaction.

Summary

It is clear that being included in social groups is important, and that being excluded from social groups has adverse emotional, psychological, and behavioral consequences. Research on the need to belong suggests that it is a fundamental human motivation, and evolutionary psychology theorizing about the nature of groups in the evolutionary environment is consistent with this argument. Moreover, research on social exclusion and ostracism suggests that exclusion results in intense negative affect, decreases in self-esteem, and negative interpersonal behaviors (e.g., aggression). However, these behaviors do not represent attempts by the excluded people to re-establish themselves with significant others. That is, these negative behaviors will not help the excluded individuals fulfill their need to belong or be accepted.

Recent work on social exclusion has demonstrated that there are instances where people respond to social exclusion in more pro-social ways. The work of Gardner, Pickett, and their colleagues has shown that people are more sensitive to social information after exclusion and pursue opportunities to affiliate when they are available, and Ouwerkerk et al. have shown cooperative behaviors in social dilemmas as a result of threatened ostracism (see chapters in this volume).

Williams and his colleagues (Williams et al., 2000; Williams & Sommer, 1997) have demonstrated several behavioral consequences of being excluded that may help to fulfill an excluded person's desire to belong and be accepted—putting effort forth in a social situation and conformity. As a whole, these results suggest that excluded people are willing to engage in behaviors that increase their likelihood of being accepted by a group, which leaves open the possibility that they might also engage in other behaviors (perhaps even automatic, nonconscious behaviors) that are related to the development of rapport and liking.

NONCONSCIOUS BEHAVIORAL MIMICRY

The idea of behavior matching has a long history in the field of psychology (James, 1890). This interest has yielded a large literature replete with fascinating examples and demonstrations of the ways in which we mimic other people (e.g., contagious laughter and yawning, adopting the speech patterns of others; for a review, see Hatfield, Cacioppo, & Rapson, 1994). Our research has focused on nonconscious behavioral mimicry, or the tendency to mimic the behaviors of others without awareness, intent, or conscious control, and the link between this particular type of mimicry and the development of affiliation and rapport (Chartrand & Bargh, 1999; Chartrand & Jefferis, 2003; Chartrand, Maddux, & Lakin, 2005; Lakin & Chartrand, 2003; Lakin, Jefferis, Cheng, & Chartrand, 2003).

There is experimental evidence that people mimic the behaviors of others. Bernieri, Reznick, and Rosenthal (1988) recorded mother–child interactions with separate cameras, and then created several different versions of the interactions, all with the mother on the right side of the screen and the child on the left. One version showed the true, real-time mother–child interaction, while other versions varied the mothers and children paired together, as well as the exact timing of the interactions. As a result, participant "judges" were unable to tell whether mothers were interacting with their own children or other peoples' children. However, analyses indicated that even under these carefully controlled conditions, judges rated mothers as more physically in sync with their own children than with other children. Bernieri (1988) replicated this effect using a teacher–student paradigm.

Idiosyncratic behaviors are also mimicked. For example, Bavelas and her colleagues have found that listeners mirror the movements of a storyteller when she ducks while telling a story (Bavelas, Black, Chovil, Lemery, & Mullett, 1988) and display an expression of pain when witnessing an experimenter experience an apparently painful injury (although the duration of the expression was affected by whether the experimenter was making eye contact with the participant; Bavelas, Black, Lemery, & Mullett, 1986).

These studies clearly demonstrate that we mimic the behaviors of those we care about (or with whom there is an ongoing relationship) and those we might want to like us. But there is also experimental evidence that people mimic the mannerisms of complete strangers, even in situations where it is unlikely that there is pre-existing rapport or a goal to develop future rapport. In one test of this idea, Chartrand and Bargh (1999) had participants sequentially interact with two unfamiliar confederates. Several steps were taken to ensure that rapport would not develop between the participant and confederates. The confederates did not make eye contact with or smile at the participant; the brief sessions (approximately 5 minutes) and mundane task (describing photographs) made this fairly easy to do. One of the two confederates was told to have a rather negative, bored, and sullen expression throughout the interaction with the participant. It was assumed that if the default tendency was to try to affiliate with the confederate and create a sense of rapport, this tendency would be overridden by the presence of the unpleasant confederate. Thus, particularly with this confederate, there was little chance that rapport would develop, or that the goal to develop rapport would be active. The question then became, would behavioral mimicry occur anyway?

Participants interacted with the two confederates (in counterbalanced order) who were trained to engage in one of two types of behaviors: face-rubbing or foot-shaking. Results revealed that participants mimicked the mannerisms of the confederates—they shook their foot more when they were with the foot-shaker than when they were with the face-rubber, and rubbed their face more when they were with the face-rubber than when they were with the foot-shaker. At the conclusion of the experiment, participants were asked about the mannerisms of both confederates, and about their own mannerisms; no participants reported noticing anything about the confederates' behaviors or their own.

The fact that participants changed their own behavior to match their environment speaks to the chameleon-like nature of mimicry behavior. Like a chameleon that changes its colors to blend or fit in with its environment, people often unwittingly change their mannerisms and behaviors to blend and fit in with their social environments. Importantly, in the Chartrand and Bargh (1999) study, even the unlikable confederate was significantly mimicked by participants, indicating that behavioral mimicry occurs under minimal conditions where there is no rapport, affiliation, or liking between interactants.

Behavioral Mimicry and Rapport

Despite the fact that mimicry can and does occur under minimal conditions, the early work in this area tended to focus on posture sharing as a potential nonverbal indicator of rapport (for a review, see Tickle-Degnen & Rosenthal, 1987). In 1964, Scheflen noted that body positioning in an ongoing interaction seemed to be an indicator of liking, understanding, and the relationships between group members. Specifically, he posited that people often adopt similar postures, and that those who share similar postures often share viewpoints as well. Charney (1966) tested Scheflen's notions in a psychotherapy context and found an association between posture sharing and positive, interpersonal speech content. These researchers foreshadowed the argument later made by Bavelas and her colleagues (e.g., Bavelas et al., 1986) that behavior matching is a tool used to communicate liking for and rapport with other people.

Subsequent research also demonstrated that posture sharing was indicative of involvement and interest in an interaction, and feelings of togetherness. Bernieri (1988) analyzed videotapes of teacher–student dyads and found that the couples whose movements were most in sync with each other also felt the most rapport. La France and her colleagues have used college classrooms to study the relationship between posture sharing and rapport. In a typical study, students were asked to report the level of rapport in their classes, and those classes were then coded for amount of posture sharing. As predicted, classes rated by students as having high rapport also manifested the greatest amount of posture sharing (La France & Broadbent, 1976; see also La France, 1979, 1982).

Although these studies hint at a causal relationship between rapport and mimicry, to truly know whether one can cause the other, one factor needs to be manipulated directly. Several early studies took this approach. Dabbs (1969) had a confederate interviewee mimic the gestures of one of two participant interviewers who were in the room at the same time. Participants who were mimicked did not report more liking for the confederate, but they did evaluate the confederate more favorably than participants who were not mimicked (e.g., they said the confederate was well-informed and had sound ideas). Mimicked participants also thought that they were more similar to the confederate (e.g., they believed that the confederate thought more like they did), and similarity has been shown to increase liking and attraction (Byrne, 1971). Maurer and Tindall (1983) also experimentally explored the link between behavioral mimicry and rapport by having counselors mimic the body positions of their clients. Under these conditions, clients perceived a greater level of empathy from the counselor.

Chartrand and Bargh (1999, Study 2) experimentally manipulated behavioral mimicry to explore the consequences for liking. They argued that perception of another's behavior automatically causes nonconscious mimicry, which in turn creates shared feelings of empathy and rapport. In their study, participants engaged in a photo-description task with a confederate. Throughout the interaction, the confederate either mimicked the behavior of the participant, or had neutral, nondescript posture and mannerisms. It was expected that when the confederate mimicked the behavior of the participant, the participant would report liking the confederate more, and also report that the interaction had been more smooth and harmonious. Results were as predicted, suggesting that one function that behavioral mimicry serves is to increase liking between interactants. This study also provides an experimental demonstration that behavioral mimicry *causes* an increase in rapport. Thus, mimicry serves the adaptive function of increasing liking and rapport between people involved in an interaction, as well as making the interaction smoother and more harmonious.

LINK BETWEEN SOCIAL EXCLUSION
AND BEHAVIORAL MIMICRY

Nonconscious behavioral mimicry has been explained by the existence of a perception-behavior link (Chartrand & Bargh, 1999; Dijksterhuis & Bargh, 2001; Dijksterhuis, Bargh, & Miedema, 2000); seeing a person engage in a behavior activates that behavioral representation, which then makes the perceiver more likely to engage in that behavior herself (James, 1890). Although the perception-behavior link provides one explanation for the occurrence of mimicry behavior (one for which there is much evidence; see Dijksterhuis & Bargh, 2001 or Dijksterhuis, 2001), its existence does not preclude the existence of other factors that also affect the likelihood of observing behavioral mimicry effects (for a review, see Chartrand et al., 2005).

Goal to Affiliate

We have been particularly interested in the role of the desire to affiliate as a motivational moderator of behavioral mimicry effects (Lakin & Chartrand, 2003). Because of the link between mimicry and rapport, we argued that a goal to affiliate with another person should reliably increase mimicry behavior. That is, behavioral mimicry would be observed in all conditions (because of the perception–behavior link), but we felt that having an active affiliation goal would further increase this tendency.

We explored this question in two separate studies. In the first, participants were given a conscious or a nonconscious affiliation goal. The conscious affiliation goal was activated through specific instructions to try to affiliate with a future interaction partner. The nonconscious affiliation goal was activated through a subliminal priming procedure (see Bargh & Chartrand, 2000). After the activation of the goal (or the absence of the activation for participants in a no goal condition), participants ostensibly watched a "live feed" of another participant in an adjoining room (actually a confederate videotaped earlier) who was engaging in several routine activities (e.g., typing, stapling papers). Importantly, the confederate was touching her face during and between the clerical tasks. Participants were surreptitiously videotaped, and the tapes were later coded to determine the extent to which participants were touching their own faces while watching the confederate. The results were as expected. Participants who had an active affiliation goal, conscious or nonconscious, mimicked the behaviors of the potential interaction partner more than participants who did not have an affiliation goal (Lakin & Chartrand, 2003, Study 1).

A second study extended this initial finding by attempting to show an increase in mimicry in a situation where there was even more pressure to create rapport with an unknown person: recent failure at an affiliation goal. Participants were subliminally primed with an affiliation goal or not, and then participated in an ostensibly unrelated second experiment. They were told that they would be interviewing two fellow students—one online, using real-time chat software, and one face-to-face—and then answering some questions about the different types of interview formats. The online interview was structured such that participants had either a successful experience (i.e., the confederate was friendly and polite) or an unsuccessful experience (i.e., the confederate was unfriendly and abrupt). Thus, participants were led to succeed or fail at their affiliation goal (if they had one). During the face-to-face interview, the other student, who was actually a confederate, shook her foot throughout the interaction. Participants were again surreptitiously videotaped, and the tapes were later coded to determine the extent to which participants shook their own feet while interacting with the confederate. Results indicated that participants who were primed with an affiliation goal and were not able to accomplish this goal in a first interaction (i.e., they failed at their goal) mimicked the behaviors of the second interaction partner more than participants who did not have an affiliation goal or participants who had an affiliation goal and succeeded in the first interaction (Lakin & Chartrand, 2003, Study 2). Presumably, participants who failed in a first attempt to achieve their goal continued to pursue their active goal with a new interaction partner by mimicking that person's behaviors.

The results of these studies suggest something interesting about nonconscious behavioral mimicry. Even though the behavioral mimicry of participants occurred without conscious intention or awareness, it was witnessed more frequently in situations where it was beneficial to participants. Participants who wanted to affiliate (even when this goal was outside of awareness) mimicked more than people who did not want to affiliate. This suggests that behavioral mimicry may be functional in that doing it helps people to accomplish their objectives; in situations where people want to create liking or rapport, they mimic more (Lakin et al., 2003).

Social Exclusion

Given the negativity that is associated with being rejected or excluded, we expected that a recent social exclusion experience may be another factor that increases nonconscious behavioral mimicry. Because exclusion is such a negative experience, people should be motivated to engage in behaviors that will help them recover from this negative state. To the extent that behavioral mimicry satisfies this objective, people who are excluded from a social group should mimic the behaviors of a subsequent interaction partner more than people who are included in a social group.

Data from two studies support our argument that mimicry should increase after being socially excluded (Lakin, 2003; Lakin, Chartrand, & Arkin, 2005). In an initial study, we recruited participants for an experiment on visualization and description. Participants were told that they would be completing two unrelated experiments. The first involved playing an online ball-tossing game (Cyberball;

Williams et al., 2000) with three other participants and trying to visualize the other players and the situation in which the game was being played. Participants were told that they would be completing a questionnaire following the mental visualization experience that would allow them to describe what they were visualizing and their experience while playing the game. With the exception of the three other players' initials (e.g., K.S.), participants had no information about their fellow players and did not expect to ever meet or interact with them. In reality, the other players were computer-controlled, and were programmed to either exclude or include participants while playing the ballgame.

Once the Cyberball game was completed and participants had answered the mental visualization questionnaire (which actually contained manipulation check items), the experimenter informed participants that the second experiment would now begin. Participants were seated in a chair that faced a hidden camera on the opposite wall and told that they would be describing a set of photographs to a partner. They were also told that their partner had not played Cyberball, and therefore knew nothing about the earlier inclusion or exclusion experience. While the experimenter ostensibly went to retrieve the participant's partner, a baseline measure of foot-shaking was obtained.

The experimenter then re-entered the room with a female confederate and instructions for the photo description task were delivered. The task was relatively mundane, and did not allow for excessive interaction between the participant and the confederate. Each person was given four photographs and told to describe them to the other person for 30 to 45 seconds without actually showing their partner the picture. The confederate's picture descriptions were scripted, and she shook her foot throughout her interaction with the participant. The interaction between the participant and the confederate was videotaped, and the tapes were later coded to determine the extent to which participants shook their own feet during the photo description task.

Analyses of the manipulation check items revealed that the manipulation of exclusion was successful. Compared to participants who were included, those who were excluded enjoyed playing Cyberball less and evaluated the individuals who were playing the game with them less favorably. With regard to the mimicry measure, we hypothesized that participants who were excluded would mimic the behaviors of the confederate more than participants who were included. This is exactly what happened. Controlling for the amount of foot-shaking that occurred during the baseline period, excluded participants mimicked the foot-shaking behavior of the confederate significantly more than participants who were included (Lakin, 2003).

Given the relationship between mimicry and affiliation (Lakin & Chartrand, 2003), the increase in mimicking tendencies seen after exclusion suggests that participants may be trying to recover from their exclusion experience by affiliating with their new interaction partner (as the social monitoring system would predict; see Gardner et al., this volume, and Pickett & Gardner, this volume). It is therefore important to note that the mimicry behavior of the participants seemed to have the desired effect. When the confederate (who was blind to condition) was asked to evaluate her interactions with each participant, she reported that the interactions with excluded participants had gone more smoothly than the interactions with included participants.

It is also important to note that the increase in mimicry by excluded participants occurred despite the fact that they reported no conscious awareness of the confederate's foot-shaking behaviors or the fact that their own behaviors were affected by the confederate. This suggests that the behavioral mimicry that occurred was indeed nonconscious, and raises the interesting issue of the adaptiveness of this behavioral tendency. Use of mimicry in situations where a person wants to affiliate is functional, as it gives people an opportunity to pursue their affiliation goal without spending limited cognitive resources on determining the best way to do so.

A second experiment was conducted to explore whether the heightened affiliation need that results from exclusion can be addressed by mimicking the behaviors of *any* interaction partner (Lakin, 2003; Lakin et al., 2005). That is, would mimicry of an interaction partner's behaviors still occur if the interaction partner did not share a salient characteristic with the excluding group? If increases in mimicry are only observed when an interaction partner shares a salient characteristic with the excluding group, then one could conclude that people may be able to "use" mimicry to re-establish themselves in groups from which they have been excluded.

In the first experiment, participants believed that the other players in the Cyberball game were other participants in the experiment. However, no information was provided about these people. Participants did not meet them (or even think that they were going to meet them), and the experimenter did not provide participants with any information about them. Participants did not even know the sex of the other players, as the initials of the players were the only information that appeared on the computer screen. In addition, effort was taken to ensure that participants thought that their photo description task partner was *not* a member of the group who played Cyberball. Therefore, participants presumably thought that the confederate was someone with whom they may have been able to develop a positive relationship. Their belongingness needs had been threatened by the Cyberball exclusion, and they attempted to affiliate with a later interaction partner who they thought could address that threatened need.

But some people may be better able to address threatened belongingness needs than others. For example, imagine a situation where a female participant is excluded by a group of females. This exclusion should be relatively threatening, since females are an ingroup. After this exclusion experience, the female participant interacts with a new person (i.e., not someone from the actual excluding group). Mimicking this particular person's behaviors may not always be a way to address the female participant's threatened belongingness need. If the new interaction partner is female, mimicry might be one potential way to restore the participant's identity in the group that excluded her; affiliating with the new (female) interaction partner addresses the female participant's need to belong to her ingroup. Significant mimicry should therefore occur. However, if the new interaction partner is male, mimicking his behavior will not help the female participant address her specific threatened belongingness need. Mimicking this (male) person could create liking or rapport more generally, but increased mimicry may be less likely to occur in this situation because it does not resolve the female participant's threatened belongingness need. Essentially, we are arguing that mimicry should occur to a greater extent in a situation where the person who can be mimicked shares a salient characteristic with the person who was excluded *and* with members of the excluding group.

To explore this idea, female participants were recruited to participate in an experiment similar to the visualization and description one described earlier. However, there were several small methodological differences. First, rather than have an inclusion control condition, the control condition in this experiment was a no exclusion condition; participants did not play Cyberball, but did complete the photo description task. Second, the participants who were randomly assigned to be excluded were given sex information about their fellow Cyberball players. In the female exclusion condition, unambiguous female name labels appeared next to the players' icons. In the male exclusion condition, unambiguous male name labels appeared next to the players' icons. Thus, participants were aware of the sex of the people who excluded them. Third, additional questions were added to the questionnaire completed after the Cyberball experience in an attempt to measure perceived threat to the needs proposed by Williams (1997, 2001; see also Williams et al., 2001) in his model of ostracism. Participants rated how much they felt that they had belonged to the group playing Cyberball (belongingness need), the extent to which they thought the other participants valued them as a person (self-esteem need), the extent to which they felt life was meaningful (meaningful existence need), and the extent to which they felt in control of their lives (control need). Finally, during the photo description task, the sex of the confederate with whom participants interacted was manipulated. Thus, this study was a 3 (condition: female exclusion, male exclusion, no exclusion) by 2 (confederate: female, male) design with behavioral mimicry as the primary dependent variable.

We expected that participants who had been excluded by females and interacted with a female confederate would mimic the foot-shaking behavior of the confederate during the photo description task more than participants in any of the other five conditions. Analyses revealed a significant interaction consistent with this prediction. Participants in the female exclusion condition mimicked the female confederate more than the male confederate, but there were no differences between mimicry of the female and male confederates in the male exclusion or control conditions. A planned contrast comparing the female exclusion/female confederate condition to all five of the other conditions was also significant (Lakin, 2003).

Surprisingly, there was less evidence to support the idea that self-esteem, meaningful existence, and control needs were threatened by the exclusion experience. Given that this lack of findings is generally inconsistent with previous research (Williams, 1997, 2001; but see Twenge at al., 2003), this discontinuity will need to be explored further. However, as predicted, there was evidence that threats to belongingness resulted in significant increases in mimicry behavior. Participants in the no exclusion conditions did not complete the belongingness threat item, because it specifically asked about the extent to which people felt that they belonged to the group playing Cyberball. All participants who were excluded reported belongingness threat; participants in both the female and male exclusion conditions scored below the midpoint of the scale. There was also a significant difference between participants in the two exclusion conditions, such that the female participants felt that they belonged to the female exclusion group more than the male exclusion group. This particular pattern was not surprising, because the females were acknowledging that the people who excluded them were members of an ingroup.

We hypothesized that the increase in mimicry in the female exclusion/female confederate condition would be a result of a threat to belongingness needs. This threat could then be addressed through mimicking the behaviors of someone who shares a salient characteristic with the participant and the group that did the excluding (in this case, being female). To explore this question, the correlation between belongingness needs and mimicry in each of the four relevant conditions was computed. Analysis indicated that belongingness needs were a stronger predictor of mimicry in the female exclusion/female confederate condition than in the other three conditions.

In a sense, then, the belongingness question used in this experiment measures both exclusion and ingroup status—participants in the female exclusion condition acknowledge feeling excluded (as do participants in the male exclusion condition), but they also acknowledge that they belong to the female group more than the male group. The correlational data support this interpretation. Participants in the female exclusion/female confederate condition feel excluded, but their belongingness to the female group is related to their mimicry of the female confederate. This is not the case in any of the other conditions. In other words, given that all participants were experiencing belongingness threat from the Cyberball group, the participants who felt that they belonged to the excluding group the most were the participants who were most likely to mimic the behaviors of a confederate sharing that group membership.

CONCLUSION

Exclusion from social groups has negative emotional, psychological, and behavioral consequences. Yet it also seems important to explore the potential positive consequences; perhaps after exclusion, individuals engage in behaviors that help them affiliate with new people or re-establish themselves in the excluding group. The research described here, along with research described elsewhere in this volume, has started to address this issue. Specifically, our research demonstrates an affiliative behavior that occurs after exclusion—nonconscious behavioral mimicry.

Prior research on behavioral mimicry has consistently demonstrated that mimicking the behaviors of others leads to increases in liking and rapport. The studies described here extend this research by demonstrating that mimicry may also be a way to directly address threatened belongingness needs. The implications of the link between exclusion, belongingness needs, and mimicry are profound. The nature of the relationship between these variables suggests that individuals may actually be able to establish themselves in desired groups by mimicking the behaviors of group members or re-establish themselves in groups from which they have been excluded by mimicking the behaviors of representative group members. This suggests that people may be able to regulate group identities through the use of mimicry, which would demonstrate yet another adaptive consequence of effortlessly and unintentionally mimicking the behaviors of others.

The results of these experiments also have implications for exclusion literatures. First, this research demonstrates that people are motivated to engage in affiliative behaviors after having been excluded (see also Williams et al., 2000; Williams & Zadro, this volume). However, given that many negative consequences of exclusion have been demonstrated (Baumeister et al., 2002; Twenge et al., 2001, 2002, 2003), the question as to when exclusion leads to negative behaviors and when it leads to positive behaviors still remains. Several interesting ideas have been proposed. Perhaps the consequences of exclusion have been measured in different ways (Williams, Govan, Case, & Warburton, 2003), or perhaps people's post-exclusion behaviors (either anti- or pro-social) will depend on their subjective probability of being able to directly address their threatened belongingness needs. For example, the mimicry studies reviewed here provided participants with an opportunity to affiliate with a *new* person, someone who knew nothing about the previous exclusion. This may be the type of situation that would lead to active attempts to affiliate (conscious or nonconscious) and recover from the recent rejection. Future research will need to continue to explore this important issue.

Second, this research shows that individuals engage in behaviors (i.e., mimicry) that help them to accomplish the goals of being included in groups and accepted by group members. Importantly, mimicking the behaviors of others is happening automatically, without conscious awareness or intention, and would therefore not be affected by self-regulation failures known to occur after exclusion (Baumeister & DeWall, this volume). Individuals who were able to effortlessly maintain relationships with others may have been more evolutionarily successful at accomplishing *all* of their survival objectives, and this functionality may be what led to behavioral mimicry becoming automatized (Bargh, 1990). The very fact that an affiliative behavior like mimicry is automatic suggests the fundamental nature of the need to be included and avoid being excluded.

REFERENCES

Aronson, E. (1999). *The social animal.* (8th ed.). New York: W. H. Freeman and Company.

Bargh, J. A. (1990). Auto-motives: Preconscious determinants of social interaction. In E. Higgins & R. Sorrentino (Eds.), *Handbook of motivation and cognition: Vol. 2* (pp. 93–130). New York: Guilford Press.

Bargh, J. A., & Chartrand, T. L. (2000). The mind in the middle: A practical guide to priming and automaticity research. In H. T. Reis & C. M. Judd (Eds.), *Handbook of research methods in social and personality psychology* (pp. 253–285). New York: Cambridge University Press.

Baumeister, R. F., & Leary, M. R. (1995). The need to belong: Desire for interpersonal attachments as a fundamental human motive. *Psychological Bulletin, 117*, 497–529.

Baumeister, R. F., & Tice, D. M. (1990). Anxiety and social exclusion. *Journal of Social and Clinical Psychology, 9*, 165–195.

Baumeister, R. F., Twenge, J. M., & Nuss, C. K. (2002). Effects of social exclusion on cognitive processes: Anticipated aloneness reduces intelligent thought. *Journal of Personality and Social Psychology, 83*, 817–827.

Bavelas, J. B., Black, A., Chovil, N., Lemery, C. R., & Mullett, J. (1988). Form and function in motor mimicry: Topographic evidence that the primary function is communication. *Human Communication Research, 14*, 275–299.

Bavelas, J. B., Black, A., Lemery, C. R., & Mullett, J. (1986). "I show how you feel": Motor mimicry as a communicative act. *Journal of Personality and Social Psychology, 50*, 322–329.

Bernieri, F. J. (1988). Coordinated movement and rapport in teacher-student interactions. *Journal of Nonverbal Behavior, 12*, 120–138.

Bernieri, F. J., Reznick, J. S., & Rosenthal, R. (1988). Synchrony, pseudosynchrony, and dissynchrony: Measuring the entertainment process in mother-infant interactions. *Journal of Personality and Social Psychology, 54*, 243–253.

Bourgeois, K. S., & Leary, M. R. (2001). Coping with rejection: Derogating those who choose us last. *Motivation and Emotion, 25*, 101–111.

Brewer, M. B. (1997). On the social origins of human nature. In C. McGarty & S. A. Haslam (Eds.), *The message of social psychology: Perspectives on mind in society* (pp. 54–62). Cambridge, MA: Blackwell Publishers.

Buss, D. M., & Kenrick, D. T. (1998). Evolutionary social psychology. In D. T. Gilbert, S. T. Fiske, & G. Lindzey (Eds.), *The handbook of social psychology* (4th ed., pp. 982–1026). New York: Oxford University Press.

Byrne, D. (1971). *The attraction paradigm.* New York: Academic Press.

Caporael, L. R. (1997). The evolution of truly social cognition: The core configurations model. *Personality and Social Psychology Bulletin, 23*, 276–298.

Caporael, L. R. (2001a). Evolutionary psychology: Toward a unifying theory and a hybrid science. *Annual Review of Psychology, 52*, 607–628.

Caporael, L. R. (2001b). Parts and wholes: The evolutionary importance of groups. In C. Sedikides & M. B. Brewer (Eds.), *Individual self, relational self, collective self* (pp. 241–258). Philadelphia: Psychology Press.

Caporael, L. R., & Brewer, M. B. (1991). Reviving evolutionary psychology: Biology meets society. *Journal of Social Issues, 47*, 187–195.

Charney, E. J. (1966). Psychosomatic manifestations of rapport in psychotherapy. *Psychosomatic Medicine, 28*, 305–315.

Chartrand, T. L. & Bargh, J. A. (1999). The chameleon effect: The perception-behavior link and social interaction. *Journal of Personality and Social Psychology, 76*, 893–910.

Chartrand, T. L., & Jefferis, V. E. (2003). Consequences of automatic goal pursuit and the case of nonconscious mimicry. In J. P. Forgas, K. D. Williams, & W. von Hippel (Eds.), *Responding to the social world: Implicit and explicit processes in social judgments and decisions* (pp. 290–305). Philadelphia: Psychology Press.

Chartrand, T. L., Maddux, W. W., & Lakin, J. L. (2005). Beyond the perception-behavior link: The ubiquitous utility and motivational moderators of nonconscious mimicry. In R. R. Hassin, J. S. Uleman, & J. A. Bargh (Eds.), *The new unconscious* (pp. 344–361). New York: Oxford University Press.

Dabbs, J. M. (1969). Similarity of gestures and interpersonal influence. *Proceedings of the 77th Annual Convention of the American Psychological Association, 4*, 337–338.

de Waal, F. (1989). *Peacemaking among primates.* Cambridge, MA: Harvard University Press.

Dijksterhuis, A. (2001). Automatic social influence:

The perception-behavior link as an explanatory mechanism for behavior matching. In J. P. Forgas & K. D. Williams (Eds.), *Social influence: Direct and indirect processes* (pp. 95–108). Philadelphia: Psychology Press.

Dijksterhuis, A. & Bargh, J. A. (2001). The perception-behavior expressway: Automatic effects of social perception on social behavior. In M. Zanna (Ed.), *Advances in Experimental Social Psychology* (pp. 1–40). San Diego, CA: Academic Press.

Dijksterhuis, A., Bargh, J. A., & Miedema, J. (2000). Of men and mackerels: Attention, subjective experience, and automatic social behavior. In H. Bless & J. P. Forgas (Eds.), *The message within: The role of subjective experience in social cognition and behavior* (pp. 37–51). Philadelphia: Psychology Press.

Ehrlich, P. R. (2000). *Human natures: Genes, cultures, and the human prospect.* Washington, DC: Island Press.

Eisenberger, N. I., Lieberman, M. D., & Williams, K. W. (2003). Does rejection hurt? An fMRI study of social exclusion. *Science, 302*, 290–292.

Gardner, W. L., Pickett, C. L., & Brewer. M. B. (2000). Social exclusion and selective memory: How the need to belong influences memory for social events. *Personality and Social Psychology Bulletin, 26*, 486–496.

Hatfield, E., Cacioppo, J. T., & Rapson, R. L. (1994). *Emotional contagion.* Cambridge: Cambridge University Press.

James, W. (1890). *Principles of psychology.* New York: Holt.

Johanson, D., & Edgar, B. (1996). *From Lucy to language.* New York: Simon & Schuster Editions.

La France, M. (1979). Nonverbal synchrony and rapport: Analysis by the cross-lag panel technique. *Social Psychology Quarterly, 42*, 66–70.

La France, M. (1982). Posture mirroring and rapport. In M. Davis (Ed.), *Interaction rhythms: Periodicity in communicative behavior* (pp. 279–298). New York: Human Sciences Press.

La France, M. & Broadbent, M. (1976). Group rapport: Posture sharing as a nonverbal indicator. *Group and Organization Studies, 1*, 328–333.

Lakin, J. L. (2003). *Exclusion and nonconscious behavioral mimicry: The role of belongingness threat.* Unpublished doctoral dissertation, The Ohio State University.

Lakin, J. L., & Chartrand, T. L. (2003). Using nonconscious behavioral mimicry to create affiliation and rapport. *Psychological Science, 14*, 334–339.

Lakin, J. L., Chartrand, T. L., & Arkin, R. M. (2005). *I am too just like you: Nonconscious mimicry as a behavioral response to social exclusion.* Manuscript submitted for publication.

Lakin, J. L., Jefferis, V. E., Cheng, C. M., & Chartrand, T. L. (2003). The Chameleon Effect as social glue: Evidence for the evolutionary significance of nonconscious mimicry. *Journal of Nonverbal Behavior, 27*, 145–162.

Leary, M. R. (1990). Responses to social exclusion: Social anxiety, jealousy, loneliness, depression, and low self-esteem. *Journal of Social and Clinical Psychology, 9*, 221–229.

Leary, M. R. (Ed.). (2001). *Interpersonal rejection.* New York: Oxford University Press.

Leary, M. R., & Baumeister, R. F. (2000). The nature and function of self-esteem: Sociometer theory. In M. Zanna (Ed.), *Advances in Experimental Social Psychology: Vol. 32* (pp. 1–62). San Diego, CA: Academic Press.

Leary, M. R., Cottrell, C. A., & Phillips, M. (2001). Deconfounding the effects of dominance and social acceptance on self-esteem. *Journal of Personality and Social Psychology, 81*, 898–909.

Leary, M. R., & MacDonald, G. (2003, February). Emotional reactions to interpersonal rejection: Why do hurt feelings hurt? In S. T. Fiske (Chair), *Rejection makes me feel bad, but also mad, sad, or had? Varieties of response to ostracism, exclusion, and negativity.* Symposium conducted at the meeting of the Society for Personality and Social Psychology, Los Angeles, CA.

Leary, M. R., Tambor, E. S., Terdal, S. K., & Downs, D. L. (1995). Self-esteem as an interpersonal monitor: The sociometer hypothesis. *Journal of Personality and Social Psychology, 68*, 518–530.

Lewin, R. (1993). *Human evolution: An illustrated introduction* (3rd ed.). Boston: Blackwell Scientific Publications.

Maurer, R. E., & Tindall, J. H. (1983). Effect of postural congruence on client's perception of counselor empathy. *Journal of Counseling Psychology, 30*, 158–163.

Pickett, C. L., Gardner, W. L., & Knowles, M. (2004). Getting a cue: The need to belong and enhanced sensitivity to social cues. *Personality and Social Psychology Bulletin, 30*, 1095–1107.

Poirier, F. E. & McKee, J. K. (1999). *Understanding human evolution* (4th ed.). Upper Saddle River, NJ: Prentice Hall.

Scheflen, A. E. (1964). The significance of posture in communication systems. *Psychiatry, 27,* 316–331.

Sommer, K. L., Williams, K. D., Ciarocco, N. J., & Baumeister, R. F. (2001). When silence speaks louder than words: Explorations into the intrapsychic and interpersonal consequences of social ostracism. *Basic and Applied Social Psychology, 23,* 225–243.

Tickle-Degnen, L., & Rosenthal, R. (1987). Group rapport and nonverbal behavior. *Review of Personality and Social Psychology, 9,* 113–136.

Twenge, J. M., Baumeister, R. F., Tice, D. M., & Stucke, T. S. (2001). Social exclusion causes self-defeating behavior. *Journal of Personality and Social Psychology, 83,* 606–615.

Twenge, J. M., Catanese, K. R., & Baumeister, R. F. (2002). If you can't join them, beat them: Effects of social exclusion on aggressive behavior. *Journal of Personality and Social Psychology, 81,* 1058–1069.

Twenge, J. M., Catanese, K. R., & Baumeister, R. F. (2003). Social exclusion and the deconstructed state: Time perception, meaninglessness, lethargy, lack of emotion, and self-awareness.

Journal of Personality and Social Psychology, 85, 409–423.

Williams, K. D. (1997). Social ostracism. In R. Kowalski (Ed.), *Aversive interpersonal behaviors* (pp.133–170). New York: Plenum Press.

Williams, K. D. (2001). *Ostracism: The power of silence.* New York: Guilford Press.

Williams, K. D., Cheung, C. K. T., & Choi, W. (2000). Cyberostracism: Effects of being ignored over the Internet. *Journal of Personality & Social Psychology, 79,* 748–762.

Williams, K. D., Govan, C. L., Case, T. I., & Warburton, W. (2003, February). When does ostracism lead to aggression? In S. T. Fiske (Chair), *Rejection makes me feel bad, but also mad, sad, or bad? Varieties of response to ostracism, exclusion, and negativity.* Symposium conducted at the meeting of the Society for Personality and Social Psychology, Los Angeles, CA.

Williams, K. D., Shore, W. J., & Grahe, J. E. (1998). The silent treatment: Perceptions of its behaviors and associated feelings. *Group Processes and Intergroup Relations, 1,* 117–141.

Williams, K. D., & Sommer, K. L. (1997). Social ostracism by coworkers: Does rejection lead to loafing or compensation? *Personality and Social Psychology Bulletin, 23,* 693–706.

18

The Effect of Rejection on Anti-Social Behaviors

Social Exclusion Produces Aggressive Behaviors

KATHLEEN R. CATANESE
DIANNE M. TICE

Manipulating Belongingness in the Laboratory
Social Exclusion Causes Aggressive Behavior
Future Work
Conclusion

Belongingness is an innate and fundamental human motivation that pervades human behavior (Baumeister & Leary, 1995). As social and cultural animals, we evolved to live in small groups and to rely on others to help us meet our basic biological needs (Baumeister, this volume). Being rejected by one's group may have been tantamount to death throughout most of history and prehistory. Proto-humans who evolved a strong need to belong probably survived better than similar creatures without this motivation, because is would have been very difficult to meet basic needs for food and shelter without the help of other group members (see Leary, this volume).

The need to belong is reflected in the universal human desire for frequent, pleasant, and reciprocal interpersonal attachments (Williams & Zadro, this volume). A fulfilled need to belong may be essential for achieving intrapersonal and interpersonal well-being (Gardner, Knowles, & Pickett, this volume; Pickett

The authors gratefully acknowledge support by grant MH65559 from the National Institutes of Health. Address correspondence to: Dianne Tice, Department of Psychology, Florida State University, Tallahassee, FL 32306-1270. E-mail: tice@psy.fsu.edu

& Gardner, this volume). In contrast, Baumeister and Leary (1995) predict that thwarting the need to belong should have serious negative consequences for the self. In other words, loneliness and rejection will have severe negative effects on people (see Cacioppo, Hawkly, & Berntson, this volume; Eisenberger & Lieberman, this volume; MacDonald, Kingsbury, & Shaw, this volume). This chapter focuses on the interpersonal consequences of feeling rejected and excluded, specifically on aggressive behavior that occurs as a result of having one's need to belong thwarted.

Correlational research supports the contention that an unfulfilled need to belong is associated with negative consequences in other domains. Lonely, disconnected, or single people suffer from more mental illness (Baumeister & Leary, 1995) and have higher rates of mortality for nearly all physical diseases (Lynch, 1979). In addition, people who are socially alienated (Durkheim, 1897/1963) or have recently experienced a broken relationship (Baumeister, 1990; Hendin, 1982) are more likely to commit suicide. This correlational research supports the idea that social exclusion is associated with negative intrapersonal consequences.

Not only is belongingness related to intrapersonal impairments, but it also seems related to negative consequences for *others* as well as society at large (see Gaertner & Iuzzini, this volume). Interpersonal violence seems to be correlated with measures of social integration. For instance, at the societal level, violent crime rates are associated with marital status. Single men and recently divorced men are most likely to commit violent crimes (Sampson & Laub, 1990, 1993, cf. Wright & Wright, 1992). Homicide rates are also correlated with marriage and divorce rates (Lester, 1994).

At a more individual level, violent young men often report feeling alienated from their families and peer groups (Garbarino, 1999). Rejected children are more disruptive and aggressive against other children (Newcomb, Bukowski, & Pattee, 1993) and bullies also seem to be socially alienated (Coie, 1990). Juvonen and Gross (this volume) summarize the findings from developmental psychology on bullies and social outcasts and conclude that rejection is a potent predictor of long-term maladaptive adjustment. Recent killings in U.S. schools were committed by frustrated and rejected adolescent men (Gaertner & Iuzzini, this volume). This violence seems to be rooted in social alienation. Indeed, Leary, Kowalski, Smith, and Phillips (2003) conducted case studies on 15 school shooters and concluded that extreme and chronic rejection precipitated all but two of these violent outbursts.

In order to supplement the correlational research described above and to examine issues of causality, we conducted a series of experiments to test whether rejection does indeed lead to aggression (Twenge, Baumeister, Tice, & Stucke, 2001). Our general hypothesis was that rejection and social exclusion would cause people to act out aggressively. In short, we have found that across manipulations and dependent measures, rejection and social exclusion caused aggressive behavior. The purpose of this chapter is to summarize the research that we have uncovered about the effects of rejection on aggressive tendencies.

MANIPULATING BELONGINGNESS IN THE LABORATORY

Our laboratory has used two main manipulations of belongingness when study-ing the effect of rejection on aggressive behaviors. These manipulations were also used by Baumeister and DeWall (this volume) and Twenge (this volume) so we will just describe them briefly here. One manipulation, which we call "future belongingness," relies on a future prediction of participants' relationship status. Participants are told that the strength of their future relationships is predicted by their score on a personality measure, and then they are randomly assigned to feedback that they are likely or unlikely to have numerous and satisfying relation-ships throughout their lives. Another manipulation of belongingness can be called the "group belongingness" manipulation. In this manipulation, newly acquainted participants are privately asked to select partners for a subsequent task. Belong-ingness is manipulated by leading participants to believe that everyone wanted to work with them or that no one wanted to work with them on the subsequent task. The use of both of these types of manipulations draws on both distal and proximal experiences of belongingness.

In the future belongingness rejection manipulation, individual participants complete a personality inventory and are given accurate feedback on their extra-version score on the inventory. Participants are told whether they are an introvert or an extrovert. The experimenter uses this accurate feedback to create credibility for a randomly assigned future prediction that follows. Participants are randomly assigned to one of three possible predictions for their future based on their extra-version score. Participants in the "Future Alone" condition are told that they will end up alone later on in life. They are told: "You're the type who will end up alone later in life. You may have friends and relationships now, but by mid-20s most of these will have drifted away. You may even marry or have several marriages, but these are likely to be short-lived and not continue into your 30s. Relationships don't last, and when you're past the age where people are constantly forming new relationships, the odds are you'll end up being alone more and more." Participants in the "Future Belong" condition are told just the opposite. They are told, "You're the type who has rewarding relationships throughout life. You're likely to have a long and stable marriage and have friendships that will last into your later years. The odds are that you'll always have friends and people who care about you." A control condition is also included to control for the negativity of the feedback in the condition where participants hear that their belongingness needs are unlikely to be met. In order to control for the negativity of this feedback, a similarly negative feedback condition informs participants that they are likely to suffer a variety of physical misfortunes, but does not mention anything about belonging-ness or relationships. The "Misfortune Control" condition is told that, "You're likely to be accident prone later in life—you might break an arm or a leg a few times, or maybe be injured in car accidents. Even if you haven't been accident prone before, these things will show up later in life, and the odds are you will have a lot of accidents." The misfortune control condition helps to eliminate the alternative explanation that any observed effects due to the rejection manipulation may be accounted for by general misfortune or the negative emotional impact of misfortune and not a failure to meet belongingness needs per se. A "No Feedback Control" condition may also accompany this design. Thus, participants are led to believe that their future relationships will be marked by closeness and belongingness, failed or absent relationships and loneliness, or misfortune that is unrelated to their relationships.

The group belongingness manipulation creates a situation in which participants believe that they have been directly rejected by their peers. This manipulation was developed as a variation on procedures used by Leary et al. (1995) and Nezlek et al. (1997). Participants are brought together in the laboratory in unacquainted and single-sex groups. They are left alone as a group to get to know one another by answering questions to induce relationship closeness (adapted from Sedikides, Campbell, Reeder, & Elliot, 1999). When the experimenter returns, participants are separated into individual rooms and asked to choose two people that they would like to work with on another task. They are specifically told to choose people who they "like and respect." The experimenter collects their choices and indicates that he or she will return later with the group assignments.

Participants are randomly assigned to be accepted or rejected by their newly acquainted peer group. The experimenter returns and tells accepted participants that everyone chose them as someone they wanted to work with. In contrast, the rejected participants are told that no one chose them as someone they wanted to work with on the next task. Both conditions are told that because of this unique outcome, the groups could not be worked out as usual, so the participant would have to do the next task alone. Although all participants complete the next task alone, the crucial difference is that some will do so believing that they were well liked and popular in the group, and others will do so believing that they were disliked and personally excluded from the group.

These laboratory manipulations are particularly powerful due to their strong ecological validity. They mirror people's real life experiences of rejection. This is especially true for the undergraduate population that has primarily been the focus of study in these experiments. Many college students ponder what their careers and relationships will be like after graduation. The future belongingness manipulation reflects the common fear that one should find oneself alone in the unknown future. The group belongingness manipulation represents direct rejection by one's peers. This type of rejection mirrors the real life acceptance and rejection that is often the result of choosing teams or groups. Nearly everyone has experienced such a situation at some time in life.

Although these manipulations reflect slightly different types of interpersonal rejection, we predicted that they would have similar effects on aggressive behaviors. Specifically, we predicted that impaired future belongingness as well as immediate rejection by a group of peers would unleash aggressive tendencies among the rejected individuals (Twenge, Baumeister, Tice, & Stucke, 2001). In the series of studies described, we gave participants the opportunity to aggress against other people after they had been exposed to these manipulations. We measured aggression both indirectly and directly. In one study, we measured the extent to which participants would negatively evaluate another person. This type of evaluation would thereby damage the target's chance of career advancement. In another study, we measured participants' choice to administer an obnoxious and painful blast of noise to another person. We predicted that compared to accepted and control participants, rejected participants would evaluate others more injuriously and harshly and that they would also be more likely to afflict aversive noise on others.

SOCIAL EXCLUSION CAUSES AGGRESSIVE BEHAVIOR

In the first experiment, we hypothesized that a future prediction of loneliness and failed relationships would lead to negative and damaging evaluations of another person. In this study, pairs of strangers were brought together in the laboratory and then separated. Each participant completed a questionnaire that they were told was a good measure of their personality type. After completing the personality questionnaire, the experimenter asked each participant to write an essay taking sides for his or her opinion on abortion. While they wrote this essay, the experimenter ostensibly scored the personality questionnaire.

The experimenter then swapped the participants' essays so that each participant could evaluate the others' essay. In actuality, all participants received a standard essay that professed the opinion opposite their own regarding abortion. In this way, participants were led to believe that the other participant, the person who was to review their own essay, was dissimilar. After evaluating the other person's essay, participants received the future belongingness manipulation. Participants were randomly assigned to hear a future prediction of strong and happy relationships, loneliness and failed relationships, a future marred by accidents (but unrelated to relationships), or no information at all.

After receiving the manipulation, the experimenter returned each participant's essay, purportedly evaluated by the other participant. In reality, most participants received a standard evaluation of their essay with a poor score and including a handwritten comment, "One of the worst essays that I have ever read!" A positive control condition consisted of participants who received no feedback about their future relationships and a positive evaluation of their essay. These participants received a standard evaluation of their essay with an excellent score and including a handwritten comment, "A very good essay!"

Our measure of aggression consisted of a personal evaluation of the person who presumably scored the participant's essay. Participants were told that their partner had applied to work in the psychology department as a research assistant. The experimenter explained that this was a highly competitive position, and requested that the participant evaluate the applicant to assist in the hiring process. Thus, the participants were being asked to evaluate the person who had just insulted their essays or praised their essays.

Results indicated that social rejection led to harsher, more critical evaluations of the offending partners. Compared to the other conditions, rejected participants gave the most negative evaluations of their offending partners. In contrast, the positive control condition resulted in highly favorable evaluations. Among the participants who all received an identical negative provocation, those who had received the provocation and the predication for a lonely future were the most aggressive. Even after receiving the same provocation, people who had received accepting and accident-prone predictions for their futures were significantly less aggressive than rejected people. In addition, the aggressive effects of being rejected went beyond those of just being provoked. A second experiment replicating these conditions confirmed that it is rejection paired with provocation that elicits the greatest degree of aggression, surpassing the degree of aggression elicited by provocation alone. In other words, rejection intensifies the aggressive response that typically follows a provocation.

These studies demonstrate that rejection has the capacity to trigger aggressive responses when rejected individuals have been provoked. Compared to the aggression that results from mere provocation, people who have been rejected and provoked retaliate even more severely. But will rejection always invoke aggression? These two studies show that rejection causes aggression directed at someone who has insulted or provoked them, but will rejected people direct aggression toward someone who has not provoked them?

Our third study was designed to determine whether provocation was necessary for producing aggression in rejected people. In effect, we were interested in testing whether rejected people would also be aggressive toward someone who was friendly and pleasant. We were primarily concerned with whether rejection would incite aggression against a partner who praised instead of insulted participants.

The third experiment was very similar to the first two. The crucial difference was that most participants received a glowing, flattering review of their essay rather than a disparaging, insulting evaluation. These participants received an evaluated essay with high scores and a handwritten comment that read, "A very good essay!" We also included a condition in which rejected individuals received an insulting evaluation in order to directly compare the effects of social exclusion on aggression for rejected participants who had been praised and rejected participants who had been insulted. We also included a measure of mood to determine whether mood differences might account for the results.

The question posed by experiment three was: Would rejection incite aggression for people who had been praised rather than insulted? The results of the study clearly indicated that it did not. Rejected participants who had their essays praised did not aggress against their partners, but rejected participants who had their essays insulted did aggress in the form of giving very negative evaluations to the partners. The praise and flattery appeared to diminish aggression following rejection. Participants who had been rejected did not displace aggression toward someone who had not provoked them. In fact, the partner evaluations for the research assistant position were indistinguishable between future belongingness conditions when the partner praised the participant. Although rejected and subsequently praised participants were not aggressive toward their partners, we replicated the finding fro the first two studies that rejected individuals provided critical and negative evaluations of their partner after being insulted on their essay. The further replication of this finding as well as the finding that praise wipes out the aggressive consequences of rejection supports the idea that rejection exacerbates aggression following a provocation. Aggression that might result from exclusion does not, however, persist following praise. These results imply that people who are rejected seem to retaliate against those who have insulted or harmed them. In contrast, they are not vindictive toward people who are nice, friendly, and amicable toward them.

But how generalizable is the finding that people who have been forecast a future of failed relationships and loneliness will negatively evaluate those who have provoked them? Is writing a negative evaluation preventing someone from being hired the same as inflicting physical violence on someone? Our final studies were conducted to provide a more proximal and concrete test of the hypothesis that rejection incites aggression. Specifically, we wanted to observe more realistic aggressive responses to a laboratory manipulation that more directly mimicked real life peer rejection.

Our fourth study used the group belongingness manipulation in which participants were told that everyone or no one wanted to work with them on another task. This belongingness manipulation was followed by the opportunity to physically aggress against another participant by administering painful blasts of noise through headphones (Bushman & Baumeister, 1998). Participants believed that they were competing in a reaction time task online with a participant located in another room. If their partner lost the competition, they could punish the partner by varying the noise intensity and duration that the loser would receive through headphones. In actuality, the game was rigged such that participants were actually playing against the computer and not a human participant.

Importantly, participants were led to believe that their opponent was not a member of the group that rejected them. In other words, the opponent had not rejected or accepted the participant earlier as the other group members unanimously had done. Participants thought they were playing the game with a new person—someone who was involved in another, unrelated experiment. Before the noise-blasting reaction time game, participants received a provocation from their opponent. Again, the provocation was a negative evaluation by the opponent of the participant's essay on abortion.

The results of this study provided further confirmation that rejection intensifies aggression following a provocation. Rejected participants blasted their opponents with longer and more intense stressful noise than accepted participants after being provoked. In particular, rejected people will aggress against someone who has provoked them, even when this person was in no way involved in rejecting them. Using a different manipulation of rejection and a different measure of aggression, the results are the same: Rejected people become aggressive when they have been provoked. Rejection intensifies aggression following provocation.

The results of these four studies provide strong evidence that rejection does indeed exacerbate aggressive responses to provocation. In particular, our studies indicated that social exclusion motivates aggression toward someone who insults but not who praises the rejected person. Rejected people become more aggressive toward people who insult and disparage them, but not toward people who praise and flatter them. But what about a neutral person? Will rejected people displace aggression toward such innocent bystanders? Would rejected people aggress against someone who did not reject them but who also did not provoke them? In a final study, we wanted to test whether a neutral target would also be the victim of hostility following social exclusion.

The design of the fifth study was identical to that of the fourth. As in the fourth study, we used the group belongingness manipulation followed by the noise-competition task. Again, the participant's opponent was a new stranger, one who had not been part of the group that accepted or rejected the participant earlier. Participants again believed that they were competing against someone who was from another, unrelated experiment. Thus, their ostensible opponent had not been involved in the group's choice to accept or reject the participant. The crucial change in this experiment was that there was no provocation or insult. Not only was the opponent uninvolved in the participants' rejection, but the opponent also provided no insult to fuel the flame of any aggressive response that might follow rejection. Would rejection alone be enough to cause participants to aggress against a completely innocent and neutral person? Indeed, it was. Compared to accepted participants, rejected participants punished an innocent, neutral individual with blasts of noise that were significantly more intense and twice as lengthy. Thus, although rejected people are not aggressive to people who are specifically nice to them (Study 3), they are aggressive to neutral, innocent bystanders whom they just happen to come across after being rejected (Study 5).

FUTURE WORK

We are just now beginning to conduct work on the psychophysiology of rejection. In collaboration with Ginette Blackhart, we are starting to examine the effects of social exclusion on salivary cortisol levels. Because salivary cortisol tends to increase with distress, we expected to find higher levels of cortisol in excluded participants than in included participants. Although we have not confirmed our hypotheses, we are continuing to collect data to address the issue of distress following exclusion.

CONCLUSION

The five studies described in this chapter attempt to demonstrated that rejection causes aggressive behaviors. Our findings are consistent with most of the chapters in this volume that have examined the effects of rejection and exclusion on aggression (see, for example, Baumeister & DeWall; Downey & Romero; Gaertner & Iuzzini; Juvonen & Gross; Sommer & Rubin; Twenge; all this volume) In a series of studies conducted using both the future belongingness manipulation and the group belongingness manipulation reported in this chapter, converging evidence strongly affirms that rejection produces and intensifies aggression. Rejected and excluded people wrote damaging and critical evaluations of someone who had insulted their essay writing skills (Study 1 and 2) but were kind toward someone who flattered them (Study 3). Peer-based rejection also caused people to afflict another with stressful blasts of noise when provoked (Study 4). Finally, rejected people aggressed against entirely innocent bystanders—people who neither rejected nor provoked them. (Study 5).

The effects of rejection on aggressive behavior were not due to general misfortune. Our misfortune control conditions were no more aggressive than other conditions. Instead, these results were directly related to impaired relationships. It was impaired relationships, not simply misfortunate life circumstances, that caused people to become aggressive.

These results occurred independent of emotional distress or bad mood. Participants who had been rejected rarely reported experiencing mood any more negative than participants in other conditions. Importantly, emotion failed to mediate any of the results of these five studies. This is consistent with the findings reported by Twenge (this volume) that emotion does not mediate the link between rejection and aggression. The results are consistent with the suggestion that rejection leads to a breakdown in self-regulation, as spelled out by Baumeister and DeWall (this volume).

The experience of social exclusion makes people hostile and aggressive. Rejection intensifies the typical aggressive responses following provocation, but it also instigates aggressive responses in the absence of any provocation. When people are alienated and excluded from the social community the results are harmful, not only to those individuals but to the community at large.

REFERENCES

Baumeister, R. F. (1990). Suicide as escape from self. *Psychological Review, 97,* 90–113.

Baumeister, R. F., & Leary, M. R. (1995). The need to belong: Desire for interpersonal attachments as a fundamental human motivation. *Psychological Bulletin, 117,* 497–529.

Bushman, B. J., & Baumeister, R. F. (1998). Threatened egotism, narcissism, self-esteem, and direct and displaced aggression: Does self-love or self-hate lead to violence? *Journal of Personality and Social Psychology, 75,* 219–229.

Coie, J. D. (1990). Toward a theory of peer

rejection. In S. R. Asher & J. D. Coie (Eds.), *Peer rejection in childhood* (pp. 365–401). New York: Cambridge University Press.

Durkheim, E. (1963). *Suicide.* New York: Free Press. (Original work published 1897).

Garbarino, J. (1999). *Lost boys: Why our sons turn violent and how we can save them.* San Francisco: Jossey-Bass.

Hendin, H. (1982). *Suicide in America.* New York: Norton.

Leary, M. R., Tambor, E. S., Terdal, S. K., & Downs, D. L. (1995). Self-esteem as an interpersonal monitor: The sociometer hypothesis. *Journal of Personality and Social Psychology, 68,* 518–530.

Leary, M. R., Kowalski, R. M., Smith, L., Phillips, S. (2003). Teasing, rejection, and violence: Case studies of the school shootings. *Aggressive Behavior, 29,* 202–214.

Lester, D. (1994). Time-series analysis of the murder and homicide rates in the USA. *Perceptual and Motor Skills, 79,* 862.

Lynch, J. J. (1979). *The broken heart: The medical consequences of loneliness.* New York: Basic Books.

Newcomb, A. F., Bukowski, W. M., & Pattee, L. (1993). Children's peer relations: A meta-analytic review of popular, rejected, neglected, controversial, and average sociometric status. *Psychological Bulletin, 113,.* 99–128.

Nezlek, J. B., Kowalski, R. M., Leary, M. R., Blevins, T., & Holgate, S. (1997). Personality moderators of reactions to interpersonal rejection: Depression and trait self-esteem. *Personality and Social Psychology Bulletin, 23,* 1235–1244.

Sampson, R. J., & Laub, J. H. (1990). Crime and deviance over the life course: The salience of adult social bonds. *American Sociological Review, 55,* 609–627.

Sampson, R. J., & Laub, J. H. (1993). *Crime in the making: Pathways and turning points through life.* Cambridge: Harvard University Press.

Sedikides, C., Campbell, W. K., Reeder, G. D., & Elliot, A. J. (1999). The relationship closeness induction task. *Representative Research in Social Psychology, 23,* 1–4.

Twenge, J. M., Baumeister, R. F., Tice, D. M., & Stucke, T. S. (2001). If you can't join them, beat them: The effects of social exclusion on aggressive behavior. *Journal of Personality and Social Psychology, 81,* 1058–1069.

Wright, K. N., & Wright, K. E. (1992). Does getting married reduce the likelihood of criminality? A review of the literature. *Federal Probation, 56,* 50–56.

19

Rejection and Entitativity

A Synergistic Model of Mass Violence

LOWELL GAERTNER
JONATHAN IUZZINI

This edited volume peers into a distressing dimension of human experience and examines the cognitive, emotional, behavioral, and explicitly social dynamics of exclusion. Humans as gregarious beings have a fundamental need to belong (Baumeister & Leary, 1995). Involuntary termination of relationships, severing of social networks, and banishment from social circles is detrimental to multiple domains of self-functioning, such as self-esteem, mood, perceived control, and a meaningful existence (Leary, Tambor, Terdal, & Downs, 1995; Leary, Haupt, Strausser, & Chokel, 1998; Williams, Cheung, & Choi, 2000; Williams et al., 2002; Williams & Zadro, this volume). Registering in the same neural regions as does physical injury, social rejection quite literally is painful (Eisenberger, Lieberman, & Williams, 2003; Eisenberger & Lieberman, this volume; MacDonald & Shaw, this volume). Our contribution to this volume examines rejection as a component of a synergistic process that instigates aggression against multiple persons (i.e., mass violence).

Address correspondence to: Lowell Gaertner, Department of Psychology, University of Tennessee, Knoxville, TN 37996-0900, USA. E-mail: gaertner@utk.edu

THE SCHOOL SHOOTINGS:
A PROCESS IMPLIED IN A DICHOTOMY

That aggression is associated with exclusionary status is a frequently documented and longstanding finding in the peer-relations literature (for reviews see Coie, Dodge, & Kupersmidt, 1990; Juvonen & Gross, this volume; for a meta-analytic integration see Newcomb, Bukowski, & Pattee, 1993). However, the correlational methodology of the externally valid peer-relations literature does not indicate conclusively whether peers are rejected because of their aggressive tendencies (e.g., Dodge, 1983) or whether rejection stimulates violence and begets aggression (e.g., DeRosier, Kupersmidt, & Patterson, 1994).

Recent controlled experiments that manipulated social rejection indicate that rejection does indeed spawn aggression (Catanese & Tice, this volume; Twenge, Baumeister, Tice, & Stucke, 2001). Those experiments included multiple manipulations of rejection and multiple measures of aggression. Some experiments, for example, manipulated expectations for chronic rejection (e.g., "you're the type of person who has rewarding relationships throughout life" vs. "...will end up alone later in life") and measured non-physical aggression (e.g., issuing a damaging job evaluation; Twenge et al., 2001, Experiments 1–3). Other experiments manipulated acute rejection (e.g., "no one chose you..." vs. "everyone chose you as someone they wanted to work with") and measured physical aggression (e.g., exposing a fellow participant to aversive noise; Twenge et al., Experiments 4 and 5). In each instance, rejected persons behaved more aggressively than did accepted persons. Furthermore, the database of controlled experiments identifying rejection as an antecedent of aggression is arguably more expansive if the insults, shocks, and frustrations received by participants in the early aggression experiments are construed as acts of rejection (e.g., Buss, 1961; Mallick & McCandless, 1966).

Our interest in social rejection was aroused by the wave of school shootings in North America and Europe, of which there have been in excess of 30 beginning in the mid 1990's. Consistent with the empirical literature, case studies indicated that in 13 of the 15 studied incidents the perpetrators previously experienced chronic or acute social rejection (Leary, Kowalski, Smith, & Phillips, 2003). However, it is not the consistency with the empirical literature that captured our attention. Despite the common element of rejection, the school shootings were not of the same form. In some shootings, the perpetrator attacked a single individual. On February 29, 2000, for example, a first-grader in Michigan shot and killed a classmate who teased him the previous day. In other shootings, the perpetrator attacked multiple persons. Perhaps the most publicized example is the April 20, 1999 shootings at Columbine High School in which Eric Harris and Dylan Klebold killed 12 students and a teacher. Similarly, on March 24, 1998, Andrew Golden and Mitchell Johnson hid in the woods near their Arkansas middle school and shot classmates exiting the building, killing 5 students and wounding 11. Furthermore, these multiple-victim incidents did not invariably involve multiple perpetrators. On May 21, 1998, for example, Kipland Kinkel shot at 400 students in the cafeteria of his Oregon high school, killing 2 students and wounding 22. Likewise, Robert Steinhäuser returned with 500 rounds of ammunition on April 26, 2002 to the high school from which he had been expelled in Germany and killed 13 teachers, 2 students, and 1 police officer.

What captured our thoughts was the dichotomy of victims: Why did some alleged instances of rejection spawn aggression against a single individual, while other instances spawned aggression against multiple persons? One plausible explanation is that each of the multiple victims in the instances of mass violence personally contributed to the rejection experience of the perpetrator. However, we were engaged by the possibility of a more flexible and generalizable explanation suggested by the groups literature. Social perception, at times, operates at the group-level (Brewer, Weber, & Carini, 1995), and individuals are perceived as undifferentiated and depersonalized group members rather than distinct and unique individuals (Hogg, this volume; Turner, Hogg, Oakes, Reicher, & Wetherell, 1987). When rejected by a member of a salient group, the rejected person may associate the group with rejection and, subsequently retaliate against the group. An attack against a group likely yields multiple victims because groups typically consist of multiple members. In other words, social rejection and perceived groupness might function synergistically to affect mass violence such that mass violence becomes likely when social rejection emanates from a perceived social group.

ENTITATIVITY: ON THE PERCEPTION OF GROUPNESS

In 1958 Donald Campbell coined the term "entitativity" (i.e., "the degree of having the nature of an entity," p. 17) to convey that aggregates of individuals vary in the extent to which they are perceived as a cohesive whole. Campbell offered the Gestalt principles of proximity, similarity, common fate, and pregnance (pattern) as potential sources of perceived entitativity.

Consistent with Campbell's ideas, research indicates that perceived entitativity is a multiply determined phenomena that is influenced by features of the aggregate, such as similarity, interdependence, interaction, shared goals, and shared outcomes among aggregate members (e.g., Dasgupta, Banaji, & Abelson, 1999; Gaertner & Schopler, 1998; Gaertner, Iuzzini, Witt, & Oriña, 2003; Kim, Song, & Lee, 1997; Knowles & Basset, 1976; Lickel et al., 2000; Lickel, Hamilton, & Sherman, 2001; McGarty, Haslam, Hutchinson, & Grace, 1995). Perceived entitativity is influenced additionally by characteristics of the perceiver (Brewer & Harasty, 1996), such as need for assimilation (Pickett & Brewer, 2001) and certainty orientation (Sorrentino, Hodson, & Huber, 2001).

Perceived entitativity dramatically shapes social judgment and behavior (e.g., Hamilton & Sherman, 1996; Hamilton, Sherman, & Lickel, 1998; Wilder, 1980). Entitativity facilitates stereotyping of group members (Crawford, Sherman, & Hamilton, 2002; Yzerbyt, Rogier, & Fiske, 1998; Yzerbyt, Corneille, & Estrada, 2001) and promotes preferential attitudes and behaviors toward the ingroup

(Castano, Yzerbyt, Paladino, & Sacchi, 2002; Gaertner & Schopler, 1998; Gaertner et al., 2003). Furthermore, perceived entitativity implicitly affects judgment without higher-level information processing (Pickett, 2001). Yzerbyt et al. (2001) suggest that to the degree an aggregate of persons is perceived as a social entity, "its members are expected to behave in a more consistent manner, they are thought to be more similar to one another, [and] they are categorized in a more undifferentiated way at the group level..." (p. 1092). Indeed, the construct of entitativity is implicitly implied, if not explicitly incorporated, in various theories of social conflict (e.g., Allport, 1954; S. L. Gaertner et al., 1993; Insko & Schopler, 1998; Brewer & Miller, 1984; Sherif, Harvey, White, Hood, & Sherif, 1961; Stephan & Stephan, 2000; Tajfel & Turner, 1979).

In the remainder of the chapter, we review two studies that provide data consistent with the synergistic effect of rejection and perceived groupness on mass violence. The first study is a laboratory experiment that addresses the internal validity of the hypothesized effect (Gaertner & Iuzzini, 2003). The second study is a questionnaire project conducted in a high school that addresses the external validity of the hypothesized effect (Gaertner, Wahler, & Iuzzini, 2003).

REJECTION X ENTITATIVITY: AN EXPERIMENT

We used a 2 x 2 between-subjects factorial to independently manipulate the perceived entitativity of a 3-person aggregate and whether a member of the aggregate socially rejected the participant. We assessed aggression with a modified noise-blast task (e.g., Bushman & Baumeister, 1998; Twenge et al., 2001; for a discussion and test of the validity of laboratory aggression-paradigms see Anderson & Bushman, 1997; Bushman & Anderson, 1998). We structured the task such that participants had to select a level of noise that would be sent simultaneously to all members of the aggregate. Consequently, participants could retaliate against the rejecter with a loud blast of noise, but only at the expense of blasting the other members of the aggregate. If rejection and entitativity synergistically affect mass violence, participants will be most willing to harm the aggregate when a member of the aggregate rejects them and the aggregate appears to be an entity-like group. That is, rejection and entitativity should interact to produce a 1-versus-3 pattern in which participants who are rejected by a member of the entity-like group blast the aggregate with louder noise than do participants in the other three conditions.

Undergraduates at Texas A&M University participated in an experiment disguised as a study of "noise tolerance." Each session consisted of one participant, one experimenter, and three confederates playing the role of other participants. We matched the sex of the experimenter and confederates to that of the participant. Confederates in the high-entitativity condition ostensibly shared membership on a recreational volleyball team and wore t-shirts displaying a volleyball and in large letters, "Bryan-College-Station Volleyball: Team United." Confederates in the low entitativity condition dressed in their regular "day-to-day" clothes, barring any university or group emblems, and appeared to be three unaffiliated individuals.

The participant and confederates sat at desks arranged in a semi-circle facing a large machine (Narco Bio-Systems, 4-channel Physiograph) with blinking lights, rotating dials, and headphones extending to each desk. To facilitate the noise task, the experimenter apologetically announced that there was one participant too many and suggested that the problem be resolved by randomly selecting a person to leave. In the non-rejection condition, the participant and confederates drew from a deck of cards with the understanding that the recipient of the "X" card would leave. We rigged the cards to ensure that the participant received the X. In the social-rejection condition, as the experimenter prepared to distribute the cards, one of the confederates glared, pointed at the participant, and scornfully suggested, "S/he should be the one who leaves!" The experimenter acted a little frazzled by the comment and, in all conditions, escorted the participant to another room.

The experimenter quietly explained that the story about having too many participants had been fabricated because the study requires two experimenters and the other experimenter had not arrived. The experimenter further explained that she decided to enlist the help of a participant rather than cancel the session. Seating the participant in front of a computer, the experimenter explained that she typically monitors the participants' reactions while her partner controls the noise level. The experimenter explained that the computer would prompt the participant to enter a noise level between 0 dB, "the lowest level of sound a human can detect," to 110 dB, "the highest level of sound to which we can expose participants." She added that the noise becomes increasingly uncomfortable as the decibels increase.

After the experimenter exited the room, the computer reiterated the instructions and prompted the participant to enter a decibel level to be sent to the participants (i.e., confederates) down the hall. Subsequent questions provided checks of the entitativity and rejection manipulations. Participants rated on 7-point semantic-differential scales the extent to which they perceived the other "participants" as (a) "1 = *not at all a group*" to "7 = *very much a group*", (b) "1 = *a collection of unconnected persons*" to "7 = *highly connected group members*", and (c) "1 = *unrelated individuals*" to "7 = *highly related group members*." Participants rated on 7-point scales (1 = *not at all*; 7 = *very much*) the extent to which four adjectives (abandoned, rejected, unwanted, and unwelcome) described how they felt when they were selected to leave the study.

We entered the entitativity index (α = .90), rejection index (α = .85), and noise level into separate 2(entitativity) x 2(rejection) x 2(sex) ANOVAs. A main effect of entitativity on the entitativity-index and a main effect of rejection on the rejection-index confirmed the respective manipulations. Participants perceived the aggregate to be more entity-like when confederates wore the common "Team United" shirt (M = 5.15) than when they wore their day-to-day clothes (M = 2.77). Likewise, participants who were rejected by a confederate reported stronger feelings of rejection (M = 3.17) than did participants who were randomly selected to leave (M = 2.89).

As displayed in Figure 19.1, the pattern of noise toward the aggregate was consistent with a synergistic effect of rejection and entitativity on mass violence. In particular, the 1 versus 3 contrast was significant, such that participants who were rejected by a member of the high-entitativity aggregate exposed the aggregate to louder noise than did participants in the other three conditions (among which the level of noise did not vary significantly). The same pattern is revealed if one were to interpret the significant Rejection x Entitativity interaction. The only significant simple effects involved the high-entitativity-social-rejection condition and indicated that (a) rejected participants exposed the high-entitativity aggregate to louder noise than did non-rejected participants and (b) rejected participants issued louder noise to the high-entitativity than low-entitativity aggregate.

Consistent with the predicted synergistic effect of entitativity and rejection, persons behaved most aggressively against the aggregate when a member of the aggregate rejected them and the aggregate appeared to be an entity-like group. In other words, rejected persons were not invariably aggressive. Persons rejected by a member of the low entitativity aggregate behaved as nonaggressively toward the aggregate as did non-rejected persons. Rejected persons ostensibly constrained their aggressive inclinations in the low entitativity condition because their behavior could harm non-rejecting confederates who shared no apparent affiliation with the rejecter. On the other hand, participants evidenced less constraint and blasted all three members with significantly louder noise in the high entitativity condition in which the non-rejecting confederates shared an affiliation with the rejecting

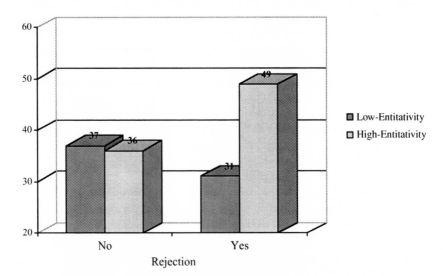

FIGURE 19.1 Noise Blast (dB) as a Function of Entitativity and Rejection

individual. These data provide evidence consistent with the possibility that social rejection and entitativity function synergistically to produce mass violence.

REJECTION X ENTITATIVITY IN A LOCAL HIGH SCHOOL

We conducted a questionnaire study in a local high school to provide an alternate test of the synergistic effect in an externally valid context. In an initial interview session, we identified 10 groups that coexist in the high school: Drama (students involved in drama or art), Druggies (students who use drugs), Gothics (students who dress in black clothes and listen to "weird" music), Jocks, Nerds/Geeks, Normals ("normal" students who do not belong to any particular clique), Popular Crowd, School Band, Skaters (students who ride skateboards), and Young Life (a religious organization). One hundred and thirty seven high school students (50 males and 87 females) subsequently answered questions about the extent to which they (a) perceive each group to be an entity, (b) experience rejection from each group, and (c) daydream (i.e., imagine or fantasize) about aggressing against each group. The order in which participants reported their experiences with a given group varied as a 10-level Latin-square design, with each group being rated first in one of the 10 orders. We assessed imagined aggression rather than actual aggression because instances of actual aggression are arguably rare and unspecified factors could inhibit the expression of aggression despite the underlying desire to harm (e.g., just as subjective norms influence whether attitudes materialize in behavior; Ajzen & Fishbein, 1980).

Measuring Entitativity

We assessed the perceived entitativity of each group with the manipulation-check items from our laboratory experiment. Participants rated on 7-point semantic-differential scales the extent to which they perceived the members of each group as (a) "0 = *not at all a group*" to "6 = *very much a group*," (b) "0 = *a collection of unconnected persons*" to "6 = *highly connected group members*," and (c) "0 = *unrelated individuals*" to "6 = *highly related group members*."

Measuring Rejection

We assessed rejection experiences with 10 items. Participants rated on 7-point scales ("*0 = never*" to "*6 = frequently*") the extent to which each group did "the following things to you:" (a) teased you, (b) made you feel rejected, (c) made you feel like an outsider, (d) made fun of you, (e) picked-on you, (f) made you feel like you don't belong, (g) hurt your feelings, (h) excluded you from their activities, (i) tried to humiliate you, and (j) made you feel unwanted.

Measuring Imagined Aggression

We assessed imagined aggression with 12 modified items from the Revised Conflict Tactics Scale (Straus, Hamby, Boney-McCoy, & Sugarman, 1996). Participants rated on 7-point scales ("*0 = never*" to "*6 = frequently*") the extent to which they "daydream about doing the following things" to members of each group: (a) insulting or swearing at members of _____, (b) shouting or yelling at members of _____, (c) destroying things that belong to members of _____, (d) throwing things at members of _____ that could hurt, (e) pushing or shoving members of _____, (f) slapping members of _____, (g) punching or hitting members of _____ with things that hurt, (h) choking members of _____, (i) attacking members of _____ with a knife, (j) shooting members of _____ with a gun, (k) slamming members of _____ against a wall, and (l) beating-up members of _____.

We formed indices of entitativity (α = .92), rejection (α = .97), and aggression (α = .97) for each participant by averaging the relevant items across each group. To test whether imagined aggression varied as a synergistic function of entitativity and rejection, we simultaneously regressed the aggression index on a factorial crossing of rejection, entitativity, and sex. We centered rejection and entitativity prior to forming interaction products to minimize collinearity (Cohen, Cohen, West, & Aiken, 2003). A model comparison test indicated that the interactions involving sex did not contribute significantly to prediction and none of those interactions were individually significant. Consequently, we retained the model that predicted aggression as a function of sex, rejection, entitativity, and Rejection x Entitativity. The model accounted for 38% of the variability in aggression and, more importantly, aggression significantly varied as a function of the Rejection x Entitativity interaction.

We decomposed the interaction by estimating the simple slope of entitativity at low and high values of rejection (i.e., 1 SD above and below the mean of rejection) and the simple slope of rejection at low and high values of entitativity (i.e., 1 SD above and below the mean of entitativity; Cohen et al., 2003). Figure 19.2 depicts the interaction. The association between imagined aggression and perceived entitativity was significantly stronger at high (B = 0.20, p = .001) than low levels of rejection (B = 0.01, p = .989). Likewise, the association between imagined aggression and rejection was significantly stronger at high (B = 0.59, p = .0001) than at low levels of entitativity (B = 0.28, p = .0004)—when we extrapolated the simple slope analyses beyond 1 SD to the lowest point on the entitativity scale the association between aggression and rejection was not significant, B = -0.06, p = .7608). In other words, when persons experienced relatively little rejection from a group, their level of fantasized aggression against the group was low and did not vary with the perceived entitativity of the group. However, when persons experienced relatively high rejection from a group, their level of fantasized aggression against the group increased with the perceived entitativity of the group.

These data are consistent with the hypothesized synergistic effect of entitativity and rejection on mass violence and replicate in a naturalistic context the results of

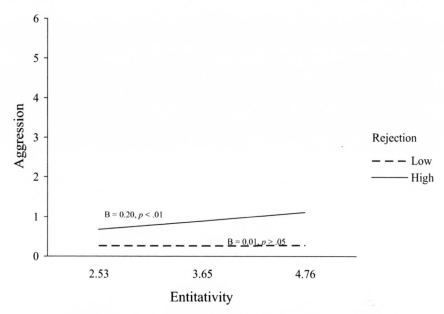

FIGURE 19.2 Imagined Aggression as a Function of Entitativity x Rejection

our internally valid laboratory research. Of course, the measure of fantasized (or imagined) aggression used in the current research does not necessarily indicate that such fantasies will affect actual behavior. Whether such fantasies translate into behavior likely depends on a host of situational and intra-personal factors. Nonetheless, the laboratory experiment evidenced a conceptually similar pattern on a behavioral measure of aggression. Such remarkably consistent findings across two methodologically divergent paradigms bolsters confidence in the validity of our conceptual analysis and suggests that mass violence arises, in part, from the synergistic effect of rejection and entitativity.

PLAUSIBLE MEDIATING PROCESSES

The group literature highlights two processes that plausibly mediate the synergistic effect of entitativity and rejection on mass violence: stereotyping and collective responsibility.

Entitativity facilitates the tendency to incorporate information inferred from an individual group member into the stereotype of the group (Crawford, Sherman, & Hamilton, 2002). That is, dispositional information more readily transfers from the perception of an individual to the perception of the individual's group when the group is perceived to be highly entity-like. Such a stereotyping process plausibly mediates the synergistic effect of rejection and entitativity on mass violence. When rejected by a member of a salient social group, rejected persons might incorporate the rejection experience into their stereotype of the group and associate (cognitively or affectively) the group with rejection.

Entitativity also facilitates judgments of collective responsibility (Lickel, Schmader, & Hamilton, 2003). Perceivers presume that members of highly entity-like groups either encouraged or failed to prevent the wrongful actions of a fellow group member and judge all group members responsible. Such a process might mediate the synergistic effect of rejection and entitativity. When rejected by a member of a salient group, rejected persons might attribute responsibility for the rejection experience to all group members.

Of course, the stereotyping and collective responsibility accounts need not be mutually exclusive. Associating group members with rejection via a group stereotype might facilitate judgments of collective responsibility and vice versa. We find both accounts relevant and plausible given their documented association with perceptions of entitativity.

INDIVIDUAL DIFFERENCES AS POTENTIAL MODERATORS

Mass violence as exemplified by the multiple victim school shootings is likely a multiply determined phenomenon that is undoubtedly more complicated than our synergistic model suggests. Indeed, our own research implies the possibility of moderators.

We replicated the high-entitativity-social-rejection condition of the previously described laboratory experiment with two major changes. Participants interacted with three confederates who shared group membership (i.e., wore "Team United" shirts) and a fourth confederate who did not share membership with the others (i.e., wore regular street clothes). One of the group members subsequently rejected the participant (i.e., "S/he should be the one who leaves!"). Rather than selecting a single noise level to be sent to all confederates, participants selected a separate noise level for each confederate. We were interested in whether participants would aggress more strongly (i.e., higher noise level) toward the two non-reject-ing group members than toward the non-rejecting non-group member. That is, does perceived groupness expand the rejected person's scope of aggression toward all group members?

The study answered our query with a resounding, "Sometimes." Approxi-mately 34% of participants evidenced a generalization of aggression against the group and blasted the non-rejecting group members with louder noise than they blasted the non-group member. However, the majority of participants did not blast the non-rejecting group members with louder noise than they blasted the non-group member (they primarily aggressed against the rejecter).

An admittedly speculative and post hoc explanation for the disparity among participants implies the moderating effect of individual-difference variables. We suspect that individual-differences interacted with the separate-noise-blast task. Setting a separate noise level for each confederate potentially prompted participants to individuate (i.e., decategorize) the confederates. Such an individuation effect likely diminished the perceived entitativity of the 3-person aggregate (Brewer & Miller, 1984). Participants who evidenced the predicted pattern and aggressed more intensely against non-rejecting group members may have been predisposed to perceive higher levels of entitativity and, consequently, were less affected by the potential individuating effect of the separate noise-blast task.

What factors predispose individuals to perceive entitativity and to potentially amplify the synergistic effect of entitativity and rejection? Individuals with heightened needs for inclusion (Pickett & Brewer, 2001) and certainty-oriented persons (Hodson & Sorrentino, 2001; Roney & Sorrentino, 1987) are particularly apt to perceive social groupings as homogenous entities. On a more speculative note, narcissists may be less inclined to differentiate among individuals and more inclined to categorize the social world at a group level due to an exacerbated preoccupation with self (e.g., Campbell, Rudich, & Sedikides, 2002). While our speculations focus on individual differences associated with entitativity, it is plausible that individual-differences that regulate reactions to social rejection also moderate the synergistic effect of rejection and entitativity. Such moderators might include rejection sensitivity (Downey & Feldman, 1996; Romero-Canyas & Downey, this volume), narcissism, (Bushman & Baumeister, 1998; Twenge & Campbell, 2003) and trait-levels of forgiveness (Lawler et al., 2003).

A CONCLUDING CAVEAT

Motivated by the rash of school shootings involving multiple victims, we attempted to identify a psychological process that underlies such incidents of mass violence. Coupling the research literatures of social rejection and entitativity, we hypothesized that rejection and entitativity synergistically precipitate mass violence such that mass violence becomes likely when social rejection emanates from a perceived social group. Data from a laboratory experiment and questionnaire study in a local high school were consistent with the hypothesized synergistic effect. Of course, we recognize that a sanctioned blast of noise in a laboratory and self-reported fantasies of aggression are a far cry from pulling a trigger or detonating a bomb in a schoolyard. Furthermore, our methodology does not enable us to state whether the coupling of rejection and entitativity precipitated any particular school shooting. What is noteworthy about our methodology is that it enables us to state that the hypothesized synergistic effect is *plausible* (e.g., Mook, 1983) and, to that extent, provides a rudimentary understanding of a process that potentially instigates lethal and destructive behavior.

REFERENCES

Ajzen, I., & Fishbein, M. (1980). *Understanding attitudes and predicting social behavior*. Englewood Cliffs, NJ: Prentice-Hall.

Allport, G. W. (1954). *The nature of prejudice*. Reading, PA: Addison-Wesley Publishing.

Anderson, C. A. & Bushman, B. J. (1997). External validity of "trivial" experiments: The case of laboratory aggression. *Review of General Psychology, 1*, 19–41.

Baumeister, R. F., & Leary, M. R. (1995). The need to belong: Desire for interpersonal attachments as a fundamental human motivation. *Psychological Bulletin, 117*, 497–529.

Brewer, M. B., & Harasty, A. S. (1996). Seeing groups as entities: The role of perceiver motivation. In R. M. Sorrentino & E. T. Higgins (Eds.), *Handbook of motivation and cognition: Vol. 3. The interpersonal context* (pp. 347–370). New York: Guilford Press.

Brewer, M. B., & Miller, N. (1984). Beyond the contact hypothesis: Theoretical perspectives on desegregation. In N. Miller & M. Brewer (Eds.) *Groups in contact: The psychology of desegregation* (pp. 281–302). New York: Academic Press.

Brewer, M. B., Weber, J. G., & Carini, B. (1995). Person memory in intergroup contexts: Categorization versus individuation. *Journal of Personality and Social Psychology, 69*, 29–40.

Bushman, B. J., & Anderson, C. A. (1998). Methodology in the study of aggression: Integrating experimental and nonexperimental findings. In R. G. Geen & E. Donnerstein (Eds.), *Human aggression: Theories, research, and implications for social policy* (pp. 23–48). San Diego, CA: Academic Press.

Bushman, B. J., & Baumeister, R. F. (1998). Threatened egotism, narcissism, self-esteem, and direct and displaced aggression: Does self-love or self-hate lead to violence? *Journal of Personality and Social Psychology, 75*, 219–229.

Buss, A. H. (1961). *The psychology of aggression*. New York: Wiley.

Campbell, D. T. (1958). Common fate, similarity, and other indices of the status of aggregates of persons as social entities. *Behavioral Science, 3*, 14–25.

Campbell, W. K., Rudich, E. A., & Sedikides, C. (2002). Narcissism, self-esteem, and the positivity of self-views: Two portraits of self-love. *Personality and Social Psychology Bulletin, 28*, 358–368.

Castano, E. Yzerbyt, V., Paladino, M., & Sacchi, S. (2002). I belong, therefore, I exist: Ingroup identification, ingroup entitativity, and ingroup bias. *Personality and Social Psychology Bulletin, 28*, 135–143.

Cohen, J., Cohen, P., West, S. G., & Aiken, L. S. (2003). *Applied multiple regression/correlation analysis for the behavioral science* (3rd ed.). Mahwah, NJ: Lawrence Erlbaum.

Coie, J., Dodge, K., & Kupersmidt, J. (1990). Peer group behavior and social status. In S. R. Asher & J. D. Coie (Eds.), *Peer rejection in childhood* (pp. 17–59). Cambridge: Cambridge University Press.

Crawford, M. T., Sherman, S. J., & Hamilton, D. L. (2002). Perceived entitativity, stereotype formation, and the interchangeability of group members. *Journal of Personality and Social Psychology, 83*, 1076–1094.

Dasgupta, N., Banaji, M. R., & Abelson, R. P. (1999). Group entitativity and group perception: Associations between physical features and psychological judgment. *Journal of Personality and Social Psychology, 5*, 991–1003.

DeRosier, M. E., Kupersmidt, J. B., & Patterson, C. J. (1994). Children's academic and behavioral adjustments as a function of the chronicity and proximity of peer rejection. *Child Development, 65*, 1799–1813.

Dodge, K. A. (1983). Behavioral antecedents of peer social status. *Child Development, 54*, 1386–1399.

Downey, G., & Feldman, S. I. (1996). Implications of rejection sensitivity for intimate relationships. *Journal of Personality and Social Psychology, 70*, 1327–1343.

Eisenberger, N. I., Lieberman, M. D., & Williams, K. D. (2003). Does rejection hurt? An fMRI study of social exclusion. *Science, 302*, 290–292

Gaertner, L. & Iuzzini, J. (2003). *Social rejection, perceived groupness, and mass violence*. Manuscript under review.

Gaertner, L., Iuzzini, J., Witt, M. & Oriña, M. M. (2003). *On the intragroup origin of positive ingroup regard*. Manuscript under review.

Gaertner, L., & Schopler, J. (1998). Perceived ingroup entitativity and intergroup bias: An interconnection of self and others. *European Journal of Social Psychology, 28*, 963–980.

Gaertner, L. Wahler, R., Iuzzini, J. (2003). *Rejection, entitativity, and violence: A high school study.* Unpublished raw data.

Gaertner, S. L., Dovidio, J. F., Anastasio, P. A., Bachman, B. A., & Rust, M. C. (1993). The common ingroup identity model: Recategorization and the reduction of intergroup bias. In W. Stroebe & M. Hewstone (Eds.), *European review of social psychology: Vol. 4* (pp. 1–26). New York: John Wiley & Sons.

Hamilton, D. L., & Sherman, S. J. (1996). Perceiving persons and groups. *Psychological Review, 103*, 336–355.

Hamilton, D. L., Sherman, S. J., & Lickel, B. (1998). Perceiving social groups: The importance of the entitativity continuum. In C. Sedikides, J. Schopler, & C. A. Insko (Eds.), *Intergroup cognition and intergroup behavior* (pp. 47–74). Hillsdale, NJ: Lawrence Erlbaum.

Hodson, G., & Sorrentino, R. M. (2001). Just who favors the in-group? Personality differences in reactions to uncertainty in the minimal group paradigm. *Group Dynamics: Theory, Research, and Practice, 5*, 92–101.

Insko, C. A., & Schopler, J. (1998). Differential distrust of groups and individuals. In C. Sedikides, J. Schopler, & C. A. Insko (Eds.), *Intergroup cognition and intergroup behavior* (pp. 75–107). Hillsdale, NJ: Lawrence Erlbaum.

Kim, B. J., Song, K. J., & Lee, H. K. (1997). The effect of group entitativity on information processing of groups. *Korean Journal of Social and Personality Psychology, 11*, 57–73.

Knowles, E. S., & Bassett, R. L. (1976). Groups and crowds as social entities: Effects of activity, size, and member similarity on nonmembers. *Journal of Personality and Social Psychology, 34*, 837–845.

Lawler, K. A., Younger, J. W., Piferi, R. L., Billington, E., Jobe, R., Edmondson, K., & Jones, W. (2003). A change of heart: Cardiovascular correlates of forgiveness in response to interpersonal conflict. *Journal of Behavioral Medicine, 26*, 373–393

Leary, M. R., Haupt, A. L., Strausser, K. S., & Chokel, J. T. (1998). Calibrating the sociometer: The relationship between interpersonal appraisals and the state self-esteem. Journal of Personality and Social Psychology, 74, 1290–1299.

Leary, M. R., Kowalski, R. M., Smith, L., & Phillips, S. (2003). Teasing, rejection, and violence: Case studies of the school shootings. *Aggressive Behavior, 292*, 202–214.

Leary, M. R., Tambor, E. S., Terdal, S. K., & Downs, D. L. (1995). Self-esteem as an interpersonal monitor: The sociometer hypothesis. *Journal of Personality and Social Psychology, 68*, 518–530.

Lickel, B., Hamilton, D. L., & Sherman, S. (2001). Elements of a lay theory of groups: Types of groups, relationship styles, and the perception of group entitativity. *Personality and Social Psychology Review, 5*, 129–140.

Lickel, B., Hamilton, D. L., Wieczorkowska, G., Lewis, A., Sherman, S., & Uhles, A. N. (2000). Varieties of groups and the perception of group entitativity. *Journal of Personality & Social Psychology, 78*, 223–246.

Lickel, B., Schmader, T., & Hamilton, D. L. (2003). A case of collective responsibility: Who else was to blame for the Columbine High School shootings? *Personality and Social Psychology Bulletin, 29*, 194–204.

Mallick, S. K., & McCandless, B. R. (1966). A study of catharsis of aggression. *Journal of Personality and Social Psychology, 4*, 591–596.

McGarty, C., Haslam, S. A., Hutchinson, K. J., & Grace, D. M. (1995). Determinants of perceived consistency: The relationship between group entitativity and the meaningfulness of categories. *British Journal of Social Psychology, 34*, 237–256.

Mook, D. G. (1983). In defense of external invalidity. *American Psychologist, 38*, 379–387.

Newcomb, A. F., Bukowski, W. M., Pattee, L. (1993). Children's peer relations: A meta-analytic review of popular, rejected, neglected, controversial, and average sociometric status. *Psychological Bulletin, 113*, 99–128.

Pickett, C. L. (2001). The effects of entitativity beliefs on implicit comparisons between group members. *Personality and Social Psychology Bulletin, 27*, 515–525.

Pickett, C. L., & Brewer, M. B. (2001). Assimilation and differentiation needs as motivational determinants of perceived in-group and outgroup homogeneity. *Journal of Experimental Social Psychology, 37*, 341–348.

Roney, C. J. R., & Sorrentino, R. M. (1987). Uncertainty orientation and person perception:

Individual differences in categorization. *Social Cognition, 5,* 369–382.

Sherif, M., Harvey, O. J., White, B. J., Hood, W. R., & Sherif, C. W. (1961). *Intergroup conflict and cooperation. The Robbers Cave Experiment.* Norman, OK: Institute of Group Relations.

Sorrentino, R. M., Hodson, G., & Huber, G. L. (2001). Uncertainty orientation and the social mind: Individual differences in the interpersonal context. In J. P. Forgas, K. D. Williams, & L. Wheeler (Eds.), *The social mind: Cognitive and motivational aspects of interpersonal behavior* (pp. 323–349). Cambridge: Cambridge University Press.

Stephan, W. G., & Stephan, C. W. (2000). An integrated threat theory of prejudice. In S. Oskamp (Ed.), *Reducing prejudice and discrimination: The Claremont Symposium on Applied Social Psychology* (pp. 23–45). Mahwah, NJ: Lawrence Erlbaum.

Straus, M. A., Hamby, S. L., Boney-McCoy, S., Sugarman, D. B. (1996). The revised conflict tactics scales (CTS2): Development and preliminary psychometric data. *Journal of Family Issues, 17,* 283–316.

Tajfel, H., & Turner, J. C. (1979). An integrative theory of intergroup conflict. In W. G. Austin & S. Worchel (Eds.), *The social psychology of intergroup relations* (pp. 33–47). Monterey, CA: Brooks/Cole.

Turner, J. C., Hogg, M. A., Oakes, P. J., Reicher, S. D., & Wetherell, M. S. (1987). *Rediscovering the social group: A self-categorization theory.* Oxford and New York: Blackwell.

Twenge, J. M., Baumeister, R. F., Tice, D. M., & Stucke, T. S. (2001). If you can't join them, beat them: Effects of social exclusion on aggressive behavior. *Journal of Personality and Social Psychology, 81,* 1058–1069.

Wilder, D. A. (1980). Perceiving persons as a group: Effects on attributions of causality and beliefs. *Social Psychology, 41,* 13–23.

Williams, K. D., Cheung, C. K. T., & Choi, W. (2000). Cyberostracism: Effects of being ignored over the internet. *Journal of Personality and Social Psychology, 79,* 748–762.

Williams, K. D., Govan, C. L., Croker, V., Tynan, D., Cruickshank, M., & Lam, A. (2002). Investigations into differences between social- and cyberostracism. *Group Dynamics, 6,* 65–77.

Yzerbyt, V. Y., Corneille, O., & Estrada, C. (2001). The interplay of subjective essentialism and entitativity in the formation of stereotypes. *Personality and Social Psychology Review, 5,* 141–155.

Yzerbyt, V. Y., Rogier, A., & Fiske, S. T. (1998). Group entitativity and social attribution: On translating situational constraints into stereotypes. *Personality and Social Psychology Bulletin, 24,* 1089–1103.

20

Avoiding the Social Death Penalty

Ostracism and Cooperation in Social Dilemmas

JAAP W. OUWERKERK
NORBERT L. KERR
MARCELLO GALLUCCI
PAUL A. M. VAN LANGE

The Social Pain and Social Function of Ostracism
The Bad Apple Effect in Social Dilemmas
Attenuating the Bad Apple Effect
Tolerance for Multiple Bad Apples
Who Gets Ostracized and How Does this Make Us Feel?
The Role of Ostracism in the Evolution of Cooperation

The Athenian democracy has been characterized as extraordinary stable. A constitutional safeguard named *ostrakismos,* which originated circa 500 B.C., was at least partly responsible for this stability (cf. Forsdyke, 2000). Each winter, the citizens of Athens decided collectively by casting votes (written on shards of pottery or *ostraca*) whether or not to banish people who had tried to become too powerful or wealthy. When a person received 6,000 votes or more, he was exiled for a period of 10 years. Interestingly, in most years the Athenian

Address correspondence to: Jaap W. Ouwerkerk, Department of Communication Science, Free University, Amsterdam, De Boelelaan 1081, 1081 HV Amsterdam, The Netherlands, jw.ouwerkerk@fsw.vu.nl

citizens chose not to exercise the power of exile, thereby suggesting that the mere threat of ostracism was a sufficient deterrent for greedy behavior.

In line with this notion, we argue in the present chapter that a threat of ostracism (as well as actual ostracism episodes) may have an important function—suppressing uncooperative behavior that is harmful to a group and its members. For this purpose, we will review some of our research programs that demonstrate positive effects of (the threat of) ostracism on cooperative behavior in social dilemmas (i.e., in situations which are characterized by a conflict between personal and collective interests). Furthermore, these programs show that people have social norms prescribing cooperation in groups and are likely to ostracize uncooperative individuals. In fact, they experience pleasure (i.e., *schadenfreude*) when uncooperative individuals are excluded from the group. We conclude with discussing the possible crucial role of ostracism in the evolution of cooperation.

THE SOCIAL PAIN AND SOCIAL FUNCTION OF OSTRACISM

When reading the various chapters in this volume, it becomes apparent that being ostracized, socially excluded, rejected, or bullied is a painful experience. It has even been suggested that the social pain resulting from exclusion episodes may arise from the same brain regions as physical pain (Eisenberger & Lieberman, this volume; see also Eisenberger, Lieberman, & Williams, 2003; MacDonald & Shaw, this volume). The question *why* ostracism hurts has been addressed extensively in the previous chapters. In short, ostracism is assumed to elicit social pain because it may threaten four fundamental needs (Williams, 2001; Williams & Zadro, 2001; this volume). First (and according to some foremost; see Leary, this volume), ostracism threatens our *need to belong*. This need for frequent, affectively pleasant interactions (Baumeister & Leary, 1995) is believed to have evolved as inclusion in a group meant increased chances of survival and reproductive benefits for our ancestors in more hostile environments (Baumeister & Tice, 1990; Buss, 1990). Second, ostracism threatens our *need for maintaining high self-esteem*, because it carries with it the implicit or explicit accusation that we have done something wrong. Third, ostracism may threaten our *need for control* over interactions with others, as well as our "interpretive control" (Rothbaum, Weisz, & Snyder, 1982) when the reason for our exclusion is ambiguous. Finally, ostracism may threaten the *need to maintain our beliefs in a meaningful existence* (James, 1890; Solomon, Greenberg, & Pyszczynski, 1991), because it may remind us of our fragile, temporary existence and even our own death (Case & Williams, 2004).

Given the threat that ostracism may pose to these four fundamental needs, it is vital that human beings are equipped with a regulatory system to monitor and maintain their level of social inclusion (see Brewer, this volume). Indeed, it has been argued that individuals posses a system that both assesses their inclusion status and activates coping strategies when this status may fall short of a desired level (Leary, Tambor, Terdal, & Downs, 1995; Pickett & Gardner, this volume).

A regulatory system at the individual level that is directed at maintaining a satisfactory level of inclusion, however, implies that a mere threat of ostracism provides social groups with a powerful means of suppressing deviant behavior that is deemed dangerous for their cohesion and survival. That is, from the perspective of a social aggregate, the presence of a threat of ostracism can be viewed as functional, because individual members will be motivated to engage in behaviors to avoid the "social death penalty" (i.e., behaviors that will benefit the group and are likely to be met with the social approval of fellow group members). Consistent with this notion, some preliminary work (Kerr, 1999) shows that a threat of ostracism can stimulate cooperation in a social dilemma situation. The focus of the research discussed in the present chapter, however, is to investigate whether a threat of ostracism (or being ostracized temporarily) may attenuate one of the most problematic behavioral tendencies in social dilemmas—the tendency to follow the bad example of others.

THE BAD APPLE EFFECT IN SOCIAL DILEMMAS

Considerable research suggests that we tend to follow the lead of other group members in social dilemma situations (e.g., Braver & Barnett, 1976; Croson & Marks, 1998; Komorita, Parks, & Hulbert, 1992; Messick, Wilke, Brewer, Kramer, Zemke, & Lui, 1983; Schroeder, Jensen, Reed, Sullivan, & Schwab, 1983). Moreover, it has been argued that we are especially prone to imitate *uncooperative* behavior of others. For example, Colman (1982, 1995) has suggested that it takes only one non-cooperator in a social dilemma (i.e., a *bad apple*) to induce others to switch to non-cooperation when the dilemma is repeated, thereby providing a plausible explanation for the finding that people tend to cooperate less in relatively large groups; if a fixed proportion of the population has a propensity to behave non-cooperatively, then the probability of one bad apple turning up in a social dilemma (and spoiling things for everyone) increases with group size.

An implicit assumption of this bad apple theory is what has been termed "the bad apple effect" (Ouwerkerk, Van Lange, Gallucci, & Van Vugt, 2004). That is, consistent with the general principle across a broad range of psychological phenomena that bad events have a stronger impact than good events (Baumeister, Bratslavsky, Finkenauer, & Vohs, 2001), it is assumed that we have a stronger tendency to follow the behavior of a single non-cooperative person in a social dilemma (i.e., a bad apple) rather than the behavior of an equivalently cooperative person (i.e., a good guy). For example, when during a drought a neighbor tells us that he is not watering his garden in order to conserve water, and a neighbor on the other side is watering his garden more intensively than usual, we are assumed to follow the behavior of the latter rather than the former (cf. Colman, 1995). Accordingly, research by Samuelson and colleagues (Samuelson & Messick, 1986a, 1986b; Samuelson, Messick, Rutte, & Wilke, 1984) demonstrates that providing high-variance harvesting feedback in a resource-conservation dilemma leads to faster depletion of the shared resource than low-variance feedback, despite the fact that the mean harvest is identical in both conditions, just as one would expect if in the high-variance feedback condition extremely low cooperators (i.e., high harvesters) had more impact on others' behavior than extremely high cooperators (i.e., low harvesters).

More direct evidence for the bad apple effect stems from research on cooperation in public good dilemmas. Public goods (e.g., infrastructure, national defense) have the property that once they are produced, any individual in the group can consume them, regardless of his or her contribution to the production of the public good. In experiments simulating public goods, a group of participants is usually faced with a decision to invest money into either an individual account or a group account (i.e., the public good). Money that is placed in the former account is kept, whereas money placed in the latter account is multiplied by a certain value greater than one and subsequently divided equally among group members. Consequently, individual earnings are maximized when everything is kept in one's individual account, although everyone would be better off if all group members contributed to the group account, thereby creating a social dilemma. Kurzban, McCabe, Smith, and Wilson (2001) have shown that in such experiments people tend to cooperate at a level slightly above the level of the least cooperative member of the group (i.e., the bad apple). This form of "minimal reciprocity" (cf. Sudgen, 1984) is believed to occur because, although individuals have a desire to achieve high levels of cooperation in their group, they are predominantly motivated by a fear or aversion of being "free ridden."[1]

Taken together, the findings of research on cooperation in social dilemmas are highly disturbing. It indeed seems that "one bad apple spoils the whole barrel," thereby making it difficult or impossible to develop and sustain cooperation in a group. However, as noted earlier, the implicit or explicit threat of ostracism provides social groups with a powerful means of suppressing deviant behavior that is deemed dangerous for their cohesion and survival. In line with this notion, Ouwerkerk, Van Lange, Gallucci, and Van Vugt (2004) designed a series of experiments to investigate whether a threat of ostracism could attenuate the bad apple effect.

ATTENUATING THE BAD APPLE EFFECT

In the experiments of Ouwerkerk, Van Lange, et al. (2004) participants played a 4-person continuous public good dilemma for 40 trials. At each trial they had to divide 4 coins between their individual account and a group account. The coins in the latter account were doubled and divided equally among group members. In their first experiment, Ouwerkerk, Van Lange, et al. manipulated the variance of individual contributions among the other 3 group members to enable them to assess a possible bad apple effect. That is, in a *homogeneous* condition all 3 players acted "normally" (from the 4 coins, they all contributed 2 coins on average to the public good). However, in a *heterogeneous* condition only 1 of the other players acted this way, whereas another player was more cooperative (contributing 3 coins on average; i.e., a good guy), while the third was less cooperative (contributing 1 coin on average; i.e., the bad apple).

In addition, the presence of a threat of ostracism was manipulated. That is, in 1 condition participants were told that after an unspecified number of trials 1 person would have to leave to group (allegedly to be able to assess how people make decisions in groups of different sizes; cf. Kerr, 1999). Who would leave the group, was to be decided by group vote. It was emphasized that the person who would be excluded had to work alone on a different task, whereas the 3 remaining participants could continue to make decisions in the public good, thereby enabling them to make more money. Thus, in this first experiment, ostracism had both psychological and economical costs.

The results show that, when a threat of ostracism was absent, the bad apple effect emerged. That is, participants cooperated less in the heterogeneous condition (i.e., when a bad apple was present) than in the homogeneous condition, despite the fact that the mean level of cooperation shown by other group members was identical in both conditions. However, when a threat of ostracism was present, the bad apple effect was attenuated and even reversed. That is, participants cooperated *more* in the heterogeneous condition (i.e., when a bad apple was present) than in the homogeneous condition, suggesting that in the heterogeneous condition they followed the example set by the good guy. In a second experiment some alternative explanations of the results were tested. What is more relevant for the present discussion, in a third experiment it was demonstrated that the mere threat of ostracism could attenuate the bad apple effect even when exclusion did not have any *economic* costs, suggesting that the anticipated *psychological* costs of ostracism are sufficient to deter people from following the bad example of an uncooperative other.

In a fourth experiment, Ouwerkerk, Van Lange, et al. (2004) studied the effect of *actual* ostracism rather than the *threat of* ostracism on the bad apple effect. Again, participants played 40 trials in a public good dilemma. In the first 20 trials, the other 3 players showed little variance in cooperation. That is, similar to the homogeneous condition of the first experiment, they all contributed 2 coins on average to the public good. After 20 trials, a group voting procedure was introduced, whereby the person with the most votes would have to leave the group. Next, participants were informed that they were either *included* or *excluded* by the group vote. Subsequently, they were told that for technical reasons the "excluded" person had to continue playing the public good dilemma with the other 3 players. Accordingly, 20 additional trials were played. However, the other three players now behaved similar to the heterogeneous condition of the first experiment (i.e., there was a normal person, a good guy, and a bad apple). The results showed that participants followed the example of the bad apple when they were included by the group vote. By contrast, they increased their cooperation when they were previously excluded by the group vote, suggesting that they tried to appease the others who had just excluded them.

The latter finding is consistent with research by Williams and Sommer (1997), who observed that women, who had previously been included during a ball-tossing game, engaged in social loafing on a collective task, whereas women who had been ostracized displayed social compensation on the task. Furthermore, this finding is also consistent with research showing increased conformity following ostracism (Williams, Cheung, & Choi, 2000), enhanced sensitivity to social cues (Pickett & Gardner, this volume), and more non-conscious mimicry in response to exclusion experiences (Lakin & Cartrand, this volume). However, the results are inconsistent with many studies showing anti-social rather than pro-social reactions to exclusion (e.g., Baumeister, Twenge, & Ciarocco, 2000; Catenese & Tice, this volume; Gaertner & Iuzzini, this volume; Twenge, Baumeister, Tice, & Stucke, 2001). It should be noted, however, that in the latter studies participants are not provided with a real opportunity for restoring group inclusion. Under such circumstances, frustration may cause aggression and other anti-social reactions (see Brewer, this volume; Twenge, this volume).

TOLERANCE FOR MULTIPLE BAD APPLES

The research by Ouwerkerk, Van Lange, et al. (2004) demonstrates that a threat of ostracism (as well as actual ostracism episodes) can deter people from following the behavior of a single bad apple in a group of four people. However, the question remains whether a mere threat of ostracism may also be effective when: (a) more than one bad apple is present in a group, and (b) groups are larger. These questions were addressed in a series of experiments by Kerr et al. (2004). Their research was inspired by an experiment of Rutte and Wilke (1992), who studied reactions to multiple bad apples. In this experiment, the number of group members ostensibly intending to defect in a dichotomous-choice prisoner's dilemma with 5 people was systematically varied from 0 to 4, after which the actual rate of cooperation of participants was measured. The function relating the number of bad apples with cooperation was a step function. That is, the rate of cooperation dropped sharply (from about 50% to 20%) with 1 bad apple, and remained at this lower level as the number of bad apples increased.

In a first experiment, Kerr et al. (2004) tried to both replicate this step function conceptually in a continuous public good dilemma and change it into a "high-resistance to temptation" function by inducing a threat of ostracism. For this purpose, participants were confronted with a continuous public good dilemma with 5 people, in which they had to divide $5 between their individual account and a group account. The money in the latter account would be doubled and divided equally among group members. Before making a decision, they learned of the choices made by members of another, randomly chosen (and hence, ostensibly representative) group, suggesting the presence of either *0*, *1*, *2*, or *3* bad apples (individuals who did not contribute anything to the public good), and other group members contributing $3 or $4. Threat of ostracism was manipulated via anonymity and means to exclude. In a *no threat* condition, participants were always anonymous and there was no way of other group members socially sanctioning them. By contrast, in the *threat* condition, participants' identities were known and there were means of socially excluding them—verbally in a group discussion and formally from future group interaction via a blackball system.

When *no threat* of ostracism was present, Kerr et al. (2004) replicated conceptually the step function obtained by Rutte and Wilke (1992), showing that the rate of cooperation dropped sharply from about \$3 to \$2.5 with 1 bad apple, and remaining at this lower level as the number of bad apples increased. When a *threat* of ostracism was present, the rate of cooperation also dropped sharply from about \$3 to \$2.5. However, this occurred only when 3 bad apples (i.e., a majority of 60%) were present. In other words, a high-resistance to temptation function was obtained. In a second experiment, Kerr et al. manipulated: (a) the presence of a minority (40%) versus a majority (60%) of bad apples, and (b) the presence versus absence of a threat of ostracism in groups of 10 or 15 people. Although participants cooperated less with a majority of bad apples than with a minority, surprisingly, a threat of ostracism had no effect on cooperative behavior, suggesting that a threat of ostracism is less effective in larger groups. The latter finding was confirmed in a third experiment. With a paradigm similar to the one used by Ouwerkerk, Van Lange, et al. (2004), Kerr et al. demonstrated that a threat of ostracism attenuated the bad apple effect in a public good dilemma with 4 people, whereas such a threat had no effect in a public good dilemma with 8 people.

WHO GETS OSTRACIZED AND HOW DOES THIS MAKE US FEEL?

One important aspect of the studies described earlier has yet to be mentioned—the negative affective reactions toward bad apples. In the experiments by Ouwerkerk, Van Lange, et al. (2004) described earlier, participants often made remarks about the simulated bad apple that cannot be repeated in print. Accordingly, bad apples were evaluated extremely negative on a number of social dimensions. Furthermore, actual voting data show that, when present, a bad apple was voted to be excluded by an overwhelming majority of participants, attesting to the importance of fairness norms in determining who gets excluded from a group.

Moreover, using the same paradigm, Ouwerkerk, Van Dijk, Spears, and Pennekamp (2004) observed that people experience more pleasure (i.e., schadenfreude) about the fact that a bad apple gets ostracized than about the fact that a good guy gets ostracized. What is more important, this effect was mediated by feelings of deservingness. We suggest that the tendency to ostracize individuals permanently when they display deviant behavior and violate social norms, as observed in our research and that of others (e.g., Juvonen & Gross, this volume; Fitness, this volume), may be functional in the sense that group cohesion can be maintained without changing behavior (cf. Brewer, this volume). Furthermore, the permanent exclusion of certain individuals may provide us with a plausible explanation for one of the long-lasting puzzles in human evolution—the evolution of cooperation.

THE ROLE OF OSTRACISM
IN THE EVOLUTION OF COOPERATION

In closing, we want to discuss the possible crucial role of ostracism in the evolution of cooperation. The dynamics underlying ostracism may help us understand how cooperation can evolve and be sustained in groups formed by individuals not related by kinship. Groups of unrelated individuals present a challenge for the evolution of cooperation, because such groups provide the highest fitness advantage to members who do not cooperate (Axelrod & Hamilton, 1981). The evolution of cooperation requires that individuals who cooperate are able to discriminate between other co-operators (with whom cooperating is beneficial) and non-cooperators (with whom cooperating is not beneficial). When this discrimination is possible, cooperation can evolve and be sustained in the long term if non-cooperators receive a punishment whenever they do not cooperate. Ostracism represents one of the strongest, most effective, and efficient punishments available to group members.

Let us consider a simplified scenario illustrating the dynamics intertwining ostracism and cooperation. We assume that individuals belonging to a population form groups in order to provide a public good, which is then divided equally among the members of the group (e.g., hunting groups that share whatever is killed). Particularly when unaided, individual survival is difficult, the outcomes of the public good represent reproductive fitness, and individuals reproduce proportionally to their fitness[2] (cf. Axelrod & Hamilton, 1981). If individuals who cooperate are able to detect non-cooperators and exclude them from the group (or from receiving the benefits of cooperation), cooperators' fitness increases proportionally to the number of cooperators in the group, whereas non-cooperators' fitness declines proportionally to the number of occasions they are excluded. In the long term, non-cooperation becomes an inefficient strategy; its bearers "die out" and are replaced by cooperators (Gintis, 2000). Ostracism functions similarly to reciprocal strategies (Axelrod, 1984) in punishing non-cooperation, but exempts the excluder from the cost of mutual non-cooperation.

A fundamental assumption of the previous logic is that non-cooperators can be detected. This is possible when groups are relatively stable, such that the same individuals are likely to meet repeatedly in the public good situation (Gintis, 2000). When groups are not stable, ostracism can support cooperation as long as non-cooperators can be detected in advance. Reputation (Nowak & Sigmund, 1998) represents an example of a mechanism of pre-emptive detection, whereby previous behavior in other groups is used to exclude people in the present situation. Other mechanisms, such as the physical ability to cooperate, or the resemblance to hostile or non-cooperative types may also work as mechanisms of detection, although they might easily produce exclusion based on social stigma, more than on realistic threats of non-cooperation (Kurzban & Leary, 2001).

Although ostracism is a strong and efficient mechanism underlying the evolution of cooperation, it is vulnerable to the presence of pure cooperators, that is, individuals who cooperate but do not exclude non-cooperators. The presence of such individuals, in fact, may nullify the effectiveness of ostracism in the long term, especially when exclusion bears a cost for the one who excludes. That is, as compared with excluding cooperators, non-excluding cooperators may not pay some costs, such as the cost of monitoring, detecting the behavior of others, and actually excluding (i.e., the social and physical costs of expelling the defector), but at the same time they enjoy the benefits of mutual cooperation and the absence of non-cooperators. In the long term, if non-excluding cooperators replace cooperators who do exclude, the group will lose its most effective weapon against non-cooperators.

This is known as the so-called "second-order problem," because a new social dilemma is created concerning who is going to carry out the exclusion. The extent to which this shortcoming of ostracism may deter its power to function as a mechanism to induce and sustain cooperation needs yet to be analyzed in detail. Indeed, despite its potentials, the evolution of cooperation through ostracism is still an uncharted territory. Social exclusion of non-cooperating members may in fact sustain cooperation in situations where other mechanisms, such as direct (Axelrod & Hamilton, 1981) and indirect reciprocity (Nowak & Sigmund, 1998), fail. Most importantly, recent studies suggest that ostracism is probably the only mechanism that can sustain cooperation in two very hostile environments: large groups and non-repeated public good situations.

Cooperation in large groups is problematic in the field of evolutionary models of cooperation. The majority of mechanisms that have been identified as capable of inducing cooperation fall short in accounting for cooperation when groups grow larger then around 8 to 10 members (Boyd & Richerson, 1988; Gallucci, Van Lange, & Ouwerkerk, 2005). This necessity is clear when we consider direct reciprocity (Axelrod & Hamilton, 1981): In couples, reciprocal behavior directly punishes defection with defection, while rewarding cooperation with cooperation. In triads, on the contrary, one's cooperation may reward cooperation of a second member who previously cooperated, but may also reward a third member who defected. As the group grows larger, the accuracy by which members' behavior can be both individually detected and rewarded or punished decreases, eventually undermining the chances of cooperation to be sustained in the long term. Social exclusion, however, prevents this indiscriminate spreading of rewards and punishments, relatively independently of the size of the group (Gallucci, Ouwerkerk, & Van Lange 2004).

The logic is surprisingly simple: By excluding a non-cooperative member, cooperative members may sustain their high level of cooperation because their cooperation will not benefit a non-cooperative member. In other words, ostracism allows separating the punishment of non-cooperation from the provision of coop-eration to the group. In virtue of this separation, punishment of non-cooperation remains specific and accurate, independently of the size of the group. Accordingly, simulation studies show that large groups can be cooperative, and remain so in the long term, provided that ostracism is possible (Gallucci, Ouwerkerk, & Van Lange, 2004).

The ability of ostracism to sustain cooperation in large groups may also ex-plain how cooperation can evolve even when large groups disband after a single public good has been provided (i.e., non-repeated interaction). When a commu-nity forms occasional big groups to solve collective problems, such as collective harvesting or hunting of big games, cooperation is exposed to exploitation by free-riders. Ostracism, however, may sustain cooperation in these situations when a few individuals have knowledge of each other from previous interactions, and the rest of the community is willing to exclude members who are "accused" of being non-cooperators. If only one member of the group spreads the word that a person is a defector, he or she would be excluded even if the remaining of the group has never met the person nor has any knowledge about this person. Interestingly, the larger the group, the easier it may be to find at least one group member with knowledge about another's behavior. When this is the case, larger groups could even provide a better environment for cooperation than smaller groups. As we previously noted, ostracism is the only known mechanism capable of sustaining cooperation in such an evolutionary scenario.

Interestingly, ostracism may not only explain cooperation in situations in which other mechanisms fail, but may also challenge the effectiveness of these mechanisms in other situations. Again a comparison with direct reciprocity may be helpful. Assume groups sustain cooperation through direct reciprocity. If individuals are willing to switch from a reciprocal strategy (by which they do not discriminate between cooperators and defectors in the group) to exclusion of non-cooperative members, those individuals will benefit from a higher level of co-operation in the group and thus outperform strictly reciprocal individuals. Hence, under suitable circumstances, social exclusion may not only sustain cooperation, but also drive out other strategies, previously considered as the most effective in enforcing cooperation in human interaction.[3] In other words, when ostracism is possible, other mechanisms may become superfluous. Thus, ostracism may very well represent the most important mechanism for the evolution of cooperation in human groups.

NOTES

1. Some evidence suggests that the tendency to cooperate slightly above the level of the least cooperative member of the group may depend on individual differences. That is, Kurzban and Houser (2001) distinguished between *coopera-tors*, who contribute a great deal regardless of what others do, *free riders*, who contribute little regardless of what others do, and, *conditional cooperators*, who are sensitive to other's rate of cooperation. Only the latter group behaved

according to the rule of minimal reciprocity. Furthermore, Reinders Folmer (2003), working with a modified version of the paradigm used by Ouwerkerk et al. (2004), has shown that individuals with a *pro-self* orientation were more inclined to follow the behavior of a bad apple than individuals with a *pro-social* orientation.

2. Although this model represents a standard in the studying of the evolution of cooperation, it can be also thought of as a model of learning, in which individuals are replaced by behavioral strategies that become more or less frequent proportionally to their effectiveness in providing fitness (Riolo, Cohen, & Axelrod, 2001).

3. The effectiveness of ostracism relative to other strategies needs further inquiring, because different characteristics of the environment may favor one strategy over the other (cf. Gallucci, Van Lange, & Ouwerkerk, 2004).

REFERENCES

Axelrod, R. (1984). *Evolution of cooperation*. New York: Basic Books.

Axelrod, R., & Hamilton, W. D. (1981). The evolution of cooperation. *Science, 211,* 1390–1396.

Baumeister, R. F., Bratslavsky, E., Finkenauer, C., & Vohs, K. D. (2001). Bad is stronger than good. *Review of General Psychology, 5,* 323–370.

Baumeister, R. F., & Leary, M. R. (1995). The need to belong: Desire for interpersonal attachments as a fundamental human motivation. *Psychological Bulletin, 117,* 497–529.

Baumeister, R. F., & Tice, D. M. (1990). Anxiety and social exclusion. *Journal of Social and Clinical Psychology, 9,* 165–195.

Baumeister, R. F., Twenge, J. M., & Ciarocco, N. (2002). The inner world of rejection: Effects of social exclusion on emotion, cognition, and self-regulation. In J. P. Forgas & K. D. Williams (Eds.), *The social self: Cognitive, interpersonal and intergroup perspectives* (pp. 161–174). New York: Psychology Press.

Boyd, R. & Richerson, P. J. (1988). The evolution of reciprocity in sizable groups. *Journal of Theoretical Biology, 132,* 337–356.

Braver, S. L., & Barnett, B. (1976). Effects of modeling cooperation in a prisoner's dilemma game. *Journal of Personality and Social Psychology, 33,* 161–169.

Buss, D. M. (1990). The evolution of anxiety and social exclusion. *Journal of Social and Clinical Psychology, 9,* 196–201.

Case, T., & Williams, K. D. (2004). Ostracism: A metaphor for death. In J. Greenberg, S. Koole, & T. Pyszczynski, (Eds.), *Handbook of experimental existential psychology* (pp. 336–351). New York: Guilford Press.

Colman, A. M. (1982). *Game theory and experimental games*. Oxford: Pergamon Press.

Colman, A. M. (1995). *Game theory and its applications in the social and biological sciences* (2nd ed.). Oxford: Butterworth Heinemann.

Croson, R., & Marks, M. (1998). Identifiability of individual contributions in a threshold public goods experiment. *Journal of Mathematical Psychology, 42,* 167–190.

Eisenberger, N. I., Lieberman, M. D., Williams, K., D. (2003). Does rejection hurt? An fMRI study of social exclusion. *Science, 302,* 290–292.

Forsdyke, S. (2000). Exile, ostracism and the Athenian democracy. *Classical Antiquity, 19,* 232–263.

Gallucci, M., Ouwerkerk, J. W., & Van Lange, P. A. M. (2004). *The evolution of cooperation through social exclusion*. Manuscript in preparation.

Gallucci, M., Van Lange, P. A. M., & Ouwerkerk, J. W. (2005). *The evolution of small cooperative groups*. Manuscript in preparation.

Gallucci, M., Van Lange, P. A. M., & Ouwerkerk, J. W. (2004). Freedom of movement: A strategic analysis of social dilemmas with the option to move. In R. D. Suleiman, D. V. Budescu, I. Fischer, & D. M. Messick (Eds.), *Contemporary Psychological Research on Social Dilemmas* (pp. 180–208). London: Cambridge University Press.

Gintis, H. (2000). Strong reciprocity and human sociality. *Journal of Theoretical Biology, 206,* 169–179.

James, W. (1890). *Principles of psychology*. New York: Holt.

Kerr, N. L. (1999). Anonimity and social control in social dilemmas. In M. Foddy, M. Smithson, S. Schneider, & M. Hogg (Eds.), *Resolving social dilemmas: Dynamic, structural, and intergroup aspects* (pp. 103–122). Philadelphia: Psychology Press.

Kerr, N. L., Rumble, A. C., Park, E. S., Ouwerkerk, J. W., Parks, C. D., Gallucci, M., et al. (2004). *One bad apple spoils the whole barrel: Social exclusion as a remedy for the one bad apple effect.* Manuscript in preparation.

Komorita, S. S., Parks, C. D., & Hulbert, L. G. (1992). Reciprocity and the induction of cooperation in social dilemmas. *Journal of Personality and Social Psychology, 62,* 607–617.

Kurzban, R., & Houser, B. J. (2001). Individual differences in cooperation in a circular public goods game. *European Journal of Social Psychology, 15,* S37–S52.

Kurzban, R., & Leary, M. R. (2001). Evolutionary origins of stigmatization: The function of social exclusion. *Psychological Bulletin, 127,* 187–208.

Kurzban, R., McCabe, K., Smith, V. L., & Wilson, B. J. (2001). Incremental commitment and reciprocity in a real-time public goods game. *Personality and Social Psychology Bulletin, 27,* 1662–1673.

Leary, M. R., Tambor, E. S., Terdal, S. K., & Downs, D. L. (1995). Self-esteem as interpersonal monitor: The sociometer hypothesis. *Journal of Personality and Social Psychology, 68,* 518–530.

Messick, D. M., Wilke, H. A. M., Brewer, M. B., Kramer, R. M., Zemke, P. E., & Lui, L. (1983). Individual adaptations and structural change as solutions to social dilemmas. *Journal of Personality and Social Psychology, 44,* 294–309.

Nowak, M. A., & Sigmund, K. (1998). Evolution of indirect reciprocity by image scoring. *Nature, 393,* 573–577.

Ouwerkerk, J. W., Van Dijk, W. W., Spears, R., & Pennekamp, S. F. (2004). *Forbidden fruit and forbidden pleasures: Interpersonal and intergroup schadenfreude following ostracism of bad apples.* Manuscript in preparation.

Ouwerkerk, J. W., Van Lange, P. A. M., Gallucci, M., & Van Vugt, M. (2004). *Ostracism and the bad apple effect.* Manuscript in preparation.

Reinders Folmer, C. (2003). *Bad apples, worse apples? The effect of framing social dilemmas on the bad apple effect.* Unpublished master's thesis. Leiden University, the Netherlands.

Riolo, R. L., Cohen, M. D., Axelrod, R. (2001). Evolution of cooperation without reciprocity. *Nature, 414,* 441–443.

Rothbaum, F., Weisz, J. R., & Snyder, S. (1982). Changing the world and changing the self: A two process model of perceived control. *Journal of Personality and Social Psychology, 42,* 5–37.

Rutte, C.. G., & Wilke, H. A. M. (1992). Goals, expectations, and behavior in a social dilemma situation. In W. B. G. Liebrand, & D. M. Messick, D. M. (Eds.), *Social dilemmas: Theoretical issues and research findings* (pp. 289–305). New York: Pergamon Press.

Samuelson, C. D., & Messick, D. M. (1986a). Alternative structural solutions to social dilemmas. *Organizational Behavior and Human Decision Processes, 37,* 139–155.

Samuelson, C. D., & Messick, D. M. (1986b). Inequities in access to and use of shared resources in social dilemmas. *Journal of Personality and Social Psychology, 51,* 960–967.

Samuelson, C. D., Messick, D. M., Rutte, C. G., & Wilke, H. A. M. (1984). Individual and structural solutions to resource dilemmas in two cultures. *Journal of Personality and Social Psychology, 47,* 94–104.

Schroeder, D. A., Jensen, T. D., Reed, A. J., Sullivan, D. K., & Schwab, M. (1983). *Journal of Experimental Social Psychology, 19,* 522–539.

Solomon, S., Greenberg, J. & Pyszczynski, T. (1991). A terror management theory of self-esteem and its role in social behavior. In M. Zanna (Ed.), *Advances in experimental social psychology* (pp. 93–159). New York: Academic Press.

Sudgen, R. (1984). Reciprocity: The supply of public goods through voluntary contributions. *Economic Journal, 94,* 772–787.

Twenge, J. M., Baumeister, R. F., Tice, D. M., & Stucke, T. S. (2001). If you can't join them, beat them: Effects of social exclusion on aggressive behavior. *Journal of Personality and Social Psychology, 81,* 1058–1069

Williams, K. D. (2001). *Ostracism: The power of silence.* NY: Guilford Press.

Williams, K. D., Cheung, C. K., & Choi, W. (2000). Cyberostracism: Effects of being ignored over the internet. *Journal of Personality and Social Psychology, 79,* 748–762.

Williams, K. D., & Sommer, K. L. (1997). Social ostracism by one's coworkers: Does rejection lead to loafing or compensation? *Personality and Social Psychology Bulletin, 23,* 693–706.

Williams, K. D., & Zadro, L. (2001). Ostracism: On being ignored, excluded, and rejected. In M. R. Leary (Ed.), *Interpersonal rejection* (pp. 21–53). NY: Oxford University Press.

21

The Psychological Impact of Social Isolation

Discussion and Commentary

MARILYNN B. BREWER

Social Inclusion as a Regulatory System
The Functions of Exclusion
The Importance of the Temporal Dimension
A Concluding Comment

*T*his volume, and the conference on which it is based, testifies to the intense interest that the study of social exclusion has garnered in recent years across the discipline of psychology. Represented among the authors in this collection are developmental psychologists, personality psychologists, social psychologists, and social neuroscientists—all bringing the conceptual and methodological tools of their respective subdisciplines to the understanding of the causes and consequences of social exclusion and rejection experiences.

Not surprisingly, studying a complex phenomenon from different perspectives generates a number of anomalies and paradoxes, along with important points of convergence and agreement. Recognizing and addressing apparent differences in findings that arise from different research paradigms is one way in which theory and research advances in a new field of inquiry, and it is my hope that this discussion chapter will contribute to that process. However, before I begin a review of some of the themes and issues that are represented in this volume, I want to highlight one important point of agreement that is shared by all of the contributors. What we have learned about the nature and intensity of response to experiences of social isolation, rejection, and exclusion attests to the profoundly

---

Address correspondence to: Marilynn B. Brewer, Department of Psychology, Ohio State University, Columbus, OH 43210, USA. E-mail: brewer.64@osu.edu

social nature of human beings. As a species, our social interdependence is, quite literally, written in our DNA.

SOCIAL INCLUSION AS A REGULATORY SYSTEM

One very useful conceptual framework that cuts across most of the chapters in this volume is that of a regulatory system that monitors and maintains an individual's level of social inclusion. This is most explicit in Williams and Zadro's coping model of ostracism (Williams, 2001) and in Pickett and Gardner's model of belonging regulation and the social monitoring system. But elements of a self-regulatory system are also represented in social pain theory (MacDonald & Shaw; Eisenberger & Lieberman), in research on rejection sensitivity (Downey), and in the sociometer model of self- esteem and self-esteem maintenance (Leary; Sommer & Rubin).

As represented in Figure 13.1 (Pickett & Gardner chapter), the components of a regulatory system include an assessment function that monitors and registers the individual's current state of need satisfaction, a comparator function that evaluates the current state against an ideal or goal state, and an activation (monitoring and coping) function that responds to discrepancies detected by the comparator and remains active until the discrepancy is reduced or eliminated (or until the system is exhausted). Much of the research discussed in this volume on individuals' perceptions of and responses to exclusion experiences can be viewed as tapping in to this regulatory system at different points in the feedback loop. Downey's programmatic research on rejection sensitivity, for example, assesses individual differences in detection of deficits in belonging. The detection stage is also the focus of Eisenberg and Lieberman's analysis of social pain as part of the body's "alarm system" registering perceived discrepancies in satisfaction of important needs. High levels of felt deficits can arise from heightened sensitivity to actual or imminent exclusion (the assessment function) or from exceptionally high standards of belonging (the comparator function), or both. Although Downey focuses on the assessment subsystem in her analysis of rejection sensitivity, it may be that some individuals high in rejection sensitivity are characterized by unrealistically high expectations for what constitutes an ideal state of belonging or inclusion.

On the response activation (coping) side of the regulatory system, Pickett and Gardner report convergent findings from several studies demonstrating that individuals experiencing temporary or chronic belonging deficit are especially attentive to social information in their environment, perhaps actively searching for what Twenge refers to as "connectedness replenishment" opportunities. This monitoring of the social environment may be a particularly important stage in the regulatory process because the selection of responses to perceived deficits may be influenced as much by the individual's understanding of available opportunities for restoring inclusion or social acceptance as it is by the level of arousal of the belonging need.

Most of the chapters in the present volume assume either explicitly or implicitly that the regulatory system controlling assessment and reactions to exclusion or rejection is associated primarily with the motive to belong as a basic human need. However, as Williams and Zadro point out, some types of exclusion experiences (particularly those classified as ostracism) also threaten other fundamental motives, including the need for self-esteem, the need for control, and existential motives. Although Leary might argue that the maintenance of self-esteem is derivative of the more fundamental need to belong, it seems clear that control needs and the need for meaningful existence are conceptually distinct from a need for social inclusion and may engage different regulatory processes. To add to the complications, my own theory of optimal distinctiveness (Brewer, 1991) is also a model of how individuals regulate their level of social inclusion, but with the added element that the need for belonging is held in check by an oppositional need for differentiation.

Optimal distinctiveness theory posits that humans are characterized by two opposing needs that govern the relationship between the self and membership in social groups. The first is a need for assimilation and inclusion, a desire for belonging that motivates immersion in social groups. The second is a need for differentiation from others that operates in opposition to the need for immersion. As group membership becomes more and more inclusive, the need for inclusion is satisfied but the need for differentiation is activated; conversely, as inclusiveness decreases, the differentiation need is reduced but the need for assimilation is activated. These competing drives assure that interests at one level are not consistently sacrificed to interests at the other. According to the model, the two opposing motives produce an emergent characteristic—social identification with optimally distinctive groups that satisfy both needs simultaneously.

Adding the need for differentiation to our theories of social motivation may be important to understanding social exclusion and rejection because it provides some insight on the other side of the coin vis à vis felt exclusion—i.e., what underlies episodes of exclusion, rejection, or disconnection in the first place. It is certainly true that both individuals and groups may use exclusion or ostracism intentionally and strategically as a mechanism of punishment and control of others' behavior. But in many cases, one individual's experience of exclusion or rejection may arise as a side effect of another person's (or group's) regulation of their own optimal distinctiveness. Individuals need recognition and differentiation, and meeting those needs may result in behaviors that draw or reinforce boundaries between self and other. Similarly, functional groups need boundaries and definition, and maintaining group identity may require marginalizing or excluding individuals who lack defining attributes. In his chapter in this volume, Michael Hogg provides an interesting account of the dynamic process by which groups both incorporate and regulate diversity. But the important point is that normal processes of group self-maintenance will result in some members feeling less included or even actively rejected.

In sum, then, the notion of a social inclusion regulatory system provides something of a meta-theory that incorporates many of the phenomena discussed in this volume. And many of the interesting questions raised within and among chapters can be framed as questions about the nature of this regulatory system. In the remainder of this section I will pose three such questions: Is the system adaptive or maladaptive? What is the regulatory focus of the system? And is belonging regulated by one system or many?

Adaptive or Maladaptive

For a system that presumably evolved to meet important survival needs for the human species, it may seem paradoxical to even raise the question of whether the social inclusion regulatory system is largely maladaptive. And yet, the research findings described in many of the chapters of the present volume provide multiple examples of maladaptive, regulatory failure—at least for some individuals or under some circumstances. An evolved system can be (or become) maladaptive if it is poorly calibrated—either because it is too recent in evolutionary history to have been fully honed by selective pressures or because the conditions of the physical or social environment in which the system originally evolved have changed dramatically. So the question can be raised as to whether the social inclusion regulatory system in general is poorly adapted to conditions of modern social life, or whether it is generally adaptive but subject to variability across individuals.

Several of the chapters in this volume explicitly characterize the social belonging system as miscalibrated and potentially maladaptive. MacDonald and Shaw, for example, describe a social pain system that is "miscalibrated" and subject to cascade effects that lead to regulatory failure. In a similar vein, Baumeister and DeWall review an extensive program of research demonstrating that the anticipation of social exclusion disrupts executive functions and impairs controlled cognitive processing and other self-regulatory behaviors. Particularly ironical, much of this research suggests that one consequence of the self-regulatory disruption associated with exclusion and belonging deficits is an increased propensity toward antisocial behaviors such as aggression and violence (see Catanese & Tice; Gaertner & Iuzzini)—responses more likely to perpetuate isolation and rejection than to restore belonging.

At a more specific level, several chapters document how certain aspects of the regulatory system can lead to maladaptive or self-defeating outcomes. Downey has documented a large number of negative consequences for mental health associated with hypersensitivity to social rejection. Similarly, Cacioppo and Hawkley discuss how chronic feelings of loneliness lead to self-defeating construals of the social environment that ultimately perpetuate isolation and lack of connection to others. In related research, Pickett and Gardner have shown that individuals characterized by chronic loneliness or rejection sensitivity also tend to be inaccurate encoders of subtle social cues. Finally, Sommer and Rubin describe how overgeneralizing exclusion experiences in the form of negative expectancies engages self-defensive processes that may operate at the expense of more socially adaptive coping strategies.

Interestingly, most of the evidence for maladaptive or miscalibrated regulation of belonging involves the effects of hypersensitivity or chronic expectations of rejection. From this perspective, it is the individuals who are in the most pain who seem to be least able to cope effectively with exclusion in a way that would restore inclusion and reduce the pain. As MacDonald and Shaw describe it, adaptive caution in the face of potential rejection is replaced by panic—an alarm system run amuck.

It is clear that at least some regulatory failures can be traced to an overly sensitive detection function. But what about those individuals who are particularly *insensitive* to social rejection? These are individuals who do not register a deficit of belonging even when others may be actively shunning them. In effect, they do not feel the pain and hence do not activate any coping strategies to restore belonging. As with physical pain, failure to register social pain may have long-term negative implications for survival in a socially interdependent species. But the feedback system may be inadequate to offset the short-term advantages of feeling no pain. As Juvonen and Gross point out, aggressive children may be insensitive to rejection, so even though they may be excluded by their peers, this does not alter their behavior. And in some groups, aggressive children or adolescents may be socially rewarded, becoming the bullies rather than the bullied. Thus, the potential maladaptive consequences of rejection insensitivity may be more difficult to document, at least at the individual level.

Despite the abundance of evidence for regulatory failure in the face of social rejection, there is also considerable research reported in this volume that documents that most individuals do successfully regulate their need for belonging most of the time. After all, Williams and Zadro report that diary studies indicate that most individuals experience some form of rejection or exclusion on a daily basis, and yet we function quite well socially. As Lakin and Chartrand's experiments on non-conscious mimicry demonstrate, strategies to restore affiliation and inclusion may be so well learned that they are engaged automatically in response to exclusion experiences. Williams and Zadro have also demonstrated that intermediate coping responses to incidents of ostracism include pro-social behaviors such as conformity, and the threat of exclusion is a strong motivator of cooperation in social groups (Ouwerkerk, vanLange, Gallucci, & Kerr).

Apart from chronic personality differences, one factor that may influence whether immediate responses to exclusion appear to be adaptive (i.e., promote inclusion) or maladaptive (perpetuate exclusion) may be what motives are aroused by the interpretation of the exclusion event. As Williams and Zadro point out, if ostracism creates deficits in felt control, then an adaptive response geared to restoring control may appear to be maladaptive in terms of inclusion needs. But even when belonging needs are aroused, the effectiveness of coping responses may depend on the social opportunities available in the immediate context. To some extent, socially healthy individuals may be able to bring their own resources to bear in the form of symbolic social bonds when they feel temporarily excluded, as demonstrated by Gardner, Pickett, and Knowles. But symbolic or internal resources may not be sufficient to cope with more severe or extended exclusion experiences, where opportunities for real social connection may be required. As Twenge reports in her chapter, the tendency to aggress following an intense social exclusion experience can be averted if a real opportunity for restoring group inclusion presents itself at the right time. Perhaps it is frustration over the lack of opportunity for restoring social bonds that underlies at least some of the aggression obtained in our experimental studies of response to social rejection.

Regulatory Focus: Promotion versus Prevention

Another factor that may underlie the nature and effectiveness of responses to actual or threatened social exclusion is the individual's regulatory focus with respect to the need to belong. Regulatory focus theory (Higgins, 1997) proposes that there are two distinct types of regulatory orientations concerned with meeting the basic needs for nurturance on the one hand, and for security and safety on the other. The two types of self-regulation (labeled promotion and prevention, respectively) fulfill these needs through the pursuit of different types of goals (or desired end-states) and the use of different behavioral means, and are characterized by differing evaluations and emotional experiences. A promotion focus involves a sensitivity to the presence or absence of gain, and employs behavioral *approach* strategies. A prevention focus, in contrast, involves a concern with the presence or absence of loss, and employs behavioral *avoidance* strategies.

When considering belonging needs and the regulation of social inclusion, one could focus either on achieving and maintaining a state of inclusion (promotion focus) or on avoiding exclusion or rejection (prevention focus), with potentially different implications for how belonging deficits are assessed and what emotional and behavioral responses are engaged. Individuals with a prevention focus in this domain are more likely to be risk-averse and more concerned with avoiding rejection than with achieving greater inclusion. Promotion-focused individuals, on the other hand, are more likely to be willing to take risks in order to improve or restore belonging and inclusion.

It is interesting that two different physical system metaphors have been employed in various chapters of this volume to describe the regulation of belonging and responses to exclusion. MacDonald and Shaw and Eisenberger and Leiberman associate social exclusion with the pain system, even suggesting that social pain and physical pain share a common neural basis. Gardner, Pickett, and Knowles, on the other hand, use hunger as a physical analogy for the belonging regulatory system. Although both pain and hunger are aversive states, pain activates escape and avoidance and is likely to be associated with prevention focus, whereas hunger activates goal-seeking and is more likely to be associated with promotion focus. It is possible that the more maladaptive consequences of social exclusion discussed above are related to prevention focus and that more adaptive responses are associated with a promotion focus. From this perspective, it is of interest to note that Pickett and Gardner report different effects of chronic loneliness versus chronic need to belong with respect to social sensitivity. Whereas chronically lonely individuals exhibit high attentiveness to social cues but poor encoding ability, individuals high in need to belong are high in attentiveness but also high on encoding ability and empathy. They speculate that loneliness may reflect a chronic deficit state, which may be associated with prevention focus; need to belong, on the other hand, may be an "appetitive" motive, more likely to correspond to a promotion focus.

Regulatory focus has been found to be a chronic individual difference variable, but it can also be influenced by temporary situational factors. Future research on responses to social exclusion might benefit from drawing on the regulatory focus research that has been conducted in other domains to determine whether the distinction between promotion versus prevention focus might prove useful in this domain as well.

Is Belonging a Single Regulatory System?

Throughout most of the chapters in this volume the terms "belonging" and "inclusion" are used interchangeably, and interpersonal rejection and exclusion from social groups are implicitly assumed to be similar (or even identical) experiences. Leary is most explicit in proposing that a single dimension—perceived relational value—underlies responses to a wide range of rejection-related experiences.

In contrast to this single-system assumption, Brewer and Gardner (1996) proposed that the "social self" is differentiated into two separate self-representations—the *relational self*, which is based on personalized relationships with significant others, and the *collective self*, which is the depersonalized representation of the self as a member of a social group or large collective. They speculated further that these are two distinct self-systems, one of which monitors and regulates the maintenance and quality of interpersonal connections with others, and the other of which monitors and regulates inclusion in large social groups. The reasoning is that interpersonal relationships (dyads and small groups) and group memberships represent different forms of social interdependence and serve different survival functions for individual humans (see Caporael, 1997, for elaboration of this point). As such, they do not substitute for each other, and socially healthy human beings must achieve both forms of connection with others in order to thrive.

The implication of this distinction between relational and collective selves is that the "need to belong" is not a single monolithic motive, but that there are at least two different belonging needs and regulatory systems. There are a few hints in the research findings reported in this volume that this distinction between different forms of social inclusion–exclusion may be useful and important. Cacioppo and Hawkley, for example, obtained evidence for three different dimensions of social embeddedness-loneliness, two of which (intimate connectedness and relational connectedness) involve the presence or lack of close interpersonal relationships (marriage and friends), and the other of which involves the presence or absence of collective connectedness (group memberships) (Hawkley, Browne, & Cacioppo, in press).

Also relevant are differences reported by Downey between males and females high in rejection sensitivity. Several of her studies suggested that high RS females respond more intensely to threats of interpersonal rejection or loss, whereas high RS males are more responsive to loss of social status, peer group rejection and/or public rejection. These findings are consistent with the idea that rejection sensitivity exacerbates sex differences that have been reported in other studies of social belonging needs. Specifically, it has been suggested that men and women differ in the relative importance placed on meeting relational versus collective forms of social attachment, with women being more relationally oriented and men more collectively oriented (Baumeister & Sommer, 1997; Kashima et al., 1995).

Gabriel and Gardner (1999) obtained a variety of support for the existence of gender differences in relational versus collective interdependence orientation. In one study involving a diary-reading paradigm, women showed better selective memory for relational items in the diary, while men showed better memory for collective items. In another study, women were found to be more likely to put their own personal desires aside for a friend, while men were more likely to sacrifice for a group (Gabriel & Gardner, 1999). In addition, related gender differences have been found with respect to the subjective importance of different types of groups (Seeley, Gardner, Pennington, & Gabriel, 2003). For women, group importance is mainly determined by the degree to which the group fulfills relational needs, while men place a greater importance on the collective identity that groups offer. Parallel differences have also been documented across cultures, with East Asians being more responsive to relational connections and Americans to shared group membership (Yuki, Maddux, Brewer, & Takemura, 2005), consistent with Fiske and Yamamoto's discussion of cultural differences in meeting belonging needs through selective, secure relationships versus wide and varied relationships.

Although there are some findings in the preceding chapters that lend support to the idea that relational connection and group inclusion represent two distinct belonging needs, some other findings cast doubt on this assertion. For instance, Juvonen and Gross's review of the developmental literature on social rejection and bullying indicates that the social distress associated with peer group rejection can be mitigated by having just one close friend—a finding that suggests that different forms of belonging are somewhat interchangeable. And the research on social pain (MacDonald & Shaw; Eisenberger & Lieberman) suggests that the affective experience of social pain (like physical pain) is not differentiated by source. So the question remains whether interpersonal connection motives and social group inclusion motives represent distinct needs—analogous to hunger versus thirst—or whether they are just different sources of satisfaction (or deprivation) of the same underlying need.

To some extent, our research paradigms limit our ability to answer this question. For the most part, our empirical studies of social exclusion and rejection focus on experiences within the context of interpersonal relationships or small, face-to-face groups. The "future alone" manipulation used in research by Baumeister and DeWall and Catanese and Tice and Twenge refers explicitly to lack of friends and close relationships. Other experimental paradigms (e.g., the ball-toss ostracism paradigm or the discussion group rejection manipulation) involve exclusion by members of relatively small social groups. (In fact, in the Baumeister et al. version of group rejection, the participant is actually rejected by each group member individually; on the other hand, the ostracism paradigm involves exclusion from the rest of the group as a unit.)

In terms of meeting belonging needs, small face-to-face groups are somewhat ambiguous. On the one hand, such groups constitute a small network of interpersonal relationships that may meet the need for relational connections. On the other hand, small groups can also be collective entities (cf. Hogg), which serve inclusion needs. Exclusion from such groups can be seen either as interpersonal rejection or group ostracism by different individuals or under different circumstances. Developmentally, young children may view classroom peer groups primarily in terms of meeting needs for interpersonal relationships (in which case, one relationship may suffice); it may not be until individuals reach adolescence that the need for collective inclusion becomes salient (see Bugental, 2000).

Among the chapters in the present volume, only those by Hogg and by Ouwerkerk et al. deal explicitly with exclusion from social groups that are relatively large collectives.[1] But these chapters focus primarily on the origin or functions of marginalization and exclusion from the group perspective, rather than the emotional or behavioral responses of those excluded. Hence there is still a great deal to be learned about the differences between social deprivation in the form of isolation or ostracism from a relationship partner and deprivation in the form of isolation or exclusion from a large social group and whether these implicate different needs, motives, subjective experience, and reparation strategies.

THE FUNCTIONS OF EXCLUSION

Thus far, the bulk of this chapter (like the volume as a whole) has focused primarily on issues related to how individuals regulate their need for social inclusion and respond to actual or threatened exclusion. However, as I mentioned briefly before, we also need to look at the other side of the coin and to explore issues associated with the causes or origins of social exclusion and rejection. Here the focus is largely that of a functional analysis of social exclusion as a mechanism of social control.

From a functional perspective, social exclusion and rejection may serve very similar purposes for both individuals (in their interpersonal relationships) and groups. First, the threat of social exclusion (or the use of rejection or ostracism as punishment) is a form of behavior control, used strategically to motivate an individual to behave in ways that benefit the partner or the group as a whole. The experimental studies of social dilemmas reported by Ouwerkerk et al. provide the clearest example of this function of social exclusion and the effectiveness of the threat of exclusion as a motivator for cooperation within groups. This behavior control mechanism is most likely to be employed when individuals are already group members (or in an existing relationship). In such cases, the threat of expulsion or ejection should be particularly powerful because such exclusion would constitute a *loss* of social inclusion and a strong signal of belonging deficit. In that respect, it is very functional for groups and individuals to have a credible threat of ejection or isolation available as a tool for social control. However, it also needs to be recognized that *implementation* of expulsion or ostracism as a punishment can be costly for the group or the relationship, if the ultimate goal is to control *future* behavior and maintain the relationship or inclusion of the group member. As a mechanism for behavior control, exclusion may be more effective as a threat the less it is actually used.

On the other hand, exclusion and rejection may be reactive rather than strategic and still serve the function of maintaining group norms (in the case of group ostracism) or individual integrity (in the case of relationship rejection). If individuals who deviate from group or relationship norms are permanently ejected (or never included in the first place), group cohesion can be maintained without changing the excluded individual's behavior. Juvonen and Gross have made a strong case that this is the function being served by peer group rejection or bullying in elementary and middle school, and Fitness applies this to the special case of family relationships, where long-term rejection or ostracism is the consequence of violation of implicit or explicit family rules.

The group norm maintenance function is served either by ejecting deviant members (who were previously in the group or relationship) or by excluding non-normative individuals from entrance into the group. However, the costs of these two forms of exclusion may be very different. As Leary points out in his taxonomy of rejection-related constructs, prior belonging status (as a group member or relationship partner or not) may have a lot to do with how an exclusion episode is defined and responded to. Expulsion, once a connection has been established, requires more effort and resources than non-inclusion. This may be one reason why groups (and perhaps also individuals) err on the side of caution when deciding whether to acknowledge a new individual as an ingroup member. When judging individuals whose group belonging is ambiguous, groups tend to be biased in the direction of overexclusion (not acknowledging individuals who do meet group membership standards) rather than inclusion (Yzerbyt, Leyens, & Bellour, 1995). Thus, for most individuals, exclusion experiences that involve noninclusion are likely to be much more frequent than experiences of ejection from existing relationships or group memberships.

Of course, belonging status is not always so clear-cut ("in" versus "out"). Michael Hogg's chapter discusses how group members may vary in prototypicality and acceptance as full-fledged group members. Marginalization is certainly a form of social isolation that should be considered among our exclusion-related constructs. Within interpersonal relationships as well, belonging status may be ambiguous rather than clear rejection versus acceptance. As Hogg points out, there may be some functions served by keeping belonging status ambiguous for at least some group members (or for a partner, some of the time). Groups may benefit in some circumstances from having moderately deviant members (diversity), but at the same time, marginalization (and the real threat of expulsion) serves as a weapon to restrain the extent of deviance that will be exhibited. This is illustrated nicely by the results of Ouwerkerk et al.'s social dilemma experiment in which individuals who had been ostracized (i.e., voted out of the group) but continued to stay in the group for further trials were highly likely to cooperate even in the face of temptation to defect.

Thus, the focus in this volume has been on the adaptive function of exclusion for the long-term benefit of groups or relationships. But as with the consequences of exclusion for individuals, it seems appropriate to ask whether the use of exclusion or rejection by groups or relationship partners can be maladaptive as well. Just as individuals can be overly sensitive to the anticipation of rejection, or react in self-defeating ways, groups (or partners) can be overly sensitive to signs of deviance from normative expectations and can use rejection, exclusion, or expulsion too often or too indiscriminately, at the cost of preservation of the group or relationship unit.

THE IMPORTANCE OF THE TEMPORAL DIMENSION

The final theme that I want to address in this review and discussion of the preceding chapters is to consider how the temporal aspects of social inclusion/exclusion are represented in our research paradigms and theories. In comparing methods and findings across different programs of research in this area, time enters the picture in a variety of ways. One obvious temporal factor is whether we are studying exclusion experiences from the past, the immediate present, or the future. Field research studies of rejection (including the developmental studies reviewed by Juvonen and Gross, or the survey research conducted by Cacioppo and Hawkley) tend to focus on the cumulative effects of past exclusion experiences. Experimental manipulations of rejection in the laboratory, on the other hand, include focusing attention on past rejection (e.g., "remember a time..."), creating an experience of exclusion in the present situation (e.g., the ball-toss paradigm or voted-out-of-the-group manipulations), or creating the anticipation of future exclusion (the "future-alone" manipulation). This variation in the temporal locus of the exclusion experience may have effects in its own right, but I suspect that the more important impact derives from its relationship to two other time-related factors: chronic versus discrete experiences, and the amount of time and opportunity for coping and repair.

Although the effects of repeated and extended rejection experiences can be expected to be generally greater than those of a single, discrete instance of exclusion or rejection, the distinction between chronic and discrete events may not always be clear. For instance, in real life are multiple mundane instances of exclusion from different sources experienced as single discrete events or are they cumulative? Are the discrete experiences we set up in our laboratory situations viewed as isolated instances, or do our participants over generalize them and react as if they were chronic (see Sommer & Rubin)? Is one effective coping mechanism the ability to discount a specific rejection experience as an isolated event and, if so, what are the conditions that make this possible?

With respect to the timeline for responding to social exclusion, the ostracism model represented in Figure 2.1 (see Williams & Zadro) is the most explicit about the importance of this temporal dimension. The distinctions made in that model among three response stages—immediate responses (which are hypothesized to be affect-laden and relatively undifferentiated by type of experience), short-term coping (potentially influenced by factors such as cognitive resources, attributional processing, and social opportunities in the immediate environment), and long-term consequences of chronic or extended exclusion (characterized by depletion of resources)—may be a very important integrative framework. This model brings yet another physical system analogy to the table since the stages are similar to those of Selye's General Adaptation System (Selye, 1956) describing the body's short- and long-term responses to stress. The comparison to stress research also raises the question of whether the stress of exclusion is responded to as a challenge or a threat (see Cacioppo and Hawkley) and whether this occurs immediately or not until the short-term coping stage of responding. For both theoretical and method- ological reasons it will be important to evaluate our diverse research paradigms to consider how they vary on this critical temporal dimension. It may be that some of the differences in quality, intensity, or type of response to exclusion experiences that have been documented in different research programs reflect what stage of coping is being tapped by the research measurement procedures and the context in which they are obtained.

A CONCLUDING COMMENT

To return to the point I was making at the outset of this chapter, I find the current explosion of interest and research on social exclusion to be particularly exciting because of its implications for the centrality of *social* psychology in the behavioral and biological sciences. Although lip service is often paid to the basic premise that human beings are adapted for group living, this premise has not been fully exploited in constructing theory in psychology. I would argue that the develop- ment of broad psychological theory would benefit from taking human social nature more seriously. It is fundamental to the science of human psychology to recognize that human beings are adapted for social living. We need to pay more attention to the implications of recognizing that all of the building blocks of human psychol- ogy—cognition, emotion, motivation—have been shaped by the demands of social interdependence. From this perspective, the research in this volume documenting the intense and often disruptive effects of social exclusion, rejection, or isolation on individual cognitive, motivational, and emotional functioning represents a potentially critical step toward a science of human sociality.

NOTES

1. Although Williams and Zadro's review of ostracism certainly includes clear cases of large group ostracism such as banishment from a country.

REFERENCES

Baumeister, R. F., & Sommer, K. L., (1997). What do men want? Gender differences and two spheres of belongingness: Comment on Cross and Madson. *Psychological Bulletin, 122,* 38–44.

Brewer, M. B. (1991). The social self: On being the same and different at the same time. *Personality and Social Psychology Bulletin, 17,* 475–482.

Brewer, M. B., & Gardner, W. (1996). Who is this "we"? Levels of collective identity and self representation. *Journal of Personality and Social Psychology, 71,* 83–93.

Bugental, D. B. (2000). Acquisition of the algorithms of social life: A domain-based approach. *Psychological Bulletin, 126,* 187–219.

Caporael, L. R. (1997). The evolution of truly social cognition: The core configurations model. *Personality and Social Psychology Review, 1,* 276–298.

Gabriel, S., & Gardner, W. L. (1999). Are there 'his' and 'hers' types of interdependence? The implications of gender differences in collective versus relational interdependence for affect, behavior, and cognition. *Journal of Personality and Social Psychology, 77,* 642–655.

Hawkley, L. C. Browne, M. W., & Cacioppo, J. T. (in press). How can I connect with thee? Let me count the ways. *Psychological Science.*

Higgins, E. T. (1997). Beyond pleasure and pain. *American Psychologist, 52,* 1280–1300.

Kashima, Y., Yamaguchi, S., Kim, U., Choi, S., Gelfand, M. J., & Yuki, M. (1995). Culture, gender, and self: A perspective from individualism-collectivism research. *Journal of Personality and Social Psychology, 69,* 925–937.

Seeley, E., Gardner, W., Pennington, G., & Gabriel, S. (2003). Circle of friends or members of a group? Sex differences in relational and collective attachment to groups. *Group Processes and Intergroup Relations,* 6, 251–263.

Selye, H. (1956). *Stress of life.* New York: McGraw-Hill

Williams, K. D. (2001). *Ostracism: The power of silence.* NY: Guilford Press.

Yuki, M., Maddux, W., Brewer, M. B., & Takemura, K. (2005). Cross-cultural differences in relationship- and group-based trust. *Personality and Social Psychology Bulletin, 31,* 48–62.

Yzerbyt, V.Y, Leyens, J-P., & Bellour, F. (1995). The ingroup overexclusion effect: Identity concerns in decisions about group membership. *European Journal of Social Psychology, 25,* 1–16.

Author Index

Subject Index